Experiential Theatres

Experiential Theatres is a collaboratively edited and curated collection that delivers key insights into the processes of developing experiential performance projects and the pedagogies behind training theatre artists of the twenty-first century.

Experiential refers to practices where the audience member becomes a crucial member of the performance world through the inclusion of immersion, participation, and play. As technologies of communication and interactivity have evolved in the postdigital era, so have modes of spectatorship and performance frameworks. This book provides readers with pedagogical tools for experiential theatre making that address these shifts in contemporary performance and audience expectations. Through case studies, interviews, and classroom applications the book offers a synthesis of theory, practical application, pedagogical tools, and practitioner guidance to develop a praxis-based model for university theatre educators training today's theatre students.

Experiential Theatres presents a holistic approach for educators and students in areas of performance, design, technology, dramaturgy, and theory to help guide them through the processes of making experiential performance.

William W. Lewis, Ph.D. is an Assistant Professor of Theatre History, Literature, and Criticism at Purdue University. His research focuses on spectatorship, politics, digital cultures, and experiential performance. As a scholar-artist he also utilizes practice-based research, where he integrates interactive technologies into live performance to better understand the relationships between contemporary audiences and mediatized culture. He has published in *Theatre Topics*, *Performance Research*, *GPS: Global Performance Studies*, *The International Journal of Performance Arts and Digital Media*, and *Theatre Research International*. Recent book chapters have appeared in *New Directions in Teaching Theatre Arts* (Palgrave, eds. Anne Flitosos and Gail S. Medford) and *Avatars, Activism and Postdigital Performance* (Bloomsbury, eds. Liam Jarvis and Karen Savage). Will is the founding co-editor of *PARtake: The Journal of Performance as Research*.

Sean Bartley, Ph.D. is an Assistant Professor of Theatre History at Northwestern State University. His research centers around contemporary site-specific, ambulatory, and immersive theatre practices and sports as performance. His work has been featured in *TDR: The Drama Review*, *Theatre History Studies*, *Theatre Journal*, *PARtake: The Journal of Performance as Research*, and *Borrowers and Lenders: The Journal of Shakespeare and Appropriation*. Recent book chapters include "You're Out! Presence and Absence at the Ballpark" in *Sporting Performances: Politics in Play* (Routledge, ed. Shannon Walsh) and "The President Makes a Play: Putin and Erdoğan's Sporting Diplomacy" with Jared Strange in *Performing Statecraft: The Postdiplomatic Theatre of Sovereigns, Citizens, and States* (Bloomsbury, ed. James R. Ball III).

Experiential Theatres

Praxis-Based Approaches to Training 21st Century Theatre Artists

Edited by William W. Lewis and Sean Bartley

Routledge
Taylor & Francis Group
NEW YORK AND LONDON

Cover image credit: Swim Pony's *Survive!*, photo by Jacques-Jean Tiziou, www.jjtiziou.net

First published 2023
by Routledge
605 Third Avenue, New York, NY 10158

and by Routledge
4 Park Square, Milton Park, Abingdon, Oxon, OX14 4RN

Routledge is an imprint of the Taylor & Francis Group, an informa business

© 2023 selection and editorial matter, William W. Lewis and Sean Bartley; individual chapters, the contributors

The right of William W. Lewis and Sean Bartley to be identified as the authors of the editorial material, and of the authors for their individual chapters, has been asserted in accordance with sections 77 and 78 of the Copyright, Designs and Patents Act 1988.

All rights reserved. No part of this book may be reprinted or reproduced or utilised in any form or by any electronic, mechanical, or other means, now known or hereafter invented, including photocopying and recording, or in any information storage or retrieval system, without permission in writing from the publishers.

Trademark notice: Product or corporate names may be trademarks or registered trademarks, and are used only for identification and explanation without intent to infringe.

Library of Congress Cataloging-in-Publication Data
Names: Lewis, William W., editor. | Bartley, Sean, editor.
Title: Experiential theatres : praxis-based approaches to training 21st century theatre artists edited William W. Lewis and Sean Bartley.
Description: New York : Routledge, 2023. | Includes bibliographical references and index.
Identifiers: LCCN 2022025343 (print) | LCCN 2022025344 (ebook) | ISBN 9781032036045 (hardback) | ISBN 9781032036038 (paperback) | ISBN 9781003188179 (ebook)
Subjects: LCSH: Theatre--Study and teaching (Higher) | Experimental theater. | Participatory theater.
Classification: LCC PN2075 .E97 2023 (print) | LCC PN2075 (ebook) | DDC 792.02/807--dc23/eng/20220819
LC record available at https://lccn.loc.gov/2022025343
LC ebook record available at https://lccn.loc.gov/2022025344

ISBN: 978-1-032-03604-5 (hbk)
ISBN: 978-1-032-03603-8 (pbk)
ISBN: 978-1-003-18817-9 (ebk)

DOI: 10.4324/9781003188179

Typeset in Minion
by MPS Limited, Dehradun

Contents

	Acknowledgments	x
	Author Biographies	xi
	Introduction	
	Experiential Theatres: An Introduction William W. Lewis and Sean Bartley	1
Section 1	**Collaborative Experience Making and Interactive Performance Practice**	23
	Section Introduction	
1	Frameworks for Making and Performing in Experiential Performance William W. Lewis and Valerie Clayman Pye	25
	Case Studies	
2	Designing Play: Game Techniques in Experiential and Interactive Performance Adrienne Mackey	35
3	Framework Design: A Curatorial Approach to Teaching Participatory Performance Jamie Harper	46
4	Intimacy in Play: Training Actors for Agentic Symmetry in Unscripted Interactions Amanda Rose Villarreal	53

vi • CONTENTS

Roundtable Interview

5 Experiential Theatres and the Value of Rethinking
Theatre Education: A Conversation with Performers and
Interactive Theatre Makers on Developing Methods for
Collaborative Experience Making 64
William W. Lewis and Valerie Clayman Pye

Praxis Essays

6 Facilitating Narrative Agency in Experiential Theatre 74
Astrid Breel

7 Training the Actor for Roleplay and Other Improv-Based
Interactive Theatre Forms 80
David Kaye

8 Standardized Patient Experience: Reframing Pedagogical
Approaches in the Acting Studio 86
Matthew Mastromatteo

9 The Significance of "Role-Play" and "Instruction-Based
Performance" as Modes of Teaching, Collaborating, and
Performing with/for Participating Audiences 91
Kesia Guillery, Persis Jadé Maravala, and Jorge Lopes Ramos

10 Collaborative Development Workshop: Approaching
Conceptualization through Audience Affordances and
Experiential Trajectories 98
William W. Lewis

Postdigital Response

11 A Postdigital Response: User Experience Design,
Interactive, Immersive, and Mixed Reality Performance 105
Lindsay Brandon Hunter and Steve Luber

Section 2 **Narrative and Dramaturgy for Experiential Forms** 113

Section Introduction

12 Models for Experiential Training in Playwriting and
Dramaturgy 115
Sean Bartley and Marshall Botvinick

CONTENTS • vii

Case Studies

13 Mapping Narrative in Pig Iron Theatre Company's *Pay Up* and *Franklin's Secret City*   120
Robert Quillen Camp

14 The Dramaturgy of Tabletop Roleplaying Games   130
Mike Sell

15 Rasa in This Is Not a Theatre Company's Experiential Productions   140
Erin B. Mee

Roundtable Interview

16 Reconfiguring Narrative and Experiential Dramaturgy: A Conversation with Professional Educators and Dramaturgs on the Future(s) of Storytelling   151
Sean Bartley and Marshal Botvinick

Praxis Essays

17 Wildwind Performance Lab: New Play Development through Abstraction   160
Sarah Johnson

18 It's Okay to Not be "Right": Incorporating Creative Thinking into Theatrical Partnerships   166
Rachel E. Bauer

19 Theatrical Immersion within Alternate Reality Games   171
Hans Vermy

Postdigital Response

20 A Postdigital Response: Experiential Dramaturgies of Online Theatre, Cyberformance, and Digital Texts   175
Christina Papagiannouli

Section 3   **Performance Technologies and Design Thinking**   183

Section Introduction

21 Pedagogies for Design Thinking and Experiential Technologies   185
Bruce Bergner and Rich Dionne

viii • CONTENTS

Case Studies

22 Storyliving: A Creative Process   194
    Justin Stichter

23 Theatre Majors and Immersive Technology:
    An Interview with HP's Joanna Popper   206
    E.B. Hunter

24 Interaction and Extended Somatechnics   212
    Johannes Birringer

Roundtable Interview

25 A Design Roundtable: The Creative Process of
    Experience   223
    Bruce Bergner, Rich Dionne, and William W. Lewis

Praxis Essays

26 Playing with the Past: Pirates in the College Classroom   234
    Samantha A. Meigs

27 Unlocking Formal Qualities to Discover the Iconography
    in Visual Design   240
    Stephen Jones

28 Designing an Interactive Production: A Practical
    Walkthrough   244
    Liz Fisher

Postdigital Response

29 A Postdigital Response: Performance Technologies and
    Design Thinking   251
    Hans Vermy and Eric Hoff

Afterword

30 An Afterword: Experience and Theatre Education   260
    William W. Lewis and Sean Bartley

Appendices

Appendix 1: Glossary of Experiential Terms   265

Appendix 2: Companies, Organizations, and Ensembles   274

Index   278

Acknowledgments

The Co-Editors of *Experiential Theatres* would like to personally thank Deb Alley, Sarah Bay-Cheng, Rachel Bowden, Scott Burrell, Bud Coleman, Mary Karen Dahl, Grace Edgar, Brett Garfinkel, Pedro Guevara, Greg Handel, Andrew Killion, Karen Laughlin, Francene Lemoine, Patrick McKelvey, Chuck Ney, Beth Osborne, Beth Osnes, Jessica Parr, Karn and Robert Richoux, Daniel Sack, Ann Shanahan, Niki Tulk, and Pia Wyatt for their personal and professional support. Special thanks to our partners, Gina and Kent, and our families for their patience, love, and encouragement during this three-year process.

We first met and discussed the earliest ideas behind this collection in an American Society for Theatre Research Working Group led by Penelope Cole and Rand Harmon. The full scope of the project began to form through a small group roundtable presented for the Association of Theatre in Higher Education. We set out to create a uniquely collaborative volume which could not have happened without all the help of the remarkable contributions from our Section Curators who added valuable insights throughout the formation and editorial process. Valerie Clayman Pye was instrumental in supporting early conversations about the project as well as offering guidance while editing and assembling Section One. She went above and beyond in her collaborative efforts and we are truly indbted. Marshall Botvinick, a trusted friend, signed up right away to help steer and support the project. Bruce Bergner and Rich Dionne introduced us to an entire area of practitioners and scholars in themed entertainment design. Throughout the stages of development, Lucia Accorsi, our anonymous reviewers, and the team at Routledge have offered kindness, encouragement, and timely logistic and editorial insight.

Our final set of thanks extends to the remarkable collection of artists, scholars, and educators who agreed to share their expertise and passion in this volume. Your overwhelmingly affirmative responses to our invitations to contribute were incredibly humbling, and your engagement with the themes and ideas we proposed, even in the earliest drafts, reassured us that we were on to something. The quality and insight of your case studies, essays, interviews, and responses pushed the project to deeper levels of engagement than we could have foreseen. We are proud to share your work with the field.

– William W. Lewis and Sean Bartley

Author Biographies

EDITORS

William W. Lewis, Ph.D. is an Assistant Professor of Theatre History, Literature, and Criticism at Purdue University. His research focuses on spectatorship, politics, digital cultures, and experiential performance. As a scholar-artist he also utilizes practice-based research where he integrates interactive technologies into live performance to better understand the relationships between contemporary audiences and mediatized culture. Will believes strongly in the ethos behind deep collaboration and collective working processes. His writing has appeared in *GPS: Global Performance Studie*s, *Theatre Topics*, *Performance Research*, the edited collection *New Directions in Teaching Theatre Arts*, and the volume *Avatars, Activism and Postdigital Performance: Precarious Intermedial Identities*. This latest essay analyzes the app-based performance work *Karen* by Blast Theory to discuss the ways algorithmic technologies usher forth a performative condition where acts of role play allow spectators the ability to hack the subjectivizing power of datafication. He is the founding co-editor of *PARtake: The Journal of Performance as Research* and has co-edited with Sonali Pahwa the special issue "Reterritorializing Digital Performance from North to South" for the *International Journal of Performance Arts and Digital Media*. Will is currently working on a monograph that tracks historical connections between interactive technologies of the latter twentieth and early twenty-first century and increased desire from spectators for increasingly personalized performance experiences.

Sean Bartley, Ph.D. is an Assistant Professor of Theatre History at Northwestern State University. His research centers on contemporary site-specific, ambulatory, and immersive theatre practices and sports as performance. His work has been featured in *TDR: The Drama Review, Theatre History Studies, Theatre Journal, PARtake: The Journal of Performance as Research,* and *Borrowers and Lenders: The Journal of Shakespeare and Appropriation*. Recent book chapters include "'You're Out! Presence and Absence at the Ballpark" in *Sporting Performances: Politics in Play* (Routledge, ed. Shannon Walsh) and "The President Makes a Play: Putin and Erdoğan's Sporting Diplomacy" with Jared Strange (Bloomsbury, ed. James R. Ball III). Recent directing projects include *TRAGEDY: a tragedy, The Government Inspector,* and *Drunk Enough To Say I Love You?*. Dramaturgy credits include work with American Repertory Theatre (*Julius Caesar, Romance*), New Repertory Theatre (*BOOM*), and Company One (*Learn to be Latina*).

xii • AUTHOR BIOGRAPHIES

SECTION CURATORS

Bruce Bergner has been an award-winning stage designer in professional theatre and opera for over 25 years. With a resume boasting 130+ realized designs at reputable companies across the United States, he has also expanded his research into the realm of Experience Design (XD): the design of live, human experiences such as those found at theme parks, museums, attractions, monuments, in retail and entertainment establishments, and in site-specific performance events. Bruce also recently published a theory book on design: *The Poetics of Stage Space: The Theory and Process of Theatrical Scene Design* to strong reviews. Bruce teaches stage design in the Department of Theatre & Dance at the University of Colorado-Boulder.

Marshall Botvinick is a playwright and dramaturg based in North Carolina. His plays have been developed at Palm Beach Dramaworks, Jewish Plays Project, Seven Devils Playwrights Conference, and South Carolina Repertory Company. As a dramaturg, he has worked with PlayMakers Repertory Company, American Repertory Theater, and Burning Coal Theatre Company. He is currently a Lecturer at the University of North Carolina Wilmington.

Valerie Clayman Pye, Ph.D. is an Associate Professor of Theatre and Chair of the Department of Theatre, Dance, and Arts Management at LIU Post, where she teaches acting, voice and speech, and Shakespeare in Performance. Valerie's research focuses on actor training pedagogy, Shakespeare's Globe, Shakespeare tourism, and on practice-as-research (PaR). Her book, *Unearthing Shakespeare: Embodied Performance and the Globe* (Routledge 2017) is the first book to consider what the unique properties of the reconstruction of Shakespeare's theatre can contribute to both the training of actors as well as to the performances of Shakespeare's plays. She is also the co-editor of *Objectives, Obstacles, and Tactics in Practice: Perspectives on Activating the Actor* and *Shakespeare and Tourism.* Her essays have appeared in *Shakespeare, Teaching Shakespeare, PARtake: The Journal of Performance as Research, Theatre Topics,* and a number of essay collections.

Rich Dionne is an Associate Professor of Practice and Chair in the Department of Theatre in the Rueff School of Design, Art, and Performance at Purdue University, as well as the co-director of Purdue's Fusion Studio for Entertainment and Engineering. Rich's work focuses on the intersection of engineering and live entertainment, including the areas of mechanical design and control systems. He also has a deep interest in the scholarship of teaching and learning.

ESSAY CONTRIBUTORS

Rachel E. Bauer, Ph.D. is Coordinator of Academic Theatre Arts and Lecturer in Theatre Arts at Sacred Heart University. In her research and teaching, Rachel highlights the transferable nature of theatre pedagogy and theatre education, focusing on the skills gained through theatre training that are useful both on the stage and across many disciplines. Additionally, her research looks at representations of gender in theatre, especially in relation to science plays and themes. In the future, Rachel plans to continue to develop the interdisciplinary relationships between the Arts and STEM fields. She received her Ph.D. from the University of Missouri (18').

Johannes Birringer is an independent choreographer/media artist. Since 1993 he has been the artistic director of AlienNation Co (www.aliennationcompany.com) and created numerous dance-theatre works, videos, digital media installations, and site-specific performances in collaboration with artists in Europe, the Americas, China, Japan, and Australia. He lives in Houston and London and co-directs the Design and Performance Lab at Brunel University

London, where he is a Professor of Performance Technologies (www.brunel.ac.uk/dap). Together with fashion designer Michèle Danjoux, he has created immersive dance works featuring electro-acoustic and sensortized wearables. DAP-Lab's "Suna no Onna" premiered in London in 2007; the mixed reality installation "UKIYO [Moveable Worlds]" premiered in 2009–10 before touring in Eastern Europe in 2010. He collaborated on the European METABODY project and developed *kimospheres,* a series of immersive installations (2015–18) that explore the convergence of physical-sensory and augmented VR spaces. The dance performance *Mourning for a dead moon* (December 2019) addresses the climate crisis. He is also the founding director of Interaktionslabor (http://interaktionslabor.de) and author of numerous books on performance and media, including *Media and Performance* (1998), *Performance on the Edge* (2000), *Performance, Technology, and Science* (2009) and *Kinetic Atmospheres: Performance and Immersion* (2021). He has co-edited three volumes on dance studies: *Dance and Cognition* (2005), *Dance & Choreomania* (2011), and *Tanz der Dinge/ Things that dance* (2019).

Lindsay Brandon Hunter, Ph.D. is an Associate Professor of Theatre and Performance Studies and Director of Undergraduate Studies in the Department of Theatre & Dance at the University at Buffalo. Lindsay's research sits at the juncture of theatre, media, and performance studies; her book, *Playing Real: Media, Mimesis, and Mischief,* was published in 2021 by Northwestern University Press, and examines the performances of authenticity and realness in contexts as varied as reality television, alternate reality gaming, and live broadcast theatre. Her essay "We Are Not Making A Movie: Constituting Theatre in Live Broadcast" won the American Theatre in Higher Education prize for Outstanding Article in 2019, and her writing has appeared in *Theatre Topics, Theatre Journal, Theatre Survey, Contemporary Theatre Review,* the *International Journal of Performing Arts and Digital Media,* and the online journal *Amodern.* At UB she is a past Honors College Faculty Fellow and Humanities Institute Faculty Fellow; she also co-organizes, with Drs. Ariel Nereson and Christian Flaugh, the HI Performance Research Workshop.

Astrid Breel, Ph.D. is a researcher and educator, whose work explores participation, agency, and impact within an interdisciplinary context. Her research explores meaning-making processes in a variety of contexts and her practice focuses on developing situations that enable two-way engagement between audiences and artists to create meaningful experiences. Current projects include exploring aesthetic experience within experiential performance forms and examining ways to capture the emergent value arising from participation in art. Astrid is the Impact Research Fellow at Bath Spa University, an Associate of Coney (who make theatre for playful audiences), and a member of artist-led organization Residence in Bristol, UK.

Robert Quillen Camp is a writer, director, and performance maker. With Pig Iron Theatre Company, he wrote the texts for *Pay Up, Franklin's Secret City,* and the Obie Award-winning *Chekhov Lizardbrain.* His other plays include *White on White* (Hoi Polloi, 2022) and *Our Ruined House* (PETE, 2019). His writing has appeared in *Conjunctions, PAJ, Theater, Comparative Drama, Chain,* and *Play A Journal of Plays,* and has been anthologized by 53rd State Press. He is an Assistant Professor and Chair of Theatre at Sweet Briar College in Sweet Briar, VA.

Liz Fisher is an interdisciplinary theatermaker based in Austin, TX. Her directing work explores applications of mixed realities, immersive theatre strategies, and game mechanics in new play development and reimaginings of classic texts. She received the Princess Grace Award in Theatre and the SDC National Directing Award [Kennedy Center]. She was a featured speaker at SXSW Interactive and other conferences on her work in building audience engagement via integrations of network technology and live performance. She is an Assistant Professor at the University of the Incarnate Word and an Associate Artistic Director of Penfold Theatre. MFA: Texas State. www.lizfisher.net

Kesia Guillery is a Research Associate with interactive theatre/digital arts company, ZU-UK. She supports delivery of ZU-UK's MA Contemporary Performance at the University of Greenwich and the company's practice-as-research processes, as a writer, and co-ordinating research projects. Her research explores interactivity and participation, the intersection between theatre and games, and role-play and fiction as tools for transformative, socially engaged experience. She has written, directed, and produced performance for venues and festivals including Shoreditch Town Hall, St Augustine's Tower Hackney, Northampton Royal & Derngate, DARE Festival, VOILA! Festival, Oslo Architecture Triennale, and spoken at State of the LARP Conference (Oslo, 2018).

Jamie Harper is a UK-based performance maker and researcher. He is a previous winner of the JMK Directors' Award, the National Theatre Cohen Bursary, and a Churchill Trust Fellowship to explore the merger of drama and games at the University of Miami. Recent participatory performance works include *The Lowland Clearances* at Camden People's Theatre, *Washing Machine* at the Baltic Centre for Contemporary Art in Newcastle, and *Nudge* which was runner-up for Headlong Theatre's Digital Artist Award. He has recently completed a practice-led Ph.D. in performance at Newcastle University and currently works as Lecturer in Drama at the University of Plymouth.

E.B. Hunter is an Assistant Professor of Drama at Washington University in St. Louis. Her digital adaptations of canonical plays have been supported by Microsoft and the Center for Interdisciplinary Research in the Arts, and her scholarship has been published in *Text and Performance Quarterly*, the *International Journal of Performance Arts and Digital Media*, *Theatre Topics,* and the edited book *Research Methods in the Digital Humanities*. Before returning to academia, Hunter founded an immersive Shakespeare company in a restored blast furnace in Birmingham, Alabama. She holds a Ph.D. in Theatre from Northwestern University and an MFA in Dramaturgy from Columbia University.

Eric Hoff is a director, dramaturg, and writer who focuses on genre-defying immersive entertainment. His work has been produced on stages across the United States. He has directed at UCLA, Cal State Long Beach, and has presented his work at SATE, CultureHub LA, Seoul Arts, and SCAD. Eric is currently the Senior Creative Director at Fever Events, which produces original content in over 80 cities around the world.

Sarah Johnson (Ph.D. in Theatre and Performance Studies: The University of Colorado Boulder, MFA in Dramaturgy: The University of Iowa) is currently the Assistant Professor of Dramaturgy and Head of Playwriting at Texas Tech University. Her research focuses on intercultural theatre, new play development, and dramaturgical methodologies. Her writing has been featured in *Asian Theatre Journal* and *Theatre Topics*. She works professionally as a dramaturg with theatre companies across the country. She serves as the Executive Director and Resident Dramaturg for WildWind Performance Lab and the Performance Review Editor for *PARtake: The Journal for Performance as Research*.

AUTHOR BIOGRAPHIES • XV

Stephen C. Jones is a Lighting and Scenic Designer (USA 829) and a Professor of Scenography at California State University-Sacramento. His professional work can be seen in Regional Theaters around the United States. Collaborative interests in the entertainment industry include serving as a beta tester with Vectorworks 3D design software. He served as the technical editor for a textbook on 3D modeling and was a Research Contributor for a book series on World Scenography. As an artist and professor, his passion for holistic storytelling revolves around the exploration of creating a unified theatrical experience.

David Kaye is a Professor of Theatre at the University of New Hampshire, specializing in acting, directing, and applied theatre. A published author and produced playwright, he has worked as an actor and director throughout the United States. He is the Artistic Director of PowerPlay, a professional interactive theatre company based at UNH. David is a Fulbright Scholar (2012) and recipient of several awards including the New England Theatre Conference Educator of the Year (2009), UNH Outstanding Associate Professor (2012), UNH Teaching Excellence Award (2009), and Spotlight on the Arts Awards for Best Director (2008), Best Supporting Actor (2012) and Best New Play (2014).

Steve Luber is Associate Director of the Ammerman Center for Arts and Technology at Connecticut College, where he teaches courses on media and performance and histories of arts and technology. His research centers on the historiography of media and performance and has published work on the Blue Man Group, Radiohole, Two-Headed Calf, and Reid Farrington, among others.

Adrienne Mackey is a multidisciplinary artist who explores the potential of performance and play. With her company, Swim Pony, she's created works including *SURVIVE!* - a 22,000 sq-ft science installation; *THE BALLAD OF JOE HILL* at Eastern State Penitentiary; *WAR OF THE WORLDS*, with Drexel's Entrepreneurial Game Studio; and *THE END* – a month-long mixed reality game exploring mortality. Most recently she's developed *TRAILOFF* – a mobile app embedding immersive audio onto nature trails and *Aqua Marooned!,* a wildlife card game. Mackey is also a classically trained soprano, former chemist, and teaches acting, directing, and devising at the University of Washington.

Persis Jadé Maravala is Artistic Director of interactive theatre/digitalarts company, ZU-UK. Ethnically Iranian/Yemeni/Indian and raised in East London, Maravala is committed to reclaiming public spaces to reduce barriers to audience participation and fairer opportunities for working-class people. Recent work focuses on mediating relationships between strangers through the use of sound and instruction-based performance. Her work has been commissioned by LIFT Festival, FACT Liverpool, Southbank Centre, Summerhall, British Council, Macau International Festival, and the Brazilian Ministry for Culture. Maravala's radical methodology is taught as an MA in Contemporary Performance by Maravala/ZU-UK at the University of Greenwich.

Matthew Mastromatteo is a New York City based actor, director, and producer whose interests lie in new play development. Matthew is an adjunct faculty member at Long Island University: Post, where he teaches acting and movement in the BFA program. In addition to his teaching, Matthew trains actors in practitioner/client simulation. He continues to work as a Standardized Patient/Client throughout the NYC metro area. An active member of the Association for Theatre in Higher Education (ATHE), Matthew serves as the chair of the Acting Program Focus Group.

Erin B. Mee is the Founding Artistic Director of This Is Not A Theatre Company, with whom she has conceived and directed *A Serious Banquet, Ferry Play, Subway Plays, Festival de la Vie, Versailles, Pool Play 2.0, Theatre In The Dark: Carpe Diem, Readymade Cabaret 2.0, Life on Earth, Play In Your Bathtub 2.0* and *Tree Confessions*, which have been performed in the United States, Argentina, Australia, China, England, France, India, Scotland, and Russia. She is the author of several books, and numerous articles for *TDR, Theatre Journal, Performance Research, Natarang*, and others. She is Assistant Arts Professor at Tisch, NYU. www.erinbmee.com

Samantha Meigs is a Professor of History and Experience Design, and Chair of the Experience Design Department at the University of Indianapolis. She holds a Master's degree from the University of Colorado and a Ph.D. from Northwestern University. Samantha is active in teaching, researching, and designing experiences related to immersive environments and story-driven design. In addition to her academic training and experience, she worked for seven summers at Conner Prairie Museum as a historical interpreter, also assisting with Visitor Studies and Program Design. Her areas of expertise include social history, themed entertainment, and game history and game design.

Christina Papagiannouli, Ph.D. is a Research Fellow in Performance and Interactive & Immersive Technology at the University of South Wales (UK), where she also lectures on performance and new media. Her research focuses on cyberformance, online theatre, and the use of interactive and immersive technologies in theatre and performance. She has published widely in the field, including a Palgrave Macmillan monograph titled *Political Cyberformance: The Etheatre Project* in 2016, and has presented her work at a range of international festivals, conferences, and other events. She is currently co-convener of IFTR's Intermediality in Theatre and Performance working group.

Jorge Lopes Ramos (Brazil-UK) is Executive Director of interactive theatre/digital arts company, ZU-UK, and Associate Professor of Contemporary Performance at the University of Greenwich. Jorge's work focuses on scaling intimacy and challenging privilege in interactive experiences using theatre, games & technology. Practice-as-research outputs have taken the form of public performances, productions, digital work, installations, and exhibitions in venues, conferences, and festivals including TaPRA, IFTR Munich, London 2012, Southbank Centre, FACT Liverpool, LIFT, The Lowry, Latitude, Summerhall Edinburgh, Festival de La Imagen (Manizales), University of Campinas (São Paulo), WorldCup 2014 Official Cultural Programme, Federal University of Rio de Janeiro, Concordia University (Montréal).

Mike Sell is a Professor of English at Indiana University of Pennsylvania. He is co-author with Michael Chemers of *Systemic Dramaturgy: A Handbook for the Digital Age* (Southern Illinois University 2022), editor of the 1960s volume of *Decades of Modern American Drama* (Methuen 2018), and co-editor with Megan Amber Condis of *Ready Reader One: The Stories We Tell With, Around, and About Videogames* (Louisiana State University Press forthcoming). He is the founder and co-director of the Digital Storygame Project, a public digital humanities project that supports K-16 teachers in the integration of game design and decision-focused storytelling in English Language Arts and other curricula.

Justin Stichter is an Attraction Designer and Project Manager for PGAV Destinations a world-renowned design firm that designs attractions, exhibits, and experiences that enrich lives. Using intuition, intellect, and imagination, the firm helps their clients create enduring memories in the minds of their guests. Justin has a Masters of Architecture and a Masters of Urban Planning from Washington University in St. Louis.

Hans Vermy is an educator, writer, theatremaker, and award-winning film editor who focuses on histories, theories, and practices of performance, media, and animation. He has also published on historical trends in lighting design and the relationship between animation and theatricality. Dr. Vermy has taught theatre at UCLA and FSU and helped found the Theatre Department at CSU, San Marcos.

Amanda Rose Villarreal serves as Assistant Faculty of Theatre Education at California State University Fullerton, where they are prompting a pedagogical shift to prepare students for the growing immersive entertainment industry. Amanda Rose has worked as an audience engagement character performer for athletic organizations; toured with American Immersion Theater (US) and Viral Ventures (AUS/US); and directed immersive performances for the ACLU's National 100th Anniversary Tour (US), Otherworld Theatre (US), Pinecone Studios (UK), and Toynbee Studios (UK). A larper and intimacy director, Amanda Rose's research focuses on consent-based practices for and learning experiences in gamified and interactive performance.

Experiential Theatres:
An Introduction

William W. Lewis and Sean Bartley

EXPERIENTIAL THEATRES: EXPERIENCE IS EVERYWHERE

American institutional theatres and university theatre training programs are stuck at similar critical impasses. Broadway, regional, and residential theatres are weathering three existential crises: the closure of theatrical spaces and budgetary cuts forced by the COVID-19 pandemic, an industry-wide demand for more inclusive, equitable, and just hiring and programming practices, spearheaded by organizations like We See You White American Theatre amidst the Black Lives Matter movement, and calls to reckon with predatory financial practices, particularly an industry-wide dependence on unpaid and low-paid internships. Theatres increasingly seem unable to understand and attract younger audiences to sustain their half-century-old subscribership models. As organizational leaders grapple with addressing this long list of crises, many cling to conventional forms of the theatrical product itself. Innovative formal practice has certainly taken place amidst the pandemic, but as theaters announce new organizational structures and accountability plans, the programming offered by most professional theaters represents a clear return to the status quo.

As American theatres navigate these new identities and structures, college theatre programs have faced their own series of life-or-death questions. How do professors teach practical skills like movement, scenic construction, or lighting design on web platforms amidst a pandemic? How do programs train young artists for the rapid structural changes forced upon institutional theaters? Why teach audition skills when theaters are dark and casting calls disappear for more than a year? Perhaps more importantly, is it *ethical* for university programs to continue to define and structure themselves as preparation for the network of Broadway, regional, and institutional theaters? If theaters continue to hire smaller and smaller numbers of our graduates, fail to hire a sufficiently diverse, equitable, and inclusive set of artists, and continue to grossly underpay them through the system of internships and short-term positions without benefits, should we continue to feed the monster? As COVID-19 laid bare, almost everyone in the American theatre faces the realities of industry-wide financial precarity: even the tiny percentage of artists who worked with a measure of job security in full-time, salaried, and benefitted positions at regional and commercial theatre organizations often found themselves fired or furloughed without a moment's notice. While this book cannot address all these issues, it does focus on how we train our students for emerging theatre-making practices and avenues for applying theatrical tools and knowledge to burgeoning experiential theatres.

DOI: 10.4324/9781003188179-1

Experiential theatre practices propose a new frame for an increasingly audience-focused series of performance methodologies. For the past half-century there has been an ongoing conversation about the form of theatrical encounters. This conversation often centers on binaries such as passive and engaged, live and mediated, or political and non-political. As these conversations have played out, we have seen a growing emphasis on the role the audience plays as a central part of these encounters. This shift has largely coincided with more participatory and experiential modes of interaction and communication in daily life fostered by both new technologies/media as well as restructuring of social codes and milieus. What we see rising is a growing emphasis on all things experiential in nearly all aspects of contemporary social life. When the experiential is foregrounded, it expands the perspective one must consider when thinking about all encounters. An experiential encounter might be something as seemingly simple as purchasing a warm morning beverage or playing with tactile artifacts that enhance the educational benefits of a science museum or something as complex as interfacing with the multiple ways a marketing campaign has designed connections between a narrative component of a film, a live theatrical event using augmented reality, and the packaging of a consumer toy based on a character from the film. If everything has become a performance in the twenty-first century (McKenzie 2001) then every individual becomes a spectator of and in their own individual theatrical event. Robin Nelson (2010) refers to these spectators as "experiencers" who do more than watch with their eyes but instead interact within the event through a fully embodied act of perception (45). This is the basis of the experiential. When everyone is at all times a spectator, then it becomes commonplace to consider them as the center of personally crafted theatrical experiences. These experiencing spectators are the central pillar of all *experiential theatres*.

This book is intended to help theatre educators better understand this perspective of twenty-first-century life so that they may set their students up for the greatest possible success as innovative future theatre artists. To do this we will push the envelope of what the term theatre means both within an artistic frame, but also towards a more expansive social frame. Experiential theatres are performative encounters where the spectator becomes both witness and performer with and in the totality of the event. This is audience-centered theatricality and performativity. These theatres are often crafted to be both singular and communal due to their focus on the overall experience of the individual audience member who is interacting through a variety of means. These theatres are often labeled immersive or participatory when accepted *as theatre* and often simply considered games or simulations that have a performative nature by those who have not been introduced to broadened theatrical horizons. Experiential theatres are also encounters whose dramaturgical frame is expanded to encompass multiple senses, ideas, and actions. These might include the way Disney, Nike, or the Hard Rock Cafe develops a distinct theatrical encounter for the consumers who enter their physical storefronts. In these instances, these spectators become what Maurya Wickstrom (2006) calls "performing consumers" where one who is simply shopping becomes the star of their own theatrical encounter. The storefront becomes the mise en scène, the flow through the designed space the character arc which connects to the eventual purchase, which is, in fact, the performing consumer's super objective. What is common amongst these examples is how the spectator becomes part of the narrative, part of the event, part of the overall experience. The authors in this collection unpack the various ways experiences are crafted through design, dramaturgy, narrative, structure, and performance in order to offer new models for praxis-based approaches to pedagogy for the twenty-first century.

To train students well for encounters of the twenty-first century we should accept that they need to learn sets of skills and methods that will be used outside of what is typically considered conventional theatrical business models. Training consciously for these expanded avenues requires softening some of the silos and specializations that have become the habitualized norm in theatre training and specifically theatre departments in US higher education. Doing so will allow our students to become more creative, collaborative, critical, innovative, and socially observant. These are the skills that are most sought after in the arts but also in areas beyond the arts where many future experiential theatres will emerge. To train students to think experientially is to help them better understand the products of their craft as experiential processes, which in turn, sets them up for the greatest possibilities of success. For educators, this means adopting a methodology steeped in a broad range of theories and pedagogical approaches.

To begin, let us first explore the overly simplistic binary of passive and engaged spectatorship that has been the focus of so much scholarship in the past twenty years. For most of human history, theatre and performance practices have been highly experiential through various forms of social participation. In antiquity many theatrical encounters centered around participatory rituals that confirmed community and social belonging. Ancient Egyptians in Abydos partook in embodied commemorations of the god Osiris, perhaps in much the same way that devotees of contemporary religions participate in masses and services. In fifth century BCE Athens, audience members sitting in their seats at the Festival Dionysia looked not at a representational set, but at the very same Aegean Sea that features prominently in *Agamemnon* and other tragedies they experienced. By connecting the sea, to the sky, to the *mise en scène*, and to the seating area built into the hillside they understood the relational position they were in as participants in a larger cosmic encounter. In many parts of Europe in the seventeenth and eighteenth centuries, wealthy audience members paid a premium to sit on the stage itself, literally and spatially inserting themselves into the action. The social performance made by these audience members was often just as important as the actors reciting the words of a dramatist. In the Egungun rituals of the Yoruba people, audience members dance with, sing to, and occasionally run from the masked and costumed performers embodying local ancestors not in a purpose-built theatrical space, but in the streets and squares of the community itself. And finally, today one might find themselves donning a nondescript mask that allows them to anonymously wander as spirits with/in an elaborate immersive scenic landscape crafted inside an empty industrial building. They might also be tasked with solving puzzles while interacting with a multi-branched narrative that is experienced across multiple parts of a bustling city scape. Across cultures and eras, theatrical practice has involved audiences spatially and experientially. The short period where audience passivity became the norm is simply a blip in the long history of engaged and interactive theatrical practices.

The most recent forms of engagement have emerged as a reaction to shifts toward media-driven passivity beginning a little over a century ago. At the end of the nineteenth century, a series of new traditions in the West that emphasized a physical, practical, and dramaturgical separation between performers and spectators emerged. Theaters shifted from elaborate boxes and spectators on the stage to more uniform, seemingly egalitarian fan-shaped seating areas. Electric lighting began to progressively dim on the audience and brighten on the stage, deemphasizing the social interactions between spectators and directing their attention onto the characters. Playwrights in the emerging Realist and Naturalist movements took advantage, writing works that shifted away from presentational acting styles suited to noble and upper-class characters declaiming their thoughts directly to audiences and moved towards more representational scenes between members of the emergent bourgeoisie. Before long, acting conventions emphasized an imaginary "fourth wall" facing the seating area, urging the actor to perform *as if the audience were not there*. This divide often became literal through the architectural mechanism of the proscenium arch, framing the onstage action like a painting or television screen. The rise of the craft of directing further solidified the separation of audience and performance product in the name of theatrical unity. What artists created for the stage had become distinctly separate from the totality of the theatrical event which included the audience as participant. Crucially, these new conventions spread in popularity in the years surrounding the two World Wars just as educational theatre programs began to emerge in American and European universities. Whereas theatre practice had been taught through apprenticeship for centuries, theatre courses and, eventually emerging from Speech and Voice or English Literature departments, theatre programs trained actors, playwrights, directors, and designers to work in the presentational conventions of professional theatres and the passive relationship they created with audience members. These traditions still foreground both the professional theatres of the United States and virtually all university training programs that prepare artists to work in them.

In the second half of the twentieth century, a wide range of interdisciplinary artists began to explore impulses that led them back towards a more experiential frame for performance events. Allan Kaprow began to stage "Happenings" which sought to give audience members embodied tasks to perform in public spaces. Performance Artists like Yoko Ono, Chris Burden, and Marina Abramović put audiences in precarious positions where they were challenged to act, often physically and emotionally endangering themselves to force the audience interaction. Inspired by Antonin Artaud, the artists of The Living Theatre sought to negate the proscenium arch by inviting the audience on stage, to dance, sing, and even disrobe with the performers. Richard Schechner's infamous Performing Garage experiments with audience interaction and environmental staging led to a renewed wave of engaged theatre that attempted to bring back some of the ritualistic and communal spirit of long forgotten traditions. In recent years, immersive, site-based, and ambulatory events, often inspired by the work of earlier artists in the United Kingdom (Mike Pearson and Brith Gof, Shunt), have seen a surge in popularity on both sides of the Atlantic. This brings us to the state of the field today where experiential practices are seeing a resurgence. This resurgence requires a distinct new set of pedagogies.

While experiential theatre practices have come into vogue in the United Kingdom, continental Europe, and many of the major cities in North America, there is a disparity between training related to these practices. In the United States a majority of theatre programs operate around a professional training format with the intentions of developing a skill set that is directly applicable to the regional theatre format of repertory productions of dramatic writing, typically focused on one area of practice (performing, directing, design, etc.) rather than embracing a more holistic approach that utilizes a "BIG C" collaborative model, one in which all involved in the creative practice have input on every area of development. This is most true in programs that embrace the MFA and BFA model but is also ingrained in the formal construction of most BA programs that honor the liberal arts tradition. In Europe, where the greatest advancement in experiential practice is seen, many programs focus more on the integration of theory and practice toward a holistic model of theatrical production. The merging of theory and practice is much more widely accepted in the UK model, where practice-led and practice-based masters and doctorate programs are abundant and serve as guideposts for undergraduate degrees. These programs often instill in students a questioning spirit while focusing on ensemble and creative practice modeled around devising practices. Outside of the few major conservatories that train artists in a specific skill set such as classical acting, the students who come out of these theatre programs more often form ensembles and companies that focus on making new work in a collaborative model. This is opposite to the training models in the US where students are typically trained in a specialization and left to fend for themselves when they enter the artistic market. No wonder many of our students end up working in other careers five to ten years beyond their degree.

Considering how theatre is heralded as a multidisciplinary artform that thrives on community and collaboration, there is an unusually predominant ethos that focuses on pre-professional training of individual artists in highly specific areas of creation. Marvin Carlson (2011) points to a paradigm of antagonism between professionalization versus scholarly investigation that came about in the US during the 1960s and 1970s. Where previous students had been trained to operate as "theatre scholar-practitioners, equally at home in the archives or onstage, and equally adept at writing a scholarly article or directing or designing a production" a new mode of theatre education emerged. In this mode theatrical production should model itself after "serious" professional practices and therefore the study of theatrical craft should eschew scholarly pursuits and instead focus on training "real artists" who expressed their creative impulses (119). Carlson continues to explain how theatre historians could only be taken seriously if they spent their energies on research and not "putting on plays" (119). With these two positions becoming more commonplace, they were solidified in the 1970s with the mass adoption of M.F.A. programs whose goals focused on professional training for theatrical vocations. This ideology bled down into undergraduate training and eventually created the binary we are left with today where most departments are staffed by a majority of creatives with M.F.A.'s training a wide range of artistic specialties and a small handful of faculty with Ph.D.'s relegated to teaching the history and theory of theatre with, problematically, little connection between the two. Within most theatre training programs most of the coursework is devoted to practice with little space allowed for reflection, exploration, and intellectual curiosity. This narrows our artists' ability to be truly creative and limits their ability to define their own artistic pursuits. Carlson concludes his essay by stating "American university theatre programs must no longer allow themselves to be drawn into the ongoing antagonism between those who study the theatre and those who create it" (123). We argue that this divide between theory/research and professional practice ultimately stifles innovation and evolution of our artform and reciprocally our pedagogies. This is why, for the good of our students and theatre as a whole, it is necessary to move forward toward new praxis-based modes of teaching and learning. We will adopt Robin Nelson's (2013) articulation of *praxis* as "theory imbricated within practice-or what some people call intelligent practice or material thinking" (5). Establishing the connection between theory and practice more broadly will allow for a greater ability to develop skills for collaborative and interdisciplinary creation versus simply specialized production. Experiential practices require these skills as they are foundationally built around the prefix *inter* that follows the dictum of both/and[1], a sense of mutual cohesiveness, and reciprocity.

Experiential theatres are uniquely interactive and interdisciplinary. The term interactivity is often applied to theatre practices, however, when one discusses interactive theatre, it often comes with a set of baggage. A 2007 ATHE white paper by Ann Fliotsos applies the term interactive theatre to formats that are largely akin to Applied Theatre practice. Applied Theatre and its distant-cousin Practice as Research (PaR) have also been often maligned in the American academy as not belonging within the conventional arena of practical theatre training but also not sufficiently rigorous to belong to true theatre scholarship. We believe this is partially due to their difficult to determine applicability to a professional training model and partially due to their emphasis on practical research which due to the binary above has been largely ignored in the United States.

Without the artificial dividing line between theory and practice or research and profession, students are led to allow inquiry and interdisciplinary collaboration to flourish as a part of theatrical creation. Due to what we consider a misalignment of the term interactivity with these other areas of practice we prefer to focus on the word experiential which is both a more expansive a model and also narrows the focus on individual experience. Experiential theatres are those that rely on multiple forms of audience interactivity and often have similar aesthetics as narrative performance events. There is often less emphasis on research, social applicability, or defined analytical outcomes related to community building and politics, though these aspects do exist in some of the most compelling experiential performances. We will utilize a simple taxonomy of experiential theatres that operate under four architectures of exchange: immersion, participation, game play, and role play (Lewis 2017, 2018a, 2021). You can see each in overlapping modalities in most of the types of practices our contributors explore in this book. It is the theory behind these terms that underpin the pedagogies and practical insights that our contributors offer.

Each term serves as a framing mechanism for a variety of practices and methodologies, but each involves some form of focus on the experience of the audience and the levels of agency that individual spectators manage with/in experiential events. These frames are distinct from an operational sense but rarely are they utilized in experiential theatre practices solely. There is often an overlap between one or more of the frames, and contemporary experiential performances often employ a combination of all these frames. But it is the distinct nature of each that educators must understand better if we are ever to develop a concrete set of pedagogies for experiential theatre making. In this project our contributors guide the reader through both the theory and methodologies behind these frames to help unpack the best practices and techniques one might lean on in their teaching. In many instances our contributors also discuss some of the ethical responsibilities one must consider when developing experiential works. This is necessary because unlike more conventional forms of theatrical practice, experiential theatres consider the overall experience of the spectator first, versus an emphasis on the event as stand-alone product for passive consumption.

Each of the four frames (See Figure 00A1) has a long history connected to interactive forms of theatrical practice but it is how they have been defined and implemented in twenty-first-century theatre methods that are of most interest to us. We will start with the term that has exploded both artistically and commercially in the past fifteen years: immersion. **Immersion** has become a sort of catch-all frame for many of the interactive practices this book explores. We, among others, find this problematic because it is in fact a more narrowly defined type of interactivity, but one that has the most marketing draw due to its powerful connection to one's affective senses. The numerous examples of scholarship (Machon 2009, 2013; Alston 2016; Biggin 2017; Lavender 2016; Jarvis, 2019; Frieze 2017) on the term beginning around 2010 have attempted to nuance its definition, but we will frame it simply as a sensory engagement that gives an audience member the feeling/idea of being enveloped by either a designed or dramaturgical world. The emphasis of immersive work is on feeling as though one is *inside* the work, and therefore it is often compared to being submerged in a body of water. Immersion does not require response, however. The spectators in an immersive event can remain passive and still interact simply through their affective senses. **Participation** on the other hand is a higher level of interactivity that is often paired with immersion but requires some form of choice making and direct action on the part of the audience member. These choices may or may not directly impact the trajectory of the narrative or the world one is immersed within, but they do alter the perception/reception of the spectator's encounter. Further up the scale of interaction is **Game Play** which capitalizes on the gamification of the choices one might make through participation. In works that focus on gameplay, one receives immediate feedback from these choices, and they are often structured in a way that the audience member is rewarded with the feeling of having achieved some form of goal/objective. Gameplay mechanics often are considered the most engaging for audience members due to the level of creative input they are allowed. The last frame we propose is **Role Play** which blends many of the above frames but is distinct in how it relies on audience members becoming more than themselves. They take on the role of a character, an operator, a guide, or some other member of the performance/narrative/designed world. They imaginatively immerse themselves in the fiction by playing an active role that belongs within the fabric of that world and ideally the choices they make while immersed in this world are informed by the role they are playing. Each of these four terms is deeply interconnected as experiential practices and is reliant on two common variables: experiential design and agency.

EXPERIENTIAL THEATRES

IMMERSION
- Sensory Engagement
- Enveloping World
- Implied Agency

PARTICIPATION
- Audience Choice
- Potential for Impact
- Heightened Agency

GAME PLAY
- Goal Oriented
- Rule Bound
- Structured Flow

ROLE PLAY
- Driven by Character
- Roles Define Choices
- Narrative Impact

Figure 00A1 Taxonomy of Interactivity in Experiential Theatres.

Experiential theatre practices take as a central point of interest the involvement of the audience. The designers, writers, dramaturgs, makers, and performers of experiential theatres are keenly focused on delivering a specific and tailored experience for each individual member of the audience. To do this they must focus on the overarching design of the project as well as the immediate sense of agency that the audience feels. Agency simply refers to a person's—in this case the spectator—ability to do something. In many instances this "ability" is simply a perceived feeling of control. One of the primary differences between the more conventional forms of "passive" spectatorship and experiential spectatorship is an emphasis on the audience member's sense of control over the encounter. This may be over the flow of the narrative or simply over their individual perspective on the event. Even in a "passive" fourth-wall event, the audience has agency to look where they want (though most skilled directors and designers manipulate the stage image in order to focus where the spectator looks). There is a common misconception that makers of experiential theatre are focused on giving the audience agency. This is a false impression. Agency simply exists. Theatrical audience conventions are the social forces that typically restrain that agency. For instance, in a fourth-wall proscenium theatre, spectator conventions set rules where the audience is trained to sit quietly facing forward in a dim lit room taking in, through eyes and ears, the product before them. The spectator has agency to break all these conventions, but they rarely do. In experiential theatre the restraints are taken off. In many ways these constraints are reconfigured to allow a specific form of agential relationship for the spectator. The way the event is designed ultimately shapes what levels of agency the audience can engage. Each of the four frames of interaction we cover allows different modes of agency based on specific operations of experiential design covered in this book.

Experiential design is a *mode of thinking* that is broader than the conventional forms of theatrical design such as scenery, lighting, sound, and costumes that are taught in traditional theatre schools. These elements can be crucial to experiential design, but as they are taught today, they are often ornamental and operate to produce a staged fiction most often intended to be seen versus felt. If they are felt, it is primarily by the performers acting within that fiction. We propose they be folded within an umbrella of overall user experience which requires a broader understanding of how each area of design defines the audience encounter. Adopting methodologies form User Experience (UX) design might be helpful. UX design is a specific area of study often related to product and software development and often is taught within fine arts, technology, and business programs. It takes as a central focus the concept of interface; the interaction between a user and the product they will use. In this manner design for experience requires thinking beyond the elements that pertain to primarily sight and sound but also to the other senses and modes of interaction. One must conceptualize and understand the thoughts, feelings, sensibilities, and expectations of the audience member. They must consider ahead of time what the user will do when they encounter the product and how they will do what they do in the encounter. These designers are architects of complex systems who develop all aspects of an encounter that will be experienced with/in: both from the outside of an event and inside an event simultaneously. The object might be the initial focus, but the overall product is the designed interaction between the spectator and the event allowed in the encounter with the object. The designer must consider both how the spectator uses the object and is also part of the event with the object. If we think about our use of technologies in the twenty-first century, it becomes easier to understand this relationship.

INTERACTIVE TECHNOLOGIES AND EXPERIENTIAL PRACTICES

The increasing rise of experiential forms of theatrical practices over the past fifty years has run in parallel to technological innovation. Where the early attempts at engaging the audience, disrupting the divide between spectacle and spectator, and expanding the spatial frame in theatre were largely motivated by an engaged sense of politics, the most recent evolutions have been influenced by the rapid adoption and integration of interactive technologies into everyday life (Causey 2006, 2016; Salter 2010). Technologies have always had an impact on theatre practices, but it is during the last quarter century that tremendous change has come both from the audiences engaging with theatre and the technologies themselves. As our environments have become more technologically interactive, so too have our daily habits related to all forms of media consumption (Couldry and Hepp 2017, Hepp 2013, Hayles 2012, McCarthy and Wright 2004). As such, theatre practices have increasingly modeled the modes of daily activity found in our technological devices.

In the first half of the twentieth century, theatre practices began to differentiate themselves from forms of visual media such as film and photography by expanding beyond notions of realism to become more abstract and theatrical in the movements of the historical avant-garde. These modernist movements reached a pinnacle during the rise of televisual mass media which also coincided with fragmentation brought about by postmodernism. While televisual media at first allowed a sense of simultaneity with the ability to creep into the living rooms of everyday life, they quickly became targets of criticism for the way they had begun to hold their users captive. Guy Debord (2005:1967) marked the 1960s as an apex in what he called the Society of the Spectacle, a society informed by image-saturated influences of television and film media. This was an artistic, political, and capitalistic paradigm where people had become consumed through their own spectatorial practices, largely led by corporatized structures that understood the power of the media delivered via airwaves. Debord argued that these corporate structures had utilized artistic media to pacify their audiences. Updating Marx's theories of society and economy, he explained that the power behind the spectacle had become the driving force for anti-revolution by engineering societies toward passivity and subservience to their media influences. During this period the unleashing of the spectator began with a new wave of avant-garde theatre artists taking up the project of those mentioned in the previous section. The first steps away from the rapture of the spectacle began by engaging with the televisual in intermedial modes of theatre and direct participation in politically motivated performance. Artists such as the Living Theatre, The Performance Group, and The Open Theatre rebelled against the society of the spectacle by capitalizing on the power of interactivity between multiple bodies in space as a mode way of activating the audience into action. Artists and companies such as the Wooster Group, Robert Wilson, Laurie Anderson, Nam Jun Paik, and Joseph Svoboda utilized the power of televisual media to engage in a more cerebral form of intermedial critique. The methods used by these artists largely stayed on the fringes for most of the latter half of the twentieth century. As technologies evolved, these practices became more mainstream and informed new practices that were increasingly experiential whether they implemented technologies or not.

Televisual media became ubiquitous in the latter part of the century and a renewed interest in interactivity and *maker culture* began to slowly rise alongside advances in digital technologies. Rising at the very beginning of the digital era, maker culture's defining trait is a "do-it -yourself" spirit ingrained in a populace who wants to do more than consume an already conceived product. Instead, they want to partake in the production as a new mode of active consumption. The making of the product itself becomes part of the product. The shift toward the paradigm began in earnest in garages across the country with the implementation of build-your-own computer systems. It was with the birth of the early Internet that this spirit really took off. It exploded with Web 2.0 and began to significantly change the way theatre makers made their products for a changing sensibility of audience members. The ethos behind maker culture is analogous to the ideologies and operations included in theatrical participation. Both users and spectators are allowed access to the agency to become more than mere consumers but instead become part of the action and the encounter that any product is wrapped up in. By being allowed the choice to impact the development and flow of this encounter, these participants now had the sense of ownership over the outcomes that the event offered. As personal computing expanded into more connected and interactive modes of use (instantaneous communication, user-generated content, postable/editable media) these users became more and more hooked on the direct feedback found in participation.

Ideologies of making the televisual more tangible through sensory interaction also took root in social structures through technologies of the virtual which the Internet supported. This is where the seed of immersion across creative industries first took root. First made famous by Jaron Lanier in 1987, virtual reality (VR) became the new technological marvel that attempted to bring together the visual fidelity of film and television with the experiential presence and ephemerality of live theatre. One only needs to look at the trends toward simulation and digital realities in the cultural zeitgeist of the late 1980s and early 1990s to understand how powerful the draw toward technological immersion was. Just consider the range of movies that played on the themes of cyberculture and machine interface. The most often cited example is *Lawnmower Man* (1992), but others such as *Johnny Mnemonic* (1995), *Virtuosity* (1995), and *Strange Days* (1995), captured the imaginations of the masses to the possibilities of jacking into cyber worlds shortly before AOL ushered in a wave of digital connectivity. With *The Matrix* (1999) came the pinnacle of this era, leading to a mainstream questioning of our ethical relationship with virtual realities in the new century. Unfortunately, the promise of the technology was about three decades ahead of its time. True immersion using VR was too expensive, cumbersome, and gimmicky to find full adoption. At the turn of the century immersive practices began to take off in theatre. Even though the technology was not fully developed, theatre makers began to use the ideas and theories behind virtual reality and simulations and co-opted them to make interactive theatre pieces that capitalized on the idea of enveloping their audiences. In the early 2000s a range of immersive artists (i.e., Blast Theory, Punchdrunk, De La Guarda, Coney, Shunt) began experimenting with a hybridization of site-specific theatre and immersive narrative. This led to a full wave of artists (i.e., Third Rail, Speakeasy Society, Cynthia Von Bulher, Nocturnal Fandango) coming into their own near the end of the decade and inspiring others to follow. It is difficult to determine explicitly where these artists learned their experiential craft though. Were they taking what they were learning from digital culture and grafting it onto their established practices in theatrical design and storytelling or were they developing something entirely new on their own?

The immersive promise of technological virtual realities found another media outlet in the 1980s. Video gaming allowed some of the same properties of VR but could also amplify the user experience through aspects of game play and flow-based immersion. Most early video games are based around four basic design fundamentals described by play theorist/maker Jane McGonigal (2011): they must have a goal, a structuring set of rules, include a system of feedback, and require volunteer participation (21). The play found in early video games is a specific form that is more structured than open-ended play described by early theorists such as Johan Huizinga (1955) and Roger Caillois (1963). They capitalize on the performances of the player as an interactive choice-maker in a relationship between a digital product and a human user. Though most video games are largely pre-scripted for specific user throughput (a framing toward linear objectives) they give the player the feeling of control and agency over their individual playing experiences. This expanded as computing power multiplied and more and more games embraced a sandbox approach to world-building. Like a child playing in their schoolyard sandbox, these games offered an almost endless environment for imagination and free exploration. These games became more immersive and engaging due to their open-ended nature to roam as one pleases through the digital environments. This is the same format that experiential theatre makers such as Punchdrunk employ in their works. When discussing gaming it is hard to miss the term "flow" which refers to a state of immersion within aspects of play. This sense of flow, which allows the player to feel fully separate from the real world and become part of the game world, is key to meaningful game experiences. What in fact is the overall effect of constant gamification in our daily lives and with our daily interactions with our devices? How might this constant state of flow impact our perceptions and expectations of theatrical events?

Gamification has become pervasive across social aspects of life as we embrace the concepts of likes, pokes, badges, milestones, and other reward systems built into social media platforms. As life becomes more gamified, we see more and more aspects of gameplay in our artistic products. Like the popular game *Pokémon Go* we see a rising trend toward experiential encounters that use Augmented Reality and other forms of locative technologies. The popular running app *Run Zombies Run* is another example of gamification of everyday routine events. By adding a soundtrack and cues to speed up or be eaten by the zombie horde at your back users are given the nudge to perform better. These nudges are folded into an ever-evolving narrative based on your individual running experience. These technologies are just now beginning to become standardized and accessible. As they continue to become more commonplace, they will ultimately create new paradigms of interaction with each other and our spatial environments. This is an outcome of our technological/media environments which are fundamentally based on relationality and mutual impact. As we engage with/in these environments we both shape and are shaped by the technologies and media. Underpinning all our technological environments is the heart of digital interactivity found in the processes of the Internet.

Under the process of digitalization driving technological change over the past fifty years, the invisible underlying construction of societies is based on complex networks of multimodal communication based on the structure of the Internet. While the Internet formally began in the 1980s as multiple small digitally connected networks primarily between academic and governmental entities, it quickly grew through the 1990s and early 2000s into a "hyper-textual" and interconnected digital backbone of the world we know today. Through protocols of computer-to-computer communication (HTTPS), a global digital infrastructure emerged and changed how communication operated and recirculated via digital, virtual, and mobile systems. These systems allow for near-instant interactivity and connectivity across vast geographical distances and give users the ability to both consume and create artistic products in a manner, unlike previous technologies. With the embeddedness of the internet into everyday lives came a shift in the way most people think about interactivity and communication. This is a shift toward the postdigital.

The tools that exist within an interconnected digital ecosystem allow their users to develop heightened sensitivity to direct response while using these tools. This causes a feedback loop where participatory action is embedded across multiple media and technological spheres. In the early 2000s when Web 2.0 ushered forth platforms such as social media spaces, user blogs, wikis, and content creation sites like YouTube, Vimeo, Instagram, and Twitch, users increasingly became producers as opposed to merely consumers of other people's information. This unprecedented shift led to what Henry Jenkins (2006) describes as Convergence Cultures that are predicated on a sense of seamless flow and interactivity between "multiple media industries," tools, and platforms (2). Jenkins' concepts align squarely with our argument for expanding the scope of inquiry and training for theatre students. The very interconnected and interactive nature of convergence cultures bleed over into all aspects of life including learning and performance. When students are born into and formed within these cultures, they develop sensibilities that replicate and encourage deeper senses of convergence, cross-platform connection, constant interactivity, and a sense of agency that comes with pervasive choice making. They are less passive receivers of information and more participatory transmitters through their daily actions. Today's students have a fundamentally different relationship to theatrical traditions and canons than any generation before them. They were also uniquely prepared for the emotional and social challenges of COVID-19 because they had already figured out how to create life experiences using digital tools such as Tik Tok and Instagram. Transitioning to making theatrical experiences with these tools seemed quite natural for them.

As Web 2.0 became pervasive, technologies continued to evolve and connect to the internet in ways that allowed innovative Apps (applications) to emerge that transformed how previous modes of work, play, communication, and interactivity occurred. Each step in the development of the internet changed how human communication worked and changed the social systems that inform how we all operate in our social worlds. The late twentieth and early twenty-first century became consumed by digitalization. In this paradigm, the internet and all the technologies connected to it go from being mere tools and networks for communication and transform into an interwoven network of mediatization driving creation, exploration, knowledge making, and experiencing. While it took nearly thirty years to reach a saturation point, this new way of experiencing reality via digital paradigms became the everyday norm by the end of the 2010s for many global societies. Once something becomes part of our everyday experience, we begin to see how it impacts our creative practices. In theatre, this meant shifting toward interactivity and ushering forth a renewed interest in the role of the spectator. You see this in the rise of interdisciplinary art groups and collaborative artists who have pushed the field wider into more experiential formats such as Blast Theory, Gob Squad, Forced Entertainment, Rimini Protocol, Punchdrunk, De La Guarda, Third Rail, and Welfare State.

MEDIATIZED LEARNING = EXPERIENTIAL KNOWLEDGE MAKING

We live in a postdigital world. Accept it. As we've explained earlier, media and technology shape our everyday realities. All life has become imbued with processes interconnected with digital traces. If we look at this concept through a generational lens, we might better understand the implications as educators. Generation Z—the generation who are now the prime college-age students—was born at the beginning of the postdigital era. Their emergence as a cohort marks a shift from analog sociality to digital selfhood. They are the first generation who are "blind to the distinction between technology and the natural behavior of certain objects" that are part of the previous analog world (Koulopoulos and Kneldsen 2014, 3). Due to their digital upbringing in a technologically intertwined social paradigm, they cannot understand fully what it means to be disconnected from *the digital*. They also have a much harder time understanding how to connect when they are asked to attempt to do so. For them everything, yes everything, is defined by digital influences. The primary influence as explained earlier is the Internet, but even more so that metal and glass brick in their pocket that serves as the symbiotic interactive gateway to all places, events, times, and ideas. This means that theatre educators can no longer hold onto the notion that theatre lives on a spectrum divorced from the world shaping influence of digitalization. There is no such thing as non-mediated theatrical performance underdigitalization. As such, educators must begin to accept and understand the influence of the digital inside a postdigital paradigm.

Crucially, today's theatre students often experienced and understood theatrical performances through digital platforms like YouTube *before* they saw them in person. The barriers of physical distance and cost keep most college theatre majors from Broadway houses, but not from voraciously watching, sharing, and discussing bootleg recordings of shows through digital forums. The COVID-19 pandemic expanded, legalized, and legitimized this digital access: commercial, regional, and institutional theatres both created new works for digital formats and made previous recordings available to thousands of new audience members who often had no previous relationship with the companies or their physical performance spaces. College-aged audiences, already familiar with digital theatergoing before COVID-19, transitioned more seamlessly into the new theatrical environment. They had already been using digital tools as a primary way to talk about theatre and understood the value of internet platforms for discussing emerging theatrical trends with others around the world. Their way of approaching theatre was inherently already postdigital.

The concept of the postdigital is surrounded by conflicting definitions depending on the agenda and the contextual framing of those engaged with its use. Florian Cramer (2015) is one of the first to discuss in detail the slippery and often un-useful ways the term is thrown around within circles of artists emerging out of the first wave of digital art. For Cramer the term is easiest to relate to as a sense of "disenchantment" (13) with the artifacts of digitalization as a visible force. Instead, the postdigital marks a periodization where the effect of the digital becomes invisible and ingrained within the fabric of sociality. For David Berry (2015) the postdigital is both a condition and an aesthetics where "'being online' or 'being offline' is now anachronistic, with our always-on smart devices, tablets, and hyperconnectivity, as, indeed, is the notion that we have 'digital' and 'analogue' worlds that are disconnected and discrete … the postdigital is hegemonic and entangled with everyday life" (50). Both Berry and Cramer discuss the postdigital in relation to artmaking practices evolving through the influence of computation, for theatre makers and theatre educators Matthew Causey's (2016) notion of "postdigital performance" as a format that is uniquely connected to postdigital culture will serve as resource closer to home. Causey explains that postdigital culture is a "social system fully familiarized and embedded in electronic communications and virtual representations (432). Like the concept of deep mediatization (Couldry and Hepp 2017), this culture reaches a point of embeddedness. This embeddedness then predicates a paradigm where it becomes less useful to argue for the separation of theatrical liveness from the effects of digitalization. Under this paradigm theatre becomes just another part of the postdigital fabric and as such is often interacted with through digital means either visible or invisible.

Communication technologies are more than mere tools in today's postdigital environment, an environment where it is no longer possible to make a clear distinction between digital and analog social worlds. These technologies act as mediators of all forms of communication that shape social life. In the twenty-first century, digital media and digital technology have become the frameworks, the tools, and the conduits shaping our realities through a process called digitalization. We both use and are used by these technologies in a manner that deeply implicates multi-modal interactivity into the very basis of our understandings of the world around us and our place within that world. Today's postdigital social world is one that fundamentally constructs the reality we perceive and experience. This world is itself constructed through communicative processes known as mediatization which encompasses all forms of technological and media-based social effects (Couldry and Hepp 2017). Mediatization is a fluid set of meta-processes whereby social and cultural networks become mediated by and mediatized through technological interactions.

The mere idea of disconnecting from these networks is anathema to contemporary students because they know nothing other than constant digital connection. The changes brought about by digitalization inside and outside the classroom require new perspectives from teachers of theatre and performance. Because our social world has reached a point where mediatization can no longer be removed from the social and the social can no longer be understood divorced from digitalization, we must begin to utilize the fundamentals of that process. Clay Shirky (2008) explains that the full social impact of technologies does not fully emerge until they have become commonplace. He states, "It's when a technology becomes normal, then ubiquitous, and finally so pervasive as to be invisible, that the really profound changes happen" (105). Shirky's argument was prescient of the changes that would occur for younger generations coming of age in the second decade of the twenty-first century. These generations were raised in digital cultures whose primary media source is the internet, delivered via multiple ubiquitous interfaces. Interfaces are increasingly tethered by smartphones, but also integrated technologies that rely on communicative and aesthetic processes such as social media, augmented reality, virtual reality, and artificial intelligence. For members of the last three generational cohorts (Gen Y, Gen Z, and Gen Alpha), perception and thought processes have been increasingly altered by constant connection due to the fragmented but interconnected nature of digital spheres. For them, their way of being is that of the postdigital. Their ways of being-in-the-world and perceiving worlds have been augmented to require constant connection and interaction with places, spaces, and identities that exist inside and through digitally assisted technological devices and media. Their connection to digital tech has caused them to evolve in a manner that mirrors the operations of their devices and media. This primarily occurs through modes of increased constant interactivity and desire for increased agency in feedback loops. We should consider this a cognitive, social, and cultural paradigm shift. This shift has impacted their ability to understand and interact with a world that does not allow constant modes of interactivity such as direct participation, choice making, editing, commenting, playmaking, and co-authoring all of which are found within the epistemologies of networked digital domains. Running parallel to these shifts toward direct participation and interaction within the digital, theatrical and performance-based modes of communication have increasingly become more interactive and participatory. We as educators must tap into a well of new knowledges and practices in order to can harness the potential of these students' novel ways of experiencing the world.

If we consider experience as a mode of reading the world around us through multiple forms of perception (embodied, cognitive, intuitive), we can then see how technologies impact that reading function. Technologies change the way people survey and interpret their environment in similar ways to the way they read literature and performance. Modes of reading and interpretation are becoming increasingly interactive and relational because our technologies and media are no longer based on static and unidirectional modes of use. Multi-directionality, non-linearity, hyper-textuality, and multi-modal interactivity have become the everyday norm. As such, performance paradigms have rapidly begun adopting these processes leading to an increasing prevalence of theatrical experiences that mirror the way we interact with digital technologies. These modes of interaction are relational, immersive, participatory, and imbued with elements of play. These interactions begin the moment the audience member hears about the event and lasts well beyond the "staged" event.

Alongside digitally induced changes to human behavior, the late twentieth and early twenty-first centuries also saw an increasing prevalence of media language framing all aspects of commercialized life as those that belong to the experiential. Joseph Pine II and James Gilmore (2011/1999) made the term experiential notorious by introducing a marketing theory based on the Experience Economy. This economy is one where capital accumulation shifts away from a commodity market toward a service market which then morphs into an experience market with theatrical underpinnings. In this market it is no longer enough for the consumer to simply purchase a product. They must instead see that product as a part of a larger experiential encounter. Products are no longer valued purely by their usefulness to the consumer. Instead, value is assumed based on the entire encounter with the product from purchase to consumption. In many instances it begins prior to the purchase. The authors use the staged event of purchasing a cup of coffee at Starbucks as a prime contemporary example. In the commodity economy a cup of coffee was valued based on its taste, aroma, and usefulness as a delivery system for caffeine. Under this long-established model, you were content with making coffee at home after finding the product that best suited your likes and purchasing it at the local market. Those aspects became secondary when the purchasing event transferred to a packaged, hip bohemian coffee house that played alluring indie music and came in a modestly designed disposable cup with your own name perfectly scribed on it by your own favorite barista. The coffee itself could actually be inferior to the one you have at home, but you are willing to let that go because the purchase is enveloped in a unique and personalized experience gained through the interaction. This experience also makes the same cup of coffee that costs ten cents to supply worth the three to seven dollars you spend at Starbucks. What you have purchased is not just the coffee but the idea and experience of being bohemian and part of a different and possibly idealized culture. Pine and Gilmore were explaining the beginnings of the experience economy in 1999. Today, the Starbucks experience has to be amped up by multiple degrees to deliver the same punch. As the experience economy became more entrenched, and the Starbucks-style experience more pervasive, the product had to become laden with more opportunities for choice-making and personalization. Now that encounter needs to be more than a coffee experience, it has to become a custom-created franken-coffee with one of six different non-dairy milks, bean roasts, and sugary add-ons delivered in your favorite Starbucks with baristas that cater to you as a unique individual. Experiences now must be based on multi-tiered modes of interaction and personalized choice-making possibilities that give you a sense of uniqueness. We have seen this in our everyday lives and increasingly in our theatres.

Theatre professionals might like to believe that our artistic practice rests outside Pine and Gilmore's experience economy in a purely aesthetic and decidedly non-commercial realm. But increasingly, a distinction between product performances and performance *as a product itself* has become blurred. And this blurring is a two-way street. Not only do multinational corporations increasingly view employees as actors and product debuts and interactions as theatrical experiences, but theatre artists and companies lend their practical expertise to corporate events and the marketing of products. Punchdrunk, for example, the wildly influential group behind *Sleep No More* and other long-running immersive theatre pieces, has recently been hired by Stella Artois, Louis Vuitton, and Sony PlayStation to craft experiences for product launches. Rather than a discrete art form wholly unconnected with commercial markets, theatre and performance are now a part of a spectrum, with a visit to Starbucks or The Apple Store on one extreme, theatricalized experiences such as theme parks somewhere in the middle, and contemporary experiential theatre pieces on the other pole. An integration of theatrical performance practices with multimodal and digital media forms is already well underway, one that Frank Rose described in 2011 as *The Art of Immersion.*

Recent attempts to better understand the trends toward constant interactivity and their relationship to theatre/performance include Andy Lavender's (2016) *Performance in the twenty-first Century.* Lavender describes a shift in societal and cultural milieus in the early part of the twenty-first century, leading to what he names *theatres of engagement.* These theatres of engagement are prompted by a shift from a "society of the spectacle to a society of involved spectaction" (29–30). He explains that contemporary spectators no longer simply watch; they interact and engage with their social surroundings. Lavender argues that theatrical performance at the end of the twentieth century became "something other than an encounter between actors, or between actor and audience," it was evolving into a form where the "separation between the space of the performance and that of spectatorship" was quickly closing (9). He is identifying the early impact of digitalization on spectators as the primary consumers of theatrical events. This points to an evolution towards interactive engagement built out of "a sharpened enjoyment of co-presence, corporeality and embodied sensation" (15). In previous paradigms, the spectator was primarily a receiver of information through sight and sound, but today's spectators crave experience that is more embodied, more personalized, and more directly linked to the ways they digitally interact in their everyday lives.

Other contemporary scholars offer increasingly useful frames for understanding these embodied and experiential notions of audience. Josephine Machon's (2013) *Immersive Theatres: Intimacy and Immediacy in Contemporary Performance* articulated a framework for "immersive" performance, a catch-all term for emerging narrative performances that has perhaps been applied too broadly outside the world of Theatre and Performance Studies to hold much meaning today. Machon's work, beginning with *(Syn)aesthetics:*

Redefining Visceral Performance (2009) is significant to this project as it starts the attempt to broaden the definition of immersive practices but does so in a manner that encapsulates other frames from within the experiential umbrella. In *Audience Participation in the Theatre: Aesthetics of the Invitation*, Gareth White (2013) focuses on the moment an embodied performance first invites the individual audience member into a new role, proposing an "aesthetics of participation" in which performance might "temporarily re-shape our social being, make it special, intensify it or bring its contours into focus, expose folds and gaps in its surfaces and depths, and, perhaps on occasion, allow us to perceive ourselves anew" (206). In *Beyond Immersive Theatre*, Adam Alston (2016) articulates a politics of immersive theatre aesthetics, arguing that current forms of these works "romanticize a .... neoliberal productivism" and envisioning a more emancipatory and subversive future for the form (226). More recently, works like Liam Jarvis' (2019) *Immersive Embodiment: Theatres of Mislocalized Sensation* and Lindsay Brandon Hunter's (2021) *Playing Real: Mimesis, Media, and Mischief* have complicated the notion of a separation between "live" immersive performance and expanding digital forms through considerations of VR, AR, and live-broadcast theatrical productions. To date, there is a dearth of formal scholarship in theatre and performance studies that unpacks game and play theory in the same manner done with immersion and participation. Where you do find this work, it often collides within frameworks of intermedial or locative media. Of specific note is *Performing Mixed Reality* by Steve Benford and Gabriella Giannachi (2011) which discusses the mechanics of developing interactivity using digital augmentation in performance through case studies created by Blast Theory. Interactivity is also broadly covered in conjunction with digital technologies in *Digital Performance: A History of New Media in Theater, Dance, Performance Art, and Installation* Steve Dixon (2007), *Multi-Media: Video – Installation – Performance* (Nick Kaye 2007) *Entangled: Technology and the Transformation of Performance* (Chris Salter 2010), *Multimedia Performance* (Klich and Sheer 2011) as well as *Mapping Intermediality in Performance* (Bay-Cheng et al., 2010) collectively assembled by the Intermediality in Theatre Working Group nested in IFTR. These last three are essential reading for anyone wanting to better understand the intricate connection between digital technologies and performance over the past fifty years and all the above are foundational readings for any educator or student interested in the development of experiential theatres of the future.

INTERDISCIPLINARY EDUCATION AS STRUCTURAL FRAMEWORK

To understand these future shifts and how we will understand new theatre, we need to adjust our thinking to include *lots* of new fields and ideas, not just technology. While we rethink training models to ensure that our theatre majors remain employable in professional theatres, we must also think expansively about the applicability of this new training to other fields, particularly as those fields reconsider approaches in the aftermath of the COVID-19 pandemic. Preparing our students for the widest potential range of outcomes is an economic and aesthetic imperative in a shifting artistic landscape. Where we've already seen how the explosion of immersive theatre creates new opportunities and training needs for performers. We need to create programs that facilitate that shift for *others* in the field. How might designers, technicians, stage managers, and arts managers take their practices in experiential and participatory performance into the experience economy?

As the younger audiences that regional and institutional theatres will need to survive increasingly demand new forms of exchange, American universities continue to resist an evolution of training programs. BA and BFA programs alike encourage a swift and conclusive "siloing" of students into tracks and emphases, often before students have had even an introductory collegiate theatre course. Programs push undergraduates to define themselves as performers, directors, designers, or technicians rather than seeing themselves as explorative theatre artists. When these declared concentrations force students down prescribed course trajectories, they prevent them from experimenting with their art form or learning truly collaborative creative practices. Designers and technicians rarely take the speech and voice classes that might offer a gateway to a career in voice acting. Performers rarely consider courses in dramaturgy that could steer them towards careers in criticism, literary management, or academia. Directors, lacking course work in ensemble-based creation, can see themselves only as leaders of a top-down creation and production model. By only concentrating on these specific areas of craft these students are at a loss when it comes to understanding the larger picture of experience. If we focus on the totality of perception and being that comes with being placed at the center of an experiential encounter through design, story, structure, and performance our students become prepared for multiple avenues of work and artistic creation. Through the current pedagogies they are instead locked into a model where they are left to operate as a cog in a machine that is getting more and more difficult to make a living in. The statistics are murky, but if we are honest with ourselves, we know that few of our students go on to make a career in the current theatrical system. There is an ethical imperative to do better. Instead of being part of the machine, let's help them become equipped to build a better system altogether.

By expanding our studies to better understand the influence of media and technologies, alongside shifts in audience expectations, as well as other philosophies of human experience, theatre educators will be better equipped to address the changing momentum toward pedagogies for future theatres. This understanding also allows educators to expand the definition of the term theatre so that our students become well versed in a creative capacity for designing, scripting, analyzing, making, and performing outside of conventional theatrical confines. While there has often been a resistance to redefine the essence of theatre, specifically as the field of performance studies has established itself (see debates on liveness, theatricality, and digital performance), doing so is imperative to our students' ultimate success. Re-definition operates as an effort to expand and bring together new and exciting voices and ideas.

As theatre educators in the twenty-first century, it is increasingly important to expand our frame of reference to better understand the forces that are changing our social spheres and in turn changing the expectations of our audiences and our students. By embracing a heightened sense of interdisciplinarity, we become more adept at evolving our practices as the world around us evolves. This sense of interdisciplinarity is at the heart of this book and the approaches we hope our readers will adopt. There are two forms of collaboration often utilized in theatre production and training: "Small C" and "Big C." The former is more common in production processes and occurs when specialists work on their particular area while addressing a larger unified concept often created or led by a director at the top of a hierarchy. This model in production is often replicated in our training practices causing the disconnect we have identified early in this chapter. In "Big C" collaboration the hierarchies are flattened, and all members of the production team have agency to impact areas outside their priority specialization. You see this mode of collaboration often in devised processes and in companies that utilize an ensemble format. Many find this form of collective creation difficult, but we argue this is due to the way we have been trained. If true collaboration and democratization are limited through specialized tracks of education and divorcing theories as connective tissue across areas, it becomes difficult to embrace this form of inter-disciplinary ethos. We can consider removing the titles of director, actor, designer, dramaturg, technical director, and playwright in favor of the term "architects of exchange" when considering how to develop experiential forms of theatre (Lewis 2018b). If each of the members of the production process focuses on the encounter and the exchange that happens with/in that encounter they can then apply their individual knowledge and talents toward a common goal: developing a meaningful experience for the audience member.

We propose three major shifts in this training model. First, a central emphasis on devising courses for all undergraduate students, fostering a sense that young artists are tasked with generating new performances rather than simply interpreting and presenting the plays of the past. Second, a new model of collaborative coursework, even after students have declared specific interests and affinities. For example, directing and design courses might be structurally intertwined, forcing undergraduate students not just to develop their individual concepts, but also to experientially learn the process of collective production development that will serve them in the larger field. Finally, an increased effort to promote interdisciplinarity in undergraduate education in small, private liberal arts colleges and large public universities alike. Under this model, students might not only take outside courses in the humanities and sciences but also create performances directly drawn from these interdisciplinary experiences.

These proposals all might function within David Kolb's (2015/2014) Experiential Learning Theory. Kolb's theory models learning as a four-part process culminating in "active experimentation," when students put concepts on their feet. As performance becomes more experiential and immersive, so too must the training behind it. Many of our courses in theatre programs already utilize Kolb's framework: acting and directing classes often end with scene showings, playwriting classes with staged readings, and even introduction to theatre courses with short performances. Kolb articulated what we might call praxis: the implementation of theory into artistic practice. This implementation or "imbrication" per Nelson (2013) will allow for greater expansion of questions that lead to creative answering through experiential methods. This notion of an increasingly praxis-based theatrical education is the central impulse behind this book.

STRUCTURE OF THE VOLUME

To model interdisciplinarity and multi-modal collaboration through praxis-based approaches to pedagogy this volume is structured in a way that brings together multiple viewpoints and expertise from across three primary areas of theatrical training: Performance Making and Performing, Dramaturgy and Writing, and Design and Technology. Each section could be read alone and will undoubtedly be helpful to educators in these focused areas, but we intend for our readers to see the connections across the areas as an impetus toward more interdisciplinary modes of pedagogies. Many scholarly resources in our field would only focus on one area in the name of narrowing a focus, but we believe this prevalence toward slicing up our craft has continued to lead to a fracturing of viewpoints and creates a disjointed sense of collaboration in the name of keeping the scope of a project manageable. We have instead opted to go broad so that our readers see both the narrow and the wide view of the new practices offered.

Each of the three major sections is co-curated by two scholars/artists who argue for deep connections between theory and practice. Section One is curated and introduced by Valerie Clayman Pye and William W. Lewis, Section Two by Marshall Botvinick and Sean Bartley, and Section Three by Bruce Bergner and Rich Dionne. We owe a debt of gratitude to these collaborators as they were instrumental in helping shape the content and selecting the contributors. To facilitate the theory/practice connections, each section is divided into five parts: An introduction with basic histories, foundational theories, and forward-looking perspectives on pedagogy; case-study chapters that more fully develop a link between theory and applied practice; a curated conversation with professional artists in the specific area; multiple praxis essays that offer direct practical application for educators in the classroom; and a response essay from scholars who return to postdigital theories to offer our readers a bridge toward technologically augmented practices. While this volume is underpinned by theories of mediatization and postdigital life, the practices we offer largely are divorced from the implementation of digital technologies. That is the work of another volume. Instead, we will focus on experiential encounters that utilize live, in-person, and embodied modes of perception and delivery. Once these encounters are understood and employed in our teaching, we can then begin to adopt technologically augmented formats in ways that are foundationally connected.

We begin with the structural toolsets required to make experiential performances and the protocols for ethical embodiment in performance. By establishing the basic structures and the questions collaborators must ask, we instigate a process where the exterior forces of interaction and experience are considered and focus an eye on the role of the audience. Next, we move on to dramaturgy and textual analysis to connect structure to the process of imagining narrative building within multi-modal experience making. The final section bookends the trio by again expanding outward to establish pedagogies of design thinking and the implementation of experiential technologies. These philosophies of design thinking help us link structure to story and story to experience.

Section One, *Collaborative Experience Making and Interactive Performance Practice* offers a broad-scale approach to the making process as well as the role that performers play within experiential encounters. The emphasis of this section is on methods of collaboration, feedback loops between spectator and event, crafting audience agency, structural flow of encounters as totality of event, and issues of ethics and safety for both performers and audiences. The section pays specific attention to aspects of audience play, both game-based and role-based while explaining how these are blended with immersion and participation. Amanda Rose Villarreal and Adrienne Mackey offer case studies based on their own experiential theatre-making practice that set the stage for the structural and ethical questions teams of makers must ask. Theories of interactivity in multiple formats are applied to theatrical practices to show how audiences become performers and co-authors in experiential theatres. Traditional performers often also take on the role of orchestrators with/in these encounters and as such they must learn to be creative interpreters and improvisers of both character and interpersonal interaction. Due to this transformation for both of these performing subjects, the ethics and concerns of safety and consent are covered for both modes of performing. The roundtable consists of theatre makers, directors, and producers of experiential content who have found success in different formats and venues. They speak to the necessity of reexamining our professional silos so we may move toward more equitable notions of collaboration. In the praxis essays, a variety of course-led methodologies are offered for teaching students to apply methods of interaction design and to craft flow and organization inside experiential performance projects. The section is concluded by reexaming structural frames of performance through a postdigital lens so we might begin thinking about how digital spaces and technologies offer the next generation of theatrical experiences for audiences.

Section Two, *Narrative and Dramaturgy for Experiential Forms* offers our readers ways to guide students toward crafting narratives and dramaturgies for participatory choice making. Courses in playwriting and dramatic structure have long centered on the inspiration and technique of the lone playwright working separately from the actual material and collaborative conditions of theatrical production. But as the field shifts from static and linear perspectives into an increased interest in multi-linear, co-authored, and branching systems of storytelling that can support experiential, multimodal, and multi-disciplinary performance formats, educators, and courses need to provide students with new collaborative models for crafting narrative. Case studies focus on contemporary ensembles already making work in these modes such as Philadelphia's Pig Iron Theatre Company and New York's This is Not A Theatre Company. Paired with these case studies are strategies for adapting campaign building in table-top role-playing games (TTRPG) to theatrical dramaturgy. A roundtable of playwriting, dramaturgy, and devising professors and practitioners assess the current state of affairs and propose new approaches, while the praxis contributors offer techniques and exercises from a wide range of experiential practices, including new play development models, augmented reality gaming, and considerations of creativity for storybuilding. The section hopes to complicate the binary framing of playwriting as an exercise of soul authorship and devising as a collective creation that excludes the playwright, highlighting artists, approaches, and tools that blur this distinction and gesture to systems outside the worlds of theatre and performance. The section is concluded by thinking of the ways narrative and theatrical storytelling have been transferred to digital spaces over the past few decades as a way of setting up new frames for theatre students telling stories in the twenty-first century.

Section Three, *Design Thinking and Experiential Technologies* offers our readers perspectives on themed entertainment, structural design, interactive technologies, and conceptualization for experience. In experiential design an emphasis is placed on the environment as a partner to the audience encounter as opposed to an ornamental element that lies subordinate to either text or performance. Elements such as space, ambience, form, and feeling are considered from the very beginning to establish a basis for a theatrical envelope from which narrative and performance may occur. The section lays out the foundations for theatrical immersion as both a form of environmental design and phenomenological condition. Unlike many "conventional" forms of training, design thinking begins by conceptualizing the entire event and the encounter as the seed for creation versus utilizing a pre-formed text as a starting point. Justin Stichter reconfigures the perspective of developing stories to encapsulate the experience of the teller and the receiver alike as a model for themed design while Johannes Birringer offers a deep and philosophical engagement with the technological tools one might utilize to immerse an audience member down to their cellular level. To supplement these essays, E.B. Hunter interviews Joanna Popper to gain more insight into the technologies contemporary corporations are considering when developing experiences that are theatrical by design. In this section, themed entertainment design becomes a central pillar where experience design, theatre design, interaction design, and technological management often collide in the most fascinating ways. The roundtable participants focus on the world of the themed entertainment industry and explain the necessary tools and practices students must learn to be successful in the rapidly changing world of experiential design. Experiential attractions such as *Star Wars: Galaxy's Edge* at Disney World Orlando are prime examples of the high-level work these students might be tasked to collaborate on. These designers work to create an experiential encounter inside a galaxy far, far away that is just beyond a set of silver turnstiles. Once inside this galaxy the guest is allowed to imagine how they might behave, become, or simply be a part of this world. They become the performers inside their own fan fiction augmented by the experiential design of environment and action. The praxis essays in the section approach methodologies for helping students understand the philosophies behind experiential design in structured projects where both spatial and aesthetic aspects of an encounter are considered in tandem with the audience backgrounds and experiences. These students are guided to think beyond the aesthetic aspects of event and to dive deep into the lived experience that audience members bring to and take from the encounter with the event. The section is concluded with a final essay responding to the previous contributions. This time Hans Vermy and Eric Hoff consider the experiential nature of the projects offered as simply a form of response itself. Bodies in time and space receiving and responding to the stimuli designed. They extrapolate this phenomenological frame to ponder how response might be different or even possibly more resonate when digital technologies are implemented. Through these technologies might the audience gain an even deeper sense of immersion in the totality of the experiential encounter?

While each of these three sections may be read on their own and out of order, we feel to truly embrace the ethos behind experiential processes it is most useful to read through each section sequentially. This will help educators to build a praxis-based framework for complete and holistic experience building which can be applied to lesson plans and course structures. By establishing a foundation on design thinking and experience through embodied immersion educators can then implement aspects of story and narrative to be experienced through structured elements of interaction. Each of these elements is integral to the overall encounter for audience members, and for students who have often been taught to focus on one particular skill set this holistic model will set them up for success in the multitude of experiential theatres the future has to offer. While we each have significant strengths in these areas, striving to become generalists of the experiential encounter can better equip us all to serve our students.

Note

1 See Bay-Cheng et al. (2010)

References

Alston, Adam. 2016. *Beyond Immersive Theatre: Aesthetics, Politics and Productive Participation.* London: Palgrave Macmillan.

Bay-Cheng, Sarah, C. Kattenbelt, A. Lavender, and R.Nelson, eds. 2010. *Mapping Intermediality in Performance.* Amsterdam: Amsterdam University Press.

Benford, Steve and Gabriella, Giannachi. 2011. *Performing Mixed Reality.* Cambridge, MA: MIT Press.

Berry, David M. 2015. "The Postdigital Constellation." In *Postdigital Aesthetics: Art, Computation and Design.* Edited by David M. Berry and Michael Dieter. London: Palgrave Macmillan UK.

Biggin, Rose. 2017. *Immersive Theatre and Audience Experience: Space, Game and Story in the Work of Punchdrunk.* London: Palgrave Macmillan UK.

Brandon Hunter, Lindsay. 2021. *Playing Real: Mimesis, Media and Mischief.* Evanston: Northwestern University Press.

Caillois, Roger. 1963. *Man, Play, and Games.* London: Thames and Hudson.

Carlson, Marvin. 2011. "Inheriting the Wind: A Personal View of the Current Crisis in Theater Higher Education in New York." *Theatre Survey* 52 (1): 117–123.

Causey, Matthew. 2006. *Theatre and Performance in Digital Culture: From Simulation to Embeddedness.* New York: Routledge.

Causey, Matthew. 2016. "Postdigital Performance." *Theatre Journal* 68 (3): 427–441.

Couldry, Nick and Andreas Hepp. 2017. *The Mediated Construction of Reality.* Cambridge, UK: Polity Press.

Cramer, Florian. 2015. "What is 'Post-Digital'." In *Postdigital Aesthetics: Art, Computation and Design.* Edited by David M. Berry and Michael Dieter. London: Palgrave Macmillan UK.

Debord, Guy. 2005/(1967). "The Society of the Spectacle." Edited by Ken Knabb. Theanarchistlibrary. Org. 2005. https://theanarchistlibrary.org/library/guy-debord-the-society-of-the-spectacle.pdf

Dixon, Steve. 2007. *Digital Performance: A History of New Media in Theater, Dance, Performance Art, and Installation.* Cambridge: MIT Press.

Fliotsos, Anne. 2007. "Interactive Theatre Group- White Paper." https://www.athe.org/page/White_Papers#IntTheatre

Frieze, James, ed. 2017. *Reframing Immersive Theatre: The Politics and Pragmatics of Participatory Performance.* London: Palgrave Macmillan.

Hayles, N. Katherine. 2012. *How We Think: Digital Media and Contemporary Technogenesis.* Chicago: University of Chicago Press.

Hepp, Andreas. 2013. *Cultures of Mediatization.* Cambridge, UK: Polity Press.

Huizinga, Johan. 1955. *Homo Ludens: A Study of the Play Element in Culture.* The Beacon Press.

Jarvis, Liam. 2019. *Immersive Embodiment: Theatres of Mislocalized Sensation.* London: Palgrave Macmillan.

Jenkins, Henry. 2006. *Convergence Culture: Where Old and New Media Collide.* New York: New York University Press.

Kaye, Nick. 2007. *Multi-Media: Video – Installation – Performance.* New York: Routledge.

Klich, Rosmary and Edward Sheer. 2011. *Multimedia Performance.* London: Bloomsbury.

Kolb, David A. 2015/2014. *Experiential Learning: Experience as the Source of Learning and Development.* 2nd ed. Upper Saddle River: Pearson Education.

Koulopoulos, Tom and Dan Kneldsen. 2014. *The Gen Z Effect: The Six Forces Shaping the Future of Business.* Brookline: Bibliomotion Inc.

Lavender, Andy. 2016. *Performance in the Twenty-First Century: Theatres of Engagement.* New York: Routledge.

Lewis, William W. 2017. "Performing 'Posthuman' Spectatorship: Digital Proximity and Variable Agencies." *Performance Research* 22 (3): 7–14.

Lewis, William W. 2018a. *Performing Posthuman Spectatorship: Contemporary Technogenesis and Experiential Architectures of Exchange.* PhD Dissertation, University of Colorado Boulder.

Lewis, William W. 2018b. "Approaches to Audience-Centered Performance: Designing Interaction for the iGeneration." In *New Directions in Teaching.* Edited by Anne Fliotsos and Gail Medford, 9–25. New York: Palgrave Macmillan.

Lewis, William W. 2021. "Performativity 3.0: Hacking Postdigital Subjectivities." In *Avatars, Activism, and Postdigital Performance. Precarious Intermedial Identities.* Edited by Liam Jarvis and Karen Savage, 39–64. London: Methuen Drama.

Machon, Josephine. 2009. *(Syn)Aesthetics: Redefining Visceral Performance.* London: Palgrave Macmillan.

Machon, Josephine. 2013. *Immersive Theatres: Intimacy and Immediacy in Contemporary Performance.* New York: Palgrave Macmillan.

McCarthy, John, and Peter Wright. 2004. *Technology as Experience.* Cambridge: MIT Press.

McGonigal, Jane. 2011. *Reality Is Broken: Why Games Make Us Better and How They Can Change the World. New York.* New York: Penguin Books.

McKenzie, Jon. 2001. *Perform or Else: From Discipline to Performance.* New York: Routledge.

Nelson, Robin. 2010. "Experiencer." In *Mapping Intermediality in Performance.* Edited by Sarah Bay-Cheng, Chiel Kattenbelt, Andy Lavender, and Robin Nelson. Amsterdam: Amsterdam University Press.

Nelson, Robin. 2013. *Practice as Research in the Arts: Principles, Protocols, Pedagogies, Resistances.* London: Palgrave Macmillan.

Pine II, Joseph B. and James H. Gilmore. 2011/1999. *The Experience Economy.* Cambridge: Harvard Business Review Press.

Rose, Frank. 2011. *The Art of Immersion: How the Digital Generation is Remaking Hollywood, Madison Avenue, and the Way We Tell Stories.* New York: W.W. Norton & Company.

Salter, Chris. 2010. *Entangled: Technology and the Transformation of Performance.* Cambridge: MIT Press.

Shirky, Clay. 2008. *Here Comes Everybody: The Power of Organizing Without Organizations.* New York: Penguin Press.

White, Gareth. 2013. *Audience Participation in Theatre: Aesthetics of the Invitation.* New York: Palgrave Macmillan.

Wickstrom, Maurya. 2006. *Performing Consumers: Global Capital and Its Theatrical Seductions.* New York: Routledge.

Section 1
Collaborative Experience Making and Interactive Performance Practice

1
Frameworks for Making and Performing in Experiential Performance

William W. Lewis and Valerie Clayman Pye

COLLABORATION AND EASING INSTITUTIONAL SILOS

Experiential theatre practices work best when they utilize a form of collaborative creation that has only recently begun to seep its way as a formalized component into many theatre training programs. While theatre-making has long been a collaborative art, we observe a noticeable shift from the type of collaboration undertaken and defined by the hierarchical structures inherent in contributors' respective roles and the emergent forms of collaborative theatre-making at the heart of experiential theatre. Experiential theatre asks artists to step outside of their proverbial lanes and occupy multiple roles in the creative process. We see the collaboration intrinsic to experiential theatre as belonging to the "Big C" model of collaboration, where each individual in the creation process has the agency to build and shape the overall product produced without institutionalized hierarchies of power.[1] This differs from what we deem "Small C" forms of collaboration, defined by a top-down approach to creation where each member of the team takes its direction from an artistic leader (often a director or producer) who then serves as a filter through which others' creative input flows. Performers in these practices are often left responsible only for the creative component directly within their control; their sole responsibility is to enact a believable reality within the confines of a predetermined fictional world. Furthermore, performers' creative agency is shaped further by directors and designers, who often work together to define that fictional world based on the source material, which then dictates how the performers might occupy it. Twentieth-century training practices have been established where the writer, the director, the designer, and the performer are taught distinct skill sets with little cross-over between them. This reinforces the restrictive qualities of "Small C" collaboration. Instead, in experiential practices, each of these specialists gains the ability to think like the other and utilize those cross-over skills to shape a more holistic and integrative production. This becomes possible because the process asks that everyone focuses on the audience member, whose role is transformed from an anonymous voyeuristic participant to the center of the performance. When the individual audience member is centralized it asks the artists to think beyond their discipline and instead focus on the collaborative nature of the entire event. By focusing on the audience, theatre artists from various disciplines learn crossover skill sets that can flatten the hierarchies that exist within siloed practices.

Formalized theatre training often remains steeped in siloed disciplines that perpetuate distinctions between creative contributions. For educators who traditionally teach courses

DOI: 10.4324/9781003188179-3

in acting and directing we intend that this section will introduce you to a variety of theories, methods, and practical advice to cultivate stronger forms of *Collaborative* processes that you can teach your students. These processes meld some of the conventional practices found in actor and director training with methodologies from devised training as well as frameworks from user-centered design, games design, social interaction, and play theory. The interlinking of these different frameworks offers a networked conceptual approach for broad interdisciplinary methodologies. Interdisciplinarity occupies one of the most dominant topics occurring across this section and the entire book. We see these interdisciplinary skills as necessary, not only for experiential theatre making, but for training holistic artists who can shape the future theatrical landscape and advance our field. Experiential theatres exist at the horizon of well-established practices and their limit is not-yet defined. This wide-open potential offers our students the capacity to shape and redefine theatre for the twenty-first century.

We introduce a more egalitarian form of collaboration where everyone on the team, no matter their specialty, serves as both leader and creative filter. This form of collaboration is already found in many forms of generative creation practices which are often geared toward collective determination due to the fact that a unifying source text—asking for interpretation and conceptualization—does not yet exist. In devised and most experiential practices the product is developed through a generative give and take from the ground up, rather than the top down. We will draw on already established practices from devising as well as theories of play and interactivity to introduce new methods for developing works that utilize immersion, participation, and new forms of interactive games and role-playing. Language and processes are also adopted from technological/design fields such as user experience (UX) design. UX design utilizes user-centered design frameworks where every step in the creative process is predicated by questions and solutions related to how a user interacts with a product. As we apply the UX framework to experiential theatre-making processes, we simply replace "user" with "audience/spectator" and "product" with "event/ encounter". By shaping the language of collaborative making through these interlinking collaborative methodologies, we are able to restructure the making process and establish a set of training protocols that delimits the siloization found in conventional theatre training. Before introducing these new methods, it is necessary to identify some of the histories that have established some of the ingrained practices we feel need to be re-examined.

HISTORICAL TRAINING PARADIGMS: EXPANDING THE FORM

Since one of our aims is to dismantle the previously established hierarchies that place the director in a position of power above the actor, we offer a brief examination of the history of formalized directing training, as it parallels the development of actor training in the Western world. The teaching of the craft of directing is historically rather new within university settings. This is in part due to the fact that having one person who artistically unifies the multiple modes of theatrical creation is a relatively recent concept having arisen at the turn of the twentieth century. It is also due to artistic disagreements about how one develops into this unifying role. English multidisciplinary director Katie Mitchell (2009) explains how many believe that becoming a director requires an "inherent talent that can only evolve on the rehearsal room floor" while others believe that directing is a skill that can be taught within an "educational context" (1). Throughout the twentieth century, a primary way of learning the craft of directing was through a combination of observerships alongside practical trial and error. If you survey most prominent books on directing, what you will find is practical advice from working directors who pass down knowledge gained from years of their own successes and failures. Not until rather recently has there been a concerted effort to examine the actual pedagogy of training directors. Mitchell argues that you can teach directing systematically at the university level and believes that directors can emerge from university programs ready for the industry similarly to actors and designers. Nonetheless, if you look at most theatre programs, directing is often taught at the undergraduate level as a stand-alone "capstone" course that integrates foundational knowledge of script analysis, performance technique, and design-based world-building in conjunction with practical staging techniques and visual tools for image making and picturization. By placing Directing as a capstone course near the end of the student's training, it reinforces the idea that the director stands atop the pyramid of the creative process. Too infrequently is there an in-depth multi-course sequence that helps expand the students' ability to theorize and conceptualize alongside deep methods of collaborative inquiry. Due to the ever-dwindling number of course credits required for the degree in many theatre programs, students, who are interested in actually creating theatre are often only given a constrained set of tools, which perpetuates this imbalance of status and reinforces the director's position as hierarchical to their collaborators. This limits their potential as emerging theatre makers to develop generative processes.

One of the driving issues with the training for directing is how its history and the texts focusing on its evolution largely focus on individual directors and the significance of their products. The nature of this framing causes impressionable students to believe that making theatre requires a singular genius whose role is to dominate the creative process. This problematic ideology is compounded by the issue that a vast majority of these directors only represent a specific cultural and gendered viewpoint. Often there is not enough regard given to the level of understanding (both theoretical and practical) for the interconnections between various areas of craft necessary for foundational frameworks of collaboration with other theatre artists. Also, these texts operate under a specific capitalistic model of top-down production. As these students leave the university, they are led to understand that to excel they must venture out on their own and rely on their singular vision and individual talent to make work. They are also led to understand directing as a rigid set of practices that often does not allow for innovation. For these students to succeed in the years beyond their university training they often need further training at the MFA level, years of unpaid observerships, and/or the resources to fund their own directing projects. Even then they often are left without the tools to push the field forward. Instead, if educators began to focus on collaborative creation that models devised work and ensemble building, students who have traditionally gravitated toward the directing track might develop skill sets that allow them greater success through collaboration and creation. To do this we might also need to rethink the pathways that actors and directors intersect.

Historically, actor training was undertaken as practical apprenticeships, as was the case with any trade. Actors learned the craft of acting by observing and imitating leading actors on the job and were often born into theatrical families, inheriting the family "business". The shift in actor training from the playhouse to the academy (as we recognize it today) can be attributed to two things in the Western world: Stanislavski's codification of an acting "system", and a reduction in the ratio between the theatrical repertory system and the number of actors who wished to undertake training. Even before the proliferation of Stanislavski's system and its impact on formalized actor training, there emerged in the early 19th century in England and the late 19th century in America, the first schools of drama: the Royal Dramatic School (1834) and the American Academy of Dramatic Arts (1884), respectively. Actor training as we currently recognize it within the European and the American traditions, however—both within and outside of the academy—traces back to Stanislavski and his proteges and is inherently steeped in a hierarchical model that centers the authority of the director.

While actors generally receive a more "developed" trajectory of training than directors (or seem to by the number of course hours offered in comparison), this undergraduate training often mirrors the hierarchical structure inherent in directing training. Actors in training are often taught to understand their craft within the larger functions of the hierarchical model. Much of the training that actors undertake centers around scripted work, and their relationship to a play's dramaturgy; they are often not explicitly taught how to apply those skills to larger applications of performance narratives and experiences. This also stifles the development of actors' creative processes. As we write this introduction, this hierarchical model is currently being challenged by the relatively recent initiatives into consent-based boundary practices, which empowers actors with agency that they were not previously granted—even as recently as a decade ago.

Overall, neither acting nor directing training (as individual skillsets) explicitly prepares theatre students to utilize the collaborative and generative skills required to conceptualize, structure, and perform within experiential theatre practices. While this lack of preparation exists in many departmental curricula, there are processes already being taught that can serve as a bridge toward more collective theatre-making practices.

DEVISING/COLLABORATION/INTERDISCIPLINARITY

Why is devising often considered a taboo word within many US academic theatre programs? What is it exactly about the process of collective creation that scares off so many educators and department season planners? Is it because devised work is hard to market, it's difficult to describe the process, or simply because it is different from standardized models of production that emulate professional regional theatres? As a form that requires multi-lateral modes of collaboration that break down more established hierarchies, we believe the model(s) that come with devising practice are a good place to begin when establishing pedagogies for experiential work.

Part of the potential of devising is that as a relatively new set of practices within academic programs—specifically American programs—the rigid structures in place for developing work are stretched and forced to evolve. In many instances, this is also the reason that there has been resistance to adopt these practices. There is no one dominant devising model in academic training—as opposed to the dominant mode of Stanislavskian actor training—instead, there are a variety of methods adopted based on a conglomeration of pedagogical focuses and professional influences. Often these models are handed down through texts that focus on histories, theories, and methodologies (Oddey 1994; Govan, Nicholson, and Normington 2007; Heddon and Milling 2005; Bogart and Landau 2005; Bicat and Baldwin 2002; Kaufman and Pitts McAdams 2018; Graham and Hoggett 2014; Robinson 2015), from workshop training with devising companies, or from formal devising experience developed through experimentation. Many of the methods that have made their way to print are from some of the most prominent theatre companies in the UK, US, and Australia. These companies include SITI Company, Tectonic Theatre, Elevator Repair Service, Frantic Assembly, Goat Island, Forced Entertainment, Complicite, and Kneehigh, amongst others. The one common denominator amongst these companies is the foundational approach to ensemble building and collective creation processes. We and many of our contributors argue this collective approach is most useful for educators who plan to use devised processes as a bridge toward experiential theatres.

Nearly all the experiential theatre practitioners we have surveyed and interviewed argue for a greater emphasis on collaborative processes and interdisciplinary connections when developing their works. As a methodology, devising has already established itself in more pronounced fashion in the educational models outside of the US. There are a few reasons for this that are complexly interlinked. One of the more foundational reasons is the emphasis that is placed on the intersection between theory and practice, and the embodiment of this praxis in rehearsal. The practice of devising trains students to pursue inquiry over technical perfection; to engage in dialogic problem solving through practice and to use performance as a mode of knowing. This can be a new process for theatre students, who may be accustomed to deciphering absolute answers that were decided long before they were engaged in the project. In a text-centric methodology, the playwright has often done the work of both asking and answering the questions for the rest of the team. The directors, designers, and actors simply work as interpretive vessels for the pre-written material. As Alison Oddey (1994) states in the opening lines of her foundational book, "Devised theatre can start from anything" (1). Those that embrace pedagogies aligned with devising help develop students who want to create theatre from scratch versus interpreting for the stage an already formed piece of literature. As Tassos Stevens remarks in this section, the term used in the formal exploration phase of development is a "scratch". To scratch is to dig into the blank surface to find what lies beneath and in the process leave a mark. Before the scratch one must develop the itch, so to speak.

We see a greater need for performance and performance-making pedagogies that address what dramaturg Mark Bly has called the *questioning spirit* in our students. By establishing this questioning spirit early on through more holistic training, students often form companies devoted to particular areas of inquiry that drive their creative practice. The questioning spirit leads to original creation within a less hierarchical model where all involved in the process ideally have equal agency. This is the basis of ensemble: the formation of a collective with co-aligned artistic goals and the agency to meet those goals. Ensemble-based creation is alchemical and transformational. Davis Robinson (2015) calls devising "the process of inventing material for performance together" (9). This shared aesthetic that comes with the togetherness of ensemble work also allows for deeper discussion and focus on the impact of the work on the proposed audience which is also a foundational principle of experiential theatres.

The funding and reception models in the UK and continental Europe also promote this type of work as it is often connected to social, regional, and community issues. Investments are often for multiple artists that form core constituencies in ensemble-based companies which means the money supports a greater share of the artistic community. Due to the already ingrained pedagogies and philosophies that link to funding models, you also see much more scholarship on devising methods and companies coming out of the UK and Australia. Each of these facets leads to more interest in devising and subsequently more devised and collectively developed work. As time has passed and devising methods have firmly established themselves as theatrical foundations it only comes naturally that experiential practices would follow. We will not go too deeply into some of the social reasons for this as this work has been covered already in other parts of the book. However, it is important to understand how methods of collaboration and creation from devising also align with forms of development and creation found in games design and user experience design. By introducing frameworks from these cognate artistic fields, we hope to help bridge the pedagogical gap between teaching devising and teaching methods for developing experiential theatres.

USER EXPERIENCE/GAME DESIGN/PLAY: FRAMEWORKS FOR INTERACTIVITY

Students who utilize tools from devising often have an upper hand when it comes to making experiential theatre because of their deep understanding of performance, character, and narrative formation. What they might be lacking though is a framework to design, develop, and test performances that do not adhere to a conventional format and rehearsal structure found in "traditional" (text-based, hierarchical) theatre settings. This is where user-centered design becomes useful. One of the most common and simplest user-centered design frameworks called "Lean UX" (Follett 2017) utilizes these three steps: (1) Think, (2) Make, (3) Check. This framework is similar to but more streamlined than iterative practices one might see introduced in devised and dance training. In Lean UX the focus is on the experiential relationship between an end user and the product they interact with. Experiential theatre makers simply need to remember that the term audience member replaces the term user in this example. The major benefit of Lean UX over other frameworks is its emphasis on collaboration through the entire process, limiting the need for specialization amongst a design team.

The first step (*Think*) asks makers to reflect broadly on what the intended experience is for the user (audience member). In essence, these makers ask, "what problem do I want to answer through the interaction?". For example, in a mobile device interaction with Google Maps, the interface is designed to help one navigate. The problem is how to help the user most easily find their way from point A to B. During step one, the team of makers brainstorm, categorize, and distill their selections of problems and possible solutions. This first step of the process operates in a similar manner to the first stage of ensemble creation where the team introduces a topic, theme, or idea from which they will develop a performance piece. This generative phase of the process is in some capacity limitless based on the imaginations of the team involved. It is in stage two that structure comes into place and we see a set of possibilities take shape.

The second step (*Make*) considers the design framework for an interaction. For theatre makers, this might mean thinking of the ways that the rules (structure) of the experience and the individual elements, known as affordances, guide an audience member through the performance. Rules offer an audience/user guidance; affordances harness that intelligence even further. This creates a dialogical system whereby all elements in the matrix, along with every possible affordance are shaped by the rules. In the example of Google Maps, a primary rule is that one must input where they want to go. Affordances include inputting this information through typing, voice commands, as well as scrolling over the map, and dropping a pin. Each method, or affordance, offers different ways to access a location which then allows directions to be generated through the software. Like an actor playing a character in a play, the affordances serve as individual tactics toward achieving an objective; in our example, getting from point A to point B. In an experiential performance the interaction might be reading a piece of writing chalked on a sidewalk or asking an actor for a password at a locked entrance. Both affordances guide the audience member forward toward their end destination. Once these affordances have been implemented into a design as prototypes of possible interactions it is up to a playing audience to offer feedback on their use in actual practice, as a form of iterative playtesting. For traditional theatre makers, this might be similar to how a piece in a company's repertoire evolves over time based on festival feedback.

The third step (*Check*) is a phase wherein the design is tested to see if the system and the rules that define it work as intended. In user-centered design this step is usually engaged in stages that introduce small elements individually allowing test audience members to give feedback about the experience. For example, the test audience might be given the opportunity to try out *both* the chalked sidewalk *and* the actor interaction above to see which one is more helpful getting them to the next point in the performance. Through this process the maker often learns something that they had not previously considered in the design process. After testing, the cycle is repeated in an iterative fashion until the full project meets the goals of the team. This is where experiential theatre-making is similar to devised processes and commercial product development cycles. There is a longer, more open-ended, timeframe for development and testing and often the final product ends up serving as simply another test for future refinement.

Many of the examples offered in this section also focus on the gamification of both performance structures as well as the ways that both actors and performing audience members play specific character roles. For the makers and performers of interactive performances based on gameplay and roleplay, it is imperative to utilize both systems thinking and user-centered design frameworks. Systems thinking refers to a complex mode of conceptualization where makers consider entire systems of interactions as well as the interactors within the system. Similar to user experience designers, the makers must always foreground how the audience member will "use" the product. In this case, the performance itself is the product and the spectatorial process is the experience delivered through interaction with and in (*with/in*) the performance. A thoughtful designer looks at both the forest and the trees together, instead of one preceding the other as a way of capturing this way of thinking.

In a system, there are multiple integrated pieces that interact in ways designed for optimal success. A game system is one that is encompassed by a specific environmental frame that allows specific forms of interactions based on sets of rules (Salen and Zimmerman 2003). The game environment contains moments of carefully designed interaction for the spectators who operate as players with/in the system. These players take part in a relational process where each has agency dictated by the rules of the game and the environmental constraints of the type of interaction the system allows. Game structures are often more defined than other forms of open-ended play which can allow potential for meaningful interactions due to most audiences' desire for structure. Working off play theorists Johan Huizinga (1955), Roger Caillois (1961), and others, Jane McGonigal (2011) argues that game-play is differentiated from other forms of play. She argues that games must contain: (1) a goal; (2) rules; (3) a feedback system; and (4) voluntary participation (21). As stated earlier, rules operate as boundaries, a framework through which makers can craft experience. The rules dictate how the players may play while also determining the basic relationships between all parts of the system.

As designers of audience experience, theatre makers can use game mechanics and structures to define what constitutes meaningful interactions. This is done by designing specific moments that allow individuals, through their selective choices, to opt into—essentially, to co-author their experience. Games theory explains that for an experience to be meaningful, the structure must be flexible enough to allow a player to make multiple personalized choices, but also rigid enough to guide those choices to the system's ideal outcome (Salen and Zimmerman 2003, 58). The experience in a game-based performance is therefore not fixed, because the player's agency to interact partially determines how it is experienced. This way of designing flexible structure based on choice also models the way an ensemble might develop a devised performance by utilizing a specific moment or idea as a prompt for creativity. The primary difference is that when structuring games often the makers will consider the ways an audience member will interact in advance to allow for specific levels of personalized agency through choice making. A well-designed experience allows for the right amount of divergence and convergence along the ideal path. Acting training that teaches facilitation skills, as well as character portrayal, allows performers to interact with these experiences as orchestrators, guiding audience members toward specific choices. In essence, they become in-game guides of an individual audience member's experience. Players embrace the agency to dictate their own experience, but when given enough guidance, via rules and through the possible orchestration of co-authoring players and performers, they gain access to personalized tension between their individual actions and structure. As many of our contributors explain, these game-based performances often take the form of or are influenced by Alternative Reality Games (ARGs).

An ARG is a framework for performance that blends fictitious narratives with real-world spaces to allow the player the ability to navigate the in-between in a manner that gives some semblance of immersion while highlighting a sense of Brechtian alienation. Think of ARGs as a blend of site-specific performance and creative role-play. ARGs have continued to gain popularity in the twenty-first century and due to advances in digital interactivity, and the gamification of multiple areas of life, it is a form of performance that has the potential to become the next avenue of exploration for theatre artists. In an ARG the audience member (player) occupies a dual reality across a hypersurface (Giannachi 2004) as they both perform as part of the fictitious narrative and also maintain their corporeal existence in the real world. This gives them a double presence that is both inside and outside the event which allows for heightened levels of critical awareness. Some of the most successful ARGs such as *Black Watchman* and *I Love Bee's* utilize digital technologies and have been connected to narratives and products in popular culture. It is the familiarity with these popular connections, and how those are encountered in daily life, that engages audience members and returns them to the experiential capacities of the ARG's gamified performance. Meaning made with(in) the performance structure becomes interlinked with their life experiences outside the game structure and offers promise for developing experiences around social causes. McGonigal (2011) argues that the best ARGs often have audacious goals that implicate the player in narratives involving "entire communities or society at large" (125) and are designed to help make our social condition better and part of a bigger picture. When a performance maker builds game structures around social or political issues from outside the game world, players gain an ability to critically connect the game world to the real world. Many forms of experiential theatre shine precisely at the intersection where empathic connections are made between the worlds of fiction/performance and the world occupied by the audience every day. Teaching our students how to navigate between these worlds is at the heart of the advice given by our contributors in this section.

SURVEY OF THE SECTION

In Section One: *Collaborative Experience Making and Interactive Performance Practice*, we offer a variety of perspectives on how training is adopted, adapted, and expanded to meet the needs of experiential theatre creation. In their respective chapters, Amanda Rose Villarreal, Jamie Harper, and Adrienne Mackey offer case studies that illuminate practice-based theoretical frameworks that model how actors may be trained to work within these immersive and experiential performance paradigms. Villarreal's essay *Lusory Intimacies: Training Actors for Agentic Symmetry in Unscripted Interactions* offers practical advice on how to develop an immersive production that capitalizes on the interactions between in-world characters and participating audiences. Through mechanisms of interaction that map on to consent-based practices, the essay offers us tools for maintaining both the immersivity of the fictive world while addressing the need for actor safety and audience agency. In *A Curatorial Approach to Teaching Participatory Performance Methods,* Harper offers makers a toolset for developing interactive larps (live action role play) in an iterative workshop method. Mackey's *Designing Play: Game Design in Immersive Performance* introduces holistic approaches to creating systems of immersion using games theory and gaming fundamentals. Each essay offers the reader new ways of considering the actor's role within an experiential model as well as offering framing mechanisms for the performances these actors might perform within.

Next, we gathered a team of international performance makers to discuss their experiences with immersive theatre, alternate reality games, and participatory performance. These thought leaders offer a variety of perspectives, both in terms of practical modalities as well as their respective artistic landscapes. By understanding how these artists work and illuminating the processes that lead to new(er) forms of performance, we hope to inspire new ways of thinking about how we can allow our theatre training to transform to meet the needs of a new theatrical landscape.

As a way of enveloping the advice and perspectives from the previous authors, we next offer a sub-section that examines the pedagogical praxis of alternative training that allows emergent theatre artists to work within participatory, immersive, and game-based performances. Offering practical advice, co-authors Jorge Lopes Ramos, Jadé Maravala, and Kesia Guillery (*The Significance of 'Role-Play' and 'Instruction-based Performance' as Modes of Teaching, Collaborating, and Performing with/for Participating Audiences*) and authors Matthew Mastromatteo (*Standardized Patient Experience: Reframing Pedagogical Approaches in the Acting Studio*), David Kaye (*Preparing the Actor for Training-Focused Inter-Active Theatre*), Astrid Breel (*Facilitating Narrative Agency in Participatory Performance*), and William Lewis (*Collaborative Development Workshop: Experiential Trajectories and Audience Affordances*) provide exercises and pedagogical approaches to teaching university students to create and perform within experiential performance environments. The educator reading this section will take with them a new arsenal of tools and practices they might integrate into their own classroom and pedagogies.

The section ends with a co-written response from Lindsay Brandon-Hunter and Steve Luber who reflect on the offerings from the section through a postdigital lens. Their essay offers ways of rethinking the process of experiencing performance events under the effects and affects of digital media. They argue that the embodied practices outlined in the section have deep connections to more digitally grounded processes and performances through the nature of twenty-first-century interactivity. This argument points toward new horizons of theatrical development that harness the power of digital tools and social interactions.

Note

1 We attribute this way of emphasizing true collaboration to performance artist and professor of dance Michelle Ellsworth who utilized this concept as part of an interdisciplinary graduate course on intermedial collaboration at the University of Colorado Boulder.

References

Bicat, Tina and Chris Baldwin. 2002. *Devised and Collaborative Theatre: A Practical Guide.* Ramsbury: Crowood Press.

Bogart, Anne and Tina Landau. 2005. *The Viewpoints Book: A Practical Guide to Viewpoints and Composition.* New York: Theatre Communications Group.

Caillois, Roger. 1961. *Man, Play and Games.* New York: The Free Press.

Follett, Jonathan. 2017. "What is Lean UX?." Oreilly.com. Accessed, August 15, 2021. https://www.oreilly.com/radar/what-is-lean-ux/

Giannachi, Gabriella. 2004. *Virtual Theatres: An Introduction.* London and New York: Routledge.

Govan, Emma, Helen Nicholson, and Katie Normington. 2007. *Making a Performance: Devising Histories and Contemporary Practices.* New York: Routledge.

Graham, Scott and Steven Hoggett. 2014. *The Frantic Assembly Book of Devising Theatre.* 2nd Edition. New York and London: Routledge.

Heddon, Deirdre and Jane Milling. 2005. *Devising Performance: A Critical History.* London: Palgrave.

Huizinga, Johan. 1955. *Homo Ludens: A Study of the Play Element in Human Nature.* Boston: The Beacon Press.

Kaufman, Moises and Barbara Pitts McAdams. 2018. *Moment Work: Tectonic Theater Project's Process of Devising Theatre*. New York: Vintage Books.

Kelly, Kevin. 2015. *The Inevitable: Understanding the 12 Technological Forces That Will Shape Our Future*. New York: Penguin Press.

McGonigal, Jane. 2011. *Reality is Broken: Why Games Make Us Better and How They Can Change the World*. New York: Penguin Press.

Mitchell, Katie. 2009. *The Director's Craft: A Handbook for the Theatre*. New York and London: Routledge.

Oddey, Allison. 1994. *Devising Theatre: A Practical and Theoretical Handbook*. New York: Routledge.

Robinson, Davis. 2015. *A Practical Guide to Ensemble Devising*. New York: Palgrave.

Salen, Katie and Eric Zimmerman. 2003. *Rules of Play: Game Design Fundamentals*. Cambridge, MA: MIT Press.

2
Designing Play: Game Techniques in Experiential and Interactive Performance

Adrienne Mackey

INTRODUCTION

In 2010, I founded Swim Pony Performing Arts to give a name to the body of work I was creating with an ever-shifting ensemble of fellow creators. Within the artistic process, I take the role of lead artist and director, visioning the central narrative arc and overseeing the design and script for its enactment. My rehearsals are highly collaborative and employ extensive research and I begin each project by defining questions around an issue critical to our contemporary moment—ecological disaster, the universe's cosmic scale, defining civic identity—and then use the generative process to discover the right experiential form to answer them. The company's first project *SURVIVE!* explored the idea of how humans do (and don't) understand the enormity of the cosmic scale, and during early rehearsals I offered my actors a prompt to create scenes that didn't just talk about these ideas but instead gave viewers a chance to *feel* the concepts we explored. While some of the results exploring audience interaction were interesting, the ensemble soon found we had little way to evaluate or iterate on the results. At that point I invited in Shane Liesgang, a former theatre maker turned game writer, to offer us some perspective on designing interaction from a game maker's perspective. That brief interaction opened an entirely new mindset for the company on how to think about cause and effect between audiences and the performances they take part in. This new orientation sparked a decade of research, exploration, and work focused on the use of immersion and interaction to find out what live interactive performances can uniquely do. Since then, our plays have explored the fertile territory where theatre and games meet, amplifying agency for our audiences, and transforming them from passive observers into active co-creators of the event. Reflecting on these experiences from my professional work, I've created a pedagogy to teach these tactics to both students and practitioners in the field. What follows is a distillation of those learnings as four major tactics—*reimagining narrative*, *fostering agency*, *centralizing subjective experience*, and *enhancing embodiment*—with examples from works in our canon that show how these ideas manifest in practice. My hope is this essay will offer readers a better understanding of the opportunities and pitfalls that emerge when developing and staging experiential performance and, more broadly, encourage dramatic artists to use games to help them embrace the power inherent to the theatrical form.

DOI: 10.4324/9781003188179-4

DEFINING WHAT MAKES A GAME A GAME

When teaching workshops on incorporating game design into live performance I begin by asking the following questions:

What is theatre?

What's a game?

How are they similar?

How are they different?

The discussion that follows tends to focus on how games require continuous engagement by their participants. While a theatrical play can be rehearsed outside the presence of an audience, a game is rendered inert without the existence of a player. Unlike the current conventional theatergoer who rarely has a direct impact on the unfolding narrative, players of games are active navigators of the stories they engage with (Frasca 2021). Dramatic scripts are generally static, proposing a singular path, but the interactive nature of game structures allows a player's objectives and actions to have a genuine impact on the progression of events, often creating experiences specific to that player's response (Juul 2004). While there are many, *many* theories about how to define what gameplay is or isn't—see (Huizinga 1949, 1–27), (Caillois 2001, 11–36), (Costikyan 2002, 24–30), (Brathwaite and Schreiber 2008, 5), (Koster 2005, 34–47) as well as (Salen and Zimmerman 2004, 70–83) for a comprehensive collection of varying definitions and their comparisons—as a theatre-maker I find it most helpful to think of games as systems that can help organize interaction, defining parameters for participant action and incentivizing them to focus on particular things.

Before we dive into practical application, let's return to that initial question of what makes games distinct as an art form. In the opening chapter of *Reality Is Broken,* Jane McGonigal (2011) cites Bernard Suits' (2005) definition of gameplay: "Playing a game is the voluntary attempt to overcome unnecessary obstacles" (22). When McGonigal unpacks this definition, she notes that part of what makes games compelling is their *inefficiency* and offers the example of golf as a means of getting a tiny ball into a hole. Though it's highly unproductive to hit a ball from far away with a weird-shaped stick, we instinctually feel that golf is a game not *in spite of* but *because of* this added difficulty. In games we undertake the labor of overcoming a challenge not solely because we desire the outcome but because we enjoy being in the *present tense* experience of playing within the structures of the game. Actors, whose skillsets require a similar state of "in the moment" presence inside the bounds of a script, might find an instinctual understanding of this willing state of playfulness, what Suits (2014) calls the *lusory* attitude. Considering the *voluntary* component to the definition, I think of theatre performances where audience participation feels like obligatory work rather than freely-offered consent. Interactive theatre fails when an audience's volition is removed, transforming an activity that could have been playful fun into obligatory work. The would-be participation designer needs to think critically about both the artistic obstacles they're asking players to surmount (emotional, physical, intellectual, narrative, etc.) and whether their audiences feel they've consented to do so.

TRANSFORMING NARRATIVE FROM LINEAR PROGRESSION INTO A LANDSCAPE OF CHOICE

Hunicke, LeBlanc, and Zubek (2004) define three levels of design they call mechanics, dynamics, and aesthetics (or MDA). Mechanics constitute the base level of design—the range of actions made available to a player. When a series of mechanics are activated, they result in the overall dynamic experience of a given moment. The sum of an event's dynamic interactions creates the overall aesthetic of the work. The more important an idea is to the overall aesthetic vision and message, the more often it should be reflected in the mechanics of interaction for participant experiences. If, for example, an audience member can only gain entry to desirable scenes by prohibiting others from gaining a spot, competition will become a theme of the theatrical world. Game designer Brenda Romero (2011) offers many potent examples of this in her "Mechanic is the Message" series on games inspired by historic atrocities, requiring players to enact actions like sacrificing pieces based on color, discovering that while focused on strategies for winning one has been inflicting harm.

Example. *Welcome to Campus* – (https://swimpony.org/shows/welcome-to-campus/)

> In 2013 Swim Pony created an interactive walking tour called *Welcome to Campus* for Drexel University, built collaboratively with students currently enrolled. Over several months of development, the ensemble settled on the form of a faux admissions tour, with audiences traveling two miles across the school's campus. The performance began with a sterile relaying of administration-sanctioned information about the school's mission, demographics, and course offerings but slowly transitioned into more personal reflections, authored by the current students who performed as "tour guides." To demonstrate one of the piece's core themes—that the polished institutional narrative often doesn't reflect the lived struggles of its actual students—the show's cast included a second group of "hidden" performers. These actors moved through the background of the tour's surroundings, coming into the foreground at moments to illustrate a guide's story: sitting on a bench while audibly venting on a phone during a recollection about feeling lonely or visibly falling asleep in a public lounge during a story about an overly heavy workload. These moments acted as mechanical encouragements for audiences to pay attention to ALL the students (both actors and not) that surrounded the audience and imagine what they might be experiencing in this place.

Using an MDA lens, my ensembles and I conceive of dramatic storytelling not as plot points forming a single line a story locks onto but as a landscape of potential narrative encounters an audience might come upon. Nearly always, theatre scripts are written and rehearsed with an assumption of ordered constancy, ascribing one sequence in which events will be performed. Even in more experimental plays like Caryl Churchill's *Love and Information*, where the director is offered freedom to select the performance order of scenes, audiences play no part in the decision of the action that unfolds. Instead, my actors and I imagine a play as a three-dimensional *landscape* of story, one whose cohesion emerges through exploration, assembly, and association rather than dependent sequencing of events. Progression of timeline may still occur across that landscape, but the audience's relationship to it might take various kinds of forms. Though we as authors lose some control over exactly how participants put our story together, the potential reward is that, when free to explore a world of their own volition, the viewer focuses on elements of a story most relevant to them. Similarly, if one has ownership in assembling the meaning of a theatrical experience, they may feel it more potently.

Example. *SURVIVE!* - (https://swimpony.org/shows/survive/)

> In 2010 Swim Pony premiered *SURVIVE!*, a 10,000-square-foot installation exploring how humans conceive the universal scale. The piece offered opportunities for audiences

to select one of several paths leading to different performance spaces, each containing a scene exploring the same idea through a different metaphor. For example, in one round, we offered audiences a choice between four scenes, each enacted by a different character, all of which examined the multi-dimensional nature of space and time. In one room, a character named The Gentle Scientist (performed by Bradley Wrenn) gave a Mr. Rogers-inspired science lesson on an overhead projector, explaining the concept of the fifth dimension by drawing a cartoon. In another, the character Kinetic Girl (Jamie McKittrick) danced a series of individual tap rhythms before layering them on top of each other in an interlocking routine, an illustration of how different dimensions can coexist in the same space. In a third, audiences walked into a vast planetarium-like installation and were led through a guided meditation encouraging them to picture the scale of the cosmos. In the final scene, Weave—a time traveler played by David Sweeny—offered a monologue in which he attempted to articulate the perceptive damage to his consciousness that his non-linear perspective had wrought. Afterwards, the audience came back together and were given a chance to share their experience with attendees of other scenes. The aim was to illustrate through action the larger concept being explored: that any one human's perception is inherently singular and limited. In SURVIVE! no single journey through the show's 128 unique variations was any more "complete" than another, underscoring that the show, like its subject, required multiple perspectives to be fully known (Figure 2.1).

Figure 2.1 The character Kinetic Girl from Swim Pony's *SURVIVE!* invites an audience member down one of several possible paths. Photograph by Jacques-Jean Tiziou.

In structuring narrative landscapes, imagine a story from a bird's eye rather than a ground-level view. For example, if telling the story of a national disaster through a chronological account from a single perspective, one could compile dozens of individual anecdotes, collaged together to highlight either the variations or similarities in what people heard, saw, and felt. It may be more useful to focus on building a cohesive world, one whose sum-total conveys your message consistently, rather than getting attached to the witnesses of any specific moment within it. Though there may be times when it's necessary for the audience to see something in a very particular way, being judicious with "required" information keeps curiosity and exploration at the center of the experience.

Example. *The End* – (https://swimpony.org/current-projects/the-end-2/)

> In 2017 Swim Pony performed *The End*, a month-long text message-based performance/game that offered space for players to contemplate their fears about death and dying. Each day of the four-week experience, players used a deck of cards to select a daily interactive prompt that explored mortality in a different way—writing one's own obituary, strolling through a cemetery, calling a family member to talk about funeral plans. Each card offered a different activity and content focus, giving players leeway to choose what kind of experience they undertook that day. We grouped the prompts into three phases: an introductory set of cards that eased into the themes and format of the show; a middle grouping with the widest variety of prompts and activities for maximum self-direction; and a final set whose challenges aimed at synthesis and post-game action. Within this overarching structure, cards could be played in any order.

A last tip is to avoid "false choices"—actions you might be tempted to offer because of their plausibility in the narrative world but don't actually want players to choose. Such options steer them to aspects of a story that aren't central to the message or require you to intervene and negate their free will, jarring players out of your world.

FOSTERING TRUE AGENCY AND HOLDING YOUR AUDIENCE IN CARE

Choices are the building blocks of a game experience, whether they occur through problem-solving to move forward, deciding on a goal to achieve, or picking which parts of an environment to explore. Audiences feel their *agency* through these choices. Creating a sense of agency for participants doesn't emerge by simply offering a massive buffet of options, but instead comes from homing in on *meaningful* decisions that have an impact within the larger narrative structure. These decisions are focused on things they care about and help them feel autonomous. Finding the right balance between curation and freedom is key. At the start of rehearsals, it's useful to be honest about what degree of control your artistic vision requires. As Nordic-style larp (or live action role play) creator Johanna Koljonen (2011) explains, the biggest lesson of leaving the world of theatre to venture into games was letting go of control at a moment-to-moment level in order to give audiences more agency in the overall experience.

In the standard theatre setting, how an audience can expect to interact with the performance is routine: a stage separates the invented world and the one the audience occupies, lights and sound indicate when the show begins and ends, and viewers have an implicit range of appropriate responses including laughter or applause. Such implicit rules are a culture of collective understanding an audience relies on. When you upend these defaults during an experiential event, remember the audience can't know which you've opted to change or keep. As such, it's imperative to clearly define the new expectations and limits (both literal and metaphoric) of your world. Game designers call this boundary the "Magic Circle," a place inside which reality is suspended and replaced by the artificial rules of the game (Salen and Zimmerman 2004; Linser, Ree-Lindstad, and Vold 2008). Janet Murray (1997) offers a useful metaphor for immersion of being dunked into water. In this state one's body functions differently and needs time to learn how to "swim." Audiences need time to learn and practice these edges, which can be tricky for artists to remember after weeks of acculturating to a world they've built. The "givens" about how to behave will inevitably feel more natural and obvious to your creative team than to someone walking into it for the first time. It may feel absurdly obvious to *you* that opening a mysterious door will set in motion an important plot event, but have you given your audience enough information to reasonably intuit this action is required of them?

Also keep in mind the status differential between you and your audience. Remember that when they arrive everything around them is unfamiliar and the social pressure to perform in such settings makes meaningful consent even harder to ensure. Consider when you ask a participant to do something if they will feel they're being given a *true* choice or if implicit factors will oblige them to play along even if they don't want to. While having a submissive audience might be useful as an author, it's also in conflict with the voluntary feeling necessary to the experience of play. Fostering *real* consent comes by vigilantly holding audiences in care, creating multiple options for them to move through an experience, and remembering the more that's asked of a player mentally, physically, or emotionally the more the creative system needs to reward their efforts. If you consistently see players respond with hesitation or resistance, take note, and consider adjustments and/ or alternatives for other options to progress through your piece. It can also be useful to offer smaller "tutorial" scenes that demonstrate important mechanics, give players feedback about your desired responses, and build patterns of understanding and trust.

Swim Pony's guiding principles in effectively teaching audiences the rules of an experience are transparency about expectations, diversity of information delivery, and repetition. Introduce rules slowly, in bite-sized doses, scaffolding complex understanding on top of previously mastered information. Give feedback that incentivizes correct behavior in lower-stakes settings before it's needed for critical scenes. Give multiple opportunities to learn the same information and do so in a variety of formats. This process can be done explicitly—sending written instructions beforehand, stating them out loud at the start of a performance, or offering a printed guide audiences can use during your show—or implicitly through trial and error within the experience, or by having performers model correct behavior, always ensuring the same action/input results in a consistent and reliable response. Most importantly, be generous with your praise and support of players as they learn. Sensing you're "not getting" something is a deeply stressful experience that can leave one paralyzed, particularly under the pressure of a performance setting. Negative or shaming tactics are rarely the most effective way to solve problems and can cause audience members to shut down. It's almost always better to be overly explicit versus too opaque.

Example. *War of the Worlds* – (https://swimpony.org/current-projects/war-of-the-worlds-philadelphia/)

When Swim Pony created our game/theatre piece *War of the Worlds*, we wanted to cast gentrification as an invading alien force affecting the city of Philadelphia. Audiences for the event were a mix of long-standing local residents and new arrivals who gathered at a local worship space for the event. We began the performance with a "readiness tutorial" structured as a series of flashcard questions that prompted players to quiz each other about what they knew about the history of space and what historical/cultural awareness they had of the surrounding area. The dialogue that ensued—gently facilitated by performers—encouraged audiences to individually reflect on their identity as an insider/outsider, note audience members with the most lived experience in the surrounding neighborhood, and reflect on their understanding of displacement before these themes were brought up in the show.

In early iterations of *The End,* rules were communicated to the player in a long thread of text messages sent on the first day. We found players rarely read big blocks of words and when they did, found it boring to do. We decided to try seeing if this information would be more readily absorbed in small doses. We reworked the opening sequence to share this content over several days, offering only one new rule at a time, which resulted in far more comprehension later in the game.

All these warnings might feel overwhelming. As theatre artists, you may feel pressure to nail the perfect balance on the first try, but game designers know it's impossible to anticipate every audience response to a system without testing. Indeed, unanticipated "emergent play" can sometimes reveal unexpectedly potent parts of your game. That's why it's important to build in time within the process to iteratively test how audiences respond.

CENTRALIZATION OF THE SUBJECTIVE EXPERIENCE

One of the biggest advantages of blending game techniques into live performance is the opportunity to shift from an objective experience to a subjective one. Though we at Swim Pony still use the term "audience" to refer to participants of our works, the function and expectation of a static observer are fundamentally different from a person who charts their own course. Games are second-person journeys that can uniquely tailor themselves to an individual and respond differently each time they are engaged. To maximize a player's subjective experience, allow them space to define a personal mission in relation to the game and/or add content to the story. Rather than designing a single ideal path, create an array of potential experiences that are fulfilling and emerge responsively to what a player does. This difference invites them in as co-creators of their distinctive playthrough.

Being open to real-time collaboration again means relinquishing a degree of control. Finding the balance can be tricky. Dictate an audience's experience too strictly and they'll feel like unwilling puppets. Hold them too loose and the journey may be muddy or vague. The sweet spot of design is found where our authorial rules satisfyingly meet the audiences' living activation of our mechanics, in other words, when audiences feel engaged in "meaningful play" (Salen and Zimmerman 2004). You need to be thoughtful in defining *your* creative goals for participants—relating a specific topic, evoking an emotional state, creating a ritual, fostering community, etc.—so you design back to mechanics that incentivize those outcomes, what game designers call win states. Though we might be more familiar with this term in the context of binary "play-to-win" games like chess (more formally called *ludic* games), Gonzalo Frasca (2003) offers an alternate aim for games like tag in which we continue engaging simply for the experience of getting to play. Such "play-to-play" (or *paidic*) games are probably familiar to theatre artists through drama games like Mirroring, Yes, Let's!, and Party Quirks. Games like these instead are "won" by creating an atmosphere of playfulness, acceptance, and ensemble. Naming a win state (either ludic or paidic) within a piece or getting players to articulate their own helps focus their actions towards meaningfully curated goals.

Because games are responsive, they also offer opportunities for players to *create* content rather than merely receiving it. When you encourage the subjectivity of the player by leaving space for them to customize the story or insert their own goals, you display that their journey is unique and significant, and by extension that *they* are as well. One way to do this is to cast them in roles they are well-primed to carry out, either by mirroring the perspective they currently occupy as an audience like an outsider, novice, or watcher.

Example. *War of the Worlds*

> In *War of the Worlds*, we began each performance with a comedic scene that invoked our audience members' obvious lack of knowledge about the narrative world and turned it into an intentional plot point. At the start of the show an actor arrives and greets the waiting audience familiarly, immediately making note of their reticence to engage and confusion about who the person is. The character quickly "realizes" the reason behind their confusion and shares exposition that explains to them that they're resistance fighters engaged in a battle against a force called The Forgetting. This alien invader attacks one's memories of local people, places, and culture. Thus, the viewer's real-life confusion becomes a central feature of the role they're tasked to play.

Subjective experiences are heightened even further when a player's journey feels witnessed, no surprise to those who have firsthand knowledge of the energy of stepping onto the stage. You might try something as simple as a performer noticing an audience member "in game" and reflecting back a positive response. Other tactics include having audiences share moments of connection with each other or creating mementos of the experience for them to take home. If the game has duration beyond a single performance, you might offer players a chance to leave a mark of their journey within the space.

ENHANCING EMBODIMENT THROUGH INTERACTION, IMMERSION, AND ROLEPLAY

Part of what makes acting so powerful for performers is the somatic experience of telling stories using one's own body. When we talk about an actor "embodying" a character, we're speaking about the way they physically transform their corporeal form as it takes on the story. Similarly, immersion into a narrative through spatial design and sensory stimulation is more transportive than observing it from a distance. In both embodied participation and immersive stimulation, we create a visceral, kinesthetic mode of learning; walking a mile in someone else's shoes in the most literal sense. It's a chance for the audience to step into the actor's "as if", to *feel* rather than merely *see* the action. Though a player may not achieve realistic portrayal at the level of a professional actor, giving them a chance to step into a character still offers empathic insight into other human experiences and practices different ways of being and thinking. It gives them the opportunity to imagine themselves differently and explore parts of their personality that don't find space in everyday life.

A quick terminology detour: the theatre field has a habit of using the words participatory, immersive, and interactive interchangeably. However, at Swim Pony we distinguish *interactive* components of our works as those that require an audience member's *action*. In other words, interaction asks audiences to *do something* within the context of the drama, ideally with some degree of impact on the outcome. *Immersive* elements, on the other hand, impart an aesthetic state of being present in an environment, a feeling of *surroundedness* within a wholly enveloping theatrical world (Machon 2013). At Swim Pony we use the word *participation* to code a general sense of "taking part" within the action in a non-traditional way that may invoke either one or both of the two preceding terms.

Example. *TrailOff.* (https://trailoff.org/)

> In 2020 we launched *TrailOff*, a GPS-triggered mobile app created for nature trails throughout the Philadelphia region. In it, users hear original audio dramas written to sync to the physical surroundings encountered as they walk. Aimed at getting more diverse populations comfortable out in nature, the experience relies heavily on the

assumed immersion a listener will have in the natural spaces that surround them on a trail. Stories use notable landscape features as backdrops for story events and also poetically invoke images of plants and geography the viewer might see. Though some stories also include interactive moments, offering a choice between forking paths, for example, the main emphasis in this work is the immersive feeling of being connected to the vistas of the trails (Figure 2.2).

Figure 2.2 An audience member walking along a trail listening to an immersive audio story as part of Swim Pony's *TrailOff*. Photograph by John Hawthorne.

Returning to embodiment for our players, we also need to keep in mind that acting is hard to do well! Performers spend years learning the needed tools to create dynamic embodiment of a character and it can be painful to watch a non-actor try to negotiate this without training. Directed interaction and immersion offered as a series of simple cues can narrow down that scope of work, anticipating the actions a player needs to perform and limiting them to those that best support the story. Much the same way actors turn objective into action, you can create game mechanics that impel your players to carry out a task in the way their character would, building performance in as a side effect of playing the game. Similarly, directions within a game like "open your arms wide" or "stare at the floor" can get players to activate their bodies in ways that, akin to "outside in" acting techniques, evoke a character's physical state. Something as simple as asking someone to slow their breathing can bring about a feeling of calm. Leading a person through a cramped hallway might create the feeling of being trapped. Offering a small bite of food in a moment of stillness tunes them into their senses. Beginning a scene with instructions for a simple task to undertake—remembering all the names of people they meet, for example—can direct their attention much more effectively than a general directive to engage. With all this in mind, remember that embodied experience can be intense and including a debrief or "cool down" may help ease your players back into the real world.

44 • ADRIENNE MACKEY

Example. *The End.*

As part of a quest offered in *The End* players were asked to roleplay the experience of receiving a terminal diagnosis. In the scene, players traveled to a simulated doctor's office where they were told they'd receive "bad news." However, to increase their sense of reality in the experience we bombarded them with physical stimuli during the conversation: as the actor playing the doctor began to talk, a hidden speaker began to play a track with music and an external voice. It demanded that audiences respond to the doctor's dialogue but also execute a series of tasks; tapping their finger while counting certain words each time they were spoken. Additionally, the voice instructed audiences to keep their eyes focused on the floor and curl their bodies inward. Every single instruction was simple to understand but added together they created a sensation of sadness and confusion. At the end of the simulation, players typically felt disoriented, agitated, and tense. In debriefs afterwards, they learned that these sensations correspond to the same feeling of helplessness and overwhelmedness that many patients report when learning of a life-threatening illness. In this way, the embodiment we manufactured gave players a chance to practice the feelings of a real-life situation without having to create them for themselves.

A FINAL CALL TO ACTION

As a theatre practitioner of the twenty-first century, my creative practice has been guided by the following question: what is the purpose of *live* performance in this contemporary moment? It's a query I pose at the start of any artistic process: "Why would someone expend the effort of leaving home to experience a play when Netflix is available only a few clicks away?" Usually, the room laughs and assumes the question to be a rhetorical one, which prompts me to repeat my provocation: "No, *really*, when the potential play-goer has so many options for compelling and easily accessible pre-recorded narratives, what justifies the unnecessary labor of transporting one's body to undertake an activity with other people at a designated time?"

People usually answer, "Because it's live" or "There's something about actually *being* there." These responses—ones we as dramatic practitioners instinctually feel—point to the underutilized superpower of theatre as a responsive artform. We dramatists can remind audiences that static media, for all its value, can never offer the viewer the reward of being *present*, of having a genuine impact on the moment they are in. This feeling of consequence, what theorist Erika Fischer-Lichte (2008) names as the *autopoietic feedback loop*, is the exciting instability and emergent response that arises when audience and performers connect and influence each other in unpredictable ways. Access to an impossible wealth of movies and television is indeed at many of our fingertips, but such stories are unresponsive and can never offer the audience more than passive viewership. Taking part in the unique ephemerality of the theatrical event might ask for more active engagement from an audience, but such voluntary "unnecessary" efforts are exactly what transforms work into joyful play. At Swim Pony we posit that theatre's true potential lies not in mere didactic storytelling, however well crafted, but in experiential communion that re-engages us with a sense of what it means to be curious, connected, and most of all, alive.

References

Brathwaite, Brenda and Ian Schreiber. 2008. *Challenges for Game Designers*. CreateSpace Independent Publishing Platform.
Caillois, Roger. 2001. *Man, Play and Games*. Urbana: University of Illinois Press.

Costikyan, Greg. 2002. "I Have No Words & I Must Design: Toward a Critical Vocabulary for Games." In *Proceedings of Computer Games and Digital Cultures Conference*. Edited by Mäyrä, 9–33. Tampere: Tampere University Press.

Fischer-Lichte, Erika. 2008. *The Transformative Power of Performance: A New Aesthetics*. New York: Routledge.

Flanagan, Mary. 2009. *Critical Play: Radical Game Design*. Cambridge: Mass. MIT Press.

Frasca, Gonzalo. ND. "Ludology Meets Narratology: Similitude and Differences between (video) games and Narrative." *Ludology.org* (blog). Accessed September 9, 2021. http://www.ludology.org/articles/ludology.htm

Frasca, Gonzalo. 2003. "Simulation vs Narrative." In *The Video Game Theory Reader*. Edited by Bernard Perron and Mark J.P. Wolf, 221–236. London: Routledge.

Huizinga, Johan. 1949. *Homo Ludens: A Study of the Play-Element in Culture*. London: Routledge and Kegan Paul.

Hunicke, Robin, Marc LeBlanc, and Robert Zubek. 2004. "MDA: A Formal Approach to Game Design and Game Research." *Proceedings of the AAAI Workshop on Challenges in Game AI* 4 (1). https://www.aaai.org/Papers/Workshops/2004/WS-04-04/WS04-04-001.pdf

Juul, Jesper. 2004. "The Definitive History of Games and Stories, Ludology and Narratology." *The Ludologist* (blog), February 22, 2004. https://www.jesperjuul.net/ludologist/2004/02/22/the-definitive-history-of-games-and-stories-ludology-and-narratology/

Koljonen, Johanna. 2011. "On Games: Painting Life With Rules." Filmed March 2011 at nordiclarptalks. Youtube video. www.youtube.com/watch?v=UOVf06NCBGQ

Koster, Raph. 2005. *A Theory of Fun for Game Design*. Scottsdale: Paraglyph Press.

Linser, Roni, Nina Ree-Lindstad, and Tone Vold. 2008. "The Magic Circle – Game Design Principles and Online Role-play Simulations." *World Conference on Educational Multimedia, Hypermedia & Telecommunications*. Ed-Media. Vienna, Austria. http://www.simplay.net/papers/MagicCircle-Linser-Lindstad-Vold08.pdf

Machon, Josephine. 2013. *Immersive Theatres: Intimacy and Immediacy in Contemporary Performance*. Houndmills, Basingstoke, Hampshire: Palgrave Macmillan.

McGonigal, Jane. 2011. *Reality Is Broken: Why Games Make Us Better and How They Can Change the World*. New York: Penguin Press.

Murray, Janet H. 1997. *Hamlet on the Holodeck the Future of Narrative in Cyberspace*. New York: The Free Press.

Romero, Brenda. Year. 2011 "Gaming for Understanding." November 2011 in Phoenix, AZ. TEDx video, https://www.ted.com/talks/brenda_brathwaite_gaming_for_understanding

Salen, Katie and Eric Zimmerman. 2004. *Rules of Play: Game Design Fundamentals*. Cambridge, Mass: MIT Press.

Suits, Bernard, et al. 2005:2014. *The Grasshopper: Games, Life and Utopia*. Peterborough: Broadview Press.

3
Framework Design: A Curatorial Approach to Teaching Participatory Performance

Jamie Harper

INTRODUCTION

The music pulsed through the speakers … "and nobody sees what we do, don't need anybody else around" … hundreds of balloons flew through the air, popping under the dancing feet … "it don't matter what they told us" … and dozens of dancing bodies responded to Ella Eyre's call … "gravity won't hold us down" (McMahon and Stein 2015). This was my experience on a summer night in 2015 in a former Soviet holiday camp in the forests of Lithuania. It was the concluding ritual of the Larpwriter Summer School, a week-long symposium on live action role-play design, organized by two cultural organizations: Fantasiforbundet from Norway and Education Center POST from Belarus. Throughout my week at the school, I danced to *Gravity* as a morning ritual and learned about how live action role-play, or larp as it is commonly known, evolved from fantasy role-play games, with Nordic larp[1] emerging in the 1990s as a specific genre that hybridizes rule-based games, improvisational drama, and participatory art (Stenros 2010).

I went to the Larpwriter Summer School (L.W.S.S.) as a disillusioned theatre director with a growing interest in participatory performance. My aim was to acquire new creative tools, but aside from the design methods that were shared, the most interesting aspect of the summer school, for me, was the way it facilitated a space of social exchange through ongoing shared reflection on the learning experience. Since attending in 2015, I have applied what I learned to my artistic practice, research, and teaching. In this essay, I discuss one of these applications: a pedagogical project, entitled Playground, which explored games, larp, and interactive performance with an interdisciplinary group of artists at Theatre Delicatessen in London over a 12-week period in the spring of 2018. Rather than focusing on the pedagogical content of Playground, I concentrate on the structure, or framing, of the creative learning space. In doing so, I argue that the co-creative design frameworks of Nordic larp can be readily transposed to teaching participatory performance, offering frameworks for co-creation that prompt learners to collaboratively construct new knowledge.

CURATORIAL PEDAGOGY AND LARP DESIGN

Larp in the Nordic tradition often includes workshop processes that invite players to co-create essential elements of the role-play, including fictional settings, characters, or narrative details (Karachun et al. 2017). This highlights that larp functions as a collaborative combination of the creative framework offered by designer(s) and the imagination of participants who play the larp into existence (Stenros 2010). Such collaboration seems to echo the pedagogical theory of Jerome Bruner (Wood, Bruner, Ross 1976), whose concept of "scaffolding" articulates the means by which the pedagogue creates frameworks for learning, with a balance of independence for students alongside teaching guidance. The scaffolding concept is underpinned by Lev Vygotsky's (1978) theory of the zone of proximal development, which conceives the learning process as an inherently social endeavor in which learning occurs "under guidance or in collaboration with more capable peers" (86). Vygotsky proposes that individuals learn by creatively imitating others with greater, or diversified, capabilities and this vision of creating new knowledge through relational exchange resonates strongly with contemporary notions of "the curatorial." Whereas traditional curating presents established knowledge to audiences by displaying artifacts, the curatorial advocates creating social contexts for the "event of knowledge," as participants engage in inter-subjective exchange (Rogoff 2013). Essentially, just as larp workshops prompt players to co-create fictional worlds, the curatorial invites groups of participants to respond to a given set of stimuli and create something new together (Szylak 2013).

In drawing connections between larp practice, scaffolding, and the curatorial, I argue that teaching participatory performance can be approached as curatorial pedagogy that not only focuses on disseminating learning content but also on the framing of learning contexts. In the development of Nordic larp, social contexts for learning have been of central importance, such as the Larpwriter Summer School, which served as a key gathering for Nordic larp practitioners over its five-year life span from 2012 to 2016. The central pedagogical tool of L.W.S.S. is the Mixing Desk of Larp. This conceptual device includes twelve binary faders which identify important variables for larp designers to consider (Stenros, Andresen, and Nielsen 2016). For example, the "Secrecy" fader refers to the minimal/extensive amount of prior information that players are given about the content of the larp, the "Environment" fader refers to the naturalistic/abstract style of the physical setting, while the "Character Creation Responsibility" fader refers to the agency of artist/player in creating character roles. Importantly, the Mixing Desk avoids stipulating which end of the fader is superior. In other words, rather than prescribing how larps should be designed, it functions as an open-ended "thing to think with" (Stenros et al. 2016). Graduates of L.W.S.S. have been invited to test the Mixing Desk at The Larporatory, a follow-up event in which small groups undertake a rapid, iterative design process, culminating in the playtesting of their larp. In considering the summer school and The Larporatory as exemplars of scaffolding, it is important to highlight that the pedagogical structure gradually recedes as participants develop their capacity to independently apply what they have learned. Having experienced L.W.S.S. and The Larporatory as a participant, I worked as a facilitator at The Larporatory for 2016 summer school graduates. Subsequently, I have re-applied insights gained from these experiences in new creative learning initiatives for performance makers, and, in the next section, I discuss my application of curatorial pedagogy in the Playground project.

SEARCHING FOR METHODS IN RELATIONAL LEARNING SPACES

The philosophy of Jacques Rancière sets out a vision of educational emancipation in which teachers encourage students to undertake their own explorations by "pointing" toward an object of attention that may be unfamiliar (Lewis 2012). According to Rancière, the object pointed toward functions as a "third thing," providing a common point of reference for teacher and learner (Rancière 1991). At L.W.S.S., the Mixing Desk served as a "third thing"

48 • JAMIE HARPER

and the range of activities I offered in Playground was certainly influenced by it. Just as the Mixing Desk sets out binaries between high levels of artist control versus player control, Playground pointed to a variety of participatory performance forms: from structured activities like rule-based games and actor-led interactive theatre scenarios to open-ended play exercises built around participatory co-creation. In offering an array of activities, my aim was to initiate a process of curatorial pointing that would highlight things that might be of interest to participants in their search for new methods.

The notion of "searching" for methods is redolent of Vygotsky's proposal that group learning is not simply a matter of passing existing methods from master to novice. Rather, the endeavor to acquire new capacities is itself the source of development. Lois Holzman (2009) describes this as a "tool and result" approach to learning, as opposed to the "tool for result" approach of "banking" education whereby students are taught how to use a tool to achieve a preconceived outcome. In the Playground project, I argue that the culture of searching for methods produced a mindset that encouraged participants to not only acquire tools but also recognize their capacity for adapting these tools and creating new ones. For example, one participant, Navdeep,[2] commented on the widely used Nordic larp practice of using workshop exercises, like sticking post-it notes on the wall to develop ideas for fictional settings:

> Because I'm such a workshop whore [referring to his frequent attendance of arts workshops] I realized early on that part of the larp must be the workshop … if we're doing a preliminary thing, we're larping … if we're doing this thing with the post-it notes–as a process of idea generation–this isn't just [an exercise]–this is actually part of the larp.
>
> (Navdeep 2018)

The key point that can be drawn from Navdeep's reflection is that his experience of using post-it notes to invent a fictional scenario was an instance of "tool and result" thinking. As well as acquiring a practical method, Navdeep's conscious awareness of having made this acquisition can be understood as a form of learning development that is independent of the tool's utilitarian function.

Central to an experimental search for method is the notion that *not knowing* can have pedagogical value. In discussing Vygostky's ideas on childhood language acquisition, Holzman suggests that "developmental activity does not require knowing how," arguing that "when babies babble, they are speaking before they know how to speak, or that they speak, by virtue of the speakers around them accepting them into the community of speakers and making conversation with them" (Holzman 2010, 34). As this reference to a "community of speakers" indicates, Vygotsky's conception of childhood learning is fundamentally based on social relationality, whereby children move beyond not knowing by imitating the behavior of more capable individuals in their vicinity (Vygotsky 1967). At L.W.S.S., creative imitation was prompted by the first larp I played: *The Family Andersson*, a piece about a group of siblings deciding what to do with their family inheritance (Nolemo and Röklander 2009). In this larp, each character is shared by two players, so that one player observes while the other plays the character. Whenever the watcher has an idea for something they would like to do, they can "tap out" their partner and take over. Although this process is not necessarily imitative, the notion of responding to the contributions of others was something that I explored in Playground by creating activities using the "tapping in/tapping out" technique. Navdeep commented on several occasions that this encouraged participants to make creative contributions in relation to the offerings of others, ensuring a collaborative shaping of the play context:

The tapping in, tapping out thing–and kind of rotating of the characters–that for me was like a brilliant gift … because you have to plug into the shared thing–how you relate it to the whole … everybody's seeing what's happening, everybody's observing.

(Navdeep 2018)

The instigation of creative imitation subsequently became something of a recurring trope, leading to exercises such as a "palimpsest" drawing, which invited players to revise each other's sketches as the basis of role-play designs. Working in small groups, players drew a picture of a place that really mattered to them, then passed their image to another player who copied the picture and added new characters to it, in preparation for short role-plays. In reflecting on this exercise, one participant, Zara, said that "building from people's memory versus then taking it into an imaginative place" was "very satisfying" (Zara 2018), suggesting that the palimpsest process encouraged a creative imitation that combined responsiveness to the original alongside imaginative transformation of it. As these examples indicate, the teaching of participatory performance can be scaffolded in such a way that relational exchange is foregrounded. By prompting an intersubjective interweaving of participants' contributions, curatorial pedagogy can cultivate a diverse creative ecology (Lampo 2015) that provides a broad array of stimuli to creatively imitate and learn from.

REFLEXIVITY AND RITUALS IN LARP PRACTICE

Nordic larp practitioners have taken a keen interest in the experience of player immersion (Bowman 2018), but recent larp scholarship has identified reflexivity as an important feature of aesthetic value (Levin 2020). At L.W.S.S., reflexive play experiences were offered through larps featuring the "meta-technique" of character and player inner monologues, which enable participants to verbally articulate the inner reflections of their character, or themselves as the player. In Playground, a notable example of this type of reflexive play came when one participant, Meg, was thinking about a role-play she had played with me, featuring a band of revolutionaries escaping to sea in a small boat, which subsequently broke down, leaving them adrift on the waves:

The moment when our play shifted was when you as a player gave like a monologue and there was something about there being introspective character roles [the use of character inner monologues] that shifted the way I was playing–like I could think about how I was feeling and I got to be like "I'm feeling really frightened right now"–and then I could pretend that I wasn't really frightened and I could deal with everything–but it allowed me to bring two layers to the way I was playing and I found that really useful.

(Meg 2018)

Meg's comment that there were "two layers" to her play connects to a key component of Vygotsky's theories of learning: the link between using language for external and internal speech. Vygotsky argues that although speech emerges first as social interaction, secondarily, as children develop complex play, language functions as a tool for internalized thought that enables a higher level of abstract imagination (Minick 2017). Essentially, the value of reflexive, internal language use is that it enables learners, or players, to reconfigure their immediate experience in abstract imaginings of how things could be different in the future.

In considering how the curatorial framing of creative learning spaces may encourage reflexivity, I suggest that reiteration in larp design is extremely important, with rich potential for gathering new knowledge as students re-apply their learnings when they become designers and teachers. As I have mentioned previously, L.W.S.S. participants were invited to test their larp design skills at The Larporatory, then re-apply their developing expertise by facilitating the next version of The Larporatory for a new group of summer school graduates. Similarly, participants in the first Playground were invited to co-facilitate a second version in the autumn of 2018. In taking up this invitation, several participants commented on how repeating an activity (as a facilitator) that they had previously experienced (as a learner) enabled them to learn something new, rather than simply reaffirming existing knowledge. For example, Jack, whose background lay in creating immersive theatre for young audiences, ran a version of my larp, *Neighbourhood*, at the National Student Drama Festival, having previously played it as part of Playground. In contrast with his usual approach, in which all facilitation is delivered within the fictional diegesis, *Neighbourhood* requires the facilitator to regularly break immersion and give instructions to players from outside the fiction, which challenged Jack to reconsider immersion as an aesthetic ideal:

> What I needed to get over throughout the course was the fact that not every bit of the setup–it doesn't have to be dramatic in itself, or theatrical … I was always trying to find ways–like menus that would tell you things, or a cup with something inside it that would give you information–and no one else seemed to care about integrating it into the fiction (he laughs) … but with your larp–it was just like "now you're doing this" and I was like "okay!" So, I definitely let go of trying to have like–an in-world way of explaining things. Actually, just saying it … learning that was a challenge. But I did learn it.
>
> (Jack 2018)

Jack went on to discuss how re-running *Neighbourhood* with a group of young people (none of whom had heard of larp before) created a context in which he could reflect on questions of theatricality and immersion at the same time as the students. As this example suggests, acts of repetition are not necessarily copies of what has gone before. Rather, they provide opportunities for reflexive learning in the gap between continuity and alteration.

The notion of continuity alongside change is readily apparent in discussions of rituals, which highlight the importance for human communities of consolidating things that are valued through recurring practices (Schechner 1985). Nordic larp practice is strongly influenced by rituals, like the tradition of the *runda*, or storytelling circle, in which players can share their thoughts and make meaning together at the conclusion of play (Bowman 2014). Following Vygotsky's idea that learning occurs through creative imitation of others, I argue that the emergence of creative communities through ritual practice creates the foundational conditions for learning to take place. So, when organizers of L.W.S.S. play *Gravity* by Ella Eyre, they are not just triggering a wave of emotions for summer school graduates of 2015, they are also maintaining a ritual and supporting a relational sociality that enables members of the group to learn from each other.

CONCLUSION

This essay has proposed that teaching participatory performance is not simply a matter of relaying practical tools to students, it also requires curatorial frameworks that support co-creation. Within these frameworks, pedagogues offer substantive content for learning, but by using "curatorial pointing" as a teaching strategy, learners are encouraged to initiate their own search for method, comparing their experiences with others to co-create new knowledge. I argue that reflexivity is of central importance in this process, both in terms of individual reflection and shared thinking within groups. Subsequently, as key insights are consolidated and repeated, ideas and methods that are valued form the basis of rituals that bind individuals into communities of practice.

The notion of community can connote stable homogeneity, but communities of larp are constantly changing as new players arrive on the scene. These provisional communities provide the foundation for learning, as individuals, whether consciously or unconsciously, creatively imitate others and learn new things. Community formation can be spontaneous, but pedagogues can actively curate frameworks for co-creation by inviting participants to make exchanges with each other, reflect on what they have exchanged, and repeat the processes that they found most useful. By offering simple prompts in this way, curatorial pedagogues can move beyond the normative model of masterful teachers instructing students and support the co-creative agency of learners as they forge their own innovations in participatory performance.

Notes

1 Role-play practitioners in the Nordic tradition tend not to use the acronym LARP. Instead, 'larp' is used as a word in its own right. Please visit nordiclarp.org for an overview of Nordic larp practices.
2 Throughout this essay, I use pseudonyms for participants to maintain confidentiality.

References

Bowman, Sarah Lynne. 2014. "Returning to the Real World." *Nordic Larp*. December 12, 2014. https://nordiclarp.org/2014/12/08/debrief-returning-to-the-real-world/
Bowman, Sarah Lynne. 2018. "Immersion and Shared Imagination in Role-Playing Games." In *Role-Playing Game Studies: Transmedia Foundations*. Edited by José P. Zagal and Sebastian Deterding, 379–394. New York: Routledge.
Holzman, Lois. 2009. *Vygotsky at Work and Play*. Hove: Routledge.
Holzman, Lois. 2010. "Without Creating ZPDs There Is No Creativity." In *Vygotsky and Creativity: A Cultural-Historical Approach to Play, Meaning Making and the Arts*. Edited by M. Cathrene Connery, Vera John-Steiner and Ana Marjanovic-Shane, 27–40. New York: Peter Lang.
Jack (pseud.) 2018. *Interview with author*. London. June 28, 2018.
Karachun, Maryia, Yauheni Karachun, Olga Rudak and Nastassia Sinitsyna. 2017. "The Workshop Pyramid." In *Once Upon a Nordic Larp … Twenty Years of Playing Stories*. Edited by Linn Carin Andreassen, Simon Brind, Elin Nilsen, Grethe Sofie Strand, and Martine Svanevik, 105–108. Oslo: Knutepunkt.
Lampo, Marjukka. 2015. "Ecological Approach to the Performance of Larping." *International Journal of Role-Playing*, 5: 35–46.
Levin, Hilda. 2020. "Metareflection." In *What Do We Do When We Play? The Player Experience in Nordic Larp*. Edited by Eleanor Saitta, 63–74. Helsinki: Ropecon.
Lewis, Tyson E. 2012. *The Aesthetics of Education: Theatre, Curiosity and Politics in the work of Jacques Rancière and Paulo Freire*. New York: Bloomsbury.
McMahon, Ella and Dan Stein. 2015. "Gravity." Track X on *Feline*. Virgin EMI, compact disc.
Meg (pseud.) 2018. *Interview with author*. London. June 27, 2018.
Minick, Norris. 2017. "The Development of Vygotsky's thought: An introduction to *Thinking and Speech*." In *Introduction to Vygotsky*. Edited by Harry Daniels, 32–56. Hove: Routledge.
Montola, Markus and Jaakko Stenros, eds. 2010. *Nordic Larp*. Stockholm: Fëa Livia.
Navdeep (pseud.) 2018. Interview with author. London. July 12, 2018.
Nolemo, Åke and Johan Röklander. 2009. *The Family Andersson*. Live Action Role-Play. Chamber Games, May 29, 2009. https://chambergames.wordpress.com/2009/05/29/the-family-andersson/
Rancière, Jacques. 1991. *The Ignorant Schoolmaster: Five Lessons in Intellectual Emancipation*, translated by Kristin Ross. Stanford, CA: Stanford University Press.
Rogoff, Irit. 2013. "The Expanding Field." In *The Curatorial: The Philosophy of Curating*. Edited by Jean-Paul Martinon, 41–48. London: Bloomsbury.

Schechner, Richard. 1985. *Between Theater and Anthropology*. Philadelphia: University of Pennsylvania Press.

Stenros, Jaakko. 2010. "Nordic Larp: Theatre, Art and Game." In *Nordic Larp*, Edited by Markus Montola and Jaakko Stenros, 300–315. Stockholm: Fëa Livia.

Stenros, Jaakko, Martin Eckhoff Andresen, and Martin Nielsen. 2016. "The Mixing Desk of Larp: History and Current State of a Design Theory." Analogue Game Studies, November 13, 2016. https://analoggamestudies.org/2016/11/the-mixing-desk-of-larp-history-and-current-state-of-a-design-theory/

Szylak, Aneta. 2013. "Curating Context." In *The Curatorial: The Philosophy of Curating*. Edited by John-Paul Martinon, 215–223. London: Bloomsbury.

Vygotsky, Lev S. 1967. "Play and its Role in the Mental Development of the Child," translated by Catherine Mulholland. *Soviet Psychology* 5 (1): 6–18.

Vygotsky, Lev S. 1978. *Mind in Society: The Development of Higher Psychological Processes*, Edited by Michael Cole, Vera John-Steiner, Sylvia Scribner, and Ellen Souberman, translated by Alexander R. Luria, Martin López-Morillas, Michael Cole, and James V. Wertsch. Cambridge. MA: Harvard University Press.

Wood, David, Jerome S. Bruner, and Gail Ross. 1976. "The Role of Tutoring in Problem Solving." *Journal of Child Psychology*, 17(17): 89–100.

Zara (pseud.) 2018. Interview with author. July 23.

4

Intimacy in Play: Training Actors for Agentic Symmetry in Unscripted Interactions

Amanda Rose Villarreal

INTRODUCTION

Performances within higher education are learning experiences for students, and immersive performances are no different; these productions are training grounds for students' future workplaces. Henry Bial (2020) acknowledges that theatrical workplaces can expose performers to harm, writing that "what appears to be 'make believe' for an audience may be all too real for a performer" (xii), exposing young actors to potential trauma in their learning environments. In the theatrical spaces Bial refers to, actors are—ideally—endowed with equal amounts of agency; they have rehearsed together, accepted the responsibility to perform agreed-upon blocking and dialogue, and adopted a common objective as an ensemble during performance. Immersive environments, however, upend this balance. Suddenly, actors are performing with asymmetrical agency, sharing the performance space with strangers who have not been choreographed. Actors, trained in rehearsal rooms to embrace their own vulnerability and maintain rehearsed blocking and dialogue, may feel unsafe when audiences are invited to follow their unscripted impulses, acting with agency to shape the performance. Recognizing this change in theatrical working environments, Erin Mee (Aviles-Rodriguez et al. 2019) issues a call to action: "one of the things that we need to talk about is a kind of performer training that has not yet been established for this work" (184).

Through experience and observation, actors are taught not to complain, despite the all-too-real physical and psychological harm they may encounter during rehearsals and performance. Chelsea Pace (2020) explains that the theatre industry's power dynamics put pressure on actors to acquiesce, writing: "performers internalize the message that saying yes is staying employed ... fearing a 'hard to work with' label might make them say 'okay' ... They might go home in tears, frustrated that the skewed power dynamic of a performer and director/producer left them feeling powerless" (8). Add to this the imbalanced, and unfamiliar, power dynamic within an immersive performance space, and students—without training—may be harmed during the learning experiences provided by immersive productions. So yes, let's talk about the kind of performer training that has not yet been widely established in this work. Let's talk about how we can approach training students to be collaborative participants in creating immersive experiences with one another and audience members.

DOI: 10.4324/9781003188179-6

VIRTUE OF REALITY: PRODUCTION CONTEXT

When the University of Colorado Boulder's Experiential Design M.F.A. students sought to cast undergraduates to help create an open-world immersive performance titled *The Virtue of Reality*, questions arose. How would the cohort prepare actors—many of whom had never *heard* of immersive theatre—for this performance? A director was selected from among the M.F.A. cohort, auditions were held, and undergraduate students were cast. I was asked to train them to safely prepare for all the unknowns that may occur when co-creating with audience participants.

Virtue of Reality was set in a techno-dystopian future in which the "VeraRev" corporation had inserted technology into every element of citizens' lives. The Experiential Design cohort created three distinct environments to fill this world: a commune of Luddites hidden away, living free from VeraRev's influence; a working-class community that strove to become—and have—more, despite social immobility imposed by disparate distribution of resources; and the elitist, conformist society in which body parts and memories were technologically enhanced, replaced, perfected. In the narrative world, these communities were incapable of contacting one another, despite being built yards away from one another in the physical performance space (Figure 4.1).

Figure 4.1 Audience players discuss technology and surveillance with a Luddite character.
Photograph by Enrique Villarreal.

The design of the production was stunning. An old gymnasium was transformed into a lushly lit, richly detailed set of environments, each uniquely textured. The rich jewel tones and foliage of the commune contrasted with the concrete grays defining the working-class area, which gave way to the neons and metallics of the third community. The Experiential Design cohort created machines that dispensed "happy pills," robotic owls that recognized and reacted to a smile, and both soundscapes and smellscapes unique to each setting. They issued this call to audiences:

Guests are ... stakeholders of massive conglomerate corporation, VeraRev. They are invited to an exclusive ... preview of their idealized future ... Visitors should be prepared to experience ... a portal to an immersive designed world that is completely free to explore. Guests will interact with the inhabitants of 2060's future and will determine what is in store for VeraRev and the rest of humanity.

("The Virtue of Reality" 2019)

Virtue of Reality was designed to encourage audiences to be "completely free" to participate in—or to *play*—the narrative, discovering the story through their unscripted interactions with the world's characters. After a short introduction in virtual reality, audience members would enter the performance to explore and improvise interactions with characters, uncovering challenges, secrets, and the plot along the way. And so, we set about training performers for these interactions, preparing them to perform emerging narratives determined by the playful, unscripted audience actions.

IMMERSIVE ACTING: A FRAMEWORK FOR FACILITATING PLAY THROUGH UNSCRIPTED INTERACTIONS

Director Veronica Rodriguez wanted the audience to "play" *Virtue of Reality*. Rodriguez's vision was distinct from larp[1]; audience players were not expected to embody characters. Instead, Rodriguez wanted audiences to engage with the world according to their own impulses, uncovering the narrative through these improvised interactions. Therefore, actors needed to *facilitate play* through their performances. Performance Studies and Game Design scholar Jane McGonigal (2011) defines games as specific form of play that contains "*a goal, rules, a feedback system, and voluntary participation*" (21, emphasis original). Actors, then, needed to introduce goals for audience undertaking, inviting players to participate in the performance. Beyond simply *assigning* goals and tasks, actors needed to learn to ensure that players felt *invited* to engage—and able to choose not to. McGonigal states that tasks undertaken in games are "work," that are effectively play when purposeful and self-selected; she stipulates that the instant *work* becomes coerced or involuntary, it ceases to be *play* (30–31). Therefore, actors needed to learn *to extend open invitations for audience-players to voluntarily participate in the work of discovering the narrative,* without crossing the line into coercion.

While immersive performance and play integrate improvisational skills, improvised performances without deep dramaturgical roots can be disruptive to play. Games scholar J. Tuomas Harviainen (2007) explains that immersive performances create systems that engage audience-players in the work of information seeking. Harviainen writes, however, that conflicting or missing information becomes a barrier to audiences' narrative discovery, interrupting play: "if the game environment, fabula and/or character-based barriers conflict with the participant's information seeking or mental state, the play becomes dysfunctional." Therefore, actors improvising with players and introducing conflicting information unintentionally (rather than as characters intending to mislead and needing to be discovered in so doing), could disrupt, rather than facilitate, play. To support play in *Virtue of Reality*, then, actors needed to collaboratively create a thorough and shared understanding of the world in which their characters existed, working directly with the design M.F.A students to create a cohesive narrative that would facilitate storytelling in the immersive environment. Therefore, exhaustive dramaturgical grounding, the process of *worldbuilding*, became the first step in actor training.

Along with supporting audience play, I also wanted to empower actors by establishing agentic symmetry among participants—actors and audience members alike. Combining a decade of immersive performance experience and training as an intimacy specialist, I developed techniques for *boundary establishment* to create a symmetrically agentic exchange between actors and audience members during play, the third prong in actor training.

As well as training actors to facilitate play while sharing agency with players, I needed to guide students in developing an interactive performance style. Participation designer Andie Nordgren (2008) invites immersive creators to focus on "the detail of the communication" (91), proposing that "*high resolution* game interaction" makes immersive experiences more powerful for participants. Nordgren defines high resolution performance as that which "enable[s] subtlety across a wide spectrum of ... interactions" (91, emphasis original). Josephine Machon (2013) similarly indicates the importance of subtlety in immersive performance, writing that audiences are attracted to this form by its capacity to create intimate encounters. In transitioning actors' skillsets from proscenium performance to intimate exchanges, I felt it was necessary for the students to experience the production *as audience participants*. Informed by both theatrical and gaming sensibilities, I developed a four-pronged approach to training undergraduate students for immersive performance—a structure to prepare them for collaboratively creating a performance with one another and their audience. The training process included *dramaturgical grounding, crafting open invitations for play, establishing clear boundaries*, and *rehearsal as audience*: a learning structure that was layered upon and interwoven with the ensemble-building activities, physical exercises, and performance-making processes included in many devising processes.

DRAMATURGICAL GROUNDING: WORLDBUILDING, LORE, AND CORES

Students had many questions about the world of the show and their roles within it. Does my character *know* these happy pills are VeraRev mind control? Can my character tell that their memories have been replaced? How do I interact with audiences? *Virtual Reality* performer Isobel Makin explains her initial confusion:

> I remember at the first rehearsal Veronica gave me a two-paragraph script. It made no sense. It was just, 'hi, my name is, I hate VeraRev, the leader of the Nest thinks technology is evil, but I think it could help people, what do you think?' And I didn't know what any of it meant. I didn't even know what immersive was, I thought I would be like one of those creepy animal things at Chuck E. Cheese.
>
> (Makin, 2021)

The design M.F.A students addressed these questions, outlining the narrative arc, hopes for the audience's experience, and how each character could support that journey. Unlike more traditional table work, actors did not analyze a script for answers. Instead, the whole company contributed ideas, enriching the original outline by collaboratively creating a consistent narrative world, adding details to the M.F.A. cohort's outline to craft a richly textured experience featuring layered characters. This is the process of *worldbuilding*. Realizing they were cast to collaborate with agency, rather than to be animatronics, students delved into worldbuilding, crafting the setting's *lore* and their characters' *cores*.

Throughout worldbuilding, we tracked the lore we developed, recording each new idea as either truth or belief and determining which characters knew the truth or held the belief, developing a deep, shared understanding of the narrative and each character's role therein. We continued adding lore throughout our rehearsal process as new questions and discoveries emerged, always consulting existing canon, closing information gaps to support players' narrative discovery. As students developed more thorough understanding of the world in which their characters existed, their improvisations—although separate from one another in the space—began to build a unified narrative. Actor Aziza Gharib (2021) named lore development as the most useful element of preparing for immersive performance:

> Building the world of our show together … made the world more cohesive and helped us all realize where we fit into each other's stories. I loved having "memories" to share with the audience that other characters in different parts of the world could mention too … Creating the lore helped us learn how to individually create our own characters while living in the same story. And we could tell that story together even though we never interacted with each other, because we had that shared knowledge.
>
> (Gharib, 2021)

Along with developing lore during worldbuilding, actors also needed to craft specific, detailed characters. Creating a deep dramaturgical rooting in their characters would guide improvisation. We called this the character's *core.* Jo Hoagland (2021), a freshman performer, highlighted this as the most beneficial aspect of training, saying:

> Building an intricate character core and practicing with mock audiences were by far the most useful exercises for me. Having a clear flushed out character core provided the solid foundation that allowed me to navigate the difficulties of immersive performance. Instead of having to take energy or panic to figure out what my character would say in the moment, I was able to answer in character automatically and put that energy into … engaging in more interesting conversation.
>
> (Hoagland, 2021)

Each character's core was rooted in three elements: status, stability, and sacrifice. Status—the character's hierarchical placement within relationships and society—was informed both by the character's social reality and by their self-perception. Students worked together, determining their characters' real and perceived statuses based on their relationships with other characters and the lore we had crafted.

Stability and Sacrifice, meanwhile, are internal—the character's psychological needs for survival. I introduced the human body as a metaphor. The core of a human body seeks to maintain a steady temperature, increasing or decreasing flow to vital organs to do so. In cold temperatures, blood flows to the core, abandoning the extremities. The body *needs* to maintain a stable temperature, functioning in a way that indicates a preference for sacrificing the extremities rather than the core, which houses vital organs. Similarly, actors determined what defined their character's core temperature: what each character *needs* to maintain stability for survival. I also asked them to identify what their character would be willing to sacrifice—and what they wouldn't—in order to attain that need. Actors determined their character's stability and sacrifice based on their roles and the lore they'd created: discovery, comfort, perfection, or the love of a specific character were needs identified for a handful of characters.

Actors rooted their improvisations in *lore* of the world and their character's *core* without blatantly stating this information to players. Instead, detailed improvisations could stem from this deep dramaturgical wellspring. Gharib describes the process:

> My character was very layered and had a core that she couldn't remember existed, but could still feel. Being able to always come back to who I am was a building block for all the improv I did. Amanda Rose helped me understand how to let my core be there for me as an actor and be there for the audience to discover without me coming straight out and saying it but through invitations.
>
> (Gharib 2021)

THE ART OF THE INVITATION: LEARNING AS ACTOR AND AUDIENCE

Extending invitations for audience participation is both an aesthetic and ethical element of immersive performance. Gareth White's (2013) *Audience Participation in Theatre* situates conventions for inviting participation well within the realm of aesthetics; his chapter "Accepting the Invitation" investigates the ethical complexities of participatory performance, as well. Aviles-Rodriquez et al (2019) more recently offers that "you want to think ahead about the kind of reaction [audiences] might have and the kind of invitation that you're offering and, in fact, the way in which you're offering the invitation" (183). As both a matter of ethics and aesthetics, the art of the invitation must be part of an actor's training for immersive performance.

In training, we began rehearsing invitations outside of the production's context, with an activity that I called "the invitation game." Rooted in game design, this activity borrowed from Chris Crawford's (2012) proclamation that "interactivity requires verb thinking" (87). Extending an invitation similarly requires verb thinking; the invitation offers an opportunity to do … *something* … and the recipient either accepts or declines the invitation. For "the invitation game," students were divided into "hosts" and "guests." Hosts extended "invitations" nonverbally to guests, who interpreted the invitation and either accepted or declined the offering.

Invitations started with simple gestures. For example, Rodrigo Gallardo Antunez, a host, raised his right hand overhead, elbow bent slightly. A guest waved back to him and moved on, without breaking stride. He approached another student, this time smiling broadly and raising his hand with a faster pace, stopping when it was overhead. The guest responded, giving him a high five. Gallardo Antunez (2021) later stated that "practicing invitations made me realize how specific we have to be but also how different players might want to engage with you differently and to accept that. I really learned to get comfortable with people not accepting invitations and not taking it personally. People want to do different things." In this activity, students practiced verb thinking and issuing invitations that allowed guests to react with variability, preparing for the eventuality in which audience-players might misunderstand, accept, or decline invitations during a performance. Invitations became more complex throughout the rehearsal process; hosts invited guests to go for piggyback rides or play leapfrog, all without speaking. Students learned from both issuing and receiving invitations: "you've got to be confident but chill," Kinari Rima (2021) explains, noting that a too-eager invitation "feels fake;" a timid one "awkward." Gharib (2021) offers that the activity taught actors "how to ask for consent without breaking character … also feeling out how comfortable an audience member was with the invitation. I learned I had to meet people where they are and modify, or sometimes even drop an invitation." Practicing outside the narrative context allowed students to learn these lessons without the pressure to perform their characters so that their learning could later inform their performances.

In-performance invitations were divided into two categories: offerings and trailheads. An *offering* invites an audience-player to join a character, delving deeper in the work of discovery. For example, Darcy Brander's character-built friendship bracelets, asking players to choose colors for the next one, sometimes offering one to a friendly passer-by. This offering invited players to stop while she tied it around their wrist, whereupon she might reward them by stating she wanted to give it to her sister but couldn't. Here, Darcy used an offering—the invitation to engage more deeply with her character.

The opposite of offerings, *trailheads* invite players to engage with a new goal, like a video game quest. This type of invitation marks the start of a trail of actions a player could take. If, for example, someone sat next to Darcy, her character might reveal that her sister disappeared: a trailhead. The player might then ask where the sister went, or why she wasn't returning, following the trail. With enough digging, the player might discover that the sister had become bionic and left home to pursue a singing career. That player might have already encountered a bionic singer elsewhere during the performance and realized that this character and Darcy were sisters. Players that further pursued this trail might eventually learn that in becoming bionic, the sister's memory had been "enhanced"—replaced with false memories. Along this trail, some audience members attempted to remind the sister of her former life. Some delivered friendship bracelets or messages from Darcy's character. One player, realizing that magnets could "short out" bionic characters, stole magnets from a store in attempt to help the sister recover her original memories—a completely unanticipated course of action that our performers rewarded with a tearful reunion not previously planned. Darcy wrote about the experience: "We planned out trails that they could take but sometimes they made their own. Because we knew our cores, we could always make it work and it was exciting to see what they would come up with. It was like we weren't just telling the same story over again through our performance, we were giving them invitations to start a story, then we were creating the story together" (Brander 2021). The process of designing and practicing extending invitations—both offerings and trailheads—during rehearsal prepared students not only to reveal unscripted moments of narrative vulnerability and intimacy along trails but to facilitate play. The process also taught students to anticipate, and appreciate, variability in the ways that audiences might respond, as illustrated by Hoagland:

Learning invitations was so helpful, especially trailheads and offerings... I had never done immersive theatre before and I was very scared of interacting with audience members and how they would react. But I knew that if I was comfortable I could use an offering … go deeper with them and if I was uncomfortable I could use a trailhead … and it would send them away. So, these tools helped me keep our audience members engaged in ways that they felt comfortable, so you were able to curate to everyone's needs and your own

(Hoagland, 2021).

ESTABLISHING BOUNDARIES: SELF-CARE CUES AND THE STING/REWARD SYSTEM

Because audiences' responses to invitations can be unpredictable, we practiced mechanics for redirecting unwanted responses. As well as using trailheads in this way, as described by Hoagland, we crafted self-care cues aligned with the setting that would alert actors to unsafe situations. For this production, one was "rebel." We practiced using these words in conversation to mask them from audience members, and we practiced simply interrupting a scene with their use. Gallardo Antunez (2021) comments on the value of practicing use of the self-care cue:

We came up with a 'SafeWord' that we were able to say to one another during the training and during the performance when we weren't feeling safe … I found that really helpful because … the SafeWord wasn't like out of context. We made it fit into the world that we were building, so I felt more like I could use it without ruining the illusion we are all working on creating.

Because students had practiced doing so and felt empowered to establish boundaries without "ruining" or interrupting the performance, they used the self-care cue readily, collaborating in facilitating players' experiences while supporting one another.

During the performance, Madelyn Wible performed as a bionic assistant at the bionic surgeon's office. When an audience member began encroaching upon her personal boundaries, she asked him, "you're not one of those nest rebels, are you?" Hearing this, the other actor in her vicinity joined the interaction, placing himself in physical proximity with Madelyn and leaning towards the player, a physical invitation for the player to back away. Madelyn later reflected: "having code words was so helpful. I remember one time [the other actor] was on break, so I just yelled, 'Rebel! Rebel!' and Amanda Rose came running. I knew that no matter what someone else had my back. It was really empowering" (Wible 2021). Because she had practiced using the self-care cue, she felt able to use this tool when needed. In this way, self-care cues became a game mechanic that performers could use to shape their own dynamic experience within the performance (Figure 4.2).

Figure 4.2 Performer Madelyn Wible rewards a player with information about bionics.
Photograph by Enrique Villarreal.

I became another element of establishing boundaries within the show. Students had requested support within the performance space. Rodriguez created a role without planned audience interactions that enmeshed me—an intimacy specialist and experienced immersive performer—in the show. I was a "rebel," someone seeking to overthrow VeraRev. If an audience member approached me, I would see their VeraRev badge and refuse to speak to them because "VeraRev is watching," thereby supporting the lore while excusing myself from further interaction. In this role, I traversed the world of the production, being available to support actors. Because these performers were students, this role served as an educational scaffold, supporting students only when they asked for that assistance.

We also practiced establishing boundaries through a system called *Stinging* and *Rewarding*. I taught the actors: *sting hard, reward fast*. This was a method students used to shape interactions with audiences. Actors *rewarded* players during interactions with information, a new invitation, or assistance helping the player progress towards their current goal. A *sting* was an in-character refusal to assist or connect with a player. Cody Snider (2021)—whose character was a bodyguard—illustrates how his sting redirected a player's tactics:

> This girl was talking about [Aziza's character] and wouldn't stop flirting with me so ... I was like "why are you touching me, you're trying to get to her, you need to leave." Later she came back ... and explained the whole trail about the sisters... She wanted to connect them so bad and she wasn't making me uncomfortable ... so I did that trail like my character didn't know about the memory erasing ... and decided to help her.

Illustrating the ways in which a participatory audience could create an agency imbalance if performers are beholden to lines and dialogue during immersive performance, this player attempted to flirt with, and touch, Snider's character. Trained to establish boundaries through improvised responses, his sting caused her to take a different approach. This illustrates both stinging—in-character refusal to assist—and rewarding—supporting the players' gamic actions—through in-character improvisation. In this way, actors were able to establish and support their own personal boundaries during performances.

In training, I repeated that actors *had every right* to break character if they felt unsafe; we established a system for this. Actors were taught to hold their hands up, palms facing outward creating a physical boundary, and say: "Stop. My name is (insert real name) and the year is 2019. I am a CU Boulder student, and you are making me feel unsafe." To my knowledge, perhaps due to the successful implementation of other methods previously described, this tactic was never utilized in performance, although we practiced using this format for establishing clear character breaks in rehearsal.

REHEARSING AS AUDIENCE

During rehearsals, actors crafted lore, character cores, and invitations, creating trails of playable action that audiences could explore; however, theorizing alone would not prepare the students for immersive performance. Therefore, we rehearsed extending these invitations and improvising in character; in this process, students rehearsed as audience as often as they performed their own roles. Students playing as audience members were given *specific* audience roles: a player seeking to troll the performers; one who was bored; one that was overeager. In this way, actors' rehearsals challenged the establishing of patterns; actors recognized the required subtlety for individual, unscripted interactions; and they deepened their understanding of the performance. We held rehearsals with other mock audiences—friends, family members, instructors, and CU staff were invited to participate and provide feedback as part of this production's iterative process—but rehearsing as audience was an integral element of realigning their acting training to fit with the more subtle, intimate performance style called for by Nordgren and Machon.

Rehearsing as audience shifted students towards performing "high resolution" gamic interactions. Gallardo Antunez (2021) outlines how this process helped: "Watching my fellow actors as a mock audience was extremely helpful so I could see where my character fit in to their worlds. How my cast mates described me ... is a huge part of what shaped my character and I created him to support people in doing the trailheads that my fellow actors started." Rima (2021) adds: "I saw them acting and I was like 'oh, that doesn't feel right.' It was too big. I thought I was better than that but when I was doing my part and Cody and

Sarah were audience I could see them having the same thought about me... It really helped me make my immersive theatre style." In this iterative process, students' experience as players helped them digest concepts we had discussed, similar to watching classmates' scenes in conventional acting coursework. Gallardo Antunez illustrates the ways in which rehearsing as audience informed his character, and Rima explains how watching others helped him develop a more intimate style of performance. A director could have *told* actors these things—in fact, I believe I did—but what cemented this was being able to partake in the audience experience. The embodied learning of experiencing improvised interactions within the narrative as both actor and audience member is a key component of engaging actors in the self-discovery that informs collaborative construction of immersive performance practices.

CONCLUSION

I approached training actors for *Virtue of Reality* from a praxis rooted in theatrical and gaming aesthetics and the ethical considerations of unscripted intimate exchanges. *Dramaturgical grounding, open invitations, boundary establishment,* and *participating as audience* members prepared actors formerly unfamiliar with the form for improvising with agency in their own immersive performance. Weaving this training framework into our devising processes provided actors with tools to facilitate play while maintaining personal safety when exploring their characters' vulnerabilities through close, improvised encounters with audience members. The ways in which actors invited players to engage in these intimate interactions, and players' unscripted responses, led to the emergence of unique details and experiences, rather than to a choreographed or scripted journey. In this way, actors collaborated with each group of audience-players to collaboratively devise new performances. Students assert that this training was "crucial" (Gharib 2021) and "empowering" (Makin 2021), agreeing with Mee (Aviles-Rodriquez et al., 2019) that the conversation about immersive performance training practices must be had, and should continue.

Note

1 Here, I choose to use larp (meaning live-action role-play) as a word in its own right, rather than in the acronym form (L.A.R.P.) more commonly used in the United States, adopting the linguistic practices of existing larp studies scholarship established by researchers in Nordic countries (Fatland 2005), rather than imposing U.S. vernacular usage into an existing scholarly discourse.

References

Aviles-Rodriguez, Guillermo, Penelope Cole, Rand Harmon, and Erin B. Mee. 2019. "Ethics and Site-Based Theatre: A Curated Discussion." *Theatre History Studies* 38 (1): 166–195. 10.1353/ths.2019.0010

Bial, Henry. 2020. "Foreword." In *Staging Sex: Best Practices, Tools, and Techniques for Theatrical Intimacy,* xii–xiii. New York, NY: Routledge.

Brander, Darcy. 2021. Remembering Virtue of Reality with Darcy, In Person.

Crawford, Chris. 2012. *Chris Crawford on Interactive Storytelling.* 2nd edition. Kindle: New Riders.

Fatland, Eirik. 2005. "Knutepunkt and Nordic Live Role-Playing: A Crash Course." In *Dissecting Larp: Collected Papers for Knutepunkt 2005.* Edited by Petter Bøckman and Ragnhild Hutchison, 11–20. Grimshei Trykkeri AS: Knutepunkt.

Gallardo Antunez, Rodrigo. 2021. Rodrigo's Reflection Google Form.

Gharib, Aziza. 2021. Responses from Aziza Google Forms.

Harviainen, J. Tuomas. 2007. "Live-Action, Role-Playing Environments as Information Systems." *Information Research* 12 (October). http://informationr.net/ir/12-4/colis/colis24.html

Hoagland, Jo. 2021. Responses from Jo Google Forms.

Machon, Josephine. 2013. *Immersive Theatres: Intimacy and Immediacy in Contemporary Performance*. 2013 edition. Houndmills, Basingstoke, Hampshire: Palgrave.

Makin, Isobel. 2021. Discussing "VR" with Wren Interview by Amanda Rose Villarreal. In Person.

McGonigal, Jane. 2011. *Reality Is Broken: Why Games Make Us Better and How They Can Change the World*. New York, NY: Penguin Books.

Nordgren, Andie, Markus Montola, and Jaako Stenros. 2008. "High Resolution Larping: Enabling Subtlety at Totem and Beyond." In *Playground Worlds: Creating and Evaluating Experiences of Role-Playing Games*, 91–101. Finland: Ropeconry.

Pace, Chelsea. 2020. *Staging Sex: Best Practices, Tools, and Techniques for Theatrical Intimacy*. Routledge Publishing.

Rima, Kinari. 2021. Kinari Virtue Reality Google Form.

Snider, Cody. 2021. (Untitled) Google Forms.

"The Virtue of Reality." 2019. University of Colorado Events Calendar. September 22, 2019. https://calendar.colorado.edu/event/the_virtue_of_reality#.YNvFcC1OKfA

White, Gareth. 2013. *Audience Participation in Theatre: The Aesthetics of the Invitation*. New York, NY: Palgrave Macmillan.

Wible, Madelyn. 2021. (Untitled) Google Form.

5

Experiential Theatres and the Value of Rethinking Theatre Education: A Conversation with Performers and Interactive Theatre Makers on Developing Methods for Collaborative Experience Making

William W. Lewis and Valerie Clayman Pye

PANEL PARTICIPANTS

Matt Adams (Blast Theory)
Tassos Stevens (Coney)
Bruce Barton and Pil Hansen (Vertical City)
Khalia Davis and Marisol Rosa-Shapiro (Spellbound Theatre)
Julianne Just and Jenny Weinbloom (The Speakeasy Society)
Mia Rovegno (Freelance Director)

How do you define experiential theatre practices? And how does it relate to your own personal practice?

Matt Adams

What I have found most strikingly different when I've worked with people who come from a traditional theatre background is that in the work that Blast Theory make, we are focused entirely on a member of the public who is taking part in the work and so that participant is then the frame of reference. We are not starting from stories or from texts, we are starting from moments of experience around the participant. That in many ways inverts the process completely.

Mia Rovegno

I'm thinking a lot about [the] importance of centering the give and take between performer and audience participant. And this exchange: asking for the act of being fully present from both participant and maker. Asking for the sort of radical listening and presence that's palpable for the audience when it's experienced, so that they feel that they're actually integrated into some kind of ecosystem that does not exist discreetly from them as a

DOI: 10.4324/9781003188179-7

EXPERIENTIAL THEATRES AND THE VALUE OF RETHINKING THEATRE EDUCATION • 65

spectator. I feel like this is a space that implicates. Sometimes it's a space that invigorates people, it's a space that invites people. It can be all these things at once, inviting a multi-pronged experience of many truths existing in the same moment, it's very much about building intimacy.

Tassos Stevens

The experience for an audience begins when they first hear about it, it only stops, if and when they stop thinking and talking about it. The experience of people inside the work as they move through it. Their presence is acknowledged and interactive, which may have some consequence on the outcome of their experience.

Marisol Rosa-Shapiro

When I think about experiential work, it is very much about getting back to something very essential and very core about what it is to take part in a connective event. There's a lot there about tradition and ritual. The very fundamental sense of connection that comes from sharing space and sharing touch and sharing other kinds of contact.

Pil Hansen

The questions we're interested in relate to the ethics, the care involved in inviting people, communities, to expand and diversify. How do they attend, what do they attend to, how do they relate, and who and what do they relate to? We ask these questions from the outset of the creative process of developing first interests and inquiries, in order to navigate the performance and experiences generated by the audience, with the audience, between the audience, and the performers, and the environment that's produced. How do we invite that, and what do we do with what's offered? Then there's the element of material contents that have been created and rehearsed. And any kind of journey that's been planned for the engagement of that audience. So, what kind of mode of engagement do we need to model and facilitate, in order to build relationships? We navigate from the very outset by asking questions and developing a work with the motivation of discovering ways of perceiving, experiencing, intending, and relating differently from what is constrained by normative processes.

Bruce Barton

We explore this idea I refer to as a "dramaturgy of embrace." You can reach out to someone, you can take hold of someone, you can hug someone. But an embrace is different; it's a two-way street. For the most part [our work] is looking to try to create this space of embrace between, on the one hand, the performance and those who have initiated it, and, on the other, those who have been invited into it. Then it really becomes a shared space. We try to create a space where everyone is feeling a similar level of vulnerability, even if the vulnerability felt by the audience is inevitably different than that felt by the performers. The audience can't help but be vulnerable if you're inviting them into a participatory context. So, we better do our work to create a space where we're as much at risk; however, you want to define that term, as they are, because then really wonderful things can happen. Which means that a lot of safety devices have to be built into the process, as well.

Khalia Davis

Something that I'm excited about when it comes to experiential theatre making especially when it comes to how we can redefine spaces that young audiences occupy is: how interactive can they get? Does it affect the artists that are doing the work and making the work? Babies crawling on their lap may now alter or shift how the artist was going to present something because they have a baby on their lap. Because we created a container that allowed a child to feel safe enough to come into the lap of an artist that they literally just met walking in that day. That to me, I think is something super exciting. And I'm interested in figuring out how we can continue to create those types of environments for young audiences so that they can feel empowered in the work that they are viewing because they know that it is a reflection of who they are, they can see themselves in that in some capacity. And then, of course, creating that sense of empathy that we're all really striving for.

Julianne Just

One of the things we talk about with our actors, when we're rehearsing an immersive experience, is the idea that the audience is your scene partner. And I think that is really captured with this idea of the baby crawling on your lap. That baby is in the moment with you and will impact, and likely change what happens in the scene. For us, as a company, it's really been a shift into an audience-first format. In this sort of work the audience is accountable, they are seen and heard and required to be fully present. For the audience, I think it's an invitation to both break personal patterns (a shy person might decide to act more boldly in the safe space of the experience) and/or to recognize those patterns and be in them more fully (a person identifies as a leader and steps into the role in the experience but get to use those skills or traits in a new dynamic or setting).

Jenny Weinbloom

So much of my work is based in gamification and interactivity in various capacities, where the role of the participant is an active one. I'm always thinking about experience and immersion as total narrative and/or total thematic immersion. So much of what we do in an experiential practice is placemaking—which is fundamentally thematic, in many ways, more than narrative. From a commercial project standpoint, you typically have to be thinking right from the start about the participant's journey. There's throughput requirements, there's facility requirements, there's a ride envelope that's in consideration, there's a strategy around technology, tools, and partnerships, interactivity, there's intellectual property, it's all of these different levers that create an increasingly narrow path of experience.

We're really looking at the story we want to tell first and foremost, and the modes of interactivity and participation need to follow and meet the needs of that story. They're so deeply, intrinsically tied. Participants are putting tremendous, tremendous trust in us. And they are going to go on the journey that we create for them and with them and co-create alongside them with the best of intentions and with open heart and mind. And we need to be aware that our authorship is also our authority and take that responsibility very seriously.

What do you think might be missing from current theatre training? What theories, methodologies, approaches, philosophies, would you recommend? And building off that question, as you've continued to develop your practices, what new trends have changed your own processes?

Pil Hansen

Many current training methods tend to teach different aspects of the process separately, and that can put up barriers between those aspects. We also, sometimes, have fewer opportunities to teach students how to build bridges, or even teach them the bridges that we have ourselves built, between those different roles and those different skill sets.

Julianne Just

I think, particularly if you're teaching or using a devising process, finding a way to bring the whole team, including management students, stage managers, production managers, and producers into that devising space is important. Then everyone has an opportunity to help create the vocabulary and world of the production, while also having the chance to step into a variety of roles, not just the one they might have been assigned, or selected. In short, you are giving people the opportunity to wear different hats. I remember when I was an undergrad, someone would be like, I'm an actor, I don't want to spend a whole semester pretending I'm a costume designer and I understand this, that is a long time to spend on something other than your interest, and yet, it has value. Doing this via a devising process, allows people to do just this, wear a variety of hats, but for a very short period on something quick and socially generative while discovering elements of the show and building a sense of the team.

I came from a literature-based theatre background. I spent a lot of time studying plays from the western theatrical canon. Despite an education in experimental theatre, I still had a limited view of what I consider theatre. Whatever it was, it was centered around a performance with a recognized performer (meaning people understood they were watching a show). And it wasn't until the very end of grad school that I was asked to consider a theme park, in its totality – not just the stage shows, through the lens of a theatrical experience. Once I got over my literary high art snobbiness, it was transformative for me. It freed me from the idea that I am meant to do work in the theatre or that my work needs to be considered theatre. I now create work that can sit in a lot of different spaces and forms. Another example, I was very dismissive of video games as art for a long time. People were telling me, "You've got to play this game. It's exactly what you're trying to do. They're telling really interesting stories. You're stepping into the role." Now I think finding ways to incorporate these sorts of thing into a theatrical curriculum is exciting.

Mia Rovegno

I think one of the biggest takeaways for me in every leg of my journey has been the importance of providing multiple creative points of view to students from mentors and artistic influences and creating spaces that encourage dialoguing between artistic team members. These might be spaces where producers are in on dramaturgy, actors collaborate with writers, or designers are seen as co-authors, from day one in the room. And I think what I've seen in some conservatory environments is a tendency, at least in America, to sort of indoctrinate students into one way of working, preparing young artists to work in one modality in the real world, which is completely unrealistic.

In my own practice, I've really moved further and further toward crossing boundaries between disciplines. I'm looking for cross-pollinating spaces between performance languages and practices. So, I love bringing musicians into a theatre space or asking game designers to work with performers, or visual artists to work with narrative, text, or playwrights. I find that the disconnect between artistic languages can provide fertile ground for creating and improvising toward new collaborative languages and expands the artistic versatility people can bring into every creative process. This practice also sharpens life skills that we are inevitably helping to cultivate with our students. So, while we're introducing them to being present and listening and remaining open-minded, we can also be asking them to be rigorous about diversifying their practice.

Tassos Stevens

I'm really struck by how people define themselves. To find your career is not necessarily like one hat. I also feel that in terms of working with performers, always encouraging people to make your own work, even if that's not what you think you want to do. Taking responsibility for the whole of the work, not just your part inside it, will really hold you in good stead. I was thinking about disciplines that have hugely influenced me: improvisation, game design, participation design, and different designer approaches. What they often share is thinking systematically and being able to see and model and map things systematically, and not just through stories, that's crucial. And also iterative, a scratch kind of process, like what gets called playtesting in game design. We're going to make something, we're going to put it out as quickly as we can, with a playing audience—my preferred catch all term—and see what happens. And then we're going to remake it, from what we learned. Rather than [it] having to be perfect before we can put it in front of people. And the mind shifts that go with this shift. I think that there's a lot around [these] skills and facilitation for this.

Jenny Weinbloom

I found conservatory actor training to be a pretty dangerous space, mentally and emotionally. My training was rooted in Grotowski-based techniques. I was always a devisor. I was always in the physical theater space. I very much did not have that kind of author/playwright-driven approach at any point in my educational process, but I never felt that I had any meaningful autonomy as a student devisor. I frequently found a very kind of authoritative atmosphere in which the teacher, the director, had a lot of control of that space. I would love to see a shift in the future towards consent-based learning and trauma-informed pedagogy. Real respect for actor autonomy, real respect for actor identities, and how that informs their experience. Thinking about crossing boundaries between creative disciplines and cultures, but also class and educational backgrounds. There can sometimes be almost a language divide between folks who come from a more academic theatre background and folks with a more practice-based background.

How are we making sure that folks who are coming to the table without a shared vocabulary, without that academic background, can feel totally confident that they have just as much to contribute from their lived experience? And most importantly, we need to invite theatre students to cultivate and enforce their boundaries, and practice acknowledging, respecting, and advocating for the boundaries of their classmates and their collaborators. Because everything we were saying at the beginning about participant journey and about audience, spectator, and participant autonomy begins with learning to listen to the self and understand your own autonomy and have the courage to enforce your own boundaries. You can't be that advocate for your audience if you can't be that advocate for yourself and your collaborators.

Marisol Rosa-Shapiro

I'll just reiterate a couple of very specific ways of working and training. Facilitation skills and the ability to feel and read the dynamics of a social space. What are the power dynamics around identities showing up in the space? How to be sensitive to, aware of, and responsive to all of that. I have a lot of skepticism about many academic spaces. I went to Italy and trained in the lineage of LeCoq, but with a teacher who is very sort of anti-establishment in the sense that he was excited about exploring an embodied opportunity through clown to understand how we show up in space, what our bodies say, when we

EXPERIENTIAL THEATRES AND THE VALUE OF RETHINKING THEATRE EDUCATION • **69**

show up in space. Becoming aware of that. It's about vulnerability and deep presence and listening. What we've done with Spellbound, there's so much of the skill set of just being able to meet the participants exactly where they are and to meet their breath, the quality of their physical presence, to build that sense of invitation and contract.

Bruce Barton

I guess what I would put up front, right off the top, is that I've never studied the practice of theatre. I began my education studying literature and painting, and then I studied poetry and drama. Then, for my doctoral work, I looked at the intersection between live performances and mediated performances (although 'live' meant something quite different then than it does today). What I do teach, a lot, is performance creation. I don't lead those classes like an acting teacher, or like a directing teacher. I lead them like a performance creator. That, for me, is often quite at odds with the approach towards teaching acting, which I think in is often a very individualistic and very competitive process. There's often an underlying assumption that a very small number of people are going to make it. And while, as a student, you go through a whole lot of polite interactions with the other people that you work with, you're the one who wants to be the star at the other end of it.

When I direct in academic contexts, they're going to be devised performances, and people are going to make their own work. It's often the more junior students who step into those roles, because by the time they're seniors, if there's not a whole lot of lines, and they're not going to be center stage for a big part of the performance, they're often not interested. That for me is a really clear indication of where we're failing our students.

I really think [that] the primary characteristics that I would love students to get hold of through their process is to learn to have humility—but not a humility based in fear. I'd love to see them have a sense of humility that is confident and that is patient. Key concepts that I work with, and that I think we could build into our training much more, is the sense of how to maintain balance in the face of what you don't know, in the face of what comes as a surprise and a change, as opposed to working so hard to nail everything down. How to be insatiably curious. I find that among many students, as they move through their programs, they become less and less curious about the world, and more and more closed down in terms of what's important to them.

The very last thing I would throw in is that it would be really healthy to complicate the idea of story, to frame it as dramaturgy as opposed to narrative. How things work, how things move, how they fit together, how they affect.

Khalia Davis

I'll address the second part of the question. Something that I am very aware of is new technologies and new devices and new apps that have broken through barriers for a lot more young people to be able to participate in art making. I was born in the 80s, raised in the 90s, and understood YouTube to be this amazing place where you can maybe make something cool and people might watch it, but you have to do a lot of work to make it happen. And now we have Tik Tok, which is so accessible and so manageable that children are able to create full productions on an app and get millions of views and get nominated for Emmys. So, something that I'm very excited about is embracing what the younger generation is finding to allow them to make the art that they want to make and to show off their identities. There's so much more confidence in the devices that they're using, that I hadn't seen in the classrooms when we take those devices away.

I am so aware of this idea that we have when we create a space with young people. The first day is like, "we are an ensemble, every single one of you is so important and vital to the creation." Again, instilling this importance, [that] every single part of the process is important, and you should have some sense of it. Then you get to universities, and it becomes more segmented, and you have to decide: "I'm going to be an actor, or I'm going to do this, or I'm going to do that." I would be very excited about programs that invite all different types of forms at the same level through your process of working at that program. Those resources you didn't have to search for? As a black identifying human—[I think] it is shameful that I don't know my history until I am searching for the elective class in the African American Studies Department. That's ridiculous! That should just be part of my educational experience from the time I'm in kindergarten. I think it's the same in artmaking if you identify as an artist, if you're excited about what art could be, then you should be exposed to all the different ways that you can be creative, as you're growing your artistry, as you're on your artistic journey. And you're picking all of these different pieces. And eventually, you're creating your own work.

Matt Adams

Firstly, interdisciplinarity is more than just, "I do two different things." There is actually a mode of thinking and understanding about what it means to be interdisciplinary. How as you move from one mode to another, different frameworks, different forms of practice are invoked. I think there's something about performing inside a structure which has been touched on by a number of different people. But I think that sense of understanding that acting can be both fully realized and subsumed within a system in the same way that someone doing Hamlet knows where their mark is. I think that there's a much more expanded notion of that approach when we're talking about experiential theatre. Thirdly, I think there's something about the wider relationship to the audience. Tassos, you mentioned about "from the very first moment to the very last moment"; that essentially means that you're involved in marketing and talking to audiences at a number of different levels. And you have to get on board with what that actually means for your practice. Rather than feeling that you're being corrupted or diluted or falling short of your artistic purity. If that happens. There are lots of situations where we're talking about how many people can do something at the same time. I think almost all good experiential theatre is doing that really well. That's all baked in.

Then the last thing I would just talk about is ethical thinking. Ethical processes for what is and is not acceptable come up all of the time in immersive and participatory work. You have to be able to understand how to think about risk and your own role in risk. To think about consent and safety, but also to think about risk and danger is equally part of that. It's not just about nailing everything down to ensure that everyone is safe all of the time. It's about understanding that good work takes risks with what it asks.

How do you think, or how might you suggest that we go about redesigning training, so that there is a participant-driven initiative or narrative at its center, rather than this kind of hierarchical, siloed experience of making that many programs are putting forth?

Jenny Weinbloom

I think it's so critical to think about that from a cross-disciplinary standpoint because if we want to believe that we're creating a laboratory approach or an R&D-oriented approach, we can't only be utilizing fellow theatre makers as our participant group. We need to be working with other departments within the university, with students of radically different backgrounds who don't identify as artists and don't identify as theatre makers.

Matt Adams

One of the ways to do that is about feedback. Put people in a position of humility, of listening carefully to feedback from audiences or participants. Shutting your mouth and taking on board what people have just said about an experience they've had, and then trying to work through problem solving, is a really important skill. I always think back to a moment of usability testing on a website that we had built, where part of our testing was saying to someone, imagine you're a student and you want to write an essay about political theatre, where would you go on the website, and then I had to sit and just watch in silence as they looked around and they went past all the routes, all the user journeys that we had designed. You're suddenly learning, for the first time, that your mental frame about how someone is participating in something is totally different from other people's mental frame. I think that links to site-specific work, or socially contextual work, which is to go into an environment where you are a stranger or an outsider, and to try and make something for that place or for those people, and to then to listen to find those processes where your artistic imperative or your artistic drive is bouncing back to you through the experience of a participant or a member of the public. That can be a very powerful experience.

Bruce Barton

I totally agree that you have to really complicate what the idea of an audience is, and what a participant is. And, therefore, I think you need to bring your students face to face with lots of different kinds of audiences and participants. Get them thinking about sports audiences, get them thinking about what it means to go to a museum, get them to think about what it means to be in a waiting room. Really try to play with that and think about all the different kinds of responsibilities and opportunities that emerge from that diversity of audiences. I think it's key to ask students to be participants, to be audiences, and to be audiences in lots of different kinds of contexts, as well.

Pil Hansen

There are two components that might be important to bring together here. One is the experience of the student being an audience member, of working with and collaborating, of trying to facilitate experience [that is] foreign with people who aren't artists themselves. Being in the space, responding to it, testing how they respond to the invitation offered. But I think the other component is distributed dramaturgical awareness: the ability to see the performance, the work as it's developing as a system, as interconnected elements, and to see the interactions that emerge in that. And you need that in order to anticipate what might happen, and both build a repertoire of possible ways of responding to that, and engaging with that, but also gaining the ability to improvise with the things that will surprise you. I think that requires a training process where you're not isolated in a specific role, and where you're also not subordinated in a master/student relationship, because you need agency. I'm talking about distributing the dramaturgical agency, so that performer[s] actually can make changes, to make choices in those situations that affect the other performers, the space, and the audience.

Tassos Stevens

How much can students be involved from the outset and also determine the direction of the course and that they have agency? Exposure to as many different practices as possible. Coney has adopted a concept of working more broadly, as an ethos of exchange, that we all have expertise to share. Making as much as possible, making, throwing away, and just kind of continuing. Critical reflection as a skill, and how to offer that and what it means.

Julianne Just

I think it is important to give everyone in the group the opportunity to talk about what's exciting them or what they are responding to in the devising or creative process. This can create a sense of agency for those working on the project, not just as a generator of content, but also as a critical thinker. Ultimately, even if indirectly, everyone can feel like they had a hand, or voice, in the decision-making process.

Khalia Davis

I was also going to bring up this idea that I noticed as the result of the pandemic; how so many theatre institutions, the first thing that they did was send out audience surveys. It has really opened my eyes to the necessity of getting feedback from your audience members and community members. It really was a great opportunity for me to reflect on how important it is that we are constantly attuned to the people that we are serving. We don't want to make things in a vacuum.

Mia Rovegno

I think it's vital to encourage a process that isn't simply preparation for spectatorship. It's important to always bring into the room a lens of the influence and context of the lived experience of each and every new person who experiences the work. To support a kind of unapologetic beta testing with participants in the delivery of production, and to consider that creative expression is useful without an endpoint. Artists can be making work that prioritizes iterating, by curating a group of specific conditions or circumstances in which an experience can evolve. This means allowing a way of making and rehearsing that embraces a kind of accumulation, or associative experience, as opposed to a fixed, linear path that we're sort of aiming to force folks down in rehearsal and in production. To me, it's about letting go of waiting for or even aiming for everyone to receive the same experience: both for maker and participant.

Matt Adams

If I was running a course, I would do a series of accessibility projects, where in three iterations, someone who has limited hearing, someone who has limited vision, and someone who has limited mobility comes in, meets the students, and communicates with them about their experience, and what they would like to see and then those students make work for that person. That person comes back a time later and students show that work to that person, and therefore get a really embodied understanding of what accessibility might look like, and they lose some of their fear of how to address issues of accessibility in a really creative way.

What are some of the obstacles that you see for artists who might be interested in making experiential theatre or performance? And what advice would you have for them?

Julianne Just

I'm really interested in the question "how do we incentivize audience participants to engage in the creative process and instill the idea in them that coming into something still in development has value?" Shifting the idea that as an audience member you are waiting to buy a ticket, or invest, in a final polished perfect version of show. Finding a way to redefine the expectations of what it means to be a part of an audience. That being in an audience is to be invited into the creative process, and getting to see a show evolve over time, is a form of audience participation, and offers an opportunity for a relationship to be formed between the audience, the artists, and the work itself based on deep engagement, which one might argue could have more value than getting to attend a polished show.

Bruce Barton

It's a twin approach of being able to frame what you do in ways that are perhaps a little bit more accessible and recognizable within conventional models, without restricting what it is you want to achieve. And to imagine that there is support and collaboration outside of traditional artistic frameworks. There are all kinds of people that will want to collaborate with you, and amazing things can happen in those contexts.

Marisol Rosa-Shapiro

I would encourage creators and educators to engage in a practice of assessing your own curiosities and also assessing what it is you bring to a creative process, what you could bring to a community process beyond your craft. Craft is very valuable in some moments. And sometimes your craft, it turns out, is actually an obstacle, right? So, what are the curiosities, the motors behind why you are making performance.

What final word of advice do you have for educators who want to engage students in this kind of work?

Matt Adams

I think we don't look enough at the transition out of training and into the beginning of the career. I feel that students are so underserved and unsupported as they graduate with a ton of debt, having to move house, change all of their arrangements. They lose access to equipment and support. I meet people regularly who are really struggling in that three, six months, nine months out of training. And I think there's so much more we can do for those people to give them tools and prepare them for that transition. It's a small thing, but it feels really important.

Jenny Weinbloom

I believe that the core value of a formal education in the theatre is participating in a cohort and the possibility that that cohort will evolve into a company or collective. The Speakeasy Society evolved out of a cohort at Cal Arts. My other creative family, Rhinestone Gorilla, evolved out of a cohort at SUNY New Paltz. Meow Wolf evolved out of a loose cohort of local artists in Santa Fe. To me, there is nothing more important that happens in an educational setting than a group of students having a shared experience, developing a common vocabulary, and becoming a creative family that can evolve together over the course of a life and welcome new voices over time. My advice to theatre students is to make finding their people their number one priority, and my advice is to theatre educators is to make assisting that effort, cultivating community, and supporting independent, peer-focused creative development their number one priority, both while their students are with them and, even more so, past graduation. As a theatre educator, my ultimate win would not be to produce a star student, but a cohort community that can eventually become a company, a collective, a movement, a school of thought that is so much bigger, more expansive, and more inclusive than the cohort that founded it.

6

Facilitating Narrative Agency in Experiential Theatre

Astrid Breel

FACILITATING NARRATIVE AGENCY IN EXPERIENTIAL THEATRE

Agency is an often-discussed term in connection to participation in theatre and performance (Alston 2016; Frieze 2016; Harpin and Nicholson 2017; Harvie 2013; Tomlin 2019; White 2013). Agency describes the ability to make decisions that in some way influence, change or impact the agent's situation (Schlosser 2015); in experiential performance this means, for instance, being able to influence the performance direction, contribute to the work's material, or change the show's outcome. It's useful to distinguish between the ability to contribute to a work during its creation and the opportunity to participate within a performance of that work (which likely happens multiple times). This essay focuses on participation *during* an experiential performance, but this does not exclude the possibility of a participatory process to create the work. Within this essay I will discuss the different types of agency in experiential theatre, strategies for facilitating audience participation, and highlight the ways that agency becomes meaningful when it is experienced by participants (which is not effectively determined through observation). As performers only have limited control over whether participants experience agency, I will discuss strategies to support performers to successfully facilitate such experiences. This essay also includes a practical exercise exploring facilitation strategies for the different types of contributions invited by experiential theatre and critical questions for reflection.

Within experiential theatre there are two main types of agency: *agency of engagement* and *narrative agency* (Breel, Forthcoming). Agency of engagement describes the ability of audience members to find their own journey through the work and the opportunity to decide on their physical relationship to the performance (i.e., getting closer to the action or exploring the space). A performance where the audience sits down throughout offers little agency of engagement, whilst a promenade performance offers a lot of agency of engagement, with different actions afforded by the way audience members are encouraged to move through the space. For instance, Punchdrunk's work offers the opportunity to explore the space to audience members, who can decide on viewing strategies such as following performers, exploring the set's corners to find details, or seeking a one-on-one encounter with a performer. Agency of engagement does not include the ability to change the performance itself, rather it is the relationship between the audience member and performance that is altered (which impacts on that audience member's individual experience).

74

DOI: 10.4324/9781003188179-8

Narrative agency is the opportunity for participants to make material contributions to or changes in the performance, which go beyond affecting the individual's experience to impact the experiences of other participants. Narrative agency can take a variety of forms, from a collective audience vote on what happens next to the contribution of a personal anecdote that becomes part of the performance text. Kaleider's *The Money*, for instance, asks participants to make a collective decision on what to do with the money on the table in front of them within the rules presented (that it must be unanimous, legal, and made within 60 minutes), meaning that they contribute the performance content as well as determine the outcome. The ability to contribute to the performance material or direction is particularly meaningful for participants as the impact of narrative agency extends beyond impacting only on their own experience (as with agency of engagement) and builds a collective experience.

Both agency of engagement and narrative agency become meaningful when they are experienced, however audience research on the experience of participation highlights that not all acts of narrative agency are automatically experienced as agency (Breel, forthcoming). Agency can be conceptualized from two perspectives: through external observation of audience actions (by makers or researchers) and through participants' reflection on their own experiences. Only audience first-person narratives can fully determine whether participants *experienced* agency during the performance, making it important to talk to audiences after any playtests during a work's development (a term from game development where a new game is tested before release to find and fix any bugs or design flaws; this is essential for experiential theatre as the work is incomplete until the audience arrives). This essay will set out an approach for teaching students about agency: by considering how to conceptualize audience agency, looking at facilitation strategies, and a practical exercise to build skills and test ideas.

CONCEPTUALIZING AGENCY

When designing, directing, or facilitating participation in experiential theatre it's important to remember that it's not possible to *give* participants agency. Agency is something all audience members already possess; however, this agency can be restricted or conducted by a performance to create the desired aesthetic experience. Most experiential performances both restrict and conduct agency, for instance, *The Money* invites contributions from participants in the form of suggestions on what to do with the money on the table as well as ideas on how to make a unanimous collective decision, whilst creating boundaries that mean these contributions can be meaningfully incorporated into the performance, such as the need for all to sign the pro forma before the time runs out.

A performance structure, including the relationship between performers and audience, the lay-out of the space, and the invitations to participants to contribute, determines the specific ways in which the work conducts and restricts participants' agency. For instance, a Punchdrunk performance invites participants to walk through the space and choose where to stand which conducts their agency of engagement but will also restrict access to certain areas (likely for audience safety). An invitation to take on a role within the narrative that includes the ability to make decisions conducts a participant's narrative agency, but it is still constrained by the existing performance narrative and might come with options to choose between to move the story forwards.

To get a more detailed picture of how narrative agency can be conducted (and restricted) it is useful to distinguish between four levels (Breel, Forthcoming):

- **Reactive:** Participants are given an explicit request or choice, such as answering a question with predefined options (verbally or physically). This enables the audience to influence the performance narrative but within clearly set boundaries. Often the

76 • ASTRID BREEL

type of response invited is explicitly set out, such as standing in a particular area of the room to indicate your choice or holding up one of three colored cards.

- **Interactive:** Participants are directly invited to respond to an element of the work, but without pre-decided responses to choose between. This enables a wider range of potential responses, which conducts narrative agency more effectively. For instance, performers might invite participants to discuss the best way forwards in relation to a challenge presented by the work; here participants can take anything they've discovered so far to come up with ideas to solve the challenge.
- **Creative:** At this level participants contribute something that responds to the affordances of the situation and adds something distinct to the performance that did not explicitly exist before. Where interactive agency asks participants to put forward their own perspective, perhaps reframing what has happened so far; for creative agency participants are encouraged to add something to the work that was not already present in a different form. This contribution might be a personal response or experience that is then incorporated into the performance, or it might be a request for participants to devise what happens next in the narrative.
- **Pro-active:** Pro-active agency consists of self-initiated contributions which are not explicitly invited by the work and where the response is situated outside of the situation's affordances. As such it is impossible to deliberately invite pro-active agency; however, it is important to be aware of it as something that might happen as some participants either misinterpret the invitations for participation or deliberately test the edges of the work. The best way to prepare for pro-active agentic acts is to be clear on the work's boundaries and acknowledge contributions that cannot be incorporated into the narrative (weaving these in as best possible, so that participants feel their contributions have been heard).

These four levels of narrative agency describe the spectrum of different types of contributions you might elicit from your audience. The specific level invited by a situation is in part determined by the interpretation of the audience member and in part responsive to the facilitation style. For instance, an invitation to contribute to the decision of what happens next in the performance narrative through conversation might be facilitated by: offering three options to choose between (reactive), inviting open conversation on events so far (interactive), or making it clear that the ending is not predetermined by asking for suggestions of what to do next (creative). The same invitation can result in both interactive and creative responses from different participants, as their contribution depends on a range of factors (including their interpretation of the task and their confidence in taking part).

FACILITATING AGENCY

It's important to remember that designing an opportunity for participants to contribute to an experiential performance will not automatically translate into an experience of agency for them (which is when agency becomes meaningful). However, a nuanced understanding of agency will support the design of more thoughtful and intentional invitations and enable effective playtesting strategies to refine the participatory elements of a work. Research on agency demonstrates that for someone to experience agency, they need to make the connection between their action and the result, even if this is not what they intended or expected (Bayne 2008; Gallagher 2005; Gallagher and Zahavi 2008). If this connection is missing, then agency is not experienced (Hallet 2011). For simple actions (i.e., pressing a button to turn a light on) a direct, and quick, result is important for someone to make the connection that leads to experienced agency. Participants'

FACILITATING NARRATIVE AGENCY IN EXPERIENTIAL THEATRE • 77

retrospective attribution of agency happens for both "planned" instances, where their actions did materially contribute to a particular moment in the performance (such as the ending), as well as for events that would have happened irrespective of any audience contributions. Although for the latter we could see this as an "incorrect" attribution, this does not make the experience any less meaningful unless the participant discovers that they have been purposefully misled as to the (lack of) consequences from their actions. In both cases, retrospective attribution is more common for complex actions, where the link between action and result is less clear and where often there are multiple contributions that together determine a result. The complicated and uncertain process of retrospective attribution of agency also highlights the importance of an iterative development process that includes playtesting and audience feedback, to develop the most effective facilitation strategies possible for the desired aesthetic experience.

Agency of engagement and narrative agency result in different types of experiences of agency for participants: in agency of engagement the connection between an action taken by a participant and the resulting impact on their experience is direct and often immediate (by moving across a room to discover something or talk to a performer). In narrative agency the relationships between acts and results are frequently more complex and longitudinal; for instance, the performance outcome might be the result of the contributions from a group of participants and this outcome might be at the end whilst contributions are made throughout the show. These aspects of narrative agency mean that it can be difficult for participants to retrospectively attribute agency to their actions within the performance; but the nature of narrative agency means that if the attribution *is* made by participants, it is a more meaningful type of agency than agency of engagement. Makers and facilitators of participatory performance can support participants to make retrospective attributions of narrative agency through the thoughtful facilitation of invitations that implicitly or explicitly make clear why participants are asked to do something (this can happen at the time of the invitation or can be made clear at the point in the performance when the result plays out). Facilitated post-performance conversations can also support participants to make the connections between their actions and the outcome(s) within the work. This process supports a better understanding for the director and performers of how agency is experienced within the work by participants.

PRACTICAL IMPLEMENTATION

This exercise is a practical exploration of different ways to restrict and conduct agency through participation to support a critical discussion of facilitation approaches. The categories listed below can also be used as a framework for the analysis of existing performances.

Preparation

Create three **sets of cards** (ten cards in total) with the bold words on each (the definition of each word is shared with the group rather than written on the card):

Types of contribution

1. **Personal:** Invite participants to contribute material to the performance that is based on or related to their own lives; for instance, past experiences, lived knowledge, or personal interpretations.
2. **Narrative:** Ask participants to make contributions that move the narrative forwards, including decisions on what happens next, voting, or influencing the performance ending by solving a problem.

78 • ASTRID BREEL

3. **Role:** Provide participants with a specific role, which might be a task to carry out or a character to play (either individually or as a group); the aspects of this role might be explicitly set out or have to be inferred from the situation.
4. **Game:** Present participants with a clear goal or objective to achieve, such as winning a challenge, solving a puzzle, or achieving a collective task.

Facilitating levels of agency

1. **Reactive:** Facilitate audience participation through presenting clear choices or options for participants to choose between.
2. **Interactive:** Invite participants to use what they have learned in the performance so far to respond to challenges, questions, or decisions that need to be made.
3. **Creative:** Encourage participants to contribute their own perspectives into the performance, with the aim of adding something new to the situation (i.e., something personal or a new perspective on existing performance content).

Participant playing style

1. **Reluctant:** Participants should be reluctant or unsure about participating (but not unwilling); this might be expressed through questions for the performer about what is desired/invited or through being slow to respond to invitations.
2. **Enthusiastic:** Participants should be keen to take part and explicitly seek out any opportunity to contribute, whilst being respectful of what the situation is asking. Once an invitation is made the response is immediate and enthusiastic.
3. **Pro-active:** Participants try to contribute something that is *not* explicitly invited by the situation, this might be by deliberately misreading the invitations made by the performers or by trying to explore the edges of the participation on offer in the scene.

EXERCISE

Divide the class into small groups (2–4 people); for each turn, one of the groups will be the Performers and the others will be Participants (depending on the overall class size the participatory scene might need to be performed multiple times). The Performer group chooses a contribution and agency card randomly (i.e., Game and Creative) and devises a short participatory scene either based around the work in development or a narrative that everyone is familiar with (good starting points are fairy tales or film plots). The aim is for the participatory situation to invite the type of contribution (Personal, Narrative, Role, or Game) and level of agency (Reactive, Interactive, or Creative) on the selected cards. Once the scene is ready, each Participant group selects a random playing style card that determines their approach to taking part (Reluctant, Enthusiastic, or Pro-active). If you have a large class, all small groups can devise their scenes simultaneously before they are played in turn; this also enables each Performer group to experience different playing styles.

In turns, let the groups experience each other's participatory scenes: the groups should not know in advance what cards the others have selected and both should be asked about their experiences before these are revealed. The facilitator of the exercise then leads a group discussion to explore whether the Performers achieved their aim (including how they succeeded, any challenges, and new ideas for improvements). If multiple groups played each scene, a discussion on how the Performers coped with the different playing styles can support the development of facilitation skills.

CRITICAL REFLECTION

The following questions are offered to support critical reflection, either as part of the above exercise or in relation to the development of an experiential performance:

- What is the purpose of participation in this work?
- What type(s) of contribution are you inviting from your audience? Why?
- How will you facilitate these contributions?
- What type(s) of agency are you hoping participants might experience? Why?
- How can you test the audience experience in your work?
- How will you communicate that participants can choose whether to take part and how can they signal that they would rather not participate?

Experiencing agency is a significant part of what can make experiential theatre meaningful for audiences, but makers and performers have limited control over whether participants experience any agency. However, an experiential performance can restrict and conduct the agency audience members already possess to create an aesthetic experience, whilst a thoughtful approach to facilitating participation can support audiences to connect their actions to the performance outcomes to make it more likely that they will experience agency. This essay has made suggestions to support participants make both immediate and retrospective attributions of narrative agency, for instance through invitations that make the outcome of their decisions clear or by facilitating reflection at the end or post-performance.

References

Alston, Adam. 2016. *Beyond Immersive Theatres: Aesthetics, Politics and Productive Participation*. Basingstoke: Palgrave Macmillan.

Bayne, Tim. 2008. "The Phenomenology of Agency." *Philosophy Compass* 3 (1): 182–202.

Breel, Astrid. (forthcoming). 'Meaningful Agency in Participatory Performance: A Contextual Approach.' Studies in Theatre and Performance.

Frieze, James, ed. 2016. *Reframing Immersive Theatre: The Politics and Pragmatics of Participatory Performance*. Basingstoke: Palgrave Macmillan.

Gallagher, Shaun. 2005. *How the body shapes the mind*. Oxford: Oxford University Press.

Gallagher, Shaun and Dan Zahavi. 2008. *The Phenomenological Mind. An Introduction to Philosophy of Mind and Cognitive Science*. Abingdon: Routledge.

Hallet, Mark. 2011. "Volition: how Physiology Speaks to the Issue of Responsibility." In *Conscious Will and Responsibility*. Edited by Walter Sinnott-Armstrong and Lynn Nadel, 61–69. Oxford: Oxford University Press.

Harpin, Anna and Helen Nicholson, eds. 2017. *Performance and Participation: Practices, Audiences, Politics*. Basingstoke: Palgrave Macmillan.

Harvie, Jen. 2013. *Fair Play: Art, Performance and Neoliberalism*. Basingstoke: Palgrave Macmillan.

Kaleider. 2013-2021. *The Money*. More information and trailer available here: https://kaleider.com/portfolio/the-money/ [Accessed 15 Oct 2021].

Schlosser, Markus. 2015. "Agency." *The Stanford Encyclopedia of Philosophy*. Fall 2015 ed., Zalta, E. (Ed.), available here: http://plato.stanford.edu/archives/fall2015/entries/agency/ [Accessed 10 April 2016].

Tomlin, Liz. 2019. *Political Dramaturgies and Theatre Spectatorship: Provocations for Change*. London: Bloomsbury.

White, Gareth. 2013. *Audience Participation in Theatre: Aesthetics of the Invitation*. Basingstoke: Palgrave Macmillan.

7

Training the Actor for Roleplay and Other Improv-Based Interactive Theatre Forms

David Kaye

INTRODUCTION

I first began training actors specifically for the application of their skills to improv-based interactive theatre models for professional development in 2006. These are theatre forms where actors take on roles to create a realistic simulation where they interact with a single participant, or a group, with the objective of building knowledge and skills. For over twenty years I had been working with various forms of highly realistic improvisational theatre as both an acting teacher and a director when I was approached by Professor Mary Banach for assistance with the students in her graduate Social Work program at the University of New Hampshire. She had her students embark in various roleplay exercises with disappointing results. It became clear to me in our discussions that the problem was that her students could easily play the role of the social worker, but not the role of the homeless teen who had just found out she was pregnant. Beyond that, her students did not have the skill to create obstacles that the student social worker needed practice over-coming. Most actor training that is rooted in Stanislavskian methods utilizes a founda-tional understanding of a character's wants and needs (objectives), impediments to those wants and needs (obstacles), and various strategies to overcome those obstacles (tactics). These actor skills, when applied to roleplay work, lift the exercise to a far more beneficial level. What Professor Banach and I quickly learned was that the trained actor allowed for a professional quality roleplay experience for her students. What I also learned was that exercises could be adapted or created to enhance the actor's foundational skills for this type of performance.

In 2011 I founded UNH PowerPlay Interactive Development, a professional applied theatre company specializing in interactive theatre. The company's work includes various roleplay formats and numerous performance models that mix scripted scene material and improvisational interactions with a participatory audience. As an educator, I had been exploring ways of applying elements of Jacob Moreno's psychodramatic techniques as well as Augusto Boal's Forum Theatre, to both the acting studio and in production rehearsals. Having trained in both these practices, as well as other improvisation-based theatre models, I experimented with adapting them in various ways with my students, ranging from character development to play devising. I found that not only were these modified exercises helping my students create more truthful and authentic performances, but they were also helping them discover and bring forth more empathy and a deeper

80   DOI: 10.4324/9781003188179-9

understanding of the roles they were playing. These attributes served as the foundation for the performance work needed to build PowerPlay's acting company. Starting with our first projects focused on developing leadership skills for public officials and then on to much of our core work centered on bias awareness and intervention, I was able to refine and refocus these techniques that began in the classroom. I now have training exercises that I can systematically apply to help actors cultivate the skillset needed for the unique performance demands of highly realistic, interactive theatre like that employed by PowerPlay. These training exercises are built on the actor's command of fundamental acting skills as well as their understanding of the basic rules utilized in most forms of improvisational performance. These exercises were conceived on the premise that the actor must develop their ability to create a fully rounded character built on given circumstances just like in a fully scripted play. In this form, however, the actor must learn how to construct these factors during an improvisation. Building on this skill, the subsequent exercises help the actor develop various improvisational skills that are critical to this type of interactive theatre. These include such abilities as creating circumstances based on audience questions, defining the purpose of a role in a scene, the capacity to incorporate changes in various circumstances into believable responses, and the skill of seamlessly mixing memorized text and improvisation. This five-step sequence uses variations of the "hot seat" exercise often used by directors for character development. The term "actor(s)" or "player(s)" will be in reference to the individual(s) who are the focus of the exercise. The term "the class" will refer to the other people taking part in the session who will often serve like a participatory audience.

EXERCISES

1. Hot Seat

Overview: The focus of this exercise is filling out the character's past and present circumstances, and learning to connect all these revealed facts into a character that is realistic and believable. In the course of this improvisational structure, the actor will also strengthen their ability to remember what has been established about their character and to utilize this knowledge to explore their wants, needs, and overall behavior.

The Exercise: A chair is set out in front of the class and an actor takes the "hot seat." The instructor gives the actor a name, an occupation, and a circumstance. For example: "Jill, you're a police officer, and you have experienced gender bias from some of your male fellow officers."

The class then begins to ask "Jill" questions and the actor playing Jill answers them as truthfully as possible. That is to say, the actor always tries to respond from the point of view of the character based on the information they have been given about them. As the exercise advances, the actor, through improvisation, will be adding facts (which are now new "truths") about this character and their circumstances and these too must now be incorporated. The actor always responds to the class as a trusted confidant.

Example:

Instructor:	*Hi Jill.*
Jill:	*Hi.*
Instructor:	*I understand you're a police officer.*
Jill:	*That's right.*
Instructor:	*How long have you been on the force?*

82 • DAVID KAYE

Jill:	Um ... going on 3 years. (Note: This is now a true fact, if the only information Jill started with is that she is a police officer).
Instructor:	Does anyone have a question for Jill?
Class Member:	I do. What is it like being one of the few women in your department?

(Just like any improv exercise, Jill must accept as a truthful fact that there are very few women in her department.)

Jill: It's ... actually been tough. Tougher than I thought it would be. There's a kind of ... a macho atmosphere, I guess, that seems to be ingrained into the culture, you know?

As the questions and answers continue, the actor must remember what has been established. This includes factual circumstances, behavior patterns, relationship dynamics, and other factors that help create a cohesive character that would live in the real world. The job of the class in this exercise is to help the actor developing their role to expand beyond the first, pre-established circumstance. In the example we are using, a question about the gender balance led Jill to reveal something about the department's "macho atmosphere." A follow-up question might be "How do the male officers in this 'macho atmosphere' treat the women in the department?" The actor playing Jill must now improvise an answer that is as truthful as she can make it, based on what facts have been established, and what her imagination informs her of what that reality might be like. Because the class is essentially playing the role of the participatory audience, they are developing their ability to understanding the dynamics of this form of interactive theatre by experiencing the exercise from the audience's perspective. The instructor engages in a debrief after each actor completes the exercise. The focus of this feedback is to note revealing responses to the questions that helped present a believable character as well as any inconsistencies or contradictions in character behavior or established circumstances.

2. Hot Seat Variation: Public/Private

Overview: This exercise adds changes to the conditions that the actor must incorporate into their responses. The next two variations of *Hot Seat* come from the work of Jeffrey Allen Steiger, an innovator and practitioner in interactive theatre who founded the CRLT Players at the University of Michigan and played an important role in the development of UNH PowerPlay.

The Exercise: Using the same format as *Hot Seat,* the exercise now includes designating if the actor's response is in a public or private setting. A public setting takes away the safe knowledge that the character is speaking with "trusted confidants." A response to a question like "are you still using drugs?" might be drastically different in a public setting due to the ramifications of who hears the answer. The same exact question can be asked first publicly and then immediately afterward, privately. This allows the actor to better understand the difference between these two realities and to bring out the subtle or drastic changes in each response. The instructor will now ask those in the class if they would like a public or private response each time they pose a question to the actor on the hot seat.

3. Expert/Find Your Lane: Group Hot Seat

Overview: This exercise is designed to transition *Hot Seat* from an individual to a group activity.

The Exercise: With no less than two and no more than six players, each actor is given a slip of paper with a simple statement written on it. For example:

Player One:	The budget is already tight.
Player Two:	We need to fill those positions.
Player Three:	Two trucks need to be replaced.
Player Four:	I've only been here for half a year.

The players are instructed to not look at their slip of paper until the start of the exercise. They must each speak their line of dialogue at some point in the exercise, though it does not have to be their first line. With the class observing, the instructor begins by asking the first question. In this example, "Is it true there's been some friction here in the public works department?" An improvised conversation then begins among the players. As the exercise proceeds, each must determine what it is they do in this department, what is their relationship with the other players, and what is important to them. The players will quickly learn that they do not have to know the first thing about paving roads or repairing public buildings. What they will have to do is capitalize on what they *do* know. For example: What is it like to have to be responsible for spending? What is it like when another person's priorities are favored over yours? What is it like to be the newest person with the most to lose?

After a few minutes, the players should have established enough foundational points to allow the class to ask them questions. These questions can be asked publicly or privately. It will be important for the other players to pretend that they are not listening to a private answer, though in reality they are taking in the response as it may be providing important information that they could incorporate as the exercise progresses. For example, Player One may say, privately, that Player Two is near retirement and Player One is eager to see them go. At the very least, Player Two now must accept the reality that they are near retirement, and perhaps they feel that Player One's refusal to fill the vacant positions they have been requesting is because their status is diminished due to their impending retirement.

This leads us to the concept of "finding your lane." So far, we have established that Player One has authority over Player Two and that Player Two is near retirement. These are "lanes" that have now been established in the improvisation. A "lane" may be an important character element, like their primary responsibility or their place in the hierarchy of the group, or perhaps a specific motivation or obstacle. We don't need two people playing the head of the department or the person being forced out. What we do need is the person who is fed up with the bureaucracy or the person who has some great ideas, but is too cautious to bring them up because of the climate of the department. This is an ensemble skill that the actors are developing as they work together to create distinction between their characters and variation in their wants and needs.

4. Hide the Monologue

Overview: This exercise is designed to help actors weave scripted text with improvisation.

The Exercise: The instructor can use text from an existing play or write text that is more applicable to the specific subject matter. The scripted monologue should be around thirty seconds long. The actor must have the monologue memorized but no context for the monologue is given. To start the exercise, the instructor gives the crucial given circumstances. For example, you are a climate scientist who has headed up a study on the effects of "monster tides" in a coastal town. You have just left a planning commission meeting where your action proposal was tabled.

84 • DAVID KAYE

Sample Monologue:
I don't think they are hearing what I am saying. It's clear to me what the problem is. The roads in this part of town are continually washing out. It's over $500,000 to repair them. The data and the projections show that in ten years they could be under five feet of water. Permanently. What more can I really do, though? The solution seems simple enough to me, but ... these people. They just don't get it. They have no idea what the real cost is that we are talking about. Par for the course in this town. I'm not sure what I am going to do next. Maybe fight it? Maybe throw in the towel? I don't know.

Before the actor delivers the monologue, the instructor gives them a single question. For example: "How did the meeting go?" The actor improvises a response of at least sixty seconds, then must seamlessly segue into the scripted text (in its entirety) and then back to improvisation. The goal is to practice making it undetectable when the actor is improvising and when they are speaking memorized text.

The same actor, or a different actor, can be given a new circumstance and role, using the same memorized text. For example: You are now a homeowner who has just been informed at this meeting that you must sell your property. A third version might be: You are a newly elected town councilor. You know the town cannot sustain the high cost of all these road repairs, but you just got publicly attacked by a property owner at the meeting.

5. What's My Line?

Overview: This is an exercise to practice incorporating lines or actions given by the audience.

The Exercise: This exercise uses the group *Hot Seat* format and can be played by two to six players. The basic circumstances and roles for this version are pre-established. For example, You are all faculty in a university English department with this basic power structure:

Player One is the department chair.

Player Two is a full professor.

Player Three is an assistant professor.

Player Four is an adjunct professor.

A circumstance prompt is stated: "The group must decide between two candidates to lead a new writing center. It is between a white female and black male for the position." For this exercise, all questions are public, and the players can interact with each other until the instructor stops them and asks the class for a line of dialogue (apropos to the moment) to be adapted by one of the players. For example, "I would like Player Three to say to Player Two, 'I'm sorry, but what you just said has really made me uncomfortable.'" Player Three says the line and the improv continues. All the players incorporate that statement and what it says about Player Two and Three's behaviors and attitudes as the exercise progresses.

CONCLUSION

I have often come across wonderful actors who fear work in interactive theatre because they are convinced they are terrible at improvisation. Through these preliminary exercises, they often discover that many of the acting skills they already have formed the base of successful, reality-focused improvisation. They learn that their own experiences and knowledge of human behavior and relationships provide them with all they need to create a believable character. They discover that improvising the role of a mechanical engineer does not require a knowledge of engineering, but simply an understanding of what human beings want, and what happens when an obstacle is placed in front of that want. Many existing exercises for improvisation can be adapted, as these have, to serve the training needs for various forms of interactive theatre. Whether preparing for roleplay work or more structured scenes, these exercises will further develop the actor's base skills while also building the confidence necessary for success.

8

Standardized Patient Experience: Reframing Pedagogical Approaches in the Acting Studio

Matthew Mastromatteo

THE EXPERIENCE

To begin, detailed below is what those in medical professional training programs (both medical schools and third-party training agencies) might call an "encounter" between a Standardized Patient (SP) and a medical student whose work will be examined (discussed below as the Learner). In short, this immersive and standardized experience is used to provide Learners an opportunity to implement skills centered around patient-physician interaction (PPI). These training organizations often hire actors as Standardized Patients because of their ability to perform truthfully and empathetically under imaginary circumstances. However, *this* experience and the duty of a Standardized Patient exists beyond our notion of an actor's role in "traditional" theatrical practice.

The work of the Standardized Patient is twofold: (a) to serve as the patient with which a Learner can interact and (b) to observe, evaluate, and critique the Learner's clinical competency and communication skills.

Commonly, during an encounter, a Standardized Patient engages (through guided improvisation) with their scene partner, the Learner, who has been tasked with collecting a detailed history from the patient. While the requirements asked of the Learners might vary greatly from case to case, the fact that our two participants have never met, nor do they "know" the other's approach to the content, remains the same. During this loosely structured improvisation the SP and Learner play off each other along the Learner's chosen line of questioning. What results is an experience that feels like a "choose your own adventure". As the Learner asks, "*tell me about your family life?*", how the SP decides to answer will often take the Learner in a particular direction. Replying, "my relationship with my parents is strained" might invite a Learner to follow that line of questioning and how that particular social factor might be impacting the patient's health. While the Learner asks about that sensitive topic, the SP watches body language, listens for tone of voice, pays close attention to language, and makes mental notes of opportunities for the Learner's growth. SPs might also undergo a non-invasive physical exam so that Learners can practice and receive feedback on execution of clinical maneuvers.

Following the encounter, the SP often completes several checklists (designed and later reviewed by the Learners' faculty) gauging the Learner's proficiency in clinical and communication skills. In *some* cases, the SP will engage in a short verbal feedback session with the Learner. In this instance the Learner has an opportunity to hear from their "patient" and receive immediate constructive feedback on their execution of communication skills throughout the encounter.

86 DOI: 10.4324/9781003188179-10

PROFICIENCIES

As we look at the brief example above, we see that there is a lot to juggle during a short ten to fifteen-minute interactive encounter. Actors, by virtue of their work, are adept at keeping track of multiple moving parts. Below are several additional proficiencies, often possessed by actors, that make for skilled SP.

Aptitude for Fleshing Out the Character and Implementing Given Circumstance: Character development is at the heart of an actors' work, and in this context, it is vital in generating a believable portrayal that affords Learners the opportunity to treat this as a "real life" scenario.

Strong Improvisation Skills: These encounters are improvisational in nature. While abbreviated given circumstances provide a skeleton for the content to be covered, the narrative flow of the dialogue is at the discretion of the SP and Learner.

Excellent Active Listening/Observational Skills: As a skilled SP moves through an encounter they are constantly responding to and making note of the Learner's performance. Observations are made and stored as mental notes for later. For example: *"Why do they keep checking their watch?" "That was really a blunt delivery of the news that I have dangerously high blood pressure." "Did they wash or sanitize their hands before touching my abdomen?"*

Proficiency in Offering Constructive Feedback: The SP converts these observations into constructive feedback by helping the Learner understand how the actions performed in the encounter made the patient feel.

We might look at these proficiencies and say, "No wonder they hire actors to be SPs. They come prepared with these skills already!" True. By amplifying proficiencies required for this experience, we will explore a model for reframing an existing acting studio exercise to prepare actors more intentionally for a broad spectrum of experiential and immersive performance settings, including Standardized Patient encounters.

REFRAMING THE PLANNED IMPROVISATION

For the purposes of this essay, we will use a planned improvisation exercise as a container in which we can investigate how one might espouse "conventional" learning objectives made more universal (within the craft of performance) when interwoven with the proficiencies needed for an interactive practice, such as Standardized Patient encounter.

The Exercise

A pair of actors are assigned two conflicting objectives and a relationship defining the connection between their characters. For example:

Actor A: *I want Actor B to say, "Yes!" to marrying me.*

Actor B: *I want Actor A to accept that I am leaving them for their sibling and keep them as a friend.*

Relationship: Cohabitating Life Partners

Actors are sent away until their next meeting with the instruction to develop given circumstances and a scenario in which they will pursue their respective objectives, *without sharing their objective with their scene partner*. Their given circumstances manifest as a paper that catalogs the character's personality and life experiences in relation to their objective. They are informed that one actor must start in the space, the other must begin outside the space, and that the educator will be side-coaching them throughout the exercise. Lastly, they are told that they may not state their objective until the educator invites them to do so during the exercise.

Actors return to the studio at the time of their showing and construct their space. They will begin as instructed: one actor outside the room (who will make an entrance) and one inside the room (who might be engaging in physical life with their environment). In the first few moments of the work, the actors have an opportunity to explore pursuing their objective without explicitly saying what they want. During the showing the actors are side-coached by their instructor who will continually be looking for opportunities to help actors succeed in achieving their objective. For instance, if Actor A is attempting to get a "yes!" to a marriage proposal, it would be difficult if Actor B continued to avoid eye contact throughout the exercise. The instructor might invite Actor A to try and make eye contact with Actor B (if this is within the actors' boundaries). It is important to remind the actors never to give up on their objective, and to invite them to keep pursuing, no matter how good the counterargument.

After about ten minutes, the educator ends the exercise and invites the participants to sit for feedback.

CONNECTING THE LINKS

The planned improvisation is broken down into three areas so that we might reframe the learning objectives with an awareness of the opportunity to train the Standardized Patient.

1. *The Prep*

It is vital in a Planned Improvisation to have a clear and expansive understanding of the characters Given Circumstances. For SP work the same is true. We want the actor to come to the room prepared with all the material possible so that they can (1) behave truthfully as the character in the space and (2) have a deep well of information to choose from as they pursue their objective. In both the planned improvisation and SP encounters, actors must reverse design their dramaturgy: they take abbreviated given circumstances and expand so to provide the foundation for thoughtful improvisational text/language choices.

Instructing actors in a planned improvisation to be the writers of their character histories vigorously flexes and stretches their storytelling muscle that often atrophies when solely depending on elaborate given circumstances provided by playwrights. For the planned improvisation it is essential to engage the actors in the writing of Given Circumstance papers prior to the improvisation. While individual educators likely have their own tools or version of character-building notation/writing, because we are building from the ground up, it is helpful here to ask actors to work in detailed paragraph form, giving them the opportunity to generate expansive and specific givens.

Actors are invited to answer: "Who Am I?", "Where Am I?", "What are the Relationships?", "What is my Recent & Distant Past?", and "Where am I going?". They are encouraged to always bring their choice-making back to the Objective and Relationship at hand. For instance, if Actor A, "wants their partner to say, 'yes' to marrying them," the Given Circumstances paper would be filled with choices that relate to their want to be engaged to their partner. We will see paragraphs of key information that might: describe them as a hopeless romantic in the "Who I am", explore events in which they have experienced true love in the "Distant Past", expand on their ideal version of life if they achieve the objective in the space in the "Where am I going?", and so on.

Learning how to author one's character in this way, using the objective (or abbreviated givens) as a guide is priceless for the performer entering a character-driven interactive improvisation. At any moment, as they are navigating obstacles in the space, the Actors can call upon and use an item from their writing to supply active text/language helping them to get what they want. "Oh, my scene partner will not marry me because they do not think I am romantic? Not true! What about the candle-lit dinner I made for you on our last anniversary!?"

The same degree of character building is essential for the SP. While a patient might be in the room because they are a college student who wants the doctor to give them medication for my aching stomach, it will be important to have a deep well of givens to draw upon when the doctor asks them about their social calendar and family ties beyond the scope of their prompt.

2. *The Exercise & Coaching*

Equally useful in this exercise is the verbal presence of a coach/instructor on the outside of the improvisation reminding actors to stay focused on the task at hand. It is easy for actors to get consumed by the big picture. In the planned improv (much like in SP encounters) we have asked our actors to think about a great deal. It can be easy to forget why they are in the room or that the answers can often be found in their scene partner. To have the outside voice helping participants remain focused both visually and aurally on what is happening in front of them is helpful in preparing actors to step into any immersive environment where what they receive from an audience/scene partner dictates the journey everyone takes as participants.

3. *The Feedback Session*

Within the feedback for this exercise the educator has an opportunity to impart critical feedback skills to the actors. As an SP, when giving feedback, it is often helpful to focus on the cause and effect of actions to help young medical professionals understand how they are perceived. This offers a model where the educator can have actors share an instance of (1) what they perceived in their scene partner, (2) how it made them feel, and (3) why they responded in the way that they did.

This articulation by the actors is dually useful. First, as an acting educator, you can quantify the participant's ability to identify obstacles in the space, articulate their impulse, and how they pursued said impulse. i.e. "You were not looking at me when I asked you if we could stay together, and I knew I had to get your attention, so I started banging pots and pans until you looked in my direction." Second, as a trainer who prepares actors that can also one day be SPs, they are practicing action-based observational verbiage that will help them share articulate constructive feedback for medical students. "You have a tendency to use very closed body language, and that made me feel that you were not interested in what I had to say, so I stopped sharing as much as I might have when you were taking my patient history."

CONCLUSION

These components: preparation, mid-exercise coaching, and feedback are not unique to the planned improvisation exercise. Nor are the proficiencies outlined specific to the Standardized Patient experience in that they speak to a wide array of immersive and experiential practices. The immersive and experiential work done by Standardized Patients has helped to shift the medical industry to be more empathetic, communication-oriented, and efficient; growth which, doubtlessly, has saved countless lives. Using the model above and allowing ourselves to look at other arenas where proficiencies align with that of our acting studios, we open actors up to endless performance and employment opportunities to support an artistic life with limited need for work that feels like the all-too-popular, "survival job." Such openness and thinking will continue to foster actors who continue to inspire positive change in industry beyond the performing arts. By allowing ourselves to identify transferable skills embedded in an exercise found in a more "conventional" studio practice—as they intersect with proficiencies needed in the experiential model of SP work—we have been able to reverse design outcomes to speak to a broader array of performance practice. An application, if made transparent, is exciting for young artists who eagerly enter an oversaturated industry, hungry for more skills to make them more widely marketable.

9

The Significance of "Role-Play" and "Instruction-Based Performance" as Modes of Teaching, Collaborating, and Performing with/for Participating Audiences

Kesia Guillery, Persis Jadé Maravala, and Jorge Lopes Ramos

INTRODUCTION

ZU-UK intends to focus learning around intentions, contextual awareness, and exploration of what it means to collaborate. Role, or role-play, and instruction-systems, have become two key structures through which ZU-UK facilitate engagement with these focal points: in formal education, in our own training and development, and in the participatory experiences we make.

The following examples of role-play and instruction in ZU-UK performance-work and workshops serve as illustrations of what we consider vital to impart to future generations of artists working with participation and live interaction. At the root of the decision-making processes we make, and wish to convey to others, lie the simple, contextual questions of:

Who is it by?

Who is it with?

Who is it for?

The ways of understanding role-play and corresponding content-creation exercises offered below are springboards from which to develop performative workshop structures that guide participants through micro-enactments of the social and political aspects of their roles as creators, and that foreground these core questions.

These priorities, and the embodied ways in which they are present in our workshop models, are the inevitable extension of our performer-training methodology, the "dramaturgy of participation" (Lopes Ramos and Maravala 2016), in turn, derived from the legacies of Augusto Boal, Jerzy Grotowski and Milon Mela, spiritual dance and theatrical practices of North-East Brazil, Capoeira Angola, Bharatanatyam, Zoroastrian religious

DOI: 10.4324/9781003188179-11

incantation, and our experience contending with the complex requirements of the overnight audience-centric multi-site performance, *Hotel Medea* (2006–12), developed over a period of seven years. What we have drawn from this combination of influences and experiences can roughly be summarized as a relational aesthetic grounded in the co-presence of human bodies and the space in between them. The body, and connections between bodies in space, as the meaningful material of politically active performance-work and the site of transformation, remain essential to the ways in which we facilitate exploration of these questions.

The following examples do not explicitly foreground any form of physical training. Physical training is, however, key to the game-making exercise detailed below. As the exercise develops, we quickly draw attention to political meanings that attach themselves to spatial relationships between the bodies present as they shift through different roles.

FRAMING ROLE-PLAY

ZU-UK's practice has emerged from a set of primarily theatrical influences, but the use of role-play in our work has come to mean something more subtle and flexible than the adoption of character or fictional circumstance associated with the term as a theatrical improvisation device, or indeed usually associated with practices like tabletop or digital RPGs (role-playing games) or LARP (live action role-play). Role-play in ZU-UK's work is usually something more like trying out versions of self, than trying on the shoes of another, and the roles to try out are usually constructed through autobiographical prompts and reflections that intensify participants' awareness of their histories, identities, and values. Correspondingly, self-reflective exercises, such as automatic writing and instruction-based activities built around personal questions, as ways into a creative process are prominent in our workshops. There is no hard and fast barrier between ZU-UK public performance structures, and ZU-UK workshop design: the fluidity between these two purposes is made sense of in the light of (1) our performances themselves being catalysts for co-creative contributions from participants (who are thus drawn out, and explore their own impulses, as creative learners, as it were), and (2) our conviction that the heightened, performative, contractually bounded state entered into through a participatory artwork is conversely of great value in pedagogical contexts: workshops are in fact always essentially designed as miniature instruction-based artworks. To contextualize the use of role- and perspective-shifting, and self-reflection in pedagogy, it is, therefore, useful to consider the nature and presence of these as tools within ZU-UK performance work.

Binaural Dinner Date (2016–), for example, (a ZU-UK experience for eighteen people, divided into nine couples) is a self-reflective audio-guided date that invites participants, with the slogan "#BeTheDate," to hack into the web of coded interactions that constitute the "secular ritual" (Lopes Ramos, Maravala, Dunne-Howrie, and Simon 2020) of dating, and inhabit its behavioral systems, as bodies. The roles it coaxes people into and out of are fluid, and relational rather than fictional. The performance establishes a shifting set of contractual boundary-lines, to elevate the performance event to an "extra-daily" (Barba 1988) realm: a plurality of frames (Calleja 2012; Consalvo 2009; Duggan 2017; Fine 2002), rather than a single "magic circle" (Huizinga 1955).

Over the course of their date, participants ask and respond to questions that call upon deeply personal, real memories, experiences, and self-perceptions. They perform themselves to the person sitting opposite them, becoming acutely aware of the Butlerian tenet (1997), also espoused by Goffman (1959), that they are always performing themselves. They often begin to ironically play into the cliché they have been invited to perform—that of the romantic dinner date. The experience invites a sway between real and self-consciously performed identities. For example, one of the games participants undertake with their date consists of a collaborative storytelling exercise, based on "choose your own adventure" structures, in which three couples create one shared imagined future for themselves as long-term partners. This imagined future, guided by a waiter-facilitator, includes church bells, babies, relationship counseling, extra-marital affairs, and dementia: participants are aware that the story is fabricated, and cannot apply to all three couples engaged in this task. It is shamelessly fictional. Magic-trick aesthetics, including a live-operated soundtrack, seemingly timed miraculously to participants' responses, allow participants to deal with such contradictions seamlessly, whilst remaining very much themselves.

In *Hotel Medea,* participants, likewise, segued between various roles, and modes of role-play—experiencing, for example, the same "micro-event" (Lopes Ramos 2015) three times, from different perspectives: as Medea's children in bunk-beds, as Jason's campaign team in a separate room filled with screens and headphones, and as Medea's guests in her bedroom—each one offering a different type of engagement through both fictional and functional roles: roles *in relation* to the narrative, or event, but not characters, as such. As Medea's children, participants were told a bedtime story, given hot cocoa, and invited to actually sleep up to twenty minutes if they wished. This perspective-switching through physically immersive role-play generates a feeling of disorientation, but also of depth of experience. Shifting participatory modes, between critical awareness and deep, active engagement in experiences, sharpens overall impact.

The role-play participants engage in, in ZU-UK's work, is thus not a pre-written role description in the usual way one might be invited to "play a role" or character, but there is an 'otherness' that participants adopt, which enables behaviors that are unusual, or even impermissible in ordinary life. Participants' contributions of their own biographical details consistently draw them back to themselves, to their own realities, and to the present moment, meaning every individual's experience is emphatically their own, and cannot be replicated.

GAME-PLAY & INSTRUCTION-SYSTEMS

Examining, experientially, who we are in relation to the social systems we function through, and in relation to each other, forms not only a huge component of what ZU-UK invite those we teach and coach to think about but also dictates the ways we structure workshops and sessions with students and mentees. As our performances invite participants to be makers of their own experiences and turn their perceptions of self into artistic material, it has been natural for us to use structures similar to those we use within performances themselves to onboard students and emerging artists to our educational programs. Exercises to spark creation become very similar to our approach with audiences. They differ, in that they tend to address participants directly as makers or researchers in active pursuit of their own goals, and thus can jump more quickly to instructions eliciting fairly high-level creative contribution, but otherwise the playful strategies used to prompt input from students are essentially the same as those forming the frameworks of ZU-UK performance work.

Key to this approach is the use of rule-systems, game mechanics, and, above all, instructions. Firstly, central to the process of creating games and rules is an understanding of "procedural rhetoric" (Bogost 2007)—the way that these systems embody ideology in their structures. By understanding how mini-social-systems like games express rhetoric in their rules, we not only gain a critical vantage point on games and structures, but also begin to consider how to think about games as social structures invented with the purpose of creating social order along very distinct lines for very distinct agendas. In designing pedagogical content, in particular, we highlight accountability and responsibility for the ways in which we, and those we teach, instruct our guests, players, and participants, and the difficulty of avoiding biases, assumptions about who your participants are, and creating spaces of exclusivity. Our workshops and exercises draw attention to the fact that we may think we are designing for a neutral player, or participant, but that there are always assumptions behind our image of this societally neutral player. We forget that "[t]he masses are made up of people and white, cis-gendered, het, middle-class men are a minority in that" (Nicklin 2019). We urge artists to design for difference and variance, rather than a mythical neutrality.

Secondly, instructions in ZU-UK work can be seen as tools handed to participants, students, or mentees, with which to create their own paths and experiences. The word, "instruction," conflates the idea of telling somebody what to do, with the process of teaching itself. It makes one synonymous with the other. ZU-UK have come to a belief, through practice, that playing into this conflation can in fact serve to challenge, subvert, and reconfigure power structures assumed within artist–audience, teacher–student relationships. They can:

a. create "pockets of agency"- focused, tiny spaces of freedom, which, in being well marked out, and subject to rules, provide the safety required for intimacy and wildness to become possible,
b. absolve participants or students, temporarily, of responsibility, to allow for unfettered self-exploration, and thus …
c. remind us, with compassion, that we are always authors of our actions and experiences within the systems that house us.

ZU-UK instructions are a gentle trick: persuading us we are not in control, to remind us of the power of response.

EXHIBIT A: SPEED-GAME MAKING (STAGE 1)

The parameters and instructions that make up the speed game-making exercise, used here as a sample, aim to guide those involved through a series of different roles in relation to creating content, and in relation to the participants in what they have created. First you are encouraged to simply make a game, without any emphasis on message, meaning, or even aesthetic intention: you embody a very early ideation stage of a process or the sort of naive relationship to artmaking that ZU-UK wants to challenge. You are then encouraged to think about the frontier between your creation and the world: how will you present and explain it to others? How will you hand it over such that participants' experience of it is theirs, but is in line with your intentions? The parameter preventing game-makers from instructing or interfering, once their game is running, highlights the importance of instruction as the interface, as it were, between artist and audience, and that the ways in which a piece is framed and contextualized form an essential part of what is experienced. How does a piece convey to participants the "right" behaviors within its temporary micro-community?

Subsequent stages of the exercise guide participants through further role shifts in their relation to the game content and aid the process of building more complex, layered systems. The example below details a research-related provocation as a gateway into a second stage, but sometimes the ZU-UK facilitators will ask students to "hack" games created by others and repurpose them with specific intentions in mind—or they might be asked to hack their own games with a more considered awareness of themselves as creators of political, rhetorical systems. We want those we teach and coach to come to an understanding of these phenomena through embodying them and modeling various roles in relation to content creation.

The sample below is limited to a description of only Stage 1 of this exercise process.

Participants are split into small groups of 3–5 people:

Choose one complete set of artefacts from the selection laid out in front of you.

(Artefacts include: a set of clothes pegs, a set of large dice, a set of mini traffic cones, a set of ribbons, etc.)

Within ten minutes, each group will create a game using only your chosen artefacts.

At the end of ten minutes you need to have created a game and decided:

ITS NAME; ITS RULES; HOW MANY PLAYERS CAN TAKE PART; HOW YOU WILL EXPLAIN & DEMO IT TO OTHERS BEFORE THEY PLAY

You will have one minute to present your game to the whole group.

Finally, allow players to play your game for no longer than one to three minutes.

A high-pressured timeframe exerts "exquisite pressure" (Bogart and Landau 2005) and helps preclude detailed critical thinking from this stage in order to heighten the impression of detached observation when creators are encouraged to add in a critical lens in subsequent stages. While players play each newly created game, the group of creators observe their players closely—however, they are also told they cannot help or instruct the players whilst they play. Only this way will they be able to observe shortcomings in their design, explanation, and demo, as well as what kinds of behaviors have been encouraged by their design. This oscillating, iterative trajectory—between making and observing—is a miniature enactment of a layer-by-layer playtesting structure common to many interactive performance-making methodologies, where analyzing the effects of specific design elements on the behavior of participants is essential to development.

EXHIBIT B: SPEED GAME-MAKING (STAGE 2)

During a speed game-making session run by ZU-UK and commissioned by UCL in 2018, ZU-UK invited researcher Malu Gatto to provide a small provocation after the first stage of the exercise, described above. Gatto spoke to the injustices and failures of democracy, with particular regard to women in Brazil (the focus of her research). ZU-UK directors then instructed game-designer groups to use Gatto's provocation to modify their design with the sole purpose of instigating anger in their players. The instructions followed:

Return to your game-making groups …

Now the task is to embed inequalities or injustices or unfairness into your game.
The idea is to keep it subtle.
The idea is to make it hidden but in plain sight.

96 • KESIA GUILLERY ET AL.

The unfairness is clear and yet justifiable.
Or worse, made the fault of the disadvantaged.
We will experience both the advantaged (read: privileged) position of the players
and the disadvantaged positions.

This is a brief example of how ZU-UK adapts its pedagogical exercise in game-making to respond to specific intentions from participants as makers—in this case, to incorporate a thematic intervention from a guest researcher to expose and explore procedural rhetoric within participation models. The content is interchangeable but makes the exercise specific every time, and the speed game-making exercise itself is the permanent scaffold. The exercise is structured to reveal, simply by a process of modeling and iterating, that by creating participatory structures as artists, we are crafting laws: artists are lawmakers, and their laws convey ideologies. Certain behaviors become permissible, or are disallowed, censored, or edited, according to the systems established. The ultimate aim is to alert students, or collaborators, participating in the exercise, to our responsibilities as makers: the models we design through which people participate in our work are persuasive, and as soon as we put them out into the world, we are responsible for what they are saying and doing. This is valid for any kind of artwork, but particularly salient for those interested in the kinds of explicitly participatory work that ZU-UK deals with. Who develops the work, who the work is tested and developed with, and ultimately who it is for are all crucial to an awareness of the maker's responsibility. Further stages of this exercise can take different routes depending on intended outcomes. One route will encourage participants to focus less on the game, and its rules, but instead on the roles that emerge for each player as a result of their design. By continuously iterating the game to support the development of "roles"—mainly practical, seldom fictional—makers also become aware of the multi-player possibilities of their design, and how audience-to-audience (or player-to-player) engagement can be developed.

CONCLUSION

ZU-UK's creative processes can take years, sometimes decades, of playtesting, iterating, and "hacking" structures with new contents for new purposes—always specific to the site and audience/players involved. Based on this lived experience, our approach to pedagogy departs from very simple, clear, and accessible starting points, which serve as a careful foundation onto which a critical process of creation and layering can begin to be built and continue to unfold—one step at a time, and brick by brick—with the inclusion of multiplayer dynamics, embodiment, role-play, and instructions. It is crucial to the politics of our participatory models that our performances are, both in format and in impact, *instructional*, and that our work as pedagogical *instructors* of makers and artists is playful, performative, and situates creativity within the freedom of response and interpretation.

References

Barba, Eugenio. 1988. "An Amulet Made of Memory: The Significance of Exercises in the Actor's Dramaturgy." *The Drama Review* 41 (4): 127–132.
Binaural Dinner Date by ZU-UK. 2016–. Directed by Persis Jadé Maravala. [Gerry's Café at Theatre Royal Stratford East, London; IndiGo at RichMix, London; York Theatre Royal, York; Square Chapel, Halifax; BrickBox, Bradford; The Lowry, Salford; Chimichanga, Hereford; Zizzi's, Salisbury; Espacio Odeon, Bogotá; Centro Cultural Banco De La República, Manizales; Café Falala, Macao].
Bogart, Anne and Tina Landau. 2005. *The Viewpoints Book: A Practical Guide to Viewpoints and Composition.* New York: Theatre Communications Group.

Bogost, Ian. 2007. *Persuasive Games: The Expressive Power of Videogames*. Cambridge, MA: The MIT Press

Butler, Judith. 1997. *Excitable Speech: A Politics of the Performative*. New York: Routledge.

Calleja, Gordon. 2012. "Erasing the Magic Circle." In *The Philosophy of Computer Games*. Edited by John Richard Sageng, Halvard Fossheim and Tarjei Mandt Larsen, 77–98. Springer [online]. Available at: https://www.researchgate.net/publication/273947262_Erasing_the_Magic_Circle (Accessed: 30 July 2021)

Consalvo, Mia. 2009. "There Is No Magic Circle." *Games and Culture* 4 (4): 408–417. DOI: 10.1177/1555412009343575

Duggan, Eddie. 2017. "Squaring the (Magic) Circle: A Brief Definition and History of Pervasive Games." In *Playable Cities: The City as a Digital Playground*. Edited by Anton Nijholt, 111–135. Springer.

Dunne-Howrie, Joseph, Jorge Lopes Ramos, Persis Jadé Maravala and Clare Qualmann. 2019. *Body Brain Bingo: Evaluation Report*. [online] Rose Bruford, London. Available at: https://bruford.repository.guildhe.ac.uk/id/eprint/15/1/brain_body_bingo_evaluation.pdf (Accessed: 30 July 2021)

Fine, Gary Allen. 2002. *Shared Fantasy: Role-Playing Games as Social Worlds*. Chicago: University of Chicago Press.

Goffman, Ervin. 1997. *The Presentation of Self in Everyday Life*. New York: Doubleday.

Hotel Medea by ZU-UK. 2006-12. Directed by Jorge Lopes Ramos and Persis Jadé Maravala. [Oi Futuro, Rio de Janeiro; Arcola Theatre, London; Salisbury Arts Centre, Salisbury; Museo Arte Contemporáneo, La Coruña; Shunt Vaults, London; Trinity Buoy Wharf, London; Summerhall, Edinburgh; Hayward Gallery at Southbank Centre, London]

Huizinga, Johan. 1955. *Homo Ludens: A Study of the Play-Element in Culture*. Boston: The Beacon Press.

Lopes Ramos, Jorge. 2015. *(Re-)Constructing the Actor-Audience Relationship in Immersive Theatre Practice*. PhD Thesis, London: University of East London.

Lopes Ramos, Jorge and Persis Jadé Maravala. 2016. "A Dramaturgy of Participation: Participatory Rituals, Immersive Environments, and Interactive Gameplay in *Hotel Medea*." In *Reframing Immersive Theatre: The Politics and Pragmatics of Participatory Performance*. Edited byJames Frieze, 151–169. London: Palgrave Macmillan.

Lopes Ramos, Jorge, Persis Jadé Maravala, Joseph Dunne-Howrie, and Bart Simon. 2020. "The Post-Immersive Manifesto." *International Journal of Performance Arts and Digital Media* 16 (2): 196–212. DOI: 10.1080/14794713.2020.1766282

Nicklin, Hannah. 2019. Keynote Talk at Freeplay Festival, Melbourne. Available at: https://www.youtube.com/watch?v=3gm97EKoypU&t=4s (Accessed: 30 July 2021)

10
Collaborative Development Workshop: Approaching Conceptualization through Audience Affordances and Experiential Trajectories

William W. Lewis

INTRODUCTION

Since the 1960s methods of conceptualization have become driving forces behind some of the most provocative and historically important theatre productions. Directors have increasingly relied on bold concepts applied to both modern and classical texts to make their productions distinct. In experiential projects conceptualization is even more important due to the fact that there is often no text to rely upon as a material resource. In this essay, I explain the foundation of a conceptualization project assignment utilized in both graduate and undergraduate directing classes.[1] The basis of conceptualization is understanding that a production concept is simply an idea plus a plan for implementing that plan (content + structure). The assignment introduces students (actors/directors, dramaturgs, designers, technicians) to forms of experiential theatre as well as methods of collaboration found in ensemble-based devised work as a way of building skills that can apply to both text-based and non-text-based productions. Through an experiential project format, the students develop the foundation for collaborative concept formation while working on team-based planning for audience throughput—the structural guidance to move the audience through the piece. Students gain the basic skill sets needed for ideation, collaboration, experimentation, logistical implementation, presentation, and critique. The project also introduces them to new methods and terminology from games studies, phenomenology, user experience design, and human–computer interaction which expand their toolbox as creatives.

The learning outcomes for the project are delivered through three stages of development: *foundational knowledge building*; *concept formation*; and *structural mapping and implementation*. Each stage is approached through an iterative process that scaffolds knowledge and methodologies. These stages also operate alongside David Kolb's (2014)) Experiential Learning Cycle.[2] *Foundational knowledge building* blends concrete experience with reflective observation; *concept formation* blends the reflective observation and abstract conceptualization, and *structural mapping and implementation* combines reflective observation and active experimentation. As a collaborative project, the differing

98   DOI: 10.4324/9781003188179-12

learning styles of the individuals in the class can significantly impact the overall success of the project. Even so, the combination of styles does not necessarily impact the overall learning outcomes. Instructors should ideally have identified these learning styles prior to moving on to this assignment so that they may create groups with synergy in order to allow the students to succeed.

FOUNDATIONAL KNOWLEDGE BUILDING

Students are first introduced to concept formation by defining what a production concept is: An Idea + a Plan. Conceptualization is more than coming up with an interesting idea, students must figure out how this idea is applicable to the overall production and if it is able to be implemented. In text-based projects this means making sure that the idea fits the material in a way that honors the world of the play, the dramatic structure, and the author's intentions. If it does not meet these expectations, it is a *conceit* that does not allow for fidelity with the text. For an experiential project, there is often no primary text so there are more possibilities for concepts as long the idea can be feasibly developed within the structure of overall experience. To make the concept work, the teams must first define what their ideal spectator experience will be.

To better understand ideal experience, students gain knowledge about frameworks for experiential theatre. To pique their interest prior to foundational definitions, students watch the 2013 "documentary" *The Institute* by Spencer McCall created as a transmedia extension of the alternate reality game *The Jejune Institute*. The project was created by the experience design company Nonchalance, which develops events that are "situated at the intersection of three core elements; Narrative, Genuine Space, and Play" (Nonchalance.com).[3] The movie documents and extends a four-part durational performance that took place in the streets, buildings, and airwaves of San Francisco through live participation and game play between 2008 and 2011. The typical response to the viewing is mind-blowing in terms of both aesthetic and structural components for those who have not been introduced to an ARG. Those who have played role-playing games or are heavy gamers tend to understand the structure better. Both become incredibly excited at the possibilities for expanding definitions and structures of theatre following experiential formats.

In class we discuss the structure of *The Jejune Institute* and what logistics were necessary for the project's success. This allows us to define and discuss the four primary architectures of experience: immersion, participation, game play, and role play. Students are then given a selection of foundational readings[4] and videos on each architecture for homework before the assignment is given. The videos, which are updated each time the course is taught, run the gamut from short interviews to games tutorials and are intended to give a brief introduction to some of the denser theories. We discuss these readings to address any questions and to see how the theories they learn might apply to events in their everyday lives. This ultimately leads to fruitful discussion of performative encounters like theme parks, flash mobs, museums, augmented reality and video games, social media, transmedia storytelling, and escape rooms. Each of these topics serve as inspiration for the project which the students are given before moving on to the next stage.

100 • WILLIAM W. LEWIS

EXPERIENTIAL THEATRE CONCEPT PROJECT ASSIGNMENT

You will work as a group to brainstorm and then design/conceptualize a seed for an experiential performance project. This project will take as its central focus the experience offered for an individual audience member. Ask yourself, "*what experience do you want that audience member to have and what is the outcome of that experience?*"

Use one of the different modes of experiential performance discussed in class (immersive, participatory, game play, or role play) as the *primary structure* for your audience members. You can combine modes, but you should make one the central focus.

The project concept must include these elements:

1. Be site specific and/or ambulatory.
2. Have a minimum of three characters played by actors.
3. Have at least three audience member tasks.
4. Utilize a narrative structure of exposition, inciting incident, crisis, climax, denouement.
5. Allow for a minimum of twelve audience members during the performance.
6. Be a performance that lasts between sixty minutes and ninety minutes.

Conceptualization and Trajectories Paper: (50% of Overall Grade)

A collectively written five-page (minimum) concept paper explaining your vision and plan for this project.

The concept will detail:

1. The Ideal Audience Experience (What you want them to experience)
2. The Narrative Arc (Plot/Story)
3. The Characters (including how your audience members serve as characters)
4. The Ideal Path Through the Experience (The Canonical Trajectory)
5. The Areas of Audience Choice (Tasks, Affordances, and Participant Trajectories)
6. How you would Develop and Rehearse (Time and Resources)
7. Design Inspiration (Include at least six representational images)

Group Presentation: (50% of Overall Grade)

A fifteen- to twenty-minute presentation delivered to the class as if they were potential producers. In both the paper and presentation, you must explain what space you plan on using and how that space is important to the story told or the experience intended for your audience. All members of the group must contribute to the presentation equally.

CONCEPT FORMATION

Once the students have been introduced to foundational knowledge on experiential performance, they are assigned groups. Groups work best with at least one member from each of the four areas identified previously as this will allow a variety of learning styles matched to interests. The students are asked to utilize their backgrounds within the group work but there is no formal hierarchy in this form of conceptualization and planning: they are all directors and designers of experience or as I define them, *architects of exchange* (Lewis 2018). They utilize two days of structured time in class to brainstorm broad ideas for their experience. This brainstorming time is often referred to as Blue Sky exploration, where no idea is off-limit, and the group learns to collectively imagine. Two in-class sessions of an hour and a half, plus at least one outside group meeting, is typically enough to establish the general framework of experience and begin thinking about steps toward structure.

Conceptualizing the world in which the encounter occurs is an important part of this first phase. At the end of each in-class session, groups deliver a brief on progress of the day. From this, brief feedback is delivered to help the students hone their ideas and frame their concepts. This iterative fashion of brainstorming and feedback helps solidify their core ideas. They are guided to think big by defining what the overall audience experience should be. Do their audiences want to know what it feels like to achieve an important goal or solve a puzzle? Do they want to have them experience what it is like to become part of another world or become another person, or might they want them to feel as though they have control over the narrative arc or other peoples' actions? This is usually the most difficult step, as they have often been trained to go directly to character and story. Without this material upfront, they are often slow to start and need prompting, but reflecting back on *The Jejune Institute* helps spur their creativity. Once they develop the broad strokes of their audience's ideal experience, they begin to go granular and structure the experience. The most common projects seen after having taught six different course sections are either modifications of escape rooms, scavenger hunts, murder mysteries, or group protest events. Each of these events has different structures built out of the four frames of experiential theatre offered but requires different emphasis during the mapping and implementation phase.

STRUCTURAL MAPPING AND IMPLEMENTATION

This phase is devoted to developing structural components of the experience and requires the students to continue to fine-tune their collaboration skills. They plan conventional elements of theatrical design similar to a pitch proposal as a director or designer while also formulating structural components of the audience interaction experience. They are asked to plan trajectories and implement affordances, terms borrowed from games studies and HCI (Human-Computer Interaction) respectively. Trajectories are pathways an audience member may follow through an experience. An ideal (canonical) trajectory allows for flexible levels of agency within the while guiding them toward the planned experience. Trajectories are comparable to dramatic arcs one finds when analyzing a linear plot. A linear structure is the easiest format for the assignment, but as a seed project in an iterative process, they can consider other structures. They can modify and expand the structure where it applies to the overall experience after the first iteration of a project.[5] Students are required to utilize mind-mapping software[6] that uses a graphical interface to show trajectories. This software allows them to interactively create flow charts that are necessary to explain the complex nature of experiential structures. In User Experience (UX) design this is considered the wireframing stage. Included below are flow-chart examples I've developed using the free program Junkyard showing the structure of experiential theatre design process (Figure 10.1) and trajectory mapping (Figure 10.2). The first example shows how experiential theatre concepts are developed by blending formal theatrical analysis (including elements from story/source, space, and design) with interaction design frameworks.

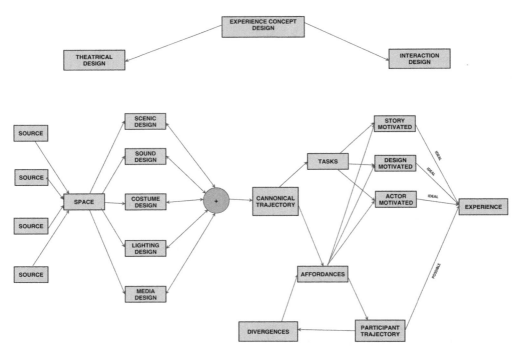

Figure 10.1 Structural map of theatrical experience design conceptualization.

Teams are tasked with designing an ideal trajectory while considering the divergences that may occur based on audience action. The points of divergence are similar to the moments of conflict a character might encounter within a play. The affordances are the tools given that help the audience member navigate these moments of conflict/interaction. In HCI and UX (User Experience) design an affordance is a clue toward the possibility of action. For instance, a door handle is designed in a way that is meant to be turned, similarly an HTML button on a web page is designed to be clicked. Both open a new pathway. A divergence might include not utilizing the affordance correctly. To emphasize the importance of affordances, the teams must implement a variety of tasks for the audience that will allow them to move forward on the trajectory. These tasks can be as simple as choosing a direction in which to move, to something as complex as unlocking a padlocked door by solving a riddle to gain the combination. The way the team plans for the use of the affordances ultimately determines whether the experience is meaningful for the audience. Planning for divergences by clearly defining the affordances helps focus the experience toward desired outcomes. Once trajectories are formulated, the team moves on to the final stages of conceptualization where traditional aspects of theatrical design are conceived as aspects to aid the audience performing within the fiction. Design elements such as lighting, scenery, or costume can also serve as additional affordances, though they may not be direct elements of interaction. For example, the level of light in a room might aid the audience member in their interaction though it is primarily an aesthetic design choice. On the other hand, the color of a wall might give a clue toward a hidden passage and serve as an interaction-based affordance. In this final stage the teams overlay all their structural elements (plan) with their aesthetic choices (idea) to cement a workable conceptualization to pitch.

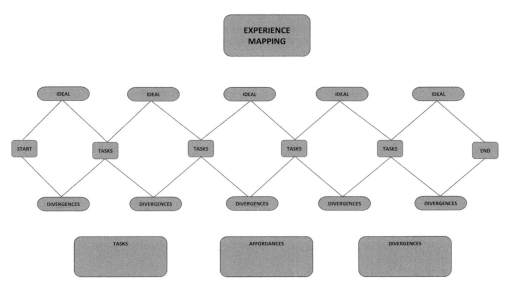

Figure 10.2 Trajectories mapping: Tasks and divergences.

The project is finalized through a collaborative written brief that details all required aspects of the concept. This brief accompanies the group pitch meeting where the team explains their concept to the remaining members of the course and instructor. They use a variety of visual and experiential formats (sight, sound, haptics, and other senses). This audience acts as a proxy-producing organization who receive the pitch and then asks questions and attempts to "poke holes" in the project. As a studio course, this critique is where the teams often learn the most about their project. It gives them the insight to re-work the project in its next iterative phase where real-world testing might occur. It also highlights the necessity of true collaboration. The projects that are least complete are often ones where individual team members only focus on one element of the concept versus working in a synergistic manner. In an ideal world these concepts would be developed further in an advanced "experimental" directing/devising class that allows a full team to practically implement the projects they have pitched. In the end, the students learn how to build tools for conceptualization by defining worlds, interactions, trajectories, and affordances in using a team-based approach. This approach delimits the emphasis of hierarchies that exist in traditional training programs and opens students up to new modes of theatre making.

Notes

1 I have modified the included assignment for various levels. For undergrad theatre students the project takes roughly three weeks, for grad students the project timeline is similar but the level of detail in planning and presentation is higher. I have also adapted this assignment for Theatre Appreciation Students to be completed in one week with no outside group work required. Surprisingly some of the most exciting pitches come from the group with the least time given.
2 David Kolb's (2014) learning style inventory, as well as psychologist Larry Rosen's (2011, 2016) work on distraction and multitasking, are useful readings to help better understand how your students learn best. Howard Gardner's (2011) Theory of Multiple Intelligences is also a useful tool for basic understanding of how different students are programmed toward specific forms of understanding and knowledge.

3 Nonchalance has made other ARG's that link live space with both digital and filmic elements. *The Jejune Institute* project officially ended with the making of *The Institute* documentary but within that documentary were easter egg style clues to their next project. AMC created a scripted series that follows the events of the Jejune Institute through the eyes of a fictional character.
4 The readings come from authors Josephine Machon (2016) on immersion, Henry Jenkins (2006) on participation, Richard Schechner (1969) on environmental theatre, Tom Pearson (2010) on site-specific performance, Katie Salen and Eric Zimmerman (2004) on game play mechanics, and Steve Benford and Gabriella Giannachi (2011) on mixed reality performance processes.
5 The project is explained as being the first seed in a potential larger project.
6 There are a variety of free software options that are either downloadable or cloud-based. Students can also utilize document software to create these maps/flow charts though if they prefer.

References

Benford, Steve and Gabriella Giannachi. 2011. *Performing Mixed Reality*. Cambridge: MIT Press.
Gazzaley, Adam and Larry Rosen. 2016. *The Distracted Mind: Ancient Brains in a High-Tech World*. Cambridge, MA: MIT Press.
Jenkins, Henry. 2006. *Convergence Culture: Where Old and New Media Collide*. New York: New York University Press.
Kolb, David A. 2014. *Experiential Learning: Experience as the Source of Learning and Development*. 2nd ed. Upper Saddle River: Pearson Education.
Lewis, William W. 2018. "Approaches to Audience-Centered Performance: Designing Interaction for the IGeneration." In *New Directions in Teaching Theater Arts*. Edited by Anne Fliotsos and Gail Medford, 9–25. New York: Palgrave Macmillan.
Machon, Josephine. 2016. "Watching, Attending, Sense-Making: Spectatorship in Immersive Theatres." *Journal of Contemporary Drama in English* 4 (1): 34–48.
McCall, Spencer. 2013. *The Institute*. United States: Argot Films.
Nonchalance. n.d. "Nonchalance." Accessed June 1, 2021. www.nonchalance.com
Pearson, Mike. 2010. *Sight Specific Performance*. New York: Palgrave Macmillan.
Rosen, Larry, Mark L. Carrier, and Nancy Cheever. 2010. *Rewired: Understanding the iGeneration and the Way They Learn*. New York: Palgrave Macmillan.
Salen, Katie and Eric Zimmerman. 2004. *Rules of Play: Game Design Fundamentals*. Cambridge, MA: MIT Press.
Schechner, Richard. 1968. "6 Axioms for Environmental Theatre." *The Drama Review: TDR* 12 (3): 41–64.

11

A Postdigital Response: User Experience Design, Interactive, Immersive, and Mixed Reality Performance

Lindsay Brandon Hunter and Steve Luber

POSTDIGTIAL RESPONSE

The breadth and depth of the chapters that precede are valuable illustrations of the impact of the postdigital in performance, how performance is mobilized in the twenty-first century, and indeed how slippery the term can be, both to the advantage and sometimes disorientation of artists and audiences. The "post" of postdigital functions much like the prefix to other discursive terms that have emerged over the past forty years—postmodern, posthuman, poststructural—that is to say not a genre or period after, but rather one that subsumes previous movements and moments. We are in no sense "after" the digital; it is difficult to imagine a future that would be (other than a post-apocalyptic one). And so, we therefore look, rather, to the term postdigital as a framework that reckons with a world and cultures that have been changed invariably by technologies of the digital.

Each of the studies featured here reflects a changing digital landscape and occasionally operates in spite of it. Performance once again proves fertile grounds for understanding these effects. We might argue that performance in the twenty-first century is always already postdigital since digital tools and economies play significant roles in generating, influencing, and expanding the reach of performance—and audiences, significantly, have little choice but to consume and read performance inflected by daily digital literacy. These essays define a diverse field of practice, including work that does not always claim the precise label "experiential," but may also be identified by authors as immersive, participatory, or interactive. As elsewhere in this volume, naming the theatres gathered here as experiential highlights common concerns that resonate across disparate sites and goals; in this section, in particular, those common concerns reflect a deep regard for the sensations, desires, and participatory offerings of audience members, constituting in many examples a foundational preoccupation with their active experience of a performed work. For Adrienne Mackey, for instance, interaction is linked to immersivity in the sense that those two qualities co-constitute a powerful catalyst that can "supercharge the inherent ephemerality of live performance," and in so doing "create embodied experiences and offer new avenues for audience agency." Matt Adams describes audience experience as the focus and fundament of Blast Theory's work when he suggests they start not "from stories or from texts," but "from moments of experience around the participant." This section of work makes clear that the experience in question in experiential theatre is emphatically

DOI: 10.4324/9781003188179-13

105

that of an audience that is not only engaged but constituting the performance event through their participation.

This widely shared concern with audience experience as central, core, and vital often keeps company with an appreciation for the seeming immediacy of live events, as Mackey notes, and in particular for the opportunities for embodied co-presence they offer. Josephine Machon (2013), in her monograph on immersive performance, reifies this apparent affinity when she cites the assertion (from David Jubb, Joint Artistic Director of BAC) that immersive work directly addresses a strong desire on the part of audiences for a particular experience, or perhaps pre-condition of experience: that of "'conviviality and congregation'." She goes on to echo Jubb's sense that "the greatest potential" for immersive work inheres in "theatrical situations where genuine human connection occurs," suggesting such connection as the product of shared space and time (23). Machon and Jubb point to liveliness (so close to liveness!) and on-site, communal gathering as valuable experiences that immersive performance can not only afford audiences but are positioned to exploit to great effect. It is tempting to posit, then, that the "experience" that immersive/experiential performance seeks to provide is specifically one of bodies meeting one another, in shared physical presence and "real" time, and that it is this synchrony and togetherness that marks the work as special and powerful—or even uniquely suited to address humanity.

This strong association might provoke questions about how experiential performance can be essayed through digital means or use modalities of production and presentation that don't rely on—or, perhaps, even allow for—the shared temporality and co-presence sometimes implied as the conditions of possibility for this kind of performance. What possibilities might be held by experiential works of performance that complicate, rather than rely on, notions of im-mediacy in order to enact experience? If conviviality, congregation, and visceral affect are important affordances of experiential or immersive work, how might we account for the insistent, resilient, connections of those affordances with liveness? How might digitally produced or presented work facilitate audience experience, with or without complicating the understanding of that experience as primarily visceral or "human"? Given that performance, as Elise Morrison, Kimberly Jannarone and Tavia Nyong'o recently noted in a call for submissions to a special issue of TDR, is "an elusive form of presence," one that, even when it seems to be frankly delivered, evokes absence by its own manifestation, it is maybe unsurprising that "privileging co-presence" within theatre and performance studies, "has sometimes been construed as naïve and even passé." If the work this volume defines as 'experiential,' however, proceeds from a lineage that prioritizes audience members' living, feeling, visceral *experience* as foundational to its execution and objective, and moreover the communal sharing of site, breath, proximity, and moment as constitutive of that experience, it seems prudent to ask what possibility there might be for performance to prioritize audience experience even as it is asynchronously delivered, experienced over distance, or essayed in solitude.

To be clear, the work described in this section does not necessarily eschew media or mediatization, and neither do the authorial voices amassed here make a project of looking askance at the possibilities of the digital. Machon's (2013) playful corruption of liveness into "live(d)ness," a quality she suggests as more apt to describe immersive performance's "potency ... in terms of an individual's experience" nevertheless results from "the fact that it *revels in liveness*" (emphasis added) and owes its "consequent live(d)ness" to that quality (43). Perhaps more importantly, a "postdigital" response to this question, as this one is intended to be, should be ready to dispense with hard taxonomic divisions between mediatized or digital works and those that present as live, or at least to map them according to reflexive and dynamic criteria, such as those set out by Sarah Bay-Cheng,

Jennifer Parker-Starbuck, and David Saltz in Performance and Media (2015). Still, responding to this section's amassed analysis of experiential work and the collaborative interaction it prizes seems like an apt place to raise questions about how some common features of experiential works—that is, sites and temporal moments held in common between performers and audience, shared atmospheres and environments, in-person collaborative engagements—might work differently in and/or beside digital landscapes. After all, work that is made or delivered digitally must depend explicitly on the mediation of interfaces, platforms, networks, devices, and systems often colloquially understood to attenuate, distance, or even pollute the "inherent ephemerality of live performance" cited by Mackey, or even something like "genuine human connection," suggested as providing a lesser, derogated substitute for the seeming purity of face-to-face interaction. The question this response poses is not so much whether digital work is categorically capable of facilitating meaningful audience experience—visceral, agentic, or otherwise—but rather how to understand those experiences' specificities within discourse that still frequently references the effects of liveness and co-presence as ideal. When performances or events enable digital facilitation across time and space, rather than within the conventionally shared duration and location of an amassed audience; when the explicit mediation of interfaces and screens highlights not the appearance of immediacy but rather the means by which engagement and interaction is achieved—how do we understand these affordances of the digital when it comes to producing or occasioning audience experience?

Certainly, the explicit mediation of devices, screens, networks, and platforms might resemble rather than diverge from complex networks of opportunity that attend the "live" experiential performances described in this section, which permit, enable, and direct interaction precisely through mediating forces—that is, of suggestion, influence, and the other tactics employed by designers and performers to shape the result. This resemblance is particularly clearly focused in William W. Lewis's invocation of user experience design (UX)—a term not unfamiliar to those who design and build the interfaces through which users interact with software products, as in a command line interface or graphical user interface—within a pedagogical project devoted to helping students conceptualize experiential performance. Amanda Rose Villarreal describes a devising a collaborative mediating system for interaction and exchange when she identifies the task of "creators" within immersive worlds as to "build ... Information systems to facilitate lusory exchanges." The suite of tools and proficiencies she describes equipping student performers with—that is, the ability and responsibility to deploy "trailheads" and "offerings," as well as "stings," code words, invitations, and the establishment and maintenance of personal boundaries—speaks to a systematicity present in the design and execution of experiential performance that does not endanger its spontaneity or rescind audience's invitations to agency (or, for that matter, visceral feeling), but rather shapes and regulates those elements as a mediating force. Something similar might be observed of the "post-immersive" practice of Lopez Ramos, Maravala, and Guillery when they describe ZU-UK's "ways of working together," ways "that reject neo-liberal pressures towards scale, reproducibility, and escape, in favor of intimacy, specificity and awareness." ZU-UK's description of praxis offers tools and tactics for engagement that structure audience action, shuttling audiences between "shifting participatory modes, between critical awareness and deep, active engagement"; the prompts and invitations that audiences encounter in the ensemble's work mediate between their contributions and the frameworks that support them, actively shaping their participation.

In this sense, experiential performance seems clearly subject to the painstaking design of cues, trajectories, and parameters designed not only to catalyze audience experience generally, but to govern and even produce its interactions in rather a similar way to a mediating interface. The priority placed by ZU-UK on intimacy and awareness, and the care taken by the artists to lay groundwork that might potentiate those experiences suggests one way that immediacy, at least figured as a pointed lack of explicit mediation, might be far less important than the artful design of useful mediating frameworks, which may, in different circumstances, work best when they are soft, subtle, responsive, occluded, or otherwise deftly honed so as to encourage and shape audience collaboration and participation. 600 Highwaymen's 2021 *A Thousand Ways, Part One: A Phone Call* might stand as a noteworthy example of experiential theatre that offers audiences an experience overwhelmingly mediated by both software and formal design, and which does so without the benefit of congregation or (much) conviviality. The piece is presented as a one-to-one, highly structured phone call of about an hour between two participating individuals who function as both performers and each other's audience, the conversation refereed by an automated, digitally produced voice adhering to a script. The robotic voice offers prompts, asks for responses, and asks the two participants to listen, imagine, and essay small tasks. The prompts that come from the automated voice are often both mundane and personal—to say the name of someone you love, for example, or to imagine the face of the conversation partner you cannot see—that exceed small talk but do not seem weighted with particular meaning or pointed attempts at intimacy. The effect of the mediated conversation, however, is frequently experienced as intimacy; the *New York Times* reviewer Laura Collins-Hughes (2020) wrote of the piece that though she was not entirely sure it qualified as theatre, part one of *A Thousand Ways* "achieves more goals of theater—telling stories, triggering imagination, nurturing empathy, fostering connection—than nearly any other show I have experienced since pre-pandemic days." Speaking, it seems, specifically of those pandemic days more than (although perhaps also of) a generalized, post-modern malaise, Collins-Hughes declares that "In this time of widespread social isolation and fragmentation, our compassion has gotten rusty. It is not nothing, then, to make even a momentary connection—to spend an hour revealing pieces of oneself and imagining the complexity of someone else's humanity."

Quite apart from its status as a pandemic-moment work that probes experiences of distance and connection in the light of ongoing quarantine and isolation, part one of *A Thousand Ways* distinguishes itself as performance devoted to audience experience quite specifically predicated on mediated connection and a pointed lack of co-presence. A similar mechanic might be observed in Blast Theory's 2007 production of *Rider Spoke*, revamped for presentation during the pandemic in 2021. In the first installations, participants cycled around urban environments in the hosting cities with computer consoles mounted on bicycles, leaving audio messages in response to prompts and listening to the messages of others, embedded in the mapped locations where previous cyclists had "hidden" them. Blast Theory (ND) described the piece as "part late night pirate radio station, part anonymized social network," and imagined its subsequent re-mount in 2021, mid-pandemic and after the advent of ubiquitous smartphones, as an auspicious match for a still-socially-distant moment. "Like a piece of theatre, you buy a ticket and come to a venue to begin. But once you start to ride, you're on your own," their website notes. "You might catch a glimpse of other riders but you are mostly looking inward." *Rider Spoke* undoubtedly catalyzes audience experience—the entire piece is nothing but, as participants bike through city neighborhoods while responding, recording, and listening-in at will—but does so without employing synchrony or co-presence, aspects of liveness often called on or understood to intensify experiential performance. Blast Theory writes that Rider Spoke is specifically "a work about intimacy through distance and anonymity," (Blast Theory) depending not on proximity to engender feeling (even as it takes advantage of shared sites) but rather on its absence, or perhaps its vacancy. Here, too, experience is mediated by aesthetic and social structures as well as software and networks, as subjects pedal through the night, interacting with *Rider Spoke*'s directives and agreements as well as with recording technologies and devices, rules of the road, and their own desires. One of the most evident strengths of *Rider Spoke*—and *A Thousand Ways, Part One*, as well—is its neat upending of any habitual linkage of pointedly meaningful experience with the promise of immediacy that stubbornly inheres in live, co-present performance. By constructing a partial, partially occluded intimacy from the distance and devices that co-constitute the performance, it subtly gives the lie to any notion that feelings, sensation, or intimacy itself is allergic to the intervention of media, or more pointedly to the ubiquitous digitality of a postdigital environment.

Like the performances described and analyzed in this section's preceding chapters, they take on a negotiation of the postdigital economies of interaction, labor, and dissemination within which they and their participants exist. The primary themes that emerge through these studies—interactivity, immersion, and the collapsing binaries of audience/performer, character/actor, and art/industry—come to the fore in large part because they align with larger characteristics enabled by digital technology, such as modularity, variability, and transcoding, all general tendencies, according to Lev Manovich (2001), "of a culture undergoing computerization" (27). And yet interactivity as integral to performance, for example, exists in performance and ritual throughout the ancient world, from Sanskrit performance to early Greek drama. Royona Mitra (2016) called to decolonize immersive performance through the lens of rasa to expand and de-center Anglicized claims on participation in the twenty-first century. Mitra's essay doubles as a commentary on contemporary performance, but also locates impulses toward postdigital phenomena in millennia-old performance practices. Liturgical dramas and traveling troupes of the medieval period and environmental performance mobilize immersion to invite an audience's engaged empathy and agency as a rehearsal for the audience (as discussed by Villareal) for the former and call to action, often political action (mentioned in Breel's typology of agency) for the latter.

With a wide range of pre-digital historical referents, it's tempting to turn the postdigital on its head, or even to suggest that until relatively recently, most theatrical performance might already have qualified as postdigital by the definitions offered here. After all, interactivity and the intersection of real and imagined spaces for both audience and performers were both defining features of performance—both ritualistic and popular—until the rise of bourgeois drama in the nineteenth century. In addition to the periods and cultures mentioned above, phenomena like groundlings, claques, and boisterous melodrama audiences all suggest a deeply participatory ethos that exposes performance as imbricated within larger, interactive systems of cultural production. The nineteenth century sees the rise of social and class distinctions become key to legitimating (and in some ways adapting) theatre in order to respond to changing socio-economic conditions, not to mention as a tool to marginalize rising middle classes that did not practice "decorum"; but also to technological changes, such as electric lights and stage machinery that radically alter possibilities for the stage picture and, significantly, the most stark division of the audience and performer since the advent of proscenia. In this sense, many of the qualities and practices this essay suggests as postdigital fall out of favor only about two hundred years ago and return in the twenty-first century to accommodate newer modes of moving through the world and balances of power. In many ways, the types of performance discussed in this section are direct reactions against narrative and material conventions of Modern and even singular undercurrents of postdramatic performance. This is not to state that the postdigital has an inherent or universal quality, but rather that the qualities of the postdigital are responsive to a complex array of socio-cultural and artistic demand.

Such adaptations, including those described here, make up one of performance's almost constant strengths—the ability to shift and speak to a moment and sensibility. One method that has become integral to this adaptation in the postindustrial age is "the double logic of remediation," as defined by Bolter and Grusin (1999): "Our culture wants both to multiply its media and to erase all traces of mediation: ideally, it wants to erase its media in the very act of multiplying them" (5). With varying degrees of reflexivity, performance slowly adopts aesthetics and tactics of other, usually newer forms of media. Shifts in quotidian interaction that feature computers and digital media over the past half-century permeate much of artistic production; cultural literacy has been greatly expanded to include hypertextual, interactive, and dynamic modes of understanding and consumption. Much immersive performance owes a great deal to video games specifically illustrated clearly by Mackey in the alignment of an MDA-inspired approach to performance making with Swim Pony, but also by the formalized branching structures of a closed system presented by Lewis and Villarreal. Even a standardized patient is, in some (possibly reductive) sense, a kind of affective chatbot (though Mastromatteo might argue for a superior one with more agency). Whether it is in the sensibility of the artists or the demand of audiences it is the ouroboros of remediation—but a composite strength, comprised of the ability to remediate newer forms joined to the draw of community and shared experience, combines to maintain a flourishing economy and aesthetics of performance.

One of the notable distinctions of recent postdigital performance's remediation of digital forms is that of gaming, and specifically the dynamic nature of interaction both as the artists as architects of exchange and the audience's agency of narrative and engagement. The type of performance hearkens back to what Janet Murray (1997) (after Deleuze) refers to as a rhizome game:

> Walking through a rhizome one enacts a story of wandering, of being enticed in conflicting directions, of remaining always open to surprise, of feeling helpless to orient oneself or to find an exit, but the story is also oddly reassuring. In the rhizome, one is constantly threatened but also continuously enclosed. The fact that the plot will not resolve means that no irreparable loss will be suffered. (133)

Murray's description bucks the binary of narrative/non-narrative storytelling, instead focusing on a work as a closed system of many, many possible developments and interactions, illustrated throughout the work of this section.

Beyond the design and dynamic thinking of performance environments, however, the postdigital and all the technologies it enables has opened-up a new ecosystem of possibilities and ways to engage with performance, from the ways of designing and participating outlined above to modes of dissemination and understanding, including through marketing and audience engagement, as well as access and proliferation of tools available to artists for design, technical support, and stagecraft. As musicians have gained an ability to build a studio in a bedroom and filmmakers can work with relatively high-quality phone cameras, so too do similar opportunities open up for those in performance. These potentialities are rooted in Sarah Bay-Cheng's (2012) thesis that "theatre is media": that history and documentation, which now in turn also has a hand in generating work, can no longer be relegated to a binary of material trace and event, but must be understood as set "within the media we use to access those sources" (27).

All this is set against an evolving economic and cultural backdrop that gives rise to the so-called Experience Economy as set forth by Pine II and Gilmore (1999). Most certainly intertwined with the rise of the digital, the experience economy represents an evolution in economic understanding and demand: "When a person buys a service, he [sic] purchases a set of intangible activities carried out on his [sic] behalf. But when he [sic] buys an experience, he [sic] pays to spend time enjoying a series of memorable events that a company stages—as in a theatrical play—to engage him [sic] in a personal way" (2). Pine and Gilmore link this shift to several factors, including technological advancements, rising global affluence, and "distintermediation," that is, a company's direct-to-consumer engagement. The irony of this last factor cannot be understated and confirms the assumptions of remediation: that a heightened value of "experience" is only possible with the proliferation of media consumption. The Harvard Business School-based analysis cleverly plays with and relentlessly exploits corollaries between brand-based marketing and theatre. And many of the impulses behind the studies in this postdigital section are a part of these "experiential" trends that Pine and Gilmore lay out; and although the *intent*—per Machon (2013)—can be debated between corporations and performance makers, many of the impulses remain the same (68).

From an audience's perspective, this desire is formed even deeper in what Henry Jenkins (2006) refers to as the "prosumer": an audience member that now has the access and tools to actively participate in and shape the media they consume. Jenkins writes, "Consumers are learning how to use these different media technologies to bring the flow of media more fully under their control and to interact with other consumers. The promises of this new media environment raise expectations of a freer flow of ideas and content" (3). While these flows of information across platforms and struggle for creative power cannot themselves fully account for postdigital performance, they go a long way to help describe the cultural literacy of a contemporary audience, as well as the interest and experiments of performance makers looking both to connect with a media-savvy audience and express artists' desires to connect. Elinor Fuchs (1996) anticipated both the Experience Economy and the prosumer when she theorized the "commodification of the theatrical unconscious" in some newer, interactive performances that she ultimately describes as "theater as shopping" (129). While Fuchs laments the boiling over of this commodification, she also quite beautifully describes a sense—or perhaps the simulacrum—of power that comes from participating in this liminal, theatrical space: "The dream of self-transformation or self-realization could not be sustained in the shopping situation without my having the power to make a choice. My capacity for pleasurable fantasy is in fact activated by the knowledge that I have this power" (134). It is this power—be it real or imagined, generative or coerced, radical or neoliberal—that may be at the heart of postdigital work; power is grappled with extensively in the pedagogical, artistic, and social studies in the chapters that comprise this section. Most of the work discussed above operates on the poles of these tensions: either for highly subsidized venues, such as the academy and service non-profits, or high-end and expensive for-profit theatres. Both, it is worth noting, remain accessible mostly to niche populations, illustrative of increasing economic disparities, and worthy of continued discourse and reflection for the field. But these remain productive sites of investigation and are empowered for as many reasons as they may be problematic.

The values of postdigital performance, therefore, contain sets of contradictory impulses and compulsions that empower artists and audiences alike but are also part of a larger economic imperative of brand-living and the commodification of experience. But within these confines, performance as form displays a remarkable cultural resilience and remains a site of radical engagement and challenge to some of the more nefarious underpinnings of postdigital, interactive culture. Performance's remediation of digital technologies both reaffirms the artform's relevance and immediacy, but also undermines some of the basic assumptions about digital interactivity, agency, and commodity fetishism. The co-presence of performers and audience members may seem quaint in one respect, but in another, it radically reevaluates our relationship and ethics as prosumers in an experience economy.

Performance materially works against the immediacy and efficiencies demanded by late-stage capitalism, even in its ability to speak to these demands. Through problem solving, agency, and attention, postdigital performance can command a radical and refreshing empathy that reminds artists and audiences of the ethics and effects of our constant state of engagement and production in a postdigital sphere.

References

Bay-Cheng. Sarah. 2012. "Theatre is Media: Some Principles for a Digital Historiography of Performance." *Theater* 42 (2): 27–41.

Bay-Cheng, Sarah, Jennifer Parker-Starbuck, and David Saltz. 2015. *Performance and Media: Taxonomies for a Changing Field*. Ann Arbor: University of Michigan Press.

Blast Theory. Nd. "Rider Spoke." https://www.blasttheory.co.uk/projects/rider-spoke/, accessed August 11, 2021.

Bolter, Jay David and Richard Grusin. 1999. *Remediation: Understanding New Media*. Cambridge, MA: MIT Press.

Cambridge University Press. Nd. "Call for papers." https://www.cambridge.org/core/journals/the-drama-review/information/call-for-papers. Accessed 3/7/2022.

Collins-Hughes, Laura. 2020. "Strangers on a Phone, Theatrically Speaking." *The New York Times. November 11, 2020.* https://www.nytimes.com/2020/11/11/theater/a-thousand-ways-600-highwaymen.html. Accessed 9/16/2021

Fuchs, Elinor. 1996. *The Death of Character: Perspectives on Theater after Modernism*. Bloomington: Indiana University Press.

Jenkins, Henry. 2006. *Convergence Culture: Where Old and New Media Collide*. New York: New York University Press.

Machon, Josephine. 2013. *Immersive Theatres: Intimacy and Immediacy in Contemporary Performance*. Basingstoke: Palgrave Macmillan.

Manovich, Lev. 2001. *The Language of New Media*. Cambridge, MA: MIT Press.

Mitra, Royona. 2016. Decolonising Immersion: Translation, Spectatorship, *Rasa* Theory, and Contemporary British Dance." *Performance Research* 21 (5): 89–90.

Murray, Janet. 1997. *Hamlet on the Holodeck: The Future of Narrative in Cyberspace*. Cambridge, MA: MIT Press.

Pine II, Joseph, and James H. Gilmore. 1999. *The Experience Economy: Work is Theatre and Every Business a Stage*. Boston: Harvard Business School Press.

Section 2
Narrative and Dramaturgy for Experiential Forms

12
Models for Experiential Training in Playwriting and Dramaturgy

Sean Bartley and Marshall Botvinick

INTRODUCTION

In the introduction to this collection, we raised concerns about an increase in specialization in university theatre programs, arguing that in order to survive in a rapidly shifting professional landscape, young theatre artists need to learn new techniques that rest outside pre-existing theatrical disciplines and models of production. Moving beyond conventional silos of training (i.e., specializations in acting, directing, design, playwriting, etc.) demands that we deconstruct some of the limitations that structure US undergraduate and graduate theatre programs. Three types of widespread degree programs exist for students hoping to establish careers in the theatre: Bachelor of Arts (BA) programs, which offer students the most broad-based introduction to various theatrical forms and disciplines while also stressing an even-broader interdisciplinary core outside the theatre department; Bachelor of Fine Arts (BFA) programs, which forgo interdisciplinarity in favor of a focused, conservatory-style training in one aspect of theatre (most commonly acting); and Master of Fine Arts (MFA) programs, which offer an even deeper dive and professional preparation into one conventionally understood career path (again, most commonly acting). More than a hundred BFA acting and more than fifty MFA acting programs exist in the United States, as do dozens of programs built for potential designers and directors. Comparatively speaking, students interested in playwriting and dramaturgy have far fewer options, particularly at the undergraduate level. Less than ten universities offer a BFA in Playwriting, and less than five offer one in Dramaturgy. As a result, students wanting to specialize in these areas follow a common trajectory: a four-year BA degree, which typically offers, at most, one course each in playwriting and dramaturgy, followed by a three-year MFA specialization in either Playwriting or Dramaturgy.

While we have typically focused on undergraduate training in the rest of this collection, the remainder of this introduction will focus on MFA Playwriting and Dramaturgy programs. Students typically leave these degree programs with massive amounts of debt and an extremely limited set of professional prospects. The lack of post-graduation opportunities for MFA Playwriting and Dramaturgy students is due in large part to the very narrow course of study offered to them. To better equip their students for life after graduation, MFA Playwriting and Dramaturgy faculty must ask themselves: How can we embrace new structures? Are training systems from outside the worlds of theatre and performance helpful models to consider?

DOI: 10.4324/9781003188179-15

115

RECENT PRACTICES IN PLAYWRITING PROGRAMS

MFA programs in Playwriting have historically and recently functioned as the most siloed, isolated, and sheltered form of US theatre training. Programs almost universally understand the playwright as the *a priori* creative artist behind a theatrical work. They train playwrights to think of the script as an inherently non-collaborative work, a battle with the empty page that must be won *before* collaboration (often with MFA Acting and Directing students at the same institution) can begin. In recent decades, the esteemed writers on the faculty of many MFA Playwriting programs have taught their students to be at best protective and, in some extremes, overtly mistrustful of their future artistic collaborators. This mindset is best summed up by Richard Nelson (2007), then-director of the MFA playwriting program at Yale University, in his speech "Thanks, but No Thanks: All This Help is Hurting Playwrights." Delivered to the Alliance of Resident Theatres/New York and later reprinted in *American Theatre*, Nelson's jeremiad begins in no uncertain terms: "the role of the playwright in today's American theatre, I believe, is under serious attack" (339). The ideal process for playwrights, he contends, is one largely free from collaboration altogether. He critiques a culture where playwrights are thought to be "in need of help—to do their work," where "they can't do their work themselves" (339). He then goes on to argue "that our mindset toward playwrights should be this: that the playwright knows what he is doing; and that perhaps the play, as presented, is as it should be" (340). But nowhere in his speech does Nelson imagine a world in which a playwright might use his creative abilities to become a co-creator of experiences. Nowhere does he allow for the possibility of joint authorship. He sees the playwright only as someone who works on a canvas that is small enough to be the property of just one person. Nelson's approach begets a world where, yes, the playwright has more ownership of the process, but in restoring that sense of ownership, Nelson sacrifices an entire realm of creative activity that can and should be open to playwrights.

The false choice Nelson advocates for has produced a generation of playwrights who are largely unprepared and unable to participate in the recent surge of collaborative immersive and experiential theatre. Examples of playwrights with MFA degrees who develop collaborative relationships with theatre ensembles that break up the *a priori* model of playwriting certainly exist (Anne Washburn's work with The Civilians, Kirk Lynn's pieces with The Rude Mechs, and Gregory S. Moss' collaboration with Pig Iron Theatre Company all come to mind), but these are the exception to the overwhelming rule. Playwrights are trained to submit finished plays to agents, awards, and companies, all in hopes of one day being picked up for production by a commercial or regional theatre. Unfortunately, those opportunities are few and far between, so most MFA playwrights graduate into a profession that traps them in an inescapable cycle of fruitless developments and workshops.

RECENT PRACTICES IN DRAMATURGY PROGRAMS

MFA programs in Dramaturgy have the opposite problem. In contrast to playwriting programs, current pedagogy in dramaturgy emphasizes a form of collaboration that takes place only after the play has been written. Dramaturgs are trained to think of themselves as advocates or servants of the play (and the playwright) rather than as artists who might help shape and author a text or experience. Coursework in dramaturgy programs can be remarkably limited when it comes to opportunities for collaboration. Classes in playwriting are often closed to dramaturgs out of deference to student playwrights who Nelson and others view as "under serious attack," and needing protection from their peers. Similarly, faculty advise dramaturgs against courses in directing and opportunities to direct productions, fearing that students might forget their role as accessories to the work of playwrights and directors.

This is not to suggest that traditional courses in dramaturgy should cease to be offered. Of course, those offerings remain a vital part of a dramaturg's training. Rather, what we are arguing is that current pedagogy needs to be supplemented with training that gives dramaturgs the tools to generate devised and experiential material. It is no longer sufficient to see dramaturgs as collaborators who join the process in *medias res*. They must also be thought of as content creators who should be present at the beginning of a collaborative endeavor.

Presently, these dramaturgy programs produce a massive surplus of graduates for a microscopic nationwide pool of literary positions. A current listing on The Playwrights' Center's website shows a dozen graduate training programs that emphasize dramaturgy. Each produces a handful of graduates each year (or each class rotation if they do not recruit each year), meaning that in a five-year period, these programs produce more than a hundred would-be dramaturgs and literary managers. But most regional theatres cannot afford a full-time literary staffer. The stark reality is that less than fifty people in the entire American theatre find full-time employment with health benefits working as dramaturgs or literary staffers for theatre companies. Only a handful of companies have more than one dramaturg, meaning that no opportunities for promotion typically exist in these jobs. Despite the entry-level pay for many of these positions, most dramaturgs cling to them desperately, knowing their prospects for landing another job among the tiny trickle of opportunities that will appear each year are slim. Professionals with Dramaturgy MFAs tend to make only two kinds of career moves from these positions: lateral moves into similar entry-level positions at other theatres, or departures from the field entirely. The COVID-19 pandemic further exacerbated this situation, as the few dozen full-time literary staffers were among the first to be cut or furloughed, and because dramaturgs have been trained to see themselves as supporters rather than creators, they are particularly ill-equipped to find other full-time theatre work or projects that would allow them to survive in the theatrical gig economy. The situation today is an ethical imperative: these graduate programs *cannot* reasonably claim that current training models are likely to result in a paid career in the field and *must* stop offering such a limited silo of training that leaves graduates unable to adapt.

ALTERNATIVE TRAINING MODELS

The introduction to this book offered three main proposals to reform MFA programs as well as undergraduate ones: reemphasize collective devising courses, embrace new models of collaborative coursework that bring the siloed areas together, and initiate a pervasive move towards interdisciplinary exchange with the other departments at our larger universities. We have argued that European universities, particularly those in the United Kingdom, are substantially ahead of US institutions in the adoption of undergraduate and graduate programs that shift the training model toward experiential and collaborative creation processes. But several universities in the United States have begun similar moves. Sarah Lawrence College, for example, now offers BA and MFA programs in Theatre that do not revolve around a professionalization focus. Faculty create individualized courses of study for each student (without the sizable "core" featured in so many undergraduate theatre programs) where interdisciplinary interests from other subject areas enter the rehearsal room as springboards for staging work. The departmental season focuses on student-created work rather than productions of extant plays. This can prove particularly empowering for students interested in playwriting and dramaturgy, who no longer need to see their roles as occurring before (or, conversely, after) the almighty text is completed. And the impetus for these newly praxis-based training models need not come solely from the academy. In recent years, the Pig Iron School, a collaboration between the Philadelphia-based University of the Arts and the Pig Iron Theatre Company, has awarded an MFA degree in Devised Performance, the first of its kind in the country.

The field is moving away from sole-authored, static, and linear perspectives and is embracing multi-linear, collaborative, and branching systems of storytelling that support experiential, multimodal, and multidisciplinary performance formats. As a result, educators need to shift too. Otherwise, we and our students will be left behind. Training programs must provide students with new collaborative models for crafting narratives. We also need to reconsider what a "successful graduate" looks like and reorient students, particularly playwrights and dramaturgs, to the myriad of job opportunities in the expanding discipline of experiential theatre.

In Section Two, *Narrative and Dramaturgy for Experiential Forms*, contributors offer tools for doing just that. Rejecting a binary between the individual authorship of a lone playwright and a collective creative that refuses to admit them, these authors share examples, models, and techniques that reshape our formulations and consider perspectives from far beyond the field of theatre as we commonly understand it. First, three Case Studies from scholars who also work as professional artists stake out new territory for theatre programs and professors to consider. In *Mapping Narrative in Pig Iron Theatre Company's* Pay Up *and* Franklin's Secret City, Robert Quillen Camp draws from two collaborations with Pig Iron, offering a map rather than a script as a central organizing document for collaborative performance making and theorizing how such a map might let us consider the perspectives of individual audience members. In *The Dramaturgy of Tabletop Roleplaying Games*, Mike Sell turns to TTRPGS such as *Dungeons and Dragons Call of Cthulhu,* arguing for their study as dramaturgical texts and their use as a practical classroom exercise for dramaturgs, playwrights, and other collaborators. Finally, Erin Mee's *Rasa in This Is Not A Theatre Company's Experiential Productions* explores how her ensemble's innovative, multi-sensory productions evoke the Sanskrit notion of *rasa* and use taste, touch, and smell to transform audience members into "partakers" of a different mode of experience.

Second, a roundtable of artists and educators situated in both university programs and professional organizations discusses the shifting landscapes for both contemporary performance and training programs. After considering how experiential performance might update our notions of authorship (and what those shifts might mean for playwrights, dramaturgs, and other theatre artists), they share hopes and ideas for how new technologies and systems might support innovative collaborative work.

Third, a Praxis section offers theatre educators exercises, tools, and examples from a wide range of experiential perspectives that they can deploy in the classroom in the short term. Sarah Johnson's *WildWind Performance Lab: New Play Development through Abstraction* outlines the unique process at WildWind where students create "abstract responses" to scripted plays in development and shares how the technique might be adapted in other programs and courses. Rachel Bauer's *It's Okay to NOT be "Right": Incorporating Creative Thinking into Theatrical Partnerships* uses theories of Creative Thinking to bridge the divide between practical and scholarly courses in many theatre programs and offers a model from team-based analysis and brainstorming that might replace dominant models of script study. Finally, Hans Vermy's *Creating Theatrical Immersion within Social Networks and Across Cyberspace* studies an Augmented Reality Game, *Arcana*, proposing a series of techniques for creating a sense of immersion in many digital modes of performance.

Taken together, these contributions offer a radical new way of thinking about playwriting and dramaturgy pedagogy and provide the beginning of a roadmap for those looking to incorporate experiential theatre practices in their classroom.

Reference

Nelson, Richard. 2007. "Thanks, but No Thanks: All This Help is Hurting Playwrights." In *The American Theatre Reader: Essays and Conversations from American Theatre Magazine*. 2009. New York: Theatre Communications Group.

13
Mapping Narrative in Pig Iron Theatre Company's *Pay Up* and *Franklin's Secret City*

Robert Quillen Camp

INTRODUCTION

I've created several works of performance with Pig Iron Theatre Company as the "playwright." What that means is not always clear, to audiences or collaborators, or to me, because Pig Iron creates work through its own bespoke devising process. Mostly it means sitting in the room and watching improvised performances and then going home and doing my own improvisation (*i.e.* writing) and then bringing the results back to the room. Then my improvisation is developed, revised, and extended by the performers. Meanwhile, I work on material that the performers have created that has been recorded and transcribed. Everything is iterated and iterated and iterated. Sometimes work that I've written makes it through more or less unchanged, and sometimes a performer's first pass on an improvisation has a fire that would only be dampened by revision. But usually, the material is *worked over*. By a bunch of people.

By *material* I'm referring to the spoken words, the movement, the stuff that happens moment-to-moment as we watch a performance. But of course, an equally significant part of making a performance is creating the overall structure, what we often think of as the *architecture* of the work. Interestingly, we often employ spatial metaphors when we try to think about the piece as a whole ("architecture"), as we attempt to flatten a temporal sequence into something that we can apprehend all at once. Architecture is difficult to improvise in the same moment-to-moment way that we use to create material, and usually gets developed in smaller groups in work sessions, in conversation, in written up and revised outlines, and spreadsheets, and diagrams, and maps. For the two experiential works that I'll be discussing here, *Pay Up* (2005–13) and *Franklin's Secret City* (2021), determining the architecture was especially involved because much of the way we interacted with the audience had to be developed along with the rest of the piece. In both cases, the physical environment of the performance was the starting point as well as the primary determinant of the final structure. In thinking through the ways in which we developed narratives for these performances, I'm especially interested in the ways we move back and forth between thinking in synchronous time with the performance and attempting to comprehend its "total" shape through abstraction. This kind of abstraction is similar to the traditional work of cartography, in which the lived experience and data collected from actual journeys (experienced and recorded in time) are assembled into a timeless projection, and I argue that the map might provide a useful alternative to the playscript as

120 DOI: 10.4324/9781003188179-16

the core organizing document of some kinds of experiential or immersive performance. I offer this idea of mapping because there is not necessarily a linear path on which audience members will travel, and because the experience of space is, from a phenomenological perspective, the ground of the audience's experience.

Pay Up

Described as a "simulated economic environment," *Pay Up* premiered in 2005 in a large white warehouse space as part of the Philly Fringe Festival. The basic idea is this: when you enter the space, we ask you to put on little booties (to protect the white floor) and we give you five dollars in cash to spend. Once inside the space, you're able to buy your way into individual scenes that take place at regular intervals inside individual cubicles. There are musical numbers offered for free in the center of the space at the midpoint and finale of the show. If you are shut out, or run out of money, there is a black market of scenes that happen outside of "authorized" locations, and little workplace dramas that you can see "behind the scenes." But not only can audience members see the individual cubicle scenes in any order, they are unable to see them all because there are only six opportunities to see eight scenes. This is by design, to draw attention to the psychological dimensions of consumer choices, inspired by the psychologist Barry Schwartz's (2003) book *The Paradox of Choice*, in which he argues that increased choice often leads to increased dissatisfaction.

The challenge presented by this structure is one well known to anyone designing a narrative experience within a non-linear context. How do you attempt to give your audience a satisfying (or, alternatively, interestingly *unsatisfying*) narrative experience while allowing it to unfold in any order, and with any number of pieces missing? The devising process itself, which tends to privilege the creation of short scenes that can remain in working memory as they are created, exacerbates the tendency to create scenes that don't build on one another in the interest of an integrated whole, and which, in the circumstances of a traditional performance, must be constantly revised with the architecture in mind. But here there is no way to follow Freytag's pyramid of rising and falling action, or any other structure that makes specific demands on the contents of the scenes. So how did we proceed to organize the material that we created? We started with the map (Figure 13.1).

David Mitchell (2018) describes the role that mapmaking plays in creating works of fiction in his essay "Imaginary Cartography":

> While none of the novels I've published as a writer contain maps, my notebooks are littered with them. Scenes (or suites of scenes) need spaces to happen in. What those spaces look like, and what is in them, can determine how the action unfolds. They can even give you ideas for what unfolds. This is why mapmaking and stage-sketching can be necessary aspects of writing. (120)

We can imagine that this principle might apply to playwriting as well, except that playwrights have two potential sources of spatial inspiration: the fictive world of, say, Grover's Corners, or the stage itself, which might afford its own potential (e.g., ladders as scenery). A playwright might oscillate between these two spatial imaginaries, or they might integrate them into a conceptual map in which one is laid over the other, an imagined living room with a missing fourth wall.

By the time we were devising the scenes that made up *Pay Up*, Anna Kiraly's set was already mostly in place. A warren of white rooms in a white warehouse with geometric shapes superimposed in stark black lines evoking packaging. In each of the rooms we hung about fifteen pairs of headphones from pegs on the wall. In performance, these were worn

PAY UP MAP

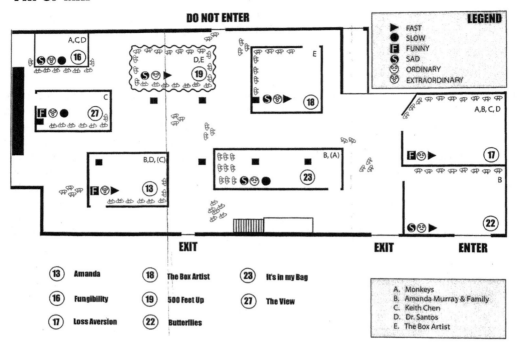

Figure 13.1 The map from the original 2005 production of *Pay Up*.

by audience members who would listen to the prerecorded audio of the scene as they watched actors wearing white jumpsuits perform in a style reminiscent of corporate demonstration videos. As we created the scenes that would fill these rooms, we thought about how participants would navigate the space and make decisions on what scenes to purchase—how much information would feel like enough to support a particular choice? We decided to give participants a map to the space on entry and create three sets of binary descriptors for scenes: whether they were funny or sad, ordinary or extraordinary, and whether they took place during day or night. We had eight rooms, and by providing one scene for each possible descriptor (*e.g.* funny, night, ordinary)[1] we would generate eight scenes (2 × 2 × 2 = 8). Each room on the map would have an icon for each of the descriptors, and audience members could use them as information to help them make decisions.

The philosopher Michel de Certeau (1984) contrasts the abstraction of the map with the lived experience of the story. "What the map cuts up," he writes, "the story cuts across" (129). Using the metaphor of a theatre, he argues that maps reify a hegemonic system of knowledge, pushing the work that formed the basis of that knowledge (i.e., people moving through the world) into the wings, along with any sense of the map's historical contingency. "It remains alone on the stage," he writes (121). By making space legible, maps instantiate a discourse of limited possibility and propriety, whereas stories create new possibilities in the spaces that they traverse. In other words, de Certeau's critique relies on the ways in which maps present themselves as *complete*, with the authority that follows therefrom.[2]

Interestingly, though, it is the *incompleteness* of the map that often attracts the writer. This impulse can be seen clearly in European writers who wrote narratives of the lands that were being assimilated into the European cartographic system during the period of European colonization. The empty spaces on the maps that appealed to nineteenth-century explorers like Henry Morton Stanley (whose cartographic legacy laid the immediate groundwork for Leopold II's brutal and disastrous colonization of the Congo)[3] also appealed to writers like Joseph Conrad, whose Marlow (1899) describes being inspired by the "blank spaces" of the map (197) just as Conrad (1926) later described his own boyhood obsession with the "exciting spaces of white paper" on nineteenth-century maps (13). In the colonial context, it's easy to see how cartography can authorize hegemonic discourse in the guise of scientific neutrality. And the urge to enter the mysterious, incomplete area of the map, the urge to escape the known, is ironically sometimes accompanied by a desire to finish the jigsaw puzzle, chart the blank spaces, eliminate mystery, or exert control. But every map is necessarily incomplete (being an abstraction) and out-of-date (being a record of the moment in time in which they were created). This incompleteness opens the space for both first-person adventure as well as third-person narrative. In a performance like *Pay Up*, in which each audience member is a protagonist exploring a fabricated world, adventure and narrative coincide. Or perhaps another way to put it is to say that the audience member's adventure takes the place of the narrative. The audience member's exploration of a fictional world is not itself a fiction.

For us, as artists, the map was an essential tool to understand the space we were creating, part of our exploration of the possibilities for the piece. But the map that we gave to the audience was also a signifier in the fictional world of the play—a representation of the *official* version of *Pay Up*. We did not place the black-market scenes on the audience map, for example. If some maps can serve to totalize, abstract, and favor the hegemonic panoptic vision that de Certeau contrasts with the lived experience of the pedestrian, our maps were self-consciously official representations, intentionally mysterious in terms of the content of the scenes aside from the descriptors, and not reflective of all of the possible paths that audience members might take through the space. Our hope was to create something interesting enough that it would propel audience members into the space without making them feel constrained by the map.

The individual scenes were all about financial transactions, especially about the social discomfort surrounding cash exchanges, and many of them had to do with real-life economist Keith Chen's efforts to get capuchin monkeys to use currency and observe their behavior. "Loss Aversion" (*Funny, Ordinary, Day*) dramatizes an experiment in which a monkey prefers a gamble in which there is a possible gain over one in which there is a possible loss, even though the statistical outcome is the same (in this, the monkey is like a human being). In "Fungibility" (*Funny, Extraordinary, Day*) audience members look through glass into a small room, as if they are researchers watching an experiment. In the scene, based on a real-life event in Chen's lab (Dubner and Levitt 2005), a monkey recognizes that money can have more than one purpose (in other words, that it is *fungible*, a key determinant of a currency) and promptly pays another monkey for sex. At the halfway point, the rules of the scene change, and the actors previously portraying the monkeys now become the researchers as they too allow their own interests to push against the confines of the experimental setting. Other scenes follow these characters in different situations (which characters appear in which scenes are also trackable on the map), but each scene is designed to be a satisfying vignette on its own, and the scenes are not plucked from a temporal sequence. We attempted to create a sense of a larger world, but not a timeline for audience members to try to reconstruct as excerpts from a temporal sequence. While each scene has its own structure, they do not participate in a larger narrative arc.

But *Pay Up* as a whole *does* have an arc, created by the structural elements (temporal and physical) that surround the scenes. When you first enter the space, you are allowed to enter

124 • ROBERT QUILLEN CAMP

and explore the warehouse on your own as white noise plays through the speakers, though you cannot enter the individual rooms. Eventually, an affectless voice echoes through the space: "*Welcome to Pay Up. Pay Up is an artificially controlled economic environment. You will have six opportunities to purchase a scene. There are eight scenes to choose from. Pause. Six opportunities. Eight scenes. You will not be able to see everything.*" In a moment that recalls flight attendants giving preflight instructions, actors standing on large white buckets demonstrate how to wear the headphones as the voice continues speaking. This is the tutorial phase of the performance, in which the rules are gradually introduced, and audience members begin to explore what agency has been afforded to them. "*Thank you,*" the voice over the loudspeaker continues, "*you have fifty-three minutes left to pay up.*" A loud buzzer sounds, followed by the sound of ticking, and the video monitors hung throughout the space begin counting down the time remaining in the performance.

After three opportunities to purchase scenes, the voice instructs the audience to assemble in the middle of the warehouse for the first of three complimentary song and dance numbers—a lament of consumer regret, ending with the line "*I feel so ba-a-d.*" After the song is over, the voice over the loudspeaker responds, "*Don't feel so bad. Don't feel so bad.*" After a pause, she continues, "*This audience has been crowding the funny scenes. I don't want to do this, but this audience is forcing my hand. The funny scenes are now two dollars. The sad scenes are good too, in their own way. All the scenes have something to offer. Please consider giving your time to scenes that might have been overlooked or misunderstood. Pause. Don't be afraid to spend your money. All money is the same. Pause. Opportunity Four will begin in 30 seconds.*" At this point in the show, the price increase raises the stakes and rising action begins to appear in the rhythm of the audience member's personal adventure, even as the scenes remain the same.

After two more opportunities to purchase scenes (or explore the off-map world of the black-market scenes and scripted "backstage" moments with the staff), the full cast of thirty actors assembles for a crowd-pleasing musical-style dance number with intricate choreography and tap routines. In the context of having to purchase your way through the play, this moment feels like a gift—a relief of tension. There is one more scene-purchasing opportunity (in which all scenes are offered on a sliding scale), and a final, mournful wordless dirge derived from the second movement of Beethoven's seventh symphony in which all the cash is pooled together and ritually carried aloft in a procession through the space. During the procession, the voice over the loudspeaker informs the audience of what they missed by attending *Pay Up*:

You could have been somewhere else.
You could have spent your money in a different way.

    Pause.

You missed the 303rd performance of Spring Awakening at the Eugene O'Neill Theatre on Broadway. Orchestra seats, $112.

    Pause.

If you stayed home, you could be meeting verified local singles now at Montclair Singles Dot Com.

    Pause.

You could have gone ice skating at the Floyd Arena, four dollars for students, seven dollars for everyone else.

    Pause.

Please remain on the blue lines ....

You could have watched The L Word on Showtime. (Tasha and Alice broke up again. Molly and Shane got back together.)

Long Pause.

*You could have spent your time somewhere else.
Now, it's gone.*

A buzzer sounds, the music ends, and the clocks reach zero all at precisely the same moment. Audience members file out past "employees" being frisked for cash. The show is over. The moment of possible anagnorisis is for the audience member, if they recognize that they have not only spent money, they have also—permanently and irrevocably—spent *time*.[4] The course of the audience's adventure—their path through the map—passes through these fixed points that give a shape to their whole experience. Though the individual scenes have their own shape, and though their subject matter—cash transactions as moments that can illuminate otherwise shadowed aspects of human relationships—mirrors the concept of the whole, from the perspective of the architecture they are interchangeable widgets. When we remounted *Pay Up* in 2008 and 2013, we replaced certain scenes (like replacing rides at an amusement park) without having to make any changes to the architecture.

Thinking about the relationship between narrative and experiential theatre, it's difficult to escape a comparison to video games, a form in which artists have long had to navigate the relationship between linear story (one in which the player is often cast as a character) and player agency. In many modern large-budget single-player role-playing games, the choices players make throughout their adventure impact the ending they get. *The Witcher 3 (2015)*, for example, has 36 different endings. Though in many cases the overarching plot of the game is only *so* responsive to player choice. The player's real agency is typically found more in how they engage in the basic game mechanics (fighting an enemy, for example). This kind of agency is subtle and intricate—it is often, though not always, embodied in the virtual world. It still does not always sit entirely comfortably with the kind of agency that affects the plot.[5] Theatre-based experiences typically have the added constraint of being multi-player, making it difficult to tailor the experience to the audience's choices, unless they are treated as collective making choices through votes, as in Aya Ogawa's *Ludic Proxy* (2015).[6] As a result, structures that allow for some exploration (especially spatial exploration) and individuated experience but bring audience members together for shared moments that drive the "arc," are not uncommon in immersive theatre. These shared moments often act like video game cutscenes, in which player agency is suspended. *Pay Up* follows this structure, though agency is suspended while you are actually watching the individual scenes as well. Ultimately, the agency of the player is low, except insofar as the player has made the original choice to see the play, the real choice that is thematized and transformed throughout the performance and finally revealed to have a slightly tragic dimension, but only because of the weight of the real-life choice the audience member has made ("*You could have spent your time in a different way. Now it's gone.*").

Franklin's Secret City

During the COVID-19 pandemic, Pig Iron co-Artistic Director Dan Rothenberg and I conceived a smartphone-based audio piece that participants could experience in pairs outdoors. Based on the world of an unproduced play that we had been commissioned to write about a fictional secret society dedicated to preserving Benjamin Franklin's technological discoveries that bordered on magic, *Franklin's Secret City* (2021) was designed to be a mix of collaborative puzzle-solving, audio narrative, and exploration. Sited on the grounds of the American Philosophical Society (founded by Franklin in 1743), the experience usually takes about forty-five minutes to an hour to complete. An open beta release of the app, freely available to download and experience in Old City, Philadelphia, was offered to the public from May through September of 2021.

The basic structure of the gameplay of *Franklin's Secret City* is inspired by games like *Spaceteam* (2012) and *Keep Talking and Nobody Explodes* (2015), in which information is distributed to players asymmetrically, and they must collaborate to move forward. In *Franklin's Secret City*, we assign one player to operate the scanner, a device not unlike a *Star Trek* tricorder, and the other player to operate the communicator, a device that can receive aural and visual messages from headquarters, as well as access society-owned computers. Players must solve puzzles in an old computer using information from the environment to move forward. The phones communicate with one another through an internet server, so they stay in sync, and we use Bluetooth beacons to track the location of the players (Figure 13.2).

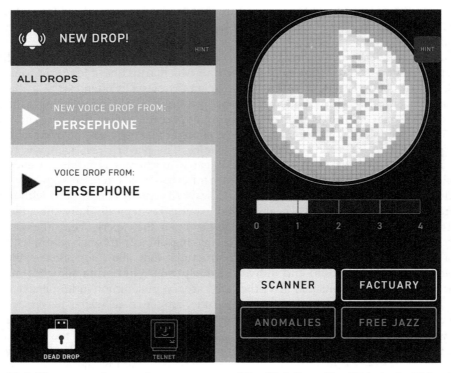

Figure 13.2 The communicator and scanner screens of *Franklin's Secret City*. UI design by Yichan Wang.

The narrative is about a member of the secret society (the New Prometheans) who has gone missing—possibly into another dimension. Using the scanner and the communicator, players go from station to station, learning more about the "secret city" in which Kenneth Moonstone, the missing scientist, is trapped. In addition to Moonstone, voiced by Johnnie Hobbs III, players hear the voices of their New Promethean guide, Persephone Poledouris, voiced by Izzy Sazak, and the scanner's AI, Diane, voiced by Grace McLean. Our goal was to create an experience in which the physical world becomes a place of technology, enchantment, and magic, one in which headphones unlock a hidden aural universe.

Part of our challenge making this piece was to develop a way of working in a game engine that made sense for a theatre company new to software development. Our lead developer, Lisa Szolovits—a theatre director herself—created a game architecture that functioned not unlike QLab, the ubiquitous show control software. We were able to imagine what we called a "robot stage manager," really a block of code, that could survey the state of the game and press go on the next cue based on whatever input it was looking for (the player moving to the right location, for example). Having a developer with a theater background on the team enabled us to communicate well and iterate fairly quickly.

Although the path we expect players to travel is fairly linear (at least in the beta version), the delivery of the narrative is complicated by the fact that both players hear entirely different things. This asymmetry not only calls to mind the games cited above but also performance pieces like Rotozaza's *Etiquette* (2005), in which pairs of audience members hear different coordinated sounds. So, once again, we were using a map as our primary way of understanding the piece. Unlike the map in *Pay Up,* though, this map is not given to the audience. Instead, the scanner registers when participants have moved to the next location and trigger the next sequence. Working around the building of the American Philosophical Society Library, we identified eight key locations that we knew we wanted our participants to visit and developed a sequence of events that would take them through the path, though there is room for participants to diverge, especially since some of the puzzles are solved through exploration.

We became especially concerned with modes of attention—as you become aware that you will have to accomplish something, even something simple, your quality of attention shifts. You want to know exactly what your power is—in video game terms, what affordances are available to you. But even more crucially, you begin to filter the information you are getting with an eye toward what will be useful to you. Moments of narrative that we might enjoy in another context can sometimes feel like an impediment to our fun. As theater makers, we are used to (a) providing narrative content and (b) tracking audience attention. But we quickly found that our instincts to make sure that people weren't bored were misplaced. We realized we were bombarding people with too much all at once, and we needed to reduce the verbiage and create what we called spaciousness—a feeling of being allowed to process, think, and explore.

We were able to recognize and respond to the audience experience because we incorporated a key element of video game development into our workflow: play-testing. We spent weeks with pairs of volunteers testing the experience and giving their feedback. We were also able to watch participants move through the experience and begin to understand which parts of the piece created too much frustration, which might be too linear, and which provoked the most joy. The play-testing component is *crucial* for experiential performances that allow audiences to explore at their own pace—to take the map and run with it—because every time you create an unconventional experience, you will make new discoveries based on watching how the audience engages. It was through this kind of play-testing that we were able to realize how important the participant's somatic engagement—their awareness of their bodies in space—was to their enjoyment of the piece.

Working with a map reminds us that we are working with space as much as we are working with time. In *Pay Up,* that was a manufactured space, while in *Franklin's Secret City* it was part of the urban landscape (albeit a highly curated and crafted space, most of it under the purview of the National Park Service). We wanted not only to take our own inspiration from the map as artists, but also to create something like that feeling of excitement in our audience members, a desire to seek out the stories of these places—stories that fill out the empty spaces of the map, or even stories that work against the logic of the map, that undermine its assumptions, that reopen the world as something finally unmappable, or rather, something that we all map and re-map as we go along.

128 • ROBERT QUILLEN CAMP

The phenomenologist David Morris (2004) argues that the *moving* body is the source not only of spatial perception but of perception more generally. Basing his analysis on Merleau-Ponty's conception of perception arising out of an interaction between body and world, Morris wants to remind us that our abstracted, geometric, topological sense of space (*e.g.* that which is represented in maps) is a consequence of our original encounter with space, as a moving body, not the other way around. An experiential performance tends to be one in which the audience's sense of space is particularly engaged, a source of context as well as meaning. I find it instructive, however, to remember the *wildness* of the spatial encounter—when we see audience members move through one of these pieces we can directly, physically, witness how variegated their experiences are, a diversity that is sometimes easy to overlook in a traditional performance, where we often consider audience responses as collective reactions. Here, we can more easily let go of the idea that there ever could be an ideal audience member (often one like ourselves) and be humbled by the knowledge that every participant's journey will deviate from the map.

Notes

1 The descriptors in the 2005 production were funny/sad, ordinary/extraordinary, and fast/slow. In the revisions that we made for later productions, fast/slow was replaced with day/night.
2 This critique is reminiscent of Derrida's critique of the book as an "idea of a totality ... of the signifier ... the encyclopedic protection of theology and of logocentrism against the disruption of writing." (Derrida 1998, 18) To extend the comparison: if, for Derrida, writing is a disruption that is contained by the book, could there be a kind of *mapping*, as a gerund, that performs a similar disruption that is finally contained by the map? This idea is probably best expressed by de Certeau as spatial practice, in which the pedestrian enunciates and appropriates the topographical system. See de Certeau, 97–99.
3 Stanley prefaces his account of his attempt to map the Congo River with a sequence of maps showing the increasing penetration of cartography into the continental interior, concluding with his own highly detailed map. (Stanley 1878, 1:2).
4 In a previous essay, I consider the tragic dimensions of the spectator's loss of time in *Pay Up* and provide a more detailed account of the performance (Camp 2014).
5 Brenda Laurel, for example, makes the argument that for player agency to be meaningful, it must impact the plot. (Laurel 2006, 19) This is not as simple as it sounds, for a few reasons. First, stories often recount what we might think of as the most interesting version of events. It's difficult to establish a set of story branches that are equally interesting. Second, frequently part of the force of narrative stems from its inevitability. The tragic impact of *The Oresteia* comes in part from an awareness that it could not be otherwise. Most importantly, though, is the relationship between plot and character ("What is character but the determination of incident? What is incident but the illustration of character?" (James 1884)) If we understand characters through their choices when their choices aren't fixed they themselves become vague, which may be useful to the extent that the player identifies with their avatar, but can also diminish their specificity and impact.
6 The 2021 version of *Ludic Proxy*'s second act, reimagined for Zoom, used Zoom's poll feature to survey the audience and move the plot forward.

References

Camp, Robert Quillen. 2014. "The Tragic Spectator." *Comparative Drama* 48 (1): 117–134.
Certeau, Michel de. 1984. *The Practice of Everyday Life*. Berkeley: University of California Press.
Conrad, Joseph. 1899. "Heart of Darkness." *Blackwood's Edinburgh Magazine* 165 (1000): 193–220.
Conrad, Joseph. 1926. "Geography and Some Explorers." In *Last Essays*. Garden City, NY: Doubleday, Page & Company.
Derrida, Jacques. 1998. *Of Grammatology*. Baltimore, MD: Johns Hopkins.
Dubner, Stephen J., and Steven D. Levitt. 2005. "Monkey Business." *The New York Times*, June 5, 2005.
James, Henry. 1884. "The Art of Fiction." *Longman's Magazine*, no. 4: 49–85.

Laurel, Brenda. 2006. "Response to Michael Mateas." In *First Person: New Media as Story, Performance, and Game*. Edited by Noah Wardrip-Fruin and Pat Harrigan, 19–22. Cambridge, MA: The MIT Press.

Mitchell, David. 2018. "Imaginary Cartography." In *The Writer's Map*. Edited by Huw Lewis-Jones, 118–125. Chicago: University of Chicago Press.

Morris, David. 2004. *The Sense of Space*. Albany, NY: State University of New York Press.

Schwartz, Barry. 2003. *The Paradox of Choice: Why More Is Less*. New York: HarperCollins.

Stanley, Henry Morton. 1878. *Through the Dark Continent: Or, The Sources of the Nile Around the Great Lakes of Equatorial Africa, and Down the Livingstone River to the Atlantic Ocean*. Vol. 1. 2 vols. London: Sampson Low, Marston, Searle & Rivington.

14
The Dramaturgy of Tabletop Roleplaying Games

Mike Sell

INTRODUCTION

Picture a world where millions of people gather every week in kitchens, hobby stores, and Zoom rooms to pretend they're someone else doing extraordinarily dramatic things in imaginary worlds. Picture them pretending to be wizards plumbing creep-infested caverns, teenage monsters thirsty for love but inevitably finding trouble, indigenous communities struggling to survive first contact with the European empire, or, well, just about anything one might imagine, as long as it's dramatic and fun. A world with so much theatre would be a kind of paradise for the dramaturg, wouldn't it?[1]

A dramaturg might sit down at the table and join the fun to promote excellence of production and performance ("I loved that moment of sharing between you two!"), highlight troubling issues ("Is anyone else uncomfortable with this kind of violence?"), and help everyone feel safe and acknowledged. They might join the community of creators, working for one of the big publishers, or consult with independent writers to offer expert advice ("We should develop the villain's motivation," "This is a stereotype"), promote diversity in content and community, and amplify new or marginalized voices. They might turn their talents towards scholarship and criticism, investigating the historical, cultural, and formal dimensions of the medium, its creators, and its enthusiasts. The best part? That world is real.

The tabletop roleplaying game (or TTRPG) is arguably the most popular theatrical form in history. The oldest and best-known, *Dungeons & Dragons*, counted more than 10 million players in 2020, many of them playing two or more times a week, with participant numbers exploding during COVID lockdown.[2] There are scores of other TTRPGs, whether enduring properties like *Call of Cthulhu* (set in the milieu of Lovecraftian "cosmic horror") and *Vampire: The Masquerade* (goth-punk vampires) or "indies" like *BLOOD & hormones* ("a cadre of trans punks trying desperately to survive in a cyberpunk future that wants them dead"), *Wait for Me* (a twenty-one-day solo journaling game "about time travel and connection"), or *Dog Eat Dog* ("a game of imperialism and assimilation on the Pacific Islands"). Those who play often create, as well, whether crafting bespoke rules and adventures for their own groups or selling their wares on direct-to-consumer websites like *DmsGuild* and *DriveThruRPG*. TTRPGs are popular to watch, too, evidenced by the hundreds of actual-play webcasts and podcasts available on YouTube and Twitch. The most popular, *Critical Role*, counts 750,000 social-media followers, as many as 116,000 live viewers, and over 24 million

130

DOI: 10.4324/9781003188179-17

THE DRAMATURGY OF TABLETOP ROLEPLAYING GAMES • 131

total views for their weekly performances (TwitchTracker). Though intended primarily for entertainment, TTRPGs are also used to facilitate group therapy, teach people to write, and encourage the neurodivergent to explore social and professional skills. Yet theatre and performance scholars have mostly ignored the tabletop roleplaying game.

Among those approaching TTRPGS as a dramaturgical practice are Todd Brian Backus, Percy Hornak, and Nicholas Orvis, who explore a range of topics in their *Dungeons + Drama Nerds* podcast, including intimacy choreography, the similarities between devised theatre and TTRPGs, the player as both performer and audience, and so on. In a similar vein, Michael Chemers and I explore the dramaturgical dimensions of roleplaying games in our book *Systemic Dramaturgy: A Handbook for the Digital Age*, demonstrating that an expanded conception of theatrical play affords formal, critical, and ethical traction on the TTRPG as a performance form. Finally, *The International Journal of Role-Playing* regularly publishes articles that are pertinent to the TTRPG dramaturg, though to date none are explicitly designated as such. While underdeveloped, these initial forays into the field have established a dynamic synergy among theoretical, critical, and practical work, a synergy that is fundamental to dramaturgy and that I will attempt to sustain in what follows.

What is a tabletop roleplaying game? Broadly speaking, the TTRPG tasks its players with collaboratively improvising a dramatic narrative according to a set of rules. Play is primarily verbal, though verbal performance varies widely. Players might talk in character at one moment ("Malanthion, your decision to negotiate with the Bloodpack Coalition moots our contract!"), about their character at another ("Dagmar turns her back on Malanthion and winks at the rest of the group"), discuss rules ("Shouldn't this be an Intimidation check rather than a Persuasion check?"), do a bit of worldbuilding ("As you turn, a cold wind begins to blow outside"), or chat about family or work. Play involves material stuff, too: rule books, paper and pencils, cards, dice, small figurines representing characters, maps, props such as letters or newspaper articles, and, almost always, food and drink. Often, the proceedings are led by a game manager (or GM), who functions as primary storyteller and referee. They would be the one who performs Malanthion's response to Dagmar, decides the appropriate ruling on whether Malanthion was intimidated or persuaded, and describes that cold wind. They'd also know who's waiting outside the door and why the fuel tanks of our heroes' sky-cycles are empty.

The argument for incorporating TTRPGs into theatre training would seem obvious, given the medium's popularity and the personal and professional opportunities they afford. As Chemers and I argue in *Systemic Dramaturgy*, the skills and perspectives of the dramaturg are useful for both producers and audiences of interactive media. On a personal level, knowledge of dramaturgical theory and practice enables players to be more attentive to the dynamic relationship among the textual, procedural, and narrative elements of TTRPGs, as well as to the complexities of their performance (more on all of this below). Professional opportunities are plentiful. The tabletop roleplaying game is in something of a golden age these days, the consequence of "increased legitimacy of the hobby in general, new audiences reaching games through streaming and podcasts, and an exploding variety of types and titles of games," all of this buoyed by a widespread (if by no means ubiquitous) desire among players and creators to increase diversity of form and community (Marks). Though as Aaron Marks has noted, reliable data about the TTRPG industry are difficult to find, it is undeniable that both traditional publishers like Wizards of the Coast (publishers of *Dungeons & Dragons*), Chaosium (*Call of Cthulhu* and *Runequest*), and Paizo (*Pathfinder* and *Starfinder*); secondary retailers like hobby stores and Amazon; and direct creator-to-consumer websites like *DM's Guild* and *DriveThruRPG* are doing quite well, driving "a high eight-figure business" (Marks). I, for one, teach TTRPG design and analysis and play in several groups as GM or player. I also sell rules supplements and adventure scenarios for two different TTRPG systems on two direct-to-consumer websites and provide consultation and editorial advice to creators. I've yet to dip my toes into the field of professional game managing, but there is good money, experience, and community to find there. And those with TTRPG design and performance experience have transferable skills of value to other interactive media, notably videogames and the rapidly growing field gameful learning design, with companies like Classcraft and Game to Grow among those focusing specifically on roleplaying games as a pedagogical framework.

But TTRPGs offer benefits to those with more conventional objectives, too. They provide fun, low-to-no-cost opportunities to engage in the traditional tasks of dramaturgy: analyzing the performance text to clarify its aesthetic and ideological architecture; working out what it takes to stage the text successfully; identifying where the text speaks most powerfully or problematically to the audience. These tasks are productively applied to the narrative scenarios GMs often use when running a roleplaying session: licensed texts published by the game's publishers or those written by independent writers and distributed on websites like *DM's Guild* or *DriveThruRpg*.

Though their format differs from game to game, they all describe a dramatic situation that involves the player-characters (or PCs), the locations in which that situation unfolds, descriptions of non-player-characters (or NPCs), and other narrative elements not covered by the game's rulebooks. TTRPG scenarios are comparable to a theatrical script in many respects. They are printed texts, inviting imagination, annotation, and critique. They are dramatically shapely narratives. They are open works, inviting creative interpretation. And they are performative texts, lifeless until infused by the imagination, energy, and emotions of performers. The tabletop roleplaying game also poses unique challenges. The audience for a TTRPG is the players themselves. TTRPGs are never rehearsed. The first moment players encounter the text is the first moment they perform it. Play is improvisatory. The question a GM most often asks is, "What do you do?" and players expect their choices to matter. Playing a TTRPG is an intensely social process, so dramaturgy necessarily encompasses the personalities and relationships of those at the table. Finally, a tabletop roleplaying game is a *game*. Performance is governed by rules: the rules of the TTRPG, the rules of the scenario, and the unwritten social rules of the group of players.

In these respects, TTRPG dramaturgy is usefully compared to devised theatre, since the whole group "must work to find the answers to the problems they have set themselves," as Chris Baldwin (2002) describes that form of dramaturgy (13). Because it is a social activity, it also shares with what Zoë Svendsen (2017) calls the "dramaturgy of spontaneity," a process in which listening, reciprocity, and spontaneity play a key role, but "habit, genre expectations, and a shared language of improvisational techniques all feature as the building blocks of potentiality in the creative present, whether or not they are acknowledged as such" (298). And because TTRPGs are games, TTRPG dramaturgy benefits from knowledge of game design, since both the rules of the TTRPG and the scenario structure player performance and interaction.

Not every tabletop roleplaying game requires a printed narrative scenario, a GM, or even other players. However, preparing a TTRPG scenario as a GM for a group of players affords a fruitful opportunity for practicing dramaturgical skills. What I will describe here are three dimensions of TTRPG dramaturgy: basic preparatory work, addressing structural flaws, and ensuring safety and fun. While these don't exhaust the pedagogical possibilities of the tabletop roleplaying game (there is significant learning to be found in the modification and design of TTRPGs or the performance of them for live or recorded audiences), they are fundamental and useful for the educator to consider.

The example text I will use is "The Haunting," an officially licensed product for *Call of Cthulhu* (or CoC). CoC was first published by Chaosium in 1981 and is now in its seventh edition. As the name suggests, the game is set in the storyworld of H.P. Lovecraft, the American writer of cosmic horror and weird fiction. In Lovecraft's stories—and in the works of those inspired by him like Stephen King, Victor LaValle, Silvia Moreno-Garcia, and Guillermo del Toro—the protagonists encounter inhuman entities and uncanny places that bespeak a reality the human mind and heart cannot abide. Unlike the heroes of *Dungeons & Dragons*, the CoC protagonists are acutely vulnerable. Their bodies are easily hurt and their minds bruised by the cosmic horrors that await them.

CoC is an excellent TTRPG for the developing dramaturg. CoC requires the GM to foster an atmosphere of mystery, dread, and horror—the theatrically inclined will find this great fun. Additionally, CoC possesses a particularly problematic mechanic involving trauma, mental illness, and madness, issues that any responsible dramaturg should approach with care. While players should always establish content preferences any time they play, this rule provides a fruitful opportunity to establish a particular group's dramaturgy of spontaneity. The basic rules of CoC and "The Haunting" are provided free by the publisher and can be found online, so the only costs are time, a table, some printouts, and energy. Finally, "The Haunting" is a simple, at times unimaginative text, inviting the GM to dramaturgically punch it up to increase the fun. And it's a flawed text in terms of its narrative structure and setting—flaws requiring some attention. In sum, it is a text that benefits from an active, imaginative, and sensitive dramaturgical hand.

BASIC PREPARATION

The work of TTRPG dramaturgy begins the same way traditional page-to-stage dramaturgy begins: reading and re-reading to ensure comprehensive understanding of the dramatic structure, conflicts, and themes. The TTRPG scenario typically starts with a brief description of the narrative premise, the objective of the player-characters (PCs), and a sketch of the overall plot. Next comes more detailed information about locations, non-player characters (NPCs), significant events, and other elements the GM needs to run it. Scenarios inevitably contain more information than will be needed during play. For example, there may be a description of an abandoned village occupied by a dragon, but the players decide their characters will not visit that location. On the flip side, scenarios always have less information than is needed; concision is valued and it is assumed the GM will improvise as needed. For example, the players might decide their characters enter a corner bodega to get a snack and directions, requiring the GM to improvise details about the place and the NPCs therein. (One of the perennial challenges of the GM is coming up with names for improvised NPCs.)

In "The Haunting," the premise is that a vampiric wizard with psychic powers has secreted himself in a house, and the owner of said house, who knows there's something supernatural afoot, hires the PCs to take care of the problem. Like most CoC scenarios, the narrative structure of "The Haunting" is divided into two phases. The first requires PCs to gather information about the supernatural problem. They might dig into archives, interview witnesses, or explore related locations to get a sense of the threat they're facing. The second phase requires the PCs to enter the house where the supernatural antagonist dwells and do something about it.

Like many scenarios, the dramatic structure of "The Haunting" is organized not in terms of events, but space. In many respects, the setting is the drama. Ninety percent of "The Haunting" is location descriptions: where the investigators meet their employer, where they acquire information (the *Boston Globe*'s clipping files, the sanitarium in which a recent victim has been committed, a ruined church, etc.), and the house itself. Most locations are described in general terms, if at all, suggesting these be played quickly, details

134 • MIKE SELL

improvised as needed. Sites of greater significance are written in more detail, those at the house in particular. That location is subdivided into fourteen rooms, each named and described (e.g., "This is the dining room, complete with a mahogany table, a built-in sideboard, and seven chairs. Three places are set and unused. Scraps of rice soup rot in a tureen" [22]). Those more verbose descriptions can be read to the players or used as the basis for improvisation. For example, to increase atmosphere and suspense, the GM might describe only the furniture and the unpleasant odor, improvising details as the PCs poke around ("On the far end of the table, there's a tureen decorated in a pattern of blue and white clouds"), then revealing the gruesomeness when a PC gets close ("You peer inside and see maggots writhing in an ashen clod of rotten rice"). Some rooms have additional information regarding game rules. The entrance to the basement, for example, has a perilous set of stairs and a magical knife that can cause harm to the investigators; the scenario describes the rules governing those and provides advice on how to make them work to optimal dramatic effect.

If the level of sensory description varies, the description of what might *happen* in each location is consistent. In TTRPGs, drama is generated in three ways: between PCs, between PCs and NPCs, and between PCs and the environment. Regardless of who or what is involved, drama is a mixture of verbal performance and following the rules and mechanics of the game. For example, in "The Haunting," one of the places where the investigators can acquire information is the clipping files of the *Boston Globe* newspaper. The scenario stipulates that the files are overseen by a curmudgeon who has no interest in helping the PCs. To get him to help, players need to verbally perform their PCs' dialogue with Arty, and neither the players nor the GM know in advance where that dialogue will go. The GM and the players decide whether their approach to Arty is best interpreted as an attempt to Charm, Persuade, Intimidate, or Fast Talk him, these interpersonal skills are determined by a numerical value and, thus, a specific chance to succeed or fail. The GM and players bring those rules and their consequences to life. A GM might say, "Sorry, you failed your Persuasion check, so Arty won't help you." A more entertaining GM might say, "Arty looks you up and down, then turns, sits down at his desk, and relights his cigar. You hear him mutter something about officious dilettantes."

This leads to one of the key challenges of TTRPG dramaturgy and a signal opportunity for the student of dramaturgy. TTRPGs are governed by the principle of "Yes, and...," and it is the GM's responsibility to make player choices matter. For this reason, a GM must prepare for the unexpected. A recent session I ran of "The Haunting" illustrates this well. Having arrived at the house and poked around a bit, a player announced that his character had discovered a cryptic sign inscribed on the foundation. He then showed us a drawing he'd made of it. There was no such sign described in the scenario's text. I held my tongue, interested in where the player was going. He explained that he had seen this sign on a trip he had recently taken to Dunluce Castle in Ireland as part of an investigation into the occult activities of the rock band Led Zeppelin (I had modified the scenario so it took place in the 1970s). The player had not informed me of this previously. Another player asked to see the drawing, then shrieked in horror (and in character!) and informed us her PC was fleeing to the backyard. I had no idea why. A third player told us their PC was following the second, concerned for her safety. A fourth player, to this point silent, then spoke in character to the first PC, telling them they had seen the same symbol while exploring case files at the Los Angeles Police Department. There had been no such symbol. I knew this because I was the one who created those files.

Moments like these require a different kind of dramaturgy, what might be called "improvisatory dramaturgy." The choices the players were making implicated not just the unfolding narrative, but the world in which the story took place, the backstory of two PCs, and, most importantly, the evolving dynamic of a group of players who had never played together before. The moment demanded thoughtful but bold dramaturgical improvisation. I needed a moment to think, so I sent a private message to the first two players (we were playing on Zoom), directing them to get their two stories in order. I made a note to myself to change a detail of the house map. By coincidence, the scenario stipulated that there actually *was* an occult sigil on the foundations, though it had not been discovered by the players. With a stroke of the pen, that sigil was now the same one the player had invented. I then turned my attention to the two PCs in the backyard. After describing the yard, I asked them to explain what was happening. Speaking in character and sobbing uncontrollably (heck of a roleplayer, that one!), she told the story of her mother's murder and the sign carved into her flesh—the very sign the first character had shown her. This, too, was invented on the spot. It was time for another bit of dramaturgical improvisation.

One of the scares I had added to the house to increase drama and atmosphere involved a framed photograph that had fallen to the floor, waiting for a PC to pick it up and discover a supernatural vision involving a friend or relative from their backstory. While preparing for this session, I had written brief, individualized descriptions of the photograph for each of the PCs. Why each PC? I couldn't predict who would pick it up, so had to be prepared for all contingencies. In light of what I had just learned, I quickly rewrote the description of that PC's photograph, incorporating the detail about the sigil. Though there was no guarantee they would pick it up, if they did, it would be brilliant. (And, as it turned out, they did!) Having accomplished my dramaturgical tasks and keeping an ear on the players who were currently the focus of roleplay, I communicated privately with the first two to see if they'd gotten everything worked out. They said they had. I didn't have time to ask for details, so I had to trust them. And off we went.

Though all the decisions I made as a GM during this passage of play were improvised, they were guided by the dramaturgical principles I identified earlier. The player decisions were compatible with the larger narrative. They worked within the game's rules. They increased dramatic tension and intensified atmosphere. They expressed and progressed character and character relationships. They strengthened the group dynamic. They aligned with player preferences and agreed-upon boundaries. Most importantly, we were all having fun. Moments such as this, particularly when experienced multiple times with different groups of players, provide a multifaceted and mercurial challenge to the TTRPG dramaturg, enabling them to practice at one and the same time textual, performance, and social dramaturgies and watch the consequences of their labor unfold in real-time.

IDENTIFYING AND ADDRESSING STRUCTURAL PROBLEMS

In a way similar to how a conventional dramatic script can pose challenges to performers and technicians—sometimes to the extent that the script must be modified—a TTRPG scenario often has structural problems that risk the delicate, but dramatically essential balance between player agency and narrative necessity. That's the case with "The Haunting," which takes us to the second dimension of TTRPG dramaturgy, assessing the narrative. To recall, "The Haunting" is divided into two parts, the first tasking players with acquiring information, the second with entering the home and confronting the supernatural entity. The flaw that a dramaturgically sensitive inspection reveals concerns the relationship and sequencing of those parts. There's no reason why the investigators shouldn't go immediately to the house after meeting with their employer—they know there's something awful dwelling there and they're being paid to get rid of it. But if the PCs don't dig into the clipping files or interview the most recent residents, the story of the house and the nature of the unnatural entity dwelling there will be poorly understood. As a result, the atmosphere of dread will be diminished and the players and their characters will lack information to help them figure out how to best deal with the baddie—in other words, both tone and dramatic shape are at risk. The designer of the scenario, Sandy Petersen et al (2019) acknowledges this problem: "Some players will be keen to head straight to the house," he warns the GM, "but you should suggest that they would be better off conducting some research first" (16). The thing is, "suggestions" don't work. They undermine player agency and disrupt the delicate process of collaborative storytelling that is the heart of the tabletop roleplaying game as a theatrical medium.

The question this poses to the student of dramaturgy requires simultaneous attention to both the text and the possibilities of play. How can we modify the text to strengthen the narrative while at the same time providing players opportunities to perform well? Here's what I did. First, I modified the script and set of the scenario. When I performed the role of the non-player character who hires the PCs, I directed them to stay out of the house until I could accompany them there. With a few clicks of my keyboard, I locked the house's doors and windows and did not allow the PC's to have a key. However, I knew the players might have their characters attempt to break in—if the reality of our storyworld deems doors and windows lockable, it deems them pickable and breakable. So, I designed in what might be called "dramatic redundancies." Since the scenario indicated the PCs could investigate the neighborhood around the house, I invented an NPC, a nosy neighbor who would conveniently appear in case of a break-in. But in the end, if the players evaded all my dramaturgical trickery with clever roleplay, then I would just need to say, "Yes, and..." and see what happened next—and no doubt, it would be great fun to do just that.

A second dramaturgical problem with "The Haunting" concerns the investigation phase. The information players gather builds atmosphere, revealing the fate of previous residents, the details of crimes committed in the house, and the connections between the resident evil and a creepy human sacrifice cult. But my dramaturgical assessment deemed it insufficiently dramatic; in TTRPG terms, it lacked rule-governed risk. Yes, the curmudgeon in the clippings files and the cops at the police station require clever roleplay and the PCs might not succeed in getting the information they desire. There's some dramatic risk there. But the information itself carries no risk, which I felt was out of alignment with both *Call of Cthulhu*'s storyworld (in which encounters with eldritch images and texts are spiritually and psychically damaging) and the rules governing the survivability of player characters. To address this issue, I revised several of the investigative documents to make the information more spine-tingling for the players and more shocking to their PCs. The former depends on the quality of my writing; the latter on a roll of the dice, e.g., what the game calls a "Sanity Check," a dice roll determined by the emotional resilience of the PC, which is defined as a numerical value. A failed check results in a penalty that is dramatically significant in game terms since Sanity is a limited resource and the PC might suffer a temporary mental-health crisis. Like the right choice and timing of music, movement, and verbal performance in a play, vivid imagery and a risky roll of the die makes for perfect drama in tabletop roleplaying games. Further, issues like this provide excellent opportunities for dramaturgs to do multiple kinds of textual assessment and modification and see their effects on play.

The third dramaturgical problem I identified was the design of the house itself, represented in the scenario by a simple map. As mentioned, unlike conventional dramatic texts, whose conflicts unfold temporally, TTRPG texts often unfold spatially, as PCs explore a dungeon, city, or other narrative-peppered space. That's the case with "The Haunting" when the PCs explore the house. From a narrative perspective, it's optimal if the PCs begin their exploration on the first floor, encountering various dreadful sights, sounds, and smells, then head upstairs, winding up in a bedroom where the scenario has prepared several high-impact scares in store. Then, again ideally, the PCs will head to the basement for the climactic encounter with the resident evil, bringing the scenario to its conclusion. However, it is entirely possible the PCs will stumble on the basement first. As with skipping a trip to the clipping files or the sanitarium, this isn't a fatal decision, but it diminishes atmosphere and moots the rich narrative elements to be found elsewhere. In this case, we have a dramaturgical problem akin to stage design. To mitigate this problem—and the need for any "suggestions"—I assessed both the narrative and spatial dimensions of the house to figure out how to steer the players along the ideal dramatic path without them suspecting what I was up to.

The original text addresses the problem to an extent. The research the investigators accomplish in the first phase of the scenario points them toward the upstairs bedroom. Further, the scenario stipulates that the necromantic nemesis doesn't want the PCs to discover him, so he focuses their attention toward the second-floor bedroom using illusory sounds and visions, which the GM can either describe or simulate. Finally, the map of the house provided in the scenario positions the basement entrance in such a way that players will likely send their characters to the second floor before looking elsewhere. But I was still concerned, so I modified both narrative and set. I moved the entrance to the basement where the investigators would be even less likely to find it. I put a chain and padlock on it, in case they did. I also had some dramaturgical improvisation at the ready. If they found the entrance and attempted to break in, that nosy NPC would swoop in. I beefed up the information about the bedroom in the research documents. And I stole a clever trick from fellow GM Joe Trier (of the *How We Roll* podcast) and added a radio in the bedroom that I could turn on (literally, using a computer and an online music account) if I sensed the Investigators' attention wandering. Not only was this a practical solution, but it worked to create a perfectly unsettling atmosphere.

In sum, the tabletop roleplaying game scenario provides a comprehensive set of learning opportunities for the dramaturg. These encompass the conventional stuff of the craft: narrative, set design, characterization, atmosphere, and performance. But they also extend beyond theatre into the particular and unique challenges of interactive media and game design.

IDENTIFYING AND MANAGING CONTROVERSIAL GAME ELEMENTS AND CONTENT BOUNDARIES

In the same way that a dramaturg needs to flag potentially problematic aspects of a script to their co-creators, the GM must do the same with their players. This can be a matter of the specific TTRPG being played. Some of the most exciting games are about big ideas, controversial content, and serious issues. I think here of Liam Liwanag Burke's *Dog Eat Dog*, a game that asks its players to imagine themselves as residents of an island recently colonized by Europeans; Jason Morningstar's *Winterhorn*, which puts players in the roles of state security forces assigned to surveil, infiltrate, and undermine radical political organizations; or Chris Spivey's *Harlem Unbound*, a supplement for *Call of Cthulhu* set in 1920s Harlem that confronts both the racist legacy of H.P. Lovecraft and foregrounds the all-too-un-supernatural horrors of racism. Part of the fun of these games is the ability to explore situations that are ideologically, interpersonally, or historically fraught.

Games might contain specific mechanics that require assessment and discussion. *Call of Cthulhu* is a game that, true to its literary origins in the work of H.P. Lovecraft, defines the threat of its supernatural entities in both physical and psychological terms. While the idea of quantifying and gamifying physical health is common in TTRPGs (i.e., hit points), doing the same with mental health is unusual and a hallmark of CoC. The current edition's rulebooks explain that "Investigators begin the game sane and rational," but encounters with "otherworldly horrors, alien creatures, and the terrible cosmic truths of the Cthulhu Mythos... will challenge their state of mind and sense of normality...," potentially causing "periods of temporary, indefinite, or even permanent madness" (Peterson et al. 2019, 154). CoC gamifies this by way of a "Sanity" mechanic, beginning with a numerical score that designates a PC's "flexibility and resilience to emotional trauma," those with higher scores being better able "to rationalize traumatic events or to repress horrific memories" (154). Sanity is also a limited resource and encounters with horror has a chance to reduce the Sanity score and cause various kinds of madness, from fainting and short-term paranoia to long-term phobias or manias.

This is an aspect of the game that needs to be frankly discussed among the players. First of all, do they want to play a game that involves this kind of content? If not, it's best to play another game altogether. If they are generally comfortable with the idea of playing with trauma and mental illness, do they have particular sensitivities? For example, a player might not want to play a game involving depression. Even if a TTRPG's rules do not contain sensitive content, its scenarios should be thoroughly assessed and players alerted to potentially troubling or triggering content. That was the case with my dramaturgically modified version of "The Haunting." In the investigation documents I created, there were images of self-harm, suicide, racist bullying, and homophobic violence. I discussed all of these with my players prior to play and, as a consequence of that discussion, eliminated some of the references, approached others with special care, and intensified others, knowing the group was comfortable going there.

However, even if a group assents to sensitive or controversial content, that does not mean the dramaturgical work is done. Part of the fun of TTRPGs is taking risks, pretending to do things we would never do in real life, imaginatively experiencing places and events that are fantastic, horrifying, hilarious, and awe-inspiring. They require improvisational collaboration among players who may not know each other well, and those improvisations can and will go in surprising directions. Thus, dramaturgical preparation must happen not just before play, but during and after it, as well, engaging Svendsen's "dramaturgy of spontaneity" in a way that ensures safety and fun for everyone involved.

Many TTRPGs and scenarios provide helpful advice about how to accomplish this. In *Harlem Unbound*, Chris Spivey (2020) includes extensive historical background about Harlem and the larger Black American community of the era along with specific advice about "battling Blackface," using the n-word ("Short answer? No."), and managing the dynamics between players of color and a white GM, among other things (90–91). In the prefatory materials for *Dream Askew*, a game about queer post-apocalyptic community, Avery Alder includes tips for how to manage players who "come to the table with different levels of familiarity and fluency" with the queer archetypes and multiple gender identities that are featured in the game (13). But the prepared dramaturg should always have at their disposal and understanding the wide range of TTRPG safety tools and instructions, including Lines and Veils; the Luxton Technique; X, N, and O cards; and Stars and Wishes; among others. All of these should be thoughtfully and thoroughly discussed and implemented by everyone at the table. In the end, the best roleplay, like the best stage performances, happens when a performer feels safe, listened to, supported, and empowered.

MODELING A PLAYFUL DRAMATURGY

In *Systemic Dramaturgy*, Michael Chemers and I advocate an expansive understanding of dramaturgy and, with that, an expanded conception of the texts, creative processes, and communities that can benefit from the insights of a well-trained, keen-eyed, critically minded, and empathetic dramaturg. We write, "Dramaturgs are, regardless of the situation, both thinkers and makers, and without a doubt, their curiosity leads us to places and problems that might not be on the radar of directors, designers, actors, and department chairs." The tabletop roleplaying game should be on our radar. As an accessible professional opportunity and multi-dimensional training tool, the TTRPG opens the dramaturgical curriculum to an emergent field of interactive media and a congeries of problems and challenges that speak both to long-lived traditions of theatre and new modes of performance and interactivity. That field already evidences a kind of organic or indigenous dramaturgy, a piecemeal practice born of practical necessity, community lore, and, in recent years, the creative ferment and critical thinking driven by those who demand greater sensitivity and inclusivity. For the dramaturg, it's a moment ripe with adventure, a moment to develop a truly playful dramaturgy.

Notes

1 Thanks to Michael M. Chemers for the advice he provided on an early version of this essay.
2 Firm numbers on the number of people who actively play are difficult to find. The producers of *D&D* claim 50 million people have played the game since its first publication in 1974 and 12 to 15 million active players in North America today (Black). Assessing various sources, M.T. Black estimates 48 million people around the world either play TTRPGs regularly or watch/listen to streaming content.

References

Baldwin, Chris. 2002. "The Director." In *Devised and Collaborative Theatre: A Practical Guide.* Edited by Tina Bicât and Chris Baldwin, 12–30. Marlborough: Crowood Press.
Black, M.T. "How many D&D Players Are There?" N.D. *M.T. Black Games.* https://www.mtblackgames.com/blog/how-many-dnd-players-are-there.
Chemers, Michael M. and Mike Sell. 2022. *Systemic Dramaturgy: A Handbook for the Digital Age.* Carbondale, IL: Southern Illinois University Press.
How We Roll. 2015. March 2. "The Haunting: Why are You Pointing that Gun at Me?" (Episode 1.30). https://howwerollpodcast.com/1-3-the-haunting-episode-3-why-are-you-pointing-that-gun-at-me/
Petersen, Sandy, Mike Mason, Paul Fricker, and Lynn Willis. 2019. *Call of Cthulhu: Keeper Rulebook.* 7th ed. Ann Arbor, MI: Chaosium, Inc.
Petersen, Sandy, Paul Fricker, Mike Mason, and Lynn Willis. 2019. *Call of Cthulhu: Seventh Edition Quick-Start Rules.* Ann Arbor, MI: Chaosium, Inc.
Spivey, Chris . 2020. *Harlem Unbound: A Sourcebook for Call of Cthulhu.* Ann Arbor: Chaosium Inc.
Svendsen, Zoë. 2017. "The Dramaturgy of Spontaneity: Improvising the Social in Theater." In *Improvisation and Social Aesthetics.* Edited by Georgina Born, Eric Lewis, and Will Straw, 288–308. Durham, NC: Duke University Press.
TwitchTracker. 2021. Dec. 4. https://twitchtracker.com/criticalrole/statistics.

15

Rasa in This Is Not a Theatre Company's Experiential Productions

Erin B. Mee

"Feel it," croons Paul in This Is Not A Theatre Company's *Ferry Play*, a podplay (or site-specific audio play) for the Staten Island Ferry in New York City.

> *Feel the wind glide around your ears, under your nails, around your waist. You. Are. Here. Smell it. Who's around you, what they're eating, the perfume they wore this morning. The sea. See it. The horizon. The sky. […] Lean against the railing. Feel that? The wind? The sun? You're inside something now. Something enormous. So just relax and breathe it in.*

This Is Not A Theatre Company produces experiential theatre in swimming pools (*Pool Play 2.0*, 2014 and 2017), on the Staten Island Ferry (*Ferry Play*, ongoing), in Manhattan apartments (*Versailles 2015*), in cafes (*Festival de la Vie*, ongoing), in restaurants (*Café Play*, 2017 and 2018), on the subway (*Subway Plays*, ongoing), at dinner tables (*A Serious Banquet*, 2014), in the dark (*Theatre In The Dark: Carpe Diem*, 2019), in bathtubs (*Play In Your Bathtub*, 2020), and under trees (*Tree Confessions*, 2021). Experiential performances are smelled, touched, and tasted as well as seen and heard; they transform spectators and audiences into partakers by inviting them to step into the performance and surround themselves with the event, engage the sensorium, and relish every aspect of what they perceive—not just what they see and hear, but what they feel on their skin, taste on their tongue, and grasp through proprioception. By asking partakers to ingest, relish, internalize, and personalize the event, engage as co-creators, and focus on affect, experiential performances are inherently rasic. However, for rasa to manifest, these productions require a dramaturgy of taste that foregrounds sensorial savoring.

Rasa is a Sanskrit term that has been variously translated as juice, flavor, taste, extract, and essence. According to *The Nātyashāstra* (The Science of Drama), the Sanskrit aesthetic treatise attributed to Bharata, it is the "aesthetic flavor or sentiment" savored in and through performance. Bharata tells us that when foods and spices are combined in different ways, they create different flavors; similarly, the mixing of different emotions and feelings arising from different situations, when expressed through the performer, gives rise to an experience or "taste" in the partaker, which is rasa (55). Rasa is what is 'tasted' when a performance is "taken in" and "digested" by a partaker. Rasa exists only as and when it is *experienced*: "the existence of rasa and the experience of rasa are identical" (qtd. Deutch Baumer 1981, 215). Similarly, rasa exists always and only as the result of an *interaction*

140

DOI: 10.4324/9781003188179-18

RASA IN THIS IS NOT A THEATRE COMPANY'S EXPERIENTIAL PRODUCTIONS • 141

between performer (or site—since, in site-based performance, the site performs) and partaker. For Abhinavagupta (CE 950–1025), who commented extensively on *The Nāṭyashāstra*, rasa is not a gift bestowed upon a passive spectator or a commodity bought by a consumer, but an attainment, an accomplishment; someone who wants to experience rasa must be an active participant in the work. Rasa and experiential performance are both active, participatory, interactive, social, experiential, sensual, tactile, multi-sensory, internal, emotional, intellectual, embodied, and an attainment. Abhinavagupta refers to rasa as an *"act of relishing"* (Deshpande 1989, 85 emphasis mine) and as such, rasa is both noun and verb: the relishing of the flavor and the flavor that is itself relished. Rasa is a mode of responding to performance, a response to performance, and a performance in and of itself.

Partakers of rasic experiential performance are implicitly or explicitly cast in the show. In *Café Play*—performed in the back room of the historic Cornelia Street Café in Greenwich Village, NYC—partakers were made aware of having been cast as restaurant customers by being seated at tables and being fed salad, risotto, and dessert at various points during the production—which also served to literalize the notion of "tasting the play." *Café Play* asked us to think about the ways we treat other human beings: do we assume the African-American woman entering the café is a waitress (as more than one partaker did)? Do we behave with a sense of entitlement toward the waitstaff? On several occasions, I was treated badly when audiences assumed I was a member of the waitstaff but was treated better when they found out I was the director of the production they had come to see, which meant that, toward the end of the play, as we had a scene about how waitresses feel when they are mistreated, partakers had to come to terms with their very real behavior. Do we think about the slavery that is embedded in the sugar we stir into our coffee? Do we think about the politics of the coffee itself—where, how, and by whom it is grown, and how it makes its way to our cup? Do we think about the class structures embedded in the ways we use our silverware? Do we think about our species-ist responses to the cockroach talking to us? As partakers looked around at other partakers as well as actors, they both received and gave information, and became aware that they were, with their presence and their visible behavior, co-creating the message both for themselves and for others in a shared network of information. Partakers and their experiences became an integral and essential part of the evening; in fact, they became what Gareth White (2013) calls "the work's aesthetic material" (9–10). Production and reception are intertwined in experiential performance.

In the finale, partakers choreographed the Dance of Chocolate.

Dear Reader, I am going to ask you to experience *this essay by performing the "Dance of Chocolate" yourself. Put down this book and find a piece of chocolate* (or some kind of fun candy that melts in your mouth and can be swirled around by your tongue).

Then type this link into a device:

https://bit.ly/3yJ8L7O

Find a comfortable chair, close your eyes, and press play. Really close your eyes. Relish your performance. After your Dance of Chocolate, resume reading.

Many people who choreograph Dance of Chocolate for the first time have never thought about the possibility that a dance can take place in the mouth, or that the tongue can be a choreographer. They have never thought about *tasting* a dance. In this case, partakers did not watch someone else dance; they were given instructions and music to create the dance themselves, simultaneously playing the roles of choreographer, dancer, and experiencer in an internal dance of flavor, smell, and mouth-feel. The Dance of Chocolate is an exercise in creativity rather than a demonstration of creativity. This shift in focus—the shift from external to internal, from observation to experience—and back again, had to be carefully choreographed throughout the evening. The dramaturgical structure had to lead partakers from one mode of engagement to the other. TINATC members spent hours debating the order of scenes not in terms of plot or character development, but in terms of the way *modes of engagement* and *sensorial experiences* developed from one scene to the next. For example, early on, one of our company members performed a dance at one of the tables; then company members led partakers in a Dance of Crayons (it so happened that the restaurant covered their tablecloths in paper and put out crayons, so we decided to create a Dance of Crayons) in which partakers danced their crayons across the paper to music. Finally, partakers choreographed the Dance of Chocolate. The dances developed from one they watched to one they participated in to one they created themselves; their dance partner developed from appetizer to main course to dessert (Figure 15.1).

Figure 15.1 The dance of crayons from *Café Play*. Photograph by Maria Baranova-Suzuki.

Theorist Jacques Ranciere (2011) claims that the audience-performance relationship in conventional proscenium theatre is designed to lure audiences into "our" (playwrights, directors, actors, designers, dramaturgs) superior understanding. The politics of experiential productions are quite different: instead of having two distinct groups – one acting and another acted upon— everyone has agency to co-create the event, to make their own meaning, and to have their experiences and understandings matter. *Versailles 2015*, an immersive cocktail party focused on income inequality and privilege, was set in an actual New York City apartment. Partakers, welcomed to the apartment as partygoers, drank wine and ate hors d'oeuvres during a scene about gentrification in the living room; they ate cake in the kitchen as a drunk woman discussed the various kinds of food one can afford to consume as a member of the 1%. Eating cake (an obvious reference to Marie Antoinette) positioned guests as members of the 1% and asked them to think about how they use their privilege as they literally internalized and became "a party to" the message through their participation. One of my students told me that as she was taking three subways to get to the play, she decided she was not part of the 1% and questioned whether the play would have any relevance for her. After the play, she realized that, simply by virtue of being a student at New York University, living in a dorm, and interacting with other privileged people at this cocktail party, she was a member of the global 1%. One reviewer wrote: "The overall tone [...] helps the show maintain a sort of 'whistling past the guillotine' balance between the obvious (yeah, we're privileged, so what) and the unsettling (but we—us in this room—not just the bankers – are actually living the kind of life that can bring about a revolution from its underclass, which should perhaps cause us more concern than it does)." In addition to being cast in the play, guests were divided into five groups and saw the scenes in a different order: we noticed that guests who had started in the kitchen and finished in the bathroom where a young woman's monologue about her health care raised the question of whether some of the privileged should not have to interrogate their privilege if they are suffering from (for example) serious health issues, came to different conclusions than those who started in the bathroom and ended in the kitchen. While all guests partook in the same scenes and came to the same overall conclusions about privilege, the nuances of their understandings were affected by the order of scenes. Which is to say that guests were invited to practice critical thinking and to come to their own conclusions, rather than simply absorbing what we told them to think (Figure 15.2).

Figure 15.2 Ashley Wren Collins in *Versailles 2015*. Photograph by Maria Baranova-Suzuki.

Artists creating experiential work quickly learn they cannot—and should not—control everything. *Ferry Play* feels very different at sunrise on a summer Sunday than it does at rush hour on a snowy winter evening—those differences are, and have to be, part of the play because partakers mix what they hear on the recording with what they see, hear, smell, and touch on the ferry. The connections between what they hear and what goes on around them create the play. Early on, one of the teenage characters says: "Look at that creepy guy over there!" If the partaker chooses to look and sees a creepy guy, that creates one kind of moment; if she looks and sees a guy who doesn't seem creepy, then she might think the teen is bring judgmental; if she looks and sees no one, she might think the teen is joking—or lying. The meaning of the moment shifts depending on what happens in the site—or the way the site interacts with the action—and the ultimate meaning is created by the partaker in the site, not by the playwright, director, or actors. In *Ferry Play*, writer Jessie Bear took into account numerous possible responses to each line, allowing for an open-ended interpretation of each moment rather than a singular interpretation. For example, riders are invited to take a selfie of themselves on the ferry with the Statue of Liberty behind them; the statue is best used as a background between four and eight minutes into the ride, so we could not begin the play with the selfie (as we had in the first draft); we had to ride the ferry, time the window of opportunity for a selfie, and use that window rather than a specific moment, in the play. Similarly, Bear invited riders to be aware of the wind and of the smells, calling their attention to their senses in a way that did not foreground or close off a particular smell, but that invited them to view that sensory information not as a "distraction" from The Play, but as an integral part of the experience.

Unlike the proscenium where the spectator believes she can see everything, experiential performance is often set up in such a way that the partaker cannot possibly see everything—and is aware of that fact. Although partakers of *Ferry Play* hear all the lines in the recording, they are well aware that they have a partial view of the set (the ferry) and the other characters (passengers on the ferry), and therefore a "partial view" of the performance. Experiential performance reveals the falseness in the very idea of objectivity (which is always already subjective), and revels in partial perceptions: the partial view is celebrated. Objectivity is not the point. Subjectivity, in all aspects, is. This extends to dramaturgical structure. Jenny Lyn Bader speaks of her experience writing one of the *Subway Plays*:

> One of the key questions I was asked [by director Erin Mee] when I began working on *Subway Plays* was, could I write a play that would be reversible? —So, on the 7 train, instead of "act one" and "act two," you would have a Queens-bound and a Manhattan-bound act and could listen to it in either order, depending on where you get on the train. [...] I did some research and could not find a precedent for this particular structure in the history of dramatic literature. There were plays with multiple sections that could be performed in different sequences, but not a two-act "reversible" model. [...] I ended up creating the characters of Daria and Steve.

> Steve keeps trying to talk to Daria on the Queens-bound ride, then confesses that he's already missed his stop and gone out of his way (to the wrong borough) in order to meet her, and finally convinces her to have coffee with him in Queens.

> In the Manhattan-bound act, when they board the train in Queens, they are holding hands. Since it's an audio play, we learn that physical fact from one of the other passengers, Chandani. It soon becomes clear they are in the initial stages of a romance:

> > STEVE: *No one's gonna believe this.*
> > DARIA: *What?*
> > STEVE: *That we met on the train. I mean, I know three couples that met on Tinder. But nothing like this.*
> > DARIA: *Are we a couple?*

STEVE: *Crap. I just meant—*
DARIA: *It's okay.*

Later in the scene, Daria is missing the sexual tension and mystery that was so palpable during the journey to Queens:

DARIA: *It was so much fun when we met. Refusing to speak to you. Wondering whether I should.*
STEVE: *Glad you enjoyed that.*
DARIA: *When we were just ... being, you know ... strangers on the train. It's hot. I love that feeling. Of first meeting someone.*
STEVE: *But this is even hotter, where we can make out on the train if we want. Right? Or are you saying the feeling's gone away?*

Indeed, she feels so much longing for their initial flirtation, with all of its interpersonal novelty and narrative suspense, she later suggests that they restage it:

DARIA: *Let's pretend to meet on the train from Times Square. But this time, I'll ignore you even more than I did when we first met. And we'll see if I'll even let you talk to me this time.*
STEVE: *Oh, that does sound hot. I'm in. Let's do it.*

Listeners of The International Local: 7 who begin in Queens hear a chronologically linear story—of an existing couple, already at the point of public displays of affection on the subway, reminiscing about how they met and then choosing to recreate an even more intense version of that moment on the trip back. For those listeners, the "meeting" journey is obviously heightened and probably takes place immediately after the journey.

Listeners who begin in Manhattan also experience a story in chronological order. A couple meets, courts, and then subsequently decides to role-play another first meeting. But those listeners may infer that some time has passed for the characters between the first two legs of the trip, though it's unclear how much time: hours or days. For those listeners, the first meeting is experienced as heightened in a different way, charged only by the reality of the interaction—and they may later even reconsider it, realizing it is someone else's "second act," and wonder how that initial encounter might be different from a reinvention of it. (Bader 2021)

Jenny Lyn Bader invented a new dramaturgical structure to allow for the fact that partakers might get on the train in different boroughs.

Readymade Cabaret invented an entirely new dramaturgical structure to ask whether our lives are determined by chance, fate, or free will. Based on Marcel Duchamp's notions of readymade art and the philosophies of Dada as practiced by Tristan Tzara, *Readymade Cabaret* consisted of twenty-eight scenes; in each performance, we performed only twenty of them. Which scenes were performed, and the order in which they were performed, was determined by partakers rolling dice. If partakers rolled ten, we performed Scene 10; if they then rolled twenty-four, we performed Scene 24. For the last scene, partakers voted between An End and Another End. Each performance had over a million possible scene combinations—and thus over a million possible interpretations. In the 2020 online iteration which spoke to the COVID moment, character-based scenes focused on characters dealing with fate and free will were interspersed with computer-generated Dada poetry, computer-generated art, partaker-created aleatory music, and Chance Dances created using prompts typed into the chat by partakers. Jessie Bear explained the process of writing the piece and its indeterminate structure in this manner:

> Western audiences are particularly primed to expect a "story" delivered to them with a beginning, middle, and end that follows a traditional rising action --> climax --> denouement structure. In developing *Readymade Cabaret*, I was excited to see what would happen if you broke a play up into its component pieces (scenes), scattered them around, and then picked them up in a random order. The scenes for *Readymade Cabaret* were structured to "fit" together in as many ways as possible—while there may have been an "order" to them in my original writing, it was crucial that they could be reorganized over and over and still make a certain kind of sense. By allowing the audience to roll the dice and determine the order of scenes, I as the playwright no longer had control over the narrative. Instead, I tried to write scenes that were open ended yet specific enough to make the play "mean" something no matter how the dice fell. Normally, as a writer, I determine the meaning and then write scenes to support that meaning. In *Readymade Cabaret*, the scenes determined the meaning, and it was up to the audience (myself included), to deduce what that meaning was on any given night. Given the "cabaret" nature of the show—it featured many wonderful multimedia/dance scenes that I didn't write—there were naturally some nights when the characters I created featured more, and other nights where they featured less. Sometimes the narrative fell into place as though I had ordered the scenes myself and created a very straightforward "story"; other nights, it was strange and lyrical. Some nights Amy and Peter were the play's protagonists, other nights, they were bit characters who only showed up in one or two scenes of an ensemble piece. No matter what, I found myself fascinated by the results, especially the way my brain insisted on forcing a traditional narrative structure even when the order defied that. I was always interested to observe what scenes I was secretly "rooting for" when an audience member rolled a dice—knowing what options were on offer, I always secretly rooted for my characters to not break up, to fulfill their dreams, to play the scenes that saw them happy, thoughtful. But that wasn't always the case. *Readymade Cabaret* was ultimately, for me, an exercise in giving up control. As a writer, I am often used to complete control over my characters, their world, and my meaning. In *RC* I had to do as much work as I could upfront to write scenes that could stand on their own after I gave up a key element of artistic control—structure. (Bear 2021)

Actors had to chart how their characters developed based on the scenes that had been chosen: on some nights Amy believed in fate; on other nights she didn't. On some nights Peter and Amy broke up with each other; on other nights they ended up together. If they broke up before they met, the meeting scene became a "flashback" and if Peter asked Amy to describe her work on a night she did believe in fate, that scene had a different set of nuances than on nights when she didn't believe in fate.

Experiential performances take place in and on the partaker's body. In *Play In Your Bathtub*, partakers sat in the tub and were submerged—or literally immersed in the subject-matter of the play. Water served both as the sensory frame and the literal dramatic text. Partakers felt the temperature and movement of the water as they danced their fingers and toes across the surface of the bath, inhaled air perfumed by scented candles and/or bath oil, tasted the tea or wine they had been asked to bring to the bath, and felt the texture of the washcloth they put over their eyes. Partakers literally touched and were touched by the production as they sat in the tub: they felt it affect them in and on their bodies.

Dear Reader, I am going to ask you to experience this essay by performing – yourself – an excerpt of Play In Your Bathtub *titled "Dance of Fingers on the Surface of the Water." Fill a tub or footbath with water. Add scented oil or bubble bath. Prepare a relaxing beverage of your choice and place it nearby. Light a candle if you wish, but do turn off the lights. Dip a washcloth in warm water.*

Click on this link and press play:

https://bit.ly/3p94bfz

After your Dance of Fingers on the Surface of the Water, resume reading.

As with Dance of Chocolate, the partaker is choreographer, dancer, and experiencer. As with TINATC's other pieces, the dramaturgical structure of *Play In Your Bathtub* was developed with modes of engagement in mind: more vigorous dances were followed by poetry using ASMR techniques to allow the water to settle while continuing to engage the body, and scents and tastes were layered onto textures to create a sensory build. The length of the piece was determined by the length of time it takes the average bath of water to cool. The goal of catharsis is immediate effect; the goal of rasa is lingering affect—a dramaturgy of the senses is required to create rasa.

A production that includes the smell of bath oil, the taste of your sugared coffee, the wind wrapping around your waist, the temperature of the air or water, and the movement of your body through space as an integral part of its meaning, privileges the feeling body. Not only did partakers' actions and experiences become "the work's aesthetic material" in *Café Play, Ferry Play*, and *Play In Your Bathtub*—the word "play" in each title being an invitation to play as verb— but their play, their physical and emotional responses, shaped and became the event: "The feeling body," as Erin Hurley (2010) claims, is "the vehicle for [experiential] theatre's images and execution. The feeling body is both the basis and the means of theatre" (36). The feeling body is an affected and affecting body. Affect can be "found in those intensities that pass body to body [...] in those resonances that circulate" about and between bodies. These are also the affective interactions in which rasa can be found. Both affect and rasa "arise in the midst of in-between-ness [and] in the capacities to act and be acted upon." If "the capacity of a body is never defined by a body alone, but by [...] the context of its force-relations," and "affect is integral to a body's perpetual becoming," (Gregg and Seigworth 2010: Kindle locations 50, 51, 72) then rasa is a mechanism for privileging the constant becoming of the affected body. Which positions experiential theatre as a force of affective change. The constant becoming of affected and affecting bodies interacting in a restaurant allows for a fluid subjectivity that is "assembled and re-assembled through" encounters with others (and with different tastes, smells, textures, props, and situations) during the course of the performance (White 2013, 24). Giovanna Colombetti's (2017) discussion of embodied, experiential, participatory, and sense making in *The Feeling Body* can be put in conversation with rasa and experiential performance to position rasa as an "affective dimension of inter-subjectivity, construed as an embodied or jointly enacted practice" of participatory sense-making (172). Colombetti argues that skills such as imitation, along with a responsiveness to others' facial expressions and physical gestures "embody [...] a *pragmatic* form of understanding others" (172) that is not based on internal simulation or mentalizing but constitutes an embodied *practice*. She refers to this as "*participatory sense making*, which is enacted in the concrete interaction between two or more autonomous agents coupled via reciprocity and coordination" (172). These skills, present in daily life and in partakers of performance, create rasa—an emotional taste—through pragmatic, participatory, and embodied sense-making in the coordinated and reciprocal interaction between performer and partaker. An

148 • ERIN B. MEE

understanding between self and other involves empathy, which is, in Colombetti's view, "an *experiential* access to the other's subjectivity," a "feeling in" (174). She stresses the "*sensual* nature of our experience of others," and refers to empathy as a process of sensing-in (174).

Crucially for a discussion of rasa as partakership, this direct body-to-body empathy occurs in the *relationship between* self and other: "I neither 'lose myself' in the others nor incorporate the others' experience into mine in a sort of extended awareness of myself" (181). Empathy, then is not self-referential: I do not convert the other person's experience into my own in order to understand it (e.g., 'I feel your pain'). "Rather, I retain an awareness of myself and the others as distinct subjects. At the same time, however, I am also aware, via basic empathy, that the others' feeling is the same as mine" (181). Colombetti's analysis of empathy functions as a description of rasa as *sensual* and *experiential*, as a *relationship* between performer and partaker, and as a *process* of sensing-in. This opens up an understanding of rasa as a *practice* of empathy in performance. If rasa is a way of experiencing another's consciousness through the embodied relationship between self and other, if rasa is an affective dimension of intersubjectivity, it is an act of empathy, a practice of empathy, and an empathetic response. Colombetti argues that the awareness of sharing a feeling leads to a "higher unity" between self and other (181). Rasa, which is an awareness of a shared feeling in that the partaker attends a performance to have a shared feeling and to be aware of that shared feeling – is then a mode of social bonding. Although rasa is most often discussed as an exchange between performer and partaker, performers partake of each others' performances, and partakers experiences each others' responses, meaning that rasa exists in the networked flow of information between performer (whether person, prop, taste, scent, or touch) and partaker, partaker and partaker, and performer and performer. As a flow of intersubjectivity, it is a tool for creating communitas. As embodied sense-making, as a way of responding to others (whether fictional or real), as a response to performance, and as an act or performance in and of itself, rasa is incorporated in(to) the self. Which is to say it participates in constituting the constantly becoming self. Rasa constitutes the constantly becoming *social* self.

What happens when partakers experience a piece entirely through taste, smell, and texture? When taste leads the experience rather than following, or supporting, text? When the relationship between performer and partaker is one between a taste or smell and a partaker? The play takes place in and on the body—allowing affect to take center stage. In *Theatre In The Dark: Carpe Diem*, partakers were blindfolded, led into a room with a clock ticking, and seated at a table with a velvet tablecloth. There they experienced an episodic piece that evoked the exquisite beauty of life through tastes and their pairings with sound, poetry, scent, and texture. There was no story; the piece was designed to evoke a desire to relish life while we can. Salt was paired with an "ocean breeze" created by fans and the scent of green tea; oranges were paired with a feather caressing the hand, a snippet of "The Love Song of J Alfred Prufrock" and French perfume; sage was paired with the smell of damp earth after rain and a love sonnet to the planet; the Dance of Chocolate was augmented by the scent of vanilla.

Dear Reader, I am going to ask you to experience this essay through an excerpt of Theatre In The Dark: Carpe Diem (Summer). *Slather yourself in sunscreen. Prepare a dish of bite-sized watermelon chunks and/or a beverage you associate with summer so you can eat and/or drink throughout the play. Find a comfortable and quiet spot.*

Click on this link, close your eyes, and press play:

https://bit.ly/3H1jxJr

After you experience this moment, resume reading.

As partaker Ana Monfared (2019) said of *Theatre In The Dark: Carpe Diem*: "It was exhilarating to be experiencing a show in which every moment was as important as the last, and I wasn't chasing a catharsis but rather learning to be present moment to moment and allowing each stimuli to affect me to the fullest degree possible." Critic Emily Cordes (2020) noted that "the absence of visuals [allowed] us to go within and witness our personal responses to, and associations with, the piece's elements" creating a situation in which "one's own mind [...] shapes the journey." Her individual associations, interacting with the material in each scene, created the dramaturgical structure and ultimate meaning of the piece. This, along with "individual tendencies to analyze what we encounter, guess what comes next, or simply absorb the experience can give the piece a different trajectory for each participant." Cordes emphasized the way in which each partaker shaped their own internal journey, applying their own frames of analysis and their own experiences to create an individual trajectory. Monfared (2019) noted that the relationship between taste and personal memory allowed her to "immediately, without trying, be taken back to different points in my life, moments with different people, and [they] even [allowed] me to create new scenarios and stories in my mind." For both Cordes and Monfared, individual associations, interacting with the material in each scene, created the dramaturgical structure and ultimate meaning of the piece, articulated by Cordes (2020) as "the ephemerality of all we perceive." Samuel Greenspan (2019) connected the dramaturgical structure to the theme, writing about *Theatre In The Dark: Carpe Diem* as a piece "about heightening our awareness and experience of the present moment. It seemed to reflect a yogic principle of being completely present, but not trapped in stasis, and maintaining an eye (or in this case, ear, nose, and tongue) to the future." Does taste as a mode of understanding matter? If so, how? Diego Ignacio Blanc Zoco (2019) explained

> *Theatre in the Dark* was about sensory experience. Rather than using a linear narrative, *Theatre in the Dark* employed my senses as actors in creating emotional responses within my body. [...] Taste triggered memory, while hearing created a context to frame my memory as a scene in the play. I was tasting/hearing the play as well as participating in it. [...] In comparison to seeing a play, I think tasting a play and having your senses fully immersed in the acting of the show creates a fuller, instinctual emotional response. With watching theatre (or any visual performance), I worry about the possibility of not have an emotional reaction. I think visual theatre depends on the actors performance visually and vocally, as well as the aesthetics of the world and our ability to suspend disbelief. However, with a blindfold on and only your ear, nose, and tongue to guide you, the experience of the theatre becomes entirely linked to your neurology. The sounds and tastes will affect and trigger memories, creating an immediate personal context for the performance. Taste theatre, as opposed to visual theatre, invites your self to become integral to their performance [...] 'taste theatre' manages to involve our entire sensory experience to create theatre.

The dramaturgical structure for *Theatre In The Dark: Carpe Diem* was designed to give partakers the growing sense—or, more accurately, sensibility—that time is short. The development of a feeling, and of tastes, rather than plot or character. The development or build of sensibility through experience. Audiences were at a loss to describe what the piece was "about," but they all said that it invited them to relish the present moment—which meant they *experienced* what it was about rather than *thinking about* what it was about. One of the common conversation-starters after a theatrical piece is: "so, what did you think?" *Theatre In the Dark* replaced this question with "how did it make you feel?" and, even more importantly, "how did the piece taste," "what was its flavor," "what did it do to you?" and "what did it evoke in you?" which invites a very different response. A response more in line with rasic *experiential* theatre.

References

Bader, Jenny Lyn. 2021. Email to the author. 23 October.
Bear, Jessie. 2021. Email to the author. 25 October.
Bharata. 1996. *The Natyasastra*. Translated by Adya Rangacharya. Delhi: Munshiram Manoharlal Publishers Pvt. Ltd.
Colombetti, Giovanna. 2017. *The Feeling Body: Affective Science Meets the Enactive Mind*. Cambridge: MIT Press.
Cordes, Emily. 2020. "Drink From The Well Of Yourself: 'Play In Your Bathtub' as Quarantine Comfort Theatre." *The Theatre Times*. 30 April.
Deshpande, G.T. 1989. *Abhinavagupta*. Delhi: The Sahitya Akademi.
Deutch, Elliott. 1981. "Reflections on Some Aspects of the Theory of Rasa." In *Sanskrit Drama in Performance*. Edited by Rachel van M. Baumer and James R. Brandon, 214–224. Honolulu: University of Hawaii Press
Greenspan, Samuel. 2019. Email to the author. 13 October.
Gregg, Melissa, and Gregory J. Seigworth, eds. 2010. *The Affect Theory Reader*. Duke University Press Books. Kindle edition.
Hurley, Erin. 2010. *Theatre & Feeling*. London: Palgrave-Macmillan.
Monfared, Ana. 2019. Email to the author. 12 October.
Ranciere, Jacques. 2011:2009. *The Emancipated Spectator*. London: Verso.
White, Gareth. 2013. *Audience Participation in Theatre: Aesthetics of the Invitation*. London: Palgrave-Macmillan.
Zoco, Diego Ignacio Blanc. 2019. Email to the author. 12 October.

16

Reconfiguring Narrative and Experiential Dramaturgy: A Conversation with Professional Educators and Dramaturgs on the Future(s) of Storytelling

Sean Bartley and Marshall Botvinick

PANEL PARTICIPANTS

Gary Garrison (Dramatists Guild)
Mark Bly (Kennedy Center Playwriting and Dramaturgy Intensives)
Carly Dwyer (Intramersive Media)
Jason Warren (AXIS Arts)

How do you define experiential theatre practices? And how does the term relate to your own personal practice?

Carly Dwyer

This question is large reason why I left education to start my company. Experiential theatre was coming to the forefront, but in my area was still slowly adopted. Experiential theatre is theatre where the audience is both participating in generating the experience and also receiving the experience in a non-detached fashion. So not only do they have an impact on the experience itself, but they're having an embodied cognitive experience, where the work is imprinting them, and they can see their imprint on the work.

Jason Warren

Experiential theatre is not actually a term that I'd heard prior to this project, but I actually quite like it as an umbrella term. It neatly sidesteps that whole "what is immersive theatre?" debate. That conversation is very hard. I've been in immersive shows that are one actor, one audience member, and neither actually leaves their two seats facing each other. But it also covers roaming across a massive warehouse with a load of other people in Punchdrunk works. I think the terminology is a place where we come unstuck because there's an implicit comparison, and maybe we don't mean it. What eventually became my book was triggered when one of my professors became a bit snippy because he felt that the term immersive theatre implies that other theatre was not immersive, which is obviously

DOI: 10.4324/9781003188179-19

not true. So experiential comes without baggage, and it maybe takes in a wider spectrum of art forms than immersive. In terms of how I might define it, I wouldn't, that's not my job. And I gladly sidestep that question. In terms of how it relates to my practice, I think this is where it becomes interesting in what it's done to reshape my issue toward training actors. I don't have a massive yearning to train actors in the genre of immersive theatre because I feel like I would always be playing catch up, because it's an evolving art form. It would already be outdated by the time it left my mouth. A thought that it provokes in me is that it fundamentally questions the nature of power in the form of experience. Or maybe agency is a better way of saying it. I don't believe this form is necessarily any more exciting than theatre that comes from the pen of one writer, I think it's just different. But what is different is the fact that the audience is required to make the immersive theatre happen. Whereas, theoretically, in a non-immersive or non-experiential play, if we made the lights bright enough that the actors didn't know that there was no audience in the room, they could still do the thing. That leads into how we train actors. We're having our own reckoning that's beginning right now in the UK about abuse of power within actor training. So the genre I think, is interesting in how it interplays with those politics. I'm interested in what the form provides for us in terms of new ways of training, but also perhaps fundamentally reshaping the power dynamics in training.

Mark Bly

Yes, so much of what Carly and Jason said counters conventional training notions of being in control; and we should not be training young artists to think that is a primary goal. Theatre that matters is so much about sharing. But for far too long our training has been about needing to be in control, and training students to think in hierarchical ways. It seems you can't start any new school or program unless it's in opposition to something. Always evolving. It has to destroy something that comes before. We are at a crucial moment right now in our society. Years ago, I worked on *Execution of Justice* with Emily Mann at the Guthrie and on Broadway. At the core of that great play is the question: why is it that in our culture, in a time of crisis, instead of staying in a middle zone, a neutral place, and having a meaningful conversation about the issues, we immediately polarize? And it seems to me here is a moment in time, when we need as artists and mentors to have meaningful conversations without jumping to opposing poles of opinions or worrying who is control.

Gary Garrison

There is power at stake when we are told where to experience our theatre when we are told to sit *here* and experience it *there*. There is a power that sits on top of that. And to me, experiential theatre happens when that power is taken away. And the space is taken away between all of us and I get to dictate my position in the room or I get to choose how long I stay in the room. As an audience member, I am in control of my participation. If that is not dictated to me, I get to control it, I get to choose. So when we subtract the classic kind of spatial arrangement, and allow everyone to experience the work, for lack of a better phrase, and on their own terms, in their own comfort, and with their own emotional accessibility, it begins to feel like it's experiential. And in all, the experiential theatre I've ever been to, I've always had the choice to leave. I can stop it. If I'm uncomfortable, if I'm unwilling to participate, if I'm angry, if I'm uncomfortable, or awkward, for whatever reason, I can leave. You can do that, obviously, in the theatre when there's prescribed distance. But when you leave a proscenium theater, you are making a statement, whereas, in experiential theatre, I think you can just disappear. And there is something to that.

What do you think might be missing from current theatre training? What theories, methodologies, approaches, philosophies, would you recommend? And building off that question, as you've continued to develop your practices, what new trends have changed your own processes?

Gary Garrison

I think theatre training is about 25 years behind the reality of the world that we're living in. And it always seems to be. It was that was the case when I was in school. And it was the case 20 years after me. And that's been the case ten years after that. It just feels like we're never caught up in this. To proudly say, "Oh, we are investigating our digital presence in the world," I'm like, what? Come on. Ten years ago, that would have been great. Because that's what your students are walking into when they graduate.

Carly Dwyer

When I do casting, I look for very unique resumes. I love working with historical interpreters. I love it if you do community theatre, you are a historical interpreter, and you also play D&D. I will hire you. Because I need to do the least amount of training with you. Because what those skill sets allow for is what I need out of an actor. When I hire an actor with a theatre degree, what I need from them is the discipline of a classically trained actor. I need somebody who knows how to take direction, I need a person who knows to take notes, who knows how to memorize when they need to, who knows how to perform under pressure, who knows how a rehearsal schedule works. But what I also need is a gamer. I need that person who is used to doing collaborative storytelling and is used to knowing a character inside and out. Because when you're playing in a collaborative storytelling setting, it's very interactive. So what I need from my actors is not just their ability to understand and memorize a script or story, but to really internalize that character and what the character's wants are. And they also have to understand the rest of the characters in the story to a point where, if they are in a heightened one-on-one situation with an audience member, they know that they are safe. Historical interpreters how to work with an audience directly in front of them and read them quickly. It's about understanding the world, understanding the priorities of the story we are working with, understanding the character, and being able to roll with the punches through an ability to really read the audience.

Jason Warren

I think there is a fundamental lack of understanding that there are multiple valid approaches and methodologies to actor training and acting, even if all you're wanting to do is Realism, or Naturalism, or whatever we want to call it. Given that we recognize that Method Acting, psychophysical approaches, and Michael Chekhov are all valid approaches. And a school may pay lip service to that idea, but how are we training our actors to actually create stuff? How do we train our actors in a society where they must be increasingly artistically promiscuous? There are no repertory theatres anymore. You need to be able to work with every damn company that you meet, no matter how different their process is. Why aren't we teaching them how to have your own process and teaching them how not to be the wanker in the room who goes "Oh, this doesn't fit with my motivation. That's not my process." I don't care about your process. Your process is to not be an idiot because that's why I'm paying you.

But how do we make that not a dictatorial thing, how do we make that something that they actually derive artistry from, the artistry of being creative within constraints, which is exactly what performing a script is. We've got constraints there, but do we view the playwright as being a dictator? No. We view them as helpful constraints. And that's not built into our training. We need to recognize within training that there is no separation between the business of acting and the craft of acting. And we are treating the business of acting as if it's dirty and smelly. And I'm seeing talented actors drop out of the industry because they've never been even told how to do their taxes. And that's criminal, especially given that more and more, we're realizing that the prevalence of dyslexia and ADHD and autism within the arts is about three times what it is in the general population. And we are not engaging with the given that these people have paid a lot of money to train, and they're not gonna make any money, even if they are successful. What value are we providing to those who are paying this money, and who are going to leave the industry, if everything we've taught them is useless and irrelevant to their lives, the minute they are no longer chasing the dream? We are charlatans. I'm not saying that we need to teach them acting techniques and say, "here's how we do the washing up." But there should be some understanding of here's how this work helps you as a teacher, here's how this work helps you as someone who wants to engage with politics in the world, here are the real-world linkages. I think increasingly, given that how much more democratic the process of creating work becomes, as we're able to bypass producers, as we're able to bypass any form of gatekeeper, the need to distinguish between what is directing and what is training an actor, which a lot of people in very high positions are not good at, becomes increasingly important.

Gary Garrison

If, in your training program right now, you are not teaching a course on how to work on a new play, you are *decades* behind. But most training programs don't have that course. If you still have a propensity to teach classical acting skills, so that your 19-year-olds can go out and work in Shakespeare and Chekhov, you're doing them a disservice. Because they're not going to go out of school and work in Chekhov or in Shakespeare. They're just not. They will, however, work on a site-specific play, an experiential play, a brand-new play.

Mark Bly

Yes, Gary is right. I believe the overall training has got to be more than taking more acting courses, but courses in other disciplines too. We should do that. More art courses, and other courses in arts and sciences to help the students become aware spatially. How they occupy space. Theatre training is not simply about the traditional six Aristotelian parts, but the potential 100 theatrical elements for the process of devising any project. I have worked with Moises Kaufman and Tectonic Theatre Project over the years and at the core of their process is Moment Work and deploying these 100 elements and expanding artists' stage vocabulary and reimagining how a stage event is created. By contrast, most training programs are sadly lacking in opening us up to that larger theatrical rainbow.

What trends are you seeing in the theatre industry, or in larger culture that you're finding impactful for your own practice?

Gary Garrison

More than I've ever experienced in my lifetime, today there is this extraordinary need to want to be seen and heard and to have one's story understood, on display for somebody or everybody's approval. Nothing speaks more to that than TikTok, where everybody is creating these extraordinary things that are rooted in the self, that are rooted in *my* story, *my* opinion, *my* values, *my* challenges, *my* politics. And at the end of the day, you come away with a million viewers. And that is mind-blowing in a way that we will never see in the theatre. But shouldn't we? So I've been wrestling with this question: is TikTok theatre? If we were smart, we would figure out what it is. Is it experiential theatre? That's really what I'm asking. Because it looks like it.

Jason Warren

For a long time, people were very flippant about immersive work, it was treated as a bit of a gimmick. But every now and then a particular piece that would come along that someone with enough clout decided, for some reason was their darling. This normally was very, very good quality work. This very much happened to Punchdrunk, who makes really good quality work. But they are not unique in having in been innovative back then. Over time, I've seen immersive work not be dismissed as much anymore, but almost more dangerously, become co-opted. Now there is a very sanitary form of immersive there. It's always a dangerous place when you start seeing brands using these artists to advertise new products. And that happened really, really swiftly. And I'm sort of conscious that although this is a story of someone speaking, and my talking to someone, and I'm so conscious that it came back to my role as an actor trainer around my role as someone who kind of dabbles in directly create an experiential theatre.

Do you think experiential performance shifts our ideas about authorship? And if so, how?

Gary Garrison

In the years that I have been at the [Dramatists] Guild, one of the things that we've been trying to focus on is this notion of: "Who is the author now?" And that is coming into question because of why we're here today. It can be anybody and it can be everybody. And the question is when it comes to the commercial theatre, where does the money go? Because that's what everybody wants to know. Right? The notion of author. I mean, aside from credit, which is another thing that also has its own value, particularly for young artists who are starting out, or an older artist who has never made a name for themselves. But credit aside, when there's so little to divide up anyway, how is that divided? And in order to understand how that is divided, you have to then define author. And that is not something that I feel we can generically define and lay down on everybody's project. They're all different. So what we're going to have to do is figure out some sort of simple parameter to begin the discussion, and then be open for the conclusion of that discussion.

Mark Bly

I've worked in theaters, advised playwrights, done a lot of "ghost dramaturging" in the shadows, and been in situations where I, frankly, worked as a dramaturg/playwright. But I didn't ask for extra credit, I didn't ask for another fee because I had already been hired by contract at a specific theater. In terms of credit I have said, "When the production bleeds I bleed ... " and if the production failed, it's failed because my lines, my notes failed as well. Along the way, there were projects like that, and I didn't need the credit. My credit was the privilege, the pleasure of working with these playwrights. If I wanted to be a playwright, I'd go be a playwright with the glories, pain, and blemishes of it. I had chosen this other pathway. I used to say this: I could live with waking up at four in the morning staring at a

156 • SEAN BARTLEY AND MARSHALL BOTVINICK

wall and accept being a second-rate dramaturg, but not living with being a third-rate playwright and knowing that was the best I could ever be. So I committed to being the best dramaturg I could be. I think somehow it does come down to case by case. You can't make some blanket statement about giving credit. You can't legislate something like that. Just our group here, we're all very like-minded in so many ways. We're very conciliatory. We're very, I believe, sensible. And yet, we're all acknowledging the challenge of defining what immersive means. So how can we possibly gather 18,000 playwrights and say, "You will do this. You will agree to this."? It's unlikely.

Are there dramatic or narrative structures that you see emerging out of an increase in experiential performance, or older narratives and structures that you see reappearing or in terms of importance in amidst the changes that we've identified in the conversation so far?

Gary Garrison

If you're not in the commercial theatre, there is a trend away from traditional narrative structure. Particularly, young people do not want to be told what to do. And what to do translates into dramatic structure. This is definitely happening in American Theatre. I'll give you an example. *The Wolves*, by Sarah DeLappe. There's no dramatic structure. It's a ball game. Several ball games. And the only thing that ends that play is that there's a death.

Carly Dwyer

The way an audience follows the narrative structure usually is associated with playwriting. But on our shows, it's easier to credit a dramaturg than it is a writer. The dramaturg does more writing of the world and the actors develop the dialog. Because the very nature and structure of the work we do is not necessarily traditional, we've had to lean on different models of storytelling than those that have worked for centuries. This helps us work in a space that is both innovative to our audience but also comfortably recognized. Something that is safe and known, but also exploratory.

Gary Garrison

I think there are two kinds of structures: there's story structure, and then there's the structure of the experience. And those are completely different things. So you can have a traditional narrative structure, the dramatic material, and then a non-traditional structure of the event. And it's interesting and fascinating how they might inform each other.

What role do dramaturgs play in the context of this emergence of forms that we're calling experiential? How is it different from their role in more traditional modes of performance?

Carly Dwyer

I have four permanent staff members, and one of them is a dramaturg. My dramaturg is so essential to what our work is. I need someone to help me build that world, research that world, give details to that world, and then break that world back down. And that's something my actors get access to. My dramaturg like, is one of the hardest workers on my staff. Because whenever we come up with a show, whether it's a history, like sitting in historical period that we're doing for museum, or we're doing something that's completely contemporary, or making a fantasy, that sense of recognizability is what allows because audience permissions to participate. She'll help do the world building and she'll pull examples. Our process is very collaborative. My dramaturg is more important to me than having a writer because she's the keeper of the world. You've heard the idea in a more traditional rehearsal setting that a dramaturg is the defender of the text? My dramaturg is the protector of the *world*.

Mark Bly

When I was teaching dramaturgy at Yale, 25 years ago the playwriting and dramaturgy programs were merged together. I didn't make that decision. But I found that I had to co-lead both of them, and I had to create a shared course. As part of that course, I believed that both sets of artists needed to be thinking about certain principles. And one of those core principles is what Carly was talking about: the "what if?" principle. What if the world behaved this way? You need to approach it that way. You have to think about it. Playwrights are constantly hitting walls or barriers. And my job is *not* to tell them what to do. My job is to stay back and ask, "Well, what if? What if? What if?" walking down the path with a playwright and continually asking questions. And at the end, maybe they'll suddenly say "Now I understand. I'm going to do this." And they look around, and I'm not there. I've disappeared. Or as Rajiv Joseph once described me as a "Mystic Dramaturg." I like to share with dramaturgs and playwrights in workshops how I "stumbled" over 30 years ago. And letting that example be an inspiration. Years ago, I worked with Joanne Akalaitis on a production of *Leon and Lena (and lenz)*. I sent her an enormous bundle of xeroxed articles. This was in the 1980s, so this was a lot of work. Six weeks passed. Nothing from her: no phone calls, no letters. Finally, a scheduled visit for casting and design at the Guthrie happened. At the end of a long day, we had a dinner with the designers. Still nothing. After a great design meeting, I drove her back to the Guthrie housing where she was staying. As I let her off I said quietly, "Joanne, it's clear. You and I are not hitting it off. Maybe you'd like to work with Michael Lupu? Maybe there's somebody else you have worked with before we could hire instead?". She started laughing, in a gentle way and said "Why? I would love to work with you. What would make you think otherwise? And I said, "Joanne, I did all this work. you haven't commented once on it." And she laughed, "Mark you sent me all of this stuff, comments from other people. I want to hear what Mark Bly has to say about the play. This is what I care about." That was a revelation. One could start from that place. What do *you* have to say? Not what some major critic or artist has to say, or what this historian has to say. Instead, what is *your* starting point? After you have done all that research, this is what I always say to dramaturgs. You bring that to the rehearsal and then you put it under the table. You do not want any barriers between you and the actors, directors, playwrights. And oh yes: you must *listen until your ears bleed*. Then you can collaborate in an active manner. That's the most important lesson I can share.

What technological innovations do you think will influence the development of playwriting and dramaturgy in the coming years?

Gary Garrison

I'm seeing cell phones enter the picture as a device to tell the story. One of my great theatre moments in the last five years has been going into the theater and being told to leave your phone *on*, and to register your number at the front desk, if you want to participate. So as you're watching a play, and you're listening to a character, the person opposite her texts you to say, "She's lying. Don't listen to what she's saying." So you are brought into the world of the play, using this thing that you use every day of your life, that you depend on for information. The writer is using that, saying, "Let's use it for information now. But *I'll* get to choose what information you get." And then you leave the theater, and the evening is through, and you're in a cab going home, and you get another text from one of the other characters. *Come on.* How good is that? Because then the production's carrying on with you. The next day, you get another message from somebody and you're like, "Okay, this has gone on forever now. I'm never going to escape the story." And that's actually the point: You are never going to escape. That's fucking brilliant.

Jason Warren

I feel like it's going to become increasingly hard to predict because the rate of technological and societal change increases. The only consistent advantage we have over film is the ability to respond to life in the moment. What Gary is describing, the characters texting us when we come home, that can be done in a gimmicky way. And I see gimmicky productions where they're just doing it because it's shiny. But that ability to have a character *actually live* in a way that they can't in other mediums because it's happening in this moment, is exciting. If you can't press pause on them, if you choose not to engage, then you, as an audience member, you have missed that moment. I hope that technology will push us more towards exploring that rather than just going "Let's do a fucking play in VR because it's shiny."

Carly Dwyer

My company, we actually are just filming our first foray into VR because one thing we learned over 2020 was a lot of lessons about accessibility. We became a fully digital company in 2020. And we learned a lot. And I think coming out of 2020, to be ignorant of what that did for accessibility for people would be to throw away a huge amount of audience that we just gained. In film, the cinematographer is telling you what to look at. And in 360 VR, they're not. We actually interact with the camera as a character. The company is having an absolute blast trying to navigate that.

How do young people understand theatre differently? What are their notions about what theatre is that we see as different?

Gary Garrison

Because of the pandemic, there's a PTSD that's happening, which we will not understand for a while. What happens when this thing that you have devoted your life to can fold up and disappear in a month's time, and your entire education is wiped out? Because no one knows what to do with this thing (the theatre) that is reliant on public assembly. And if the public doesn't want to assemble, you're in trouble. It's an exciting time. Let's use AR and VR. Let's learn to tell stories differently in a way that doesn't require an audience to sit in front of actors with quiet respect, and listen, and then go home and eat tacos at the end of the night. Let's figure out a different way of doing this. Let's explore the idea that an audience is anything that we direct it to be.

Jason Warren

I have a suspicion and a hope that we're about to see in theatre what we saw happen with films and music in the mid-seventies to mid-eighties, the moment where punk changed so much. Theatre has held onto gatekeepers long after other art forms have dismissed them. I think the current generation of young theatre artists is very, very, very different than my

RECONFIGURING NARRATIVE AND EXPERIENTIAL DRAMATURGY • 159

generation. When I was 25, we were rebelling against theatre. We were trying to make punk stuff, to be like the punks of theatre. But to rebel, you have to *care*. You have to care what gatekeepers think. These students, they don't care. They see it as an irrelevance. They don't have strong opinions about what the National Theatre is doing, even when they're doing good stuff. Because that would require them to invest. And why would they need to? They can make theatre in any space. That's been legitimized. They can make theatre without any space at all. The pandemic has legitimized that. They've already realized this before being told by our government that there will be no funding in the arts at any point. They already didn't need the approval of people who are going to give them money. None of them think they're going to make a living financially. So they've stopped checking in with us. I'm scared of that on a selfish level, but I'm really excited by it.

Carly Dwyer

One thing I'm noticing with the younger audiences coming up is that they're really using theatre and storytelling devices to identify community. When we talk about the PTSD of social media, it's not so much that people are looking to stand out as individuals is that they're definitely trying to *belong*. I was born in 1981. Rugged individualism was pushed on me as a young American person. As Jason was saying, they're not looking for rugged individualism anymore, they're looking to find their community. When we think about theatre as a gathering point, which it has been since inception, we have to ask: are we creating an opportunity for community? Or are we sitting there and being didactic?

Mark Bly

We need to be more nimble than ever now artistically and politically, especially in the aftermath of the deep, volatile divisions that have emerged in our country in the past few years. That's how we have to think about ourselves. Young people I have encountered in workshops understand that better than we do. During the Summer of 2020 Kennedy Center Dramaturgy Intensive, everyone's spirits were low, because they faced this enormous debt coming out of school, the Covid-19 pandemic, racial unrest, and a Presidential Election Crisis. So I invited a diverse group of different people from many fields over five, six months to meet with them on Zoom to talk to them about alternate careers deploying their dramaturgical skills. They learned their future did not have to be about an old, calcified notion of dramaturgy. They were encouraged to think about theatre in other ways, too. This was the start of my sharing with students and other artists in workshops a personal mantra that I was beginning to evolve: that I would "Break old measuring sticks for success" that I had used in the past and that I would begin searching for new ones. And I believe that is a core value that young people, emerging artists understand is key if the future of theatre is not to stagnate.

Gary Garrison

I just want to say that every generation of theatre artists that I can remember has said "theatre is dying!". Every generation, every ten years, this comes up again. Before the pandemic, it actually felt like we were miring down in our sameness. And here is an extraordinary opportunity where the world stopped. And we have a chance to reboot and redefine the theatre in a way that it won't die because young people will want to be a part of it.

17
WildWind Performance Lab: New Play Development through Abstraction

Sarah Johnson

WILDWIND PERFORMANCE LAB

Each June, the WildWind Performance Lab (WWPL) convenes at Texas Tech University (TTU). Described to students and guest artists as an "immersive and intensive" course, the lab (called WildWind or WWPL) results in something akin to a conference, intensive training workshop, and new play development festival all in one. Participants in the course deeply involve themselves in each aspect of the lab and surround themselves and interact with the plays, guest artists, and material of WWPL all day, every weekday, for four consecutive weeks (our definition of intensive and immersive). One of the key missions of WWPL, as both a course and new play development opportunity, is to connect TTU students with exciting artists from around the world. Lubbock, TX is fairly isolated, a five-hour drive to a city in any direction. While we have a thriving local arts scene, we dedicate resources to facilitating our students' professional development through travel and bringing world-class artists to the TTU campus to offset the deficit of a theatre education outside of a major metropolitan area. We also collaborate with institutions such as the Kennedy Center American College Theatre Festival and Hong Kong Performing Arts Academy to include a diverse set of WildWind participants in addition to our students. We joke that the campus leisure pool (with the longest lazy river on a college campus) brings many of our exceptional guest artists to Lubbock, but I suspect that the reason for our exciting slate of artists has more to do with the unique environment we offer. Guest artists, particularly playwrights, get the benefits of both an intensive rehearsal process over the week and the feeling of remote writing retreat with time to focus on their work in the windy desert of West Texas. The inclusion of experiential dramaturgical feedback also draws excellent artists and teachers to Lubbock. Each week, a group of students we call "Abstracters" responds to a play in development by generating creative work inspired by the play. These "abstractions" function as embodied or object-based dramaturgical feedback to the play. The holistic experience of WildWind includes both pedagogical and new play development tactics founded in experiential learning and art making. At WildWind lounging by the river, eating a meal together, and making performance art inspired by a play in development work together to create a cohesive experience; an immersive whole greater than the sum of its parts.

Each week, a set of professional artists arrive for their residency. Students choose a workshop to participate in each morning for the full week. The afternoons are dedicated to

160

DOI: 10.4324/9781003188179-20

question and answer sessions with guests from around the world via video conferencing. The guests range from actors and designers to artistic directors and agents. We dedicate the last part of each day to developing a new play from a guest professional playwright. During the week we rehearse the play and the playwright explores revisions as desired. Playwrights have no obligations outside of their rehearsals, so they have time to write in the mornings and afternoons each day. Any student not cast in the play, or serving as a stage manager, assistant director, assistant dramaturg, or any other role in the rehearsal room joins the abstracter team. These students generate artistic responses to the play in a process detailed below. Each Friday, WildWind Participants, our TTU School of Theatre and Dance family, and the Lubbock community attend a public staged reading of the play in progress. We celebrate the completion of each week with a shared meal. On Monday, we start again, with new guest artists teaching new workshops and a new play in development. Each student ends WildWind having attended four workshops, spoken to over thirty guest artists in our Q&A sessions, and taken part in the development of four new plays (Figure 17.1).

WEEK FOUR - June 21st to June 25th, 2021

	6/21		6/22		6/23		6/24		6/25	
9:00-9:30	Meet and Greet									
9:30-11:45	Workshop 1 Solo Performance	Workshop 2 Seeing/Listening to the world as a DJ	Workshop 1 Solo Performance	Workshop 2 Seeing/Listening to the world as a DJ	Workshop 1 Solo Performance	Workshop 2 Seeing/Listening to the world as a DJ	Workshop 1 Solo Performance	Workshop 2 Seeing/Listening to the world as a DJ	Workshop 1 Solo Performance	Workshop 2 Seeing/Listening to the world as a DJ
11:45-1:00	Lunch		Lunch		Lunch		Lunch		Lunch	
1:00-2:15	Zoom Guest Diep Tran		Zoom Guest Chay Yew		Zoom Guest Stephen Graybill		Zoom Guest Reginald L. Douglas		Zoom Guest John Leguizamo	
2:15-2:30	Break		Break		Break		Break		Break	
2:30-5:30	Play Workshop The Snake Eater	Abstracter Sessions	Play Workshop The Snake Eater	Abstracter Sessions	Play Workshop The Snake Eater	Abstracter Sessions	Play Workshop The Snake Eater	Abstracter Sessions	Play Workshop The Snake Eater	Abstracter Sessions
5:30-7:00									Dinner	
7:00-7:30									Abstractor Presentations	
7:30-10:00									Play Reading The Snake Eater	

Figure 17.1 Workshop schedule, summer 2021.

The abstracting process was developed out of the chaos of the pandemic. In June of 2020, WWPL was canceled, and WildWind Pandemic Lab was born. While the focus of the lab remained the same, the necessity of hosting the experience online using video-conferencing had our team of faculty[1] creatively adapting the lab to an online format. Of the many changes we made to facilitate the online modality and combat screen fatigue, one resulted in the creation of the Abstracters. In previous years, WildWind Participants not cast in or otherwise directly involved in the new play development process would find themselves mostly observing. The faculty felt whatever benefit in observing rehearsals might have existed in face-to-face modalities would be transformed into cruel and unusual punishment in Zoom-land. In brainstorming the involvement of these students online, we remembered that previously one of the guest artists leading a design workshop had the students design the show in development, similar to the "dream design" concept of the O'Neill National Playwrights Conference and Seven Devils Playwrights Conference's design meetings. This seemed a valuable addition to the lab but did not meet the needs of all of our students, many of whom were performers, directors, dramaturgs, playwrights, and arts administrators. This prompted us to pivot towards the notion of abstraction and students working creatively in response to the play. We asked ourselves: How could our students abstractly respond to the play in development using a wide variety of media? Could this response be useful to both the students creating and the audience receiving the product, in particular the playwright? We landed on asking the Abstracters to use the play as a prompt to create an artistic response in any media of their choice. Abstracters listened to the cold reading of the play on Monday, brainstormed ideas as a group on Tuesday, created their abstractions on Wednesday, shared their work in progress and gave each other feedback on Thursday, and finalized their pieces for presentation in the lobby before the public staged reading on Friday. Here are our Context and Guidelines[2] given to the Abstracters at the start of each week:

> Everyone will be responding to the sum total of what they encounter at WWPL, in writing, by journaling. Some will also have the privilege and challenge of responding to the plays in development as an "Abstracter". If your interests naturally lie within design and technology, or if you are not cast in or immediately tied to the nightly rehearsal process, you will be "abstracting." This means you will approach new play development less through direct involvement in the rehearsal room and more by creatively responding to the work in progress in different and unique ways. This is a crucial part of the new play development process and can greatly enhance the early work of the playwright, and the whole production team. In part we are choosing to characterize your method of working as a kind of "abstracting" in order to keep as many options open to you, and to the playwright, as possible. We want you to find your own ways of responding to texts (the plays, assigned readings), conversations, ideas, play readings etc. Your responses can borrow from the many forms of the word 'abstract':
>
> - in the sense that an abstract (usually to an academic paper) is about research and serves as a point-of-entry or an outline to a larger work and often compiles and synthesizes information
> - in the sense that it relates to in-depth analysis of something
> - in the sense that it need not be director literal but instead can be more theoretical, conceptual, imaginative, and in the case of abstract art, non-representational
> - in the sense that it can be a process of extracting the essence of something from its original form

Whatever your individual approach, you all have the plays in development as common reference points. The plays, along with the assigned readings, discussions, guest artist talks, and rehearsals that relate to the plays, are to what you will be responding. For those of you familiar with the typical design process in theatre, there are some similarities here. As per usual, you may find yourself doing initial intuitive and visual research, historical research, sketching, rendering, modeling, maybe even drafting. The typical design process starts somewhat abstract but rather quickly moves into a process where experts in particular areas start making very practical decisions in response to the director's vision, the budget, the build time, the inventory, and staff, etc. We design sometimes with wild creative abandon, but always within a range of real-world limitations. Typically, we do all of this for a play that was finished by a playwright, sometimes long ago, and possibly produced by countless directors and production teams before us. But here at WWPL, a play could be an idea sketched on the back of a birthday card, or it could be 200 pages of dialogue that will change in form and content by tomorrow, or it could be the cassette demo of a single song. In whatever state the play may be, it probably has never been realized by a director with a production team. Here, the playwright doesn't know the contours of what this world is yet, and they tend to be rather open to suggestions (otherwise, they wouldn't be here).

So, it follows that we, as "designers", need a different approach for this process than what is typical. First and foremost, please note, none of you have specific design roles and none of you are designing a show that needs to be realized. That is not the point. Our work as Abtracters is more of a freewheeling prequel of possibilities to the typical design process. The pressure is not to work out the details for one realization but to expand the conversation about the many conceptual potentialities. The goal is less to provide the playwright with solutions to challenges baked into a finished script and more to provide questions about the current state of the script, and feedback about what the world they are creating looks, feels, smells, and sounds like. So don't think of this process as normal design at all; no one is designing a show, but everyone is finding unique ways of creatively responding to a play in the process of being born. Later, the playwright will draw from the experimentation that happens here and some or none of that may one day become the flesh and blood of a finished play. Who knows, you might influence how a play grows up...?

The goal of the abstracter should be, at first anyway, to quickly and frequently respond using whatever tools they have at their disposal, are comfortable with, or want to experiment with and learn about. Soon after that (we are generally working within the confines of short weeks only), you will need to make specific decisions about what your creative response is: what to keep and what to cut, how to stitch disparate elements together to form a comprehensive creative gesture. You will be doing this for the mid-process showing drafts as well as for final showings. You may be thinking, "cool, but I still don't know what the heck a 'creative response' is?!". The answer is: your main assignment during WWPL, along with journaling, is to figure that out! Be bold, be creative! Our hope is that you surprise us with additional possibilities by the end of the process.

Shared Parameters

- We don't bypass the mighty tools of critical thinking and intellectual research and rely on some mystical "gut", but we do examine what intuition means, and learn to develop and trust it, in the name of making decisions much faster than usual.
- We rely on readily available material that we can find at our homes and around campus. We do not need to spend a lot of money and lean on university resources to make compelling artistic gestures. Creating complex and surprising art out of simple means is our goal (and all we have time for), not highly produced and technologically-driven spectacle.
- We find ways to use our individual strengths but within an artistic format that has some sort of over-arching connection, relating to the play in process. For our final showing each week, we collectively create a "world" of some sort. It may have many unique facets, but it is a somehow *interconnected* world, similar to how the play in development – whatever state it is in – is some kind of interconnected world.

The sky (or maybe we should say the planet that is the play or your response to it) is the limit.

Have fun.

Our Abstracters created a wide variety of responses drawing on their unique skillsets. We had embroidery swatches, illustrated maps of play worlds, immersive ambulatory performance art, a graduation ceremony, sculpture, a bug's eye view tour of a model set, a music video, a Minecraft space, live-looping demonstrations, food tastings, poetry and so much more. As an educator, I couldn't have predicted the wild and exciting results of this process, and as a dramaturg, I was thrilled by the experiential dramaturgical feedback the playwrights received on their work. The students got to flex creative muscles while also contributing to the new play development process in targeted ways. Overall, this process guided students to the most useful form of feedback for playwrights (what did you experience in this play) and away from the less useful and sometimes damaging feedback that folks inexperienced in new play development land (what I liked or didn't like) (Figure 17.2).

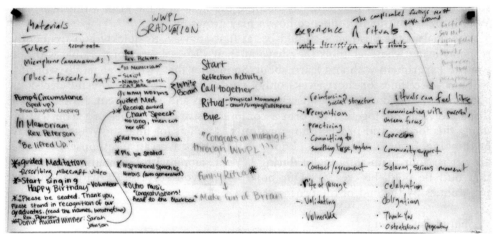

Figure 17.2 White board image: brainstorming for an abstracter-devised performance-art response to Bradley Hewlett's play, *The Snake Eaters*.

I can see variations on this assignment being valuable in spaces of new play development, including playwriting and dramaturgy courses as well as directing and design courses, where students form responses to plays before working on them. The abstracting assignment also lends itself to a devising modality of its own, foregrounding the designing of experience. Using this practice of responding to the world of already created plays (or other art) in abstract form can generate new theatrical work. While we created the assignment as a form of dramaturgical feedback for the existing plays in development at WildWind, it could be used to create new immersive dramaturgies that are performances unto themselves. In many ways it already has. The pieces created by the abstracters can be engaged with as distinct theatrical experiences of their own. The abstracting process encourages critical and sensory responses to plays that directly bypass the pitfalls of traditional feedback on new plays. Students engage with dramaturgy experientially from multiple entry points: new play development dramaturgy, the dramaturgy of the "prompt" play, and the dramaturgy of the response itself. This results in nuanced engagement with new plays, doing dramaturgy in tangibles ways, and new theatrical work that exists apart from the original play in development. Theatre begets more theatre.

Notes

1 Faculty for WWPL 2020 included Seth Warren-Crow, Rachel Hirshorn-Johnston, Kyla Olsen, and the author (who also serves as WWPL's Executive Director).
2 Written in collaboration by both the WWPL 2020 and 2021 faculty including Seth Warren-Crow (who wrote most of the guidelines and facilitated the Abstracters), Dr. Tanya Calamoneri, Kyla Olsen, and Rachel Hirshorn-Johnston.

18
It's Okay to NOT be "Right": Incorporating Creative Thinking into Theatrical Partnerships

Rachel E. Bauer

INTRODUCTION

Creative thinking and the confidence to take chances are especially important when we consider ways to practice, encounter, and interact with new forms of theatre. To situate ourselves into conversations relating to new theatrical forms, we first need to push for innovative thinking. We need to think about *how* we think to disrupt our preconceived ideas of writing and creating new works, evaluating merit of an idea as right/wrong, and working as collaborative partners. If we are to be responsible for creating new works, breaking the boundaries of traditional performance, to engage in immersive and experimental theatres, we must also lean into the *experience* of thinking. Thinking creatively can guide us to new discoveries during production team discussions, through interpretation and analysis, collaborations with a dramaturg, and in play development. However, it can also dramatically change the way that we think of theatre as a form; new ways of thinking can—and should—inspire innovations in playwriting, dramaturgy, collaboration, and experiential practices of theatre. By focusing on idea generation, and group brainstorming, we can work to disrupt hierarchies of whose ideas are privileged in traditional models of rehearsal, focusing instead on collaborative practices. As such, creative thinking is an important skill set outside of what is usually used in theatre training. Thinking experimentally allows theatre students to push past preconceived notions of their abilities and sets them up to succeed in the ever-changing landscape of theatre.

Even when seen as exemplars of creativity, theatre students can struggle with open-ended calls for creativity in and outside of the classroom, stymied by the fear of being wrong. Thus, we can choose to *practice* thinking, ensuring our thinking is *purposeful*. In doing so, we strive to move past more stringent constraints of right and wrong to encourage young artists to feel comfortable sharing ideas, leading discussions, and embracing new ways of working with artistic partners. This approach highlights creative thinking within theatre practice, allowing for brainstorming and adjudicating ideas, as well as collaboration, to foster increased confidence in one's creative skills. As a theatre educator and artist, I use drafting and revising of ideas, team-based approaches to analysis, and reflection in traditional theatre arts settings and classrooms to encourage students to think non-traditionally, supporting the idea of being closer to "right," not the duality of right and wrong. However, these methods can be applied outside the classroom to encourage us to think about how we make art, examining the voices and ideas we allow to inspire us. In

166   DOI: 10.4324/9781003188179-21

this essay, I explore the ways in which I include and utilize elements of creativity theory and creative approaches in the hopes of providing new tools to foster discovery and collaboration for training innovative theatre artists of the future.

USING A CREATIVE APPROACH

In a classroom setting, educational and theatrical texts often provide the basis for exploration, and within a conventional theatrical context, we tend to know the steps to lead us from page to stage and how to work with a creative team. But what happens when we are working with new, experimental forms of theatre? We can't always rely on existing ways of thinking when working with new ways of creating.

As Tom Kelley's (2001) *The Art of Innovation* points out, the issue with brainstorming is most people think they do it already (55). Therefore, it is not something they need to work for. Unfortunately, the truth is we do not utilize brainstorming, or, more accurately, we do not brainstorm in a way that is actually *useful*. In fact, most of us take brainstorming for granted in the creative process. Keith Sawyer (2013) adds, "to be creative, you have to generate boatloads of ideas. To be creative successfully, you have to let most of them sink, because the real genius lies in picking good ideas" (173). However, it's not as simple as generating tons of ideas and picking the very best one. Instead, "people generate better ideas when they're guided by clear criteria" (176).

As important as brainstorming is to thinking creatively, it will only go so far without thoughtful evaluation and revision of ideas. After spending time generating many ideas, it is time to hold them to an identified criteria to see which ideas are useful. Thus, I turn to Kathy Goff's (2005) four creative abilities: fluency, flexibility, originality, and elaboration (23). She notes, "there is considerable evidence that the more ideas we have, the more likely we are to find a useful solution or answer," (24) but that we need to utilize other skills, including "the ability to process information or objects in different ways given the same stimulus" (25). Goff pushes us to look at originality, "getting away from the obvious and commonplace or breaking away from habit-bound thinking," (30) and elaboration, "the ability to embellish ideas with details" (34).

How does this translate to practicing *purposeful* creative thinking? After spending time brainstorming and thinking through ideas, do not settle on initial instincts. Rather, take ideas generated and dig deeper, revising and expanding where needed, to fine-tune the thought process. When working through the elaboration of ideas, focus on thoroughness and clarity, as elaboration does not always mean longest. With these concepts in mind, look at the array of ideas developed during brainstorming and begin to evaluate them by using Goff's creative abilities to stretch and push each idea beyond our initial thoughts. Finally, the idea is ready to be fine-tuned by drafting, revising, and reflecting to ensure the final product remains in line with the original purpose of the endeavor.

In the section below, I provide step-by-step exercises for working through and promoting creative thinking to enhance work within a theatrical context. While all three exercises can be used independently, they can also be used in tandem—in order or out of order—building on each other. Additionally, small adjustments can be made to meet the needs of the specific topic and participants involved. I hope these prove helpful for you and your creative partners.

EXERCISE #1: BRAINSTORMING AND BEYOND

As noted above by our creativity experts, brainstorming is a fantastic tool when it is used in conjunction with clear, set criteria. We engage with brainstorming activities like the one below to become more practiced in our brainstorming abilities. Since the application of these exercises is broad, anything from texts, to objects, to the very beginning ideas for a new piece can be used as prompts and criteria. For example, a script, established or being created, can serve as a guide, providing us clear criteria and expectations for idea generation. We know what we are looking for; therefore, we aren't brainstorming directionless into the ether. To do this, participants are led through this step-by-step activity that focuses on idea generation, before moving onto idea adjudication. This distinction is key, as it is always good to begin with a reminder that brainstorming is a part of the creative process that is not to be evaluated. Finally, we'll take our idea generation to the next level by engaging with Goff's four creative abilities to stretch our ideas.

1. **Set parameters**: Before beginning the brainstorming session, it's important to know what we're going to be focusing on. Whether it's an analysis, play development, or dramaturgical element, we have a guide to look to. The focus of the brainstorm could be to establish a production concept based on images, but it is certainly not limited to traditional theatrical work.
2. **Clear expectations**: Next, be sure to communicate all expectations associated with the session. What is the specific task? What is the product/products we hope to have after the brainstorm?
3. **Brainstorming Fluency**: Timed idea generation. Ten to fifteen minutes is a suitable time frame for solo brainstorming. Check in periodically, if needed, for encouragement! Here, we call on Goff's first ability: fluency.
4. **Adjudicate ideas (ongoing)**: Take a good hard look at the generated list of ideas: the product of the brainstorm. Is there anything that stands out from the rest? Why does it stand out?
5. **Push for Flexibility**: See where the ideas differ from each other. Are the statements all responding to the initial prompt in the same way? Or did the brainstorming session produce a variety of options? Goff's call for flexibility allows us to examine the range of our ideas.
6. **Identify the Originality**: Identify any ideas that stick out as original and/or unique from the others. By seeing what stands out from the crowd of ideas, we can test how well we achieve Goff's idea of originality.
7. **Pick one**: Now, it is time to choose a statement, or two, that works with your purpose. Note, this does not have to be a final decision; there is always time to revisit ideas passed over for the time being.
8. **Time for Elaboration**: Is there enough information to communicate the idea to another, or do we need more detail or clarification to ensure our idea can be transferred to another? Finally, we use Goff's focus on elaboration to expand and flesh out our thoughts, to see how much they can—and have—grown.
9. **Revision, revision, revision**: No idea is final, and there is always room to change or improve ideas. Feel free to revise statements as necessary, sometimes several times.

One potential challenge to this approach is participants may compare themselves to others, noting "I only came up with three" when another shares they generated more ideas. However, I find this attitude is mitigated by reminding us of the purpose: we're here to support idea exploration and that looks different for all of us. All ideas are valuable. We celebrate every idea, no matter how small they may seem, because it will bring us one step closer to understanding a play, collaborating on a new project, or fostering idea exchange.

EXERCISE #2: TEAM-BASED ANALYSIS

While solo brainstorming is a useful tool, generating ideas with a team is an important skill to practice in terms of establishing fruitful collaboration. Given the nature of theatre, it's important to spend time working through team-based approaches to brainstorming and analysis. This approach uses many of the same basic tools stated above; however, it utilizes a different approach in working towards collaboration. First, participants generate ideas and evaluate them as a group, going over the merits of each. Then, the team selects an idea to go forward with, revising and elaborating, until they feel it meets their needs. This exercise works well with groups who are working on a collective project, allowing opportunity for multiple perspectives on the same prompt.

1. **Set parameters and expectations**: Like Exercise #1, the first steps are to communicate (1) the focus of the brainstorming session and (2) all expectations associated with the session.
2. **Brainstorm**: Set a timer and give each group the time, and room, to brainstorm. They can start by making separate lists or by working together to create one. Ten to fifteen minutes may suffice, but with group brainstorming, more time may be needed.
3. **Encourage discussion**: Instead of moving into the evaluation phase as we did in Exercise #1, we're going to prioritize group discussion. What did you discover? What ideas stand out?
4. **Evaluate**: Though it's likely some evaluation creeps in during Step #4, now is the time to dig into the ideas to see which ones, or ones, best fit our needs. Feel free to revisit Goff's four creative abilities, as we did in Exercise #1, to test, stretch, and expand.
5. **Choosing the "best"**: Focus in and choose one idea to use for the final steps. As a group, choose one of your ideas that "best" fits the circumstances and needs.
6. **Revision, revision, revision**: Spend some time revising and redrafting the idea the group has picked. The current idea is draft #1. Try revising the idea into a second and third draft and see where that leads you. Keep all drafts so you can revisit them if needed.
7. **Final thoughts**: It's important for the group to check back in with a final discussion or check-in to ensure the revision did not take us away from our original intent. Or, if we did stray, are we happy with where we have wandered?

Giving the opportunity for open discussion and adjudication, without judgment to expectation of "correctness," allows for the drafting and revising of ideas. Not only does this approach to thinking creatively take some of the pressure off the individual, it allows for practice in team-based collaboration. Additionally, it provides an opportunity for reflection. With each attempt at this exercise, we do not look for "wrong" or "right" when examining our ideas. Rather, we celebrated the thought that went into a discovery and turn toward revision.

EXERCISE #3: LARGE-GROUP ANALYSIS

When working with a large group, we can use each other as a sounding board for ideas—another way to test our conclusions after generating, adjudicating, and revising. After smaller teams fine-tune their ideas, each chooses a representative to present to the full group. Again, the focus is open, constructive discussion, rather than the right or wrong of the ideas. To do this, participants are encouraged to respond using phrasing grounded in active listening techniques such as, "This statement tells me _____ about _____. Is that what you are trying to say?" If the large group is not receiving what the team intended, then the idea goes back for another round of revision. Large-group discussion is a tool to test more finalized products of brainstorming and evaluation; after all, when developing a performance, our productions have their test in others as well: the audience.

FINAL THOUGHTS

With these exercises, participants are encouraged to explore new perspectives and the more-right approach helps them get comfortable with creativity, rather than being intimidated by a daunting and unfamiliar task. While these exercises work well in a pedagogical setting, their uses within the field of theatre are broad. For example, incorporating brainstorming, evaluation, drafting, and revising of ideas, either from an individual perspective or through teamwork, can be useful in collaborative, non-traditional rehearsal settings. Additionally, these exercises are transferable to situations where creative partners, like a playwright and dramaturg, are collaborating in new play development. I plan to continue this work, building upon what I learn, and I hope you consider adding these methods to your pedagogical and collaborative arsenal.

References

Goff, Kathy. 2005. *Everyday Creativity*. 3rd ed., Mannford: Little Ox Books.
Kelley, Tom and Jonathan Littman. 2001. *The Art of Innovation: Lessons in Creativity from IDEO, America's Leading Design Firm*. New York, NY: Currency.
Sawyer, Keith. 2013. *Zig Zag: The Surprising Path to Greater Creativity*. San Francisco: Jossey-Bass.

19
Theatrical Immersion within Alternate Reality Games

Hans Vermy

INTRODUCTION

More and more the mobility of digital networks merge the internet into our everyday experiences and our everyday experiences onto the internet. Theatre absorbs and reflects *everything* the world has to offer; yet, when theatre moved online during Covid-19 we mostly witnessed performances akin to film and TV instead of shows encouraging a merger of *living participation* online with the *presence* of a theatre audience. There were a few exceptions but one that stood out in its embrace of an internet-located audience was an Alternate Reality Game called *Arcana*—garnering glowing reviews and awards. The online immersive tactics employed by the creators of *Arcana* offer invaluable strategies for developing any kind of experiential narrative that utilize online spaces and social networks. In this essay, I explore the nature and challenges of creating experiential projects like Alternate Reality Games and *Arcana*. To contextualize this exploration, I end the essay by turning to its creators, concluding with their insights into the organization and dramaturgy of making immersive performance a safe, multi-layered, and accessible experience for many kinds of viewers.

ALTERNATE REALITY GAMES AS MEDIATED DRAMA

What is an Alternate Reality Game? An ARG is like a scavenger hunt. Some begin online but rarely stay confined there. The "Alternate Reality" part of the game comes into play because clues for a fictional narrative are dropped inside real-world events. For example, the famous Alternate Reality Game *The Beast* began with a fictional credit on a trailer and poster for the Stephen Spielberg film *A.I* (2001). The credit read: "Jeanine Salla, Sentient Machine Therapist." If one googled "Jeanine Salla," navigating to her webpage would begin the game; without necessarily knowing it was a game. This idea is famously championed for immersive aesthetics by Jane McGonigal (2003) in "'This is Not a Game' Immersive Aesthetics and Collective Play." In a similar play on words, the most comprehensive website for finding information on immersive theatre and games is called *No Proscenium*; in other words, "no frame of performance." Denial of the game is strongly attached to ARGs just as performance art, devising ensembles, and live artists sometimes resist the title "theatre" in order to reframe their audience. McGonigal finds immersive power in a "This is Not a Game" form: "[no frame] made the game world less of a 'virtual' (simulated) reality or an 'augmented' (enhanced) reality, and more of an 'alternate' (layered) reality."

DOI: 10.4324/9781003188179-22

McGonigal wrote hoping to point out the collective community-building and real-world action achieved by ARG players but also noted the obvious dangers: "Are collective intelligences potentially reactionary, rather than (r)evolutionary? Might collective intelligence, operating as a kind of emergent 'hive mind', manifest itself as a more perilous mob mentality?" If you haven't noticed already, this question about the dangers of group puzzle-solving within ARGs has been answered by QAnon. Framing an alternate reality with "this is not a game" creates a *persuasive* element, the same element empowering conspiracy theories that tell followers to "do internet research" to find the truth—where that research leads one deeper into the conspiracy itself, not a network of critique and review of the truth. ARGs are nearly always based around "internet research" that leads one down a rabbit hole of the *real* internet. Theatre is a great lens through which to construct immersive experiences online because theatre too presents an art that is consistently and pervasively identical *in material* to the world it mirrors. Recently called out for being problematic, ARGs are at a crossroads. Their salvation? Ditch "this is not a game" mentality and embrace theatre with its obvious prosceniums.

Arcana offers theatre makers a model for harnessing social realities online into something similar to the immersive experience of a performance. The creators of *Arcana* have shared their process which utilized theatrical frames in order to expand their audience to include those who just watch as well as to *protect* those who chose to participate in full immersion: "Our success in Arcana is due to coming back to our goal: a *new* way to tell an ARG. We wanted to make it accessible with different levels of engagement" (AOTW 2021). Making an Alternate Reality Game accessible on many levels of engagement is to embrace its theatrical proscenium with an offer for the audience to cross through the proscenium and become players. But they don't have to. The audience can sit back and watch on their phones as the main character of *Arcana*, Jade, begins posting to a new account on Instagram. The following is from the official post-show walk-through found on Arcana-game.com:

> *A flyer with the website for Arcana circulates. If participants read... carefully, they discover the enigmatic phrase PROVIDENCE AWAITS. Once they read the rules, participants are directed to the Instagram of a stranger—a fun-loving young artist named JADE. We see her apartment—artsy knick-knacks scattered here and there. Participants may or may not figure out that some of these images contain clues.*

Jade begins to feel haunted as the riddles and her own story begin to collide with the real-life 1927 murder of Marion Parker. Real-life Los Angeles historian Hadley Meares enters the story playing herself, giving the narrative a more powerful connection to the real world. It also opens up the narrative rabbit hole away from Instagram and onto real-world journalism surrounding Marion Parker, which then has clues and puzzles that feed back into the narrative of Jade's story. During the four-week run, the audience had the option to interact through comments, emails, and postings helping shape the complex narrative. Alternate Reality Games are filled with puzzles, like the hiding of the "enigmatic phrase Providence Awaits" within the advertising flyer for *Arcana*, the clues hidden within the sets and props of Jade's apartment, and the story of Marion Parker. It is also a powerfully easy way to engage the audience on multiple levels.

Is *Arcana* theatre or a game? Games and theatrical plays are historically and phenomenologically entangled in many ways. In "Games of the Middle English Religious Drama," Peter Ramey (2013) reveals a deep history of interactive, multi-location theatre performances that allowed for audiences to either watch or participate. What about it being all online? Digital games may seem like they are all about game engineering, but video games have been since their birth on a trajectory towards being a writer-led form

THEATRICAL IMMERSION WITHIN ALTERNATE REALITY GAMES • 173

that unites audience/players into a shared cyberspace—similarly to the way a playwright "leads" a production that eventually brings an audience into a shared space for witnessing a story. When video games were born, the developing technology required technicians to lead, letting writers and designers know what could be done (Bissell 2010). But now designers and writers are leading the way. *Arcana* was one of the best theatre performances of the pandemic; alive, present, and responsive to an engaged audience. It also had puzzles, was performed across social networks, and ran in real-time over four weeks. Experiential theatres aim to embrace a wider audience through more levels of engagement. *Arcana* was astoundingly successful at just that, which is why I asked All of Them Witches, the creative group behind *Arcana*, to share their theories and practices for creating experiential theatre. Theatre educators looking new strategies for teaching their students how to develop the dramaturgy of experiential theatre, like ARGs, can use their insights as a starting point.

All of Them Witches offered a lot of advice which I placed into seven categories followed by their comments. They began by recommending a focus on the *guest experience* and to dramaturgically keep in mind that both guest and experience are plural in immersive art.

1. **Learn and participate in many immersive guest experiences.**
   Go to experiential spaces and performances. Play immersive games; watch the players; learn how different people engage with immersive content. Come to planning an immersive experience with the question, *how will it go wrong?* That is an important question when dealing with immersion and consent. But it's also important to think at scale (when the game has thousands of players). Which is why being familiar with and playing immersive theatre and online games are important.

2. **Protect the guest experience with strong borders and frames.**
   Historically ARGs were used to push the boundaries of consent (extreme haunts, kidnapping storylines, moments that became non-consensual torture); that easily happens with a horror story. Don't make an immersive project that hurts its players. Post #metoo it is no longer appropriate to push the boundaries of consent. Creators need to think through how consent works online and off and maximize thinking about safety. Think ahead: might some misinterpretation of a puzzle lead an audience member to go hunting for treasure somewhere dangerous? And most importantly, say "it's a game. It's a show." And make it easy to see what is in game and what is not.

3. **A braided story allows for braided experiences and various levels of access.**
   If you are new to experiential games, you might have missed some of the puzzles and clues that would stand out for veteran players. So, how does one make a narrative that works for those who just want to watch and those who know to look for deep clues in images and names? [In *Arcana*] we created three tracks within the narrative. The first, was the social track, for those who signed up to follow the show. The second track was for those who would go a step further and investigate the true crime mystery that surrounded the fictions of *Arcana*—such as the Marion Parker murder. The third track was for those who also knew how to look for embedded puzzles and clues.

   [Our large-scale writing process] was broken down over months of collaborative writing where two writers wrote in broad strokes at first and then shared with the whole group, refining, over time and meetings, down to details such as dialogue.

   Sometimes [in the writing process] the puzzle was introduced first and that then affected the story. To the writers, this was gold.

4. **Every guest experience needs a time frame and to be forced into a clear, mostly shared ending.**
   For successful connection with your audience, add that true ending/curtain. Consider what days and times are active [for the audience] and which aren't.

Remember as puppet masters (immersive creators) you need to go to bed, so have a set bedtime when all work must stop. Work breaks into the logic of the narrative as well (lost phone, characters go to sleep or are in transit, etc.) Tell the audience/players when to stop. Have daily endings. Don't let those who want to get fully sucked in suck all your time as creators.

5. **Keep in mind that guest experiences need to account for many different bodies and minds.**
Offer accessibility options up front! We had deaf participants set up on slack, but you have to ask, "what other considerations for accessibility?" Think about even color-blind participants if making color-coded or hidden messages and puzzles. The challenge [when making experiential works is]: can you make more reasonable accommodations, especially since online works can gain so many players so quickly?

6. **Build narrative with the materials you have access to and make sure you know how to keep your online guest experience open for the duration.**
Taking stock of what you and what your audience has. For example, if your audience is on a college campus that changes how they share space (computer labs) versus a giant urban space. In choosing to present on Instagram we knew some players would ethically object to Facebook's ownership. In the end you have to make choices that might leave some audience members out. The smartest decision we made was to write on the Insta bio line, "this is an in-game character." That kept the game online because Instagram can kick you off, shut down access paths, if you don't play by their rules.

7. **Keeping tabs on guest experience is itself a creative experience. Because the ending might not be set until the audience chimes in, creators go along for the whole ride; they don't stop when the curtain goes up.**
For the entire duration of *Arcana*, we observed from beyond the veil, keeping tabs on player delight and frustration to ensure we could adapt narrative and puzzles and access alongside our audience's needs. This was real-time adaptation with pivoting, which enhanced our ability to give the audience real agency. When making a durational immersive experience, plan on working as hard as it runs.

All of Them Witches is comprised of Eva Anderson, Mali Elfman, Eric Hoff, Tommy Honton, and E3W Productions (Aaron Keeling, Austin Keeling, and Natalie Jones). Hans Vermy interviewed them collectively over Zoom in April of 2021.

References

All of Them Witches (AOTW). 2020. "Arcana Game Walkthrough" Online. https://www.arcana-game.com/walkthrough

Bissell, Tom. 2010. *Extra Lives: Why Video Games Matter*. New York: Pantheon.

McGonigal, Jane. 2003. "This is Not a Game: Immersive Aesthetics and Collective Play." Online. PDF: 1–10. ttps://janemcgonigal.files.wordpress.com/2010/12/mcgonigal-jane-this-is-not-a-game.pdf

Ramey, Peter. 2013. "The Audience-Interactive Games of the Middle English Religious Drama." *Comparative Drama* 47 (1): 55–83.

20

A Postdigital Response: Experiential Dramaturgies of Online Theatre, Cyberformance, and Digital Texts

Christina Papagiannouli

POSTDIGITAL RESPONSE

In 2010, I started exploring online theatre[1] as part of my practice research[2] titled *The Etheatre Project: Directing Political Cyberformance*. At the time, I was constantly challenged for using the term theatre, "a very heavily laden word [...], tied to [...] mainstream theatre" (Jamieson 2012) and specific aesthetics, which require a certain code of behavior, a dress code and procedures. At the Sixth International Conference of the Arts in Society (2011), a participant argued that cyberformance—"the genre of digital performance that uses the Internet as a performance space" (Papagiannouli 2016, x)—is not theatre because it misses the "theatrical ritual" of indoor theatre where people dress well to meet friends. Ten years later, the dystopian reality of COVID-19 pandemic "forced" the whole theatre industry to move "online." What I was challenged for not being theatre, became the new theatrical "norm-al." This new normality found many unprepared and clashed with conservative theatre circles who could only see this new norm as an enemy for theatre. As Twyla Mitchell (1999) argues, theatre sees computers as "enemies", fearing that new technology will replace theatre, similarly to humans' fear that computers will replace people, or, in the case of *Matrix*, that avatars will replace humans (10–11). With most theatres across Europe and the rest of the world choosing to stream pre-recorded versions of pre-COVID-19 performances for free to online audiences, instead of creating new live theatre shows online, it indeed raised a key risk for theatre, making its most core characteristic, *liveness*, into a less important element during the pandemic. It did, however, open the path for new forms of sharing theatre recordings and digital archives to entertain a new type of audience who prefer to watch digitized versions of theatre shows than the actual shows in the theatre; first with NTLive's[3] theatre in cinemas, then with National Theatre at Home's[4] YouTube live streamings during the pandemic. The "Narrative and Dramaturgy for Experiential Forms" section incorporates key debates, discussions and examples related to this new "norm-ality" of experiential theatre, demonstrating a real need for new and/or updated approaches and methodologies. Written from a practice-based perspective, this chapter offers a post-digital response to the section, historizing experiential dramaturgies of online theatre, cyberformance, and digital texts.

Although the vast majority of audiences encountered online theatre during the COVID-19 pandemic, it is important to note that cyberformance is not a COVID-19 product, nor a passive form of entertainment. Since its birth, online theatre is primarily about preserving

DOI: 10.4324/9781003188179-23

and strengthening the direct communication between performers and audiences. Shortly after the introduction of the world wide web in the 1990s, theatre-makers started exploring and experimenting with new ways of performing online, recognizing the experiential and interactive character of the internet. Since "[m]any early works were never documented" (Abrahams et al 2021), I am not going to attempt to give a historical record, but rather a brief glimpse of some of theatre makers' early online shows.

In 1993, The Hamnet Players debuted the concept of "Internet Theatre" with their 80-line version of *Hamlet, Hamnet,* using Internet Relay Chat[5] (irc) software and world-wide-web (www) links (irc Theatre, Live!!!, no date). The Hamnet Players produced six online participatory performances, *Hamnet* in December 1993 and February 1994, *PCBeth* (an IBM clone of Macbeth) in April and July 2014, and *An irc Channel Named #desire* in October 1994 and February 1995. The actors, who were based in various locations, received their lines and cues by e-mail and, without rehearsals, adapted and delivered their lines via keyboard in real-time during the performances (irc Theatre, Live!!!, no date). Here, performers and audience shared the same virtual space, communicating with each other via text. This can be considered a collective writing exercise, where the mistakes of the "damned actors" (Kidder 1994) and the responses of the audience re-adapted the play during the live performance. In The Hamnet Players performances, the performativity of writing was enhanced by the use of text-made sets and props. For an example, see the boar's head image at the following link. https://www.marmot.org.uk/hamnet/pscript.htm.

Similarly, since 1994, the Plaintext Players (founded by new media artist Antoinette LaFarge) performed live text-based online theatre performances using multi-user cross platforms (such as MOOS)[6] to explore new ways of interactive play-writing as live performance. The Plaintext Players invited their audiences to "witness the process of composition of a work of art—and the work of art as a process of composition" (Corcoran 1999, 359). Their LittleHamlet project, for instance, was a "reworking of the Hamlet story that inverted text and subtext" to allow "all of the characters" formerly unspoken needs, fears, and desires [to come] to the fore" (Plaintext Players 1995, in Papagiannouli 2016, 4). As Marlena Corcoran (1999) highlights, "[t]here is no point in looking for the author's intention, because there are about half a dozen writers performing together" (359).

In 1997, Desktop Theater (Adriene Jenik and Lisa Brenneis) performed a web adaptation of *Waiting for Godot* by Samuel Beckett, *waitingforgodot.com* in The Palace[7]—a program with graphical chat room servers in which users interact using avatars with their messages appearing as chat bubbles, similarly to comic books. In Desktop Theater's performances in The Palace, audiences as avatars shared the same virtual space with the performers, allowing for pure moments of interaction to take place. *Waitingforgodot.com* is known as the "the only performance of Beckett"s *Waiting for Godot* where Godot has actually arrived" (Jamieson 2008, 26, see also Papagiannouli 2018, 429), as during the live event a participant changed their avatar's name into Godot and announced his arrival. Despite using graphic elements, Desktop Theater's performances were also primarily text-based, as the communication of the text was through chat bubbles. As Toni Sant and Kim Flintoff rightly argue, these text-based platforms "are perfect for performers and audiences to mingle; the creation of the environment is a co-production between all who come to participate" (2007) in the same vein of the notion of *partakers* as co-creators discussed by Erin Mee.

With most platforms being primarily text-based,[8] the initial experiments of online theatre have been seen as a new way of performing writing. Even when technologies improved, and online theatre purpose-built platforms started appearing, text-based communication remained a significant tool to allow interaction and co-production with the audience. The use of chat-box and chat bubbles remained key tools of the UpStage platform, a venue for online theatre produced in 2004 by Douglas Bagnall for the Avatar Body Collision (Helen Varley Jamieson, Karla Ptacek, Leena Saarinen, and Vicki Smith), and are still used in the new UpStage version launched in October 2021. In the meantime, theatre companies started experimenting with social media platforms, such as Twitter, Facebook and Instagram, combining the use of text, image, sound, and video communication tools. In 2010, the Royal Shakespeare Company (RSC) staged *Such Tweet Sorrow,* a Twitter adaptation of *Romeo and Juliet,* with the actors posting tweets of up to 140 characters. RSC's five-week durational performance engaged audiences in a co-production experience, "with the live version of the play [...] created and completed by both the actors" and "the audience's tweets" (Papagiannouli 2016, 3). Adapting classics, and especially Shakespeare, is another common characteristic of online theatre's initial experiments that we still see in more recent examples. As John H. Muse (2012) highlights, "[t]o date, the most popular Twitter stagings have been adaptations" (45). Even during the pandemic, readings of classic plays on Zoom overtook the online theatre landscape. One of the first projects that emerged was Robert Myles' *The Show Must Go Online*—weekly readings of the complete Shakespeare's plays on Zoom by an international cast. Moreover, Forced Entertainment shared an at home version of their *Complete Works*, a series of broadcasts of Tabletop retellings of all Shakespeare's plays, using household objects.

PREPARING OURSELVES

Looking at the history of online theatre from a transmedia, postdigital, post-internet and now from a post-Covid future, it is important to highlight its experiential character. The Internet might be the biggest archive in the world, but it is simultaneously an interactive space, a medium for communication and a collaborative platform that brings geographically distant users together in real-time. When in 2018 Richard Gough (General Editor of Performance Research Journal) invited me to write a response on the *Performance Research* issue "On Line" (Allsopp and Scott de Lahunta 1999) for the celebratory 100th issue (Gough 2018), I argued that little, if anything, had changed since the 1990s initial experiments and discussions on online theatre and performance in the period until 2018, and made a call for more experiential forms of practice:

> If I wish for anything to have changed in the field of online performance since 1999, it is for more Godots [referring to Desktop Theater"s *waitingforgodot.com*] to keep on appearing and creatively changing, disturbing, disrupting, challenging, trolling and motivating pure interactivity, immersion and participation in online theatre and performance. (Papagiannouli 2018, 430).

But how can we prepare ourselves for the future? Online adaptations offer new narrative, dramaturgy and collective writing approaches for experiential forms of theatre. Artists and performers can now use social media to explore and build their characters, connect and interact with their audiences and with other performers/characters through chat or live streaming communication, and incorporate intermedial and interdisciplinary approaches to performance. In 2019, we asked: "What do we do with a cohort of student-performers who show more interest in Instagram than in Konstantin Stanislavski, in Facebook than in Peter Brook and in Google than in Bertolt Brecht?" (Crews and Papagiannouli 2019). The *InstaStan – FaceBrook – Brecht+:a performer training methodology for the age of the internet* offers some exercises and approaches, focusing on a laboratory-style and critical-creative processes (for *creativity* as pedagogical approach, see Rachel E. Bauer's chapter) and engaging students/performers as both participants and facilitators of creative practice, allowing them to make strong connections between everyday digital tools and theatre and performance methods and techniques. As Maria Kapsali (2020) notes in the introduction of the *Performer Training and Technology: Preparing Ourselves* book—a more complete study of technology-informed performer training methods written before Covid-19 but published in the middle of the pandemic—"the aim is to kick start an approach towards performer training that acknowledges its deep affinities with technology and thus catalyses the (re)consideration of past, present or future encounters with technology" (23).

Indeed, we need to become more flexible and start incorporating new technologies in theatre training, preparing tomorrow's performers, directors, playwrights and dramaturgs for the theatre(s) of the present and future. New technologies in theatre are not anymore a "privilege" for multimedia companies and digital artists. Mainstream theatres, such as the Royal Shakespeare Company and the Royal National Theatre in London, a.k.a. National Theatre (NT), are now incorporating interactive and immersive technologies into their work. RSC continues to experiment with new technologies, producing the *Dream* performance in 2021, a virtual performance using motion capture, while the National Theatre has its own Immersive Storytelling Studio, working with "artists and emerging technologies to develop new dramatic work and experiences" (NT).

New forms of experiential narratives, such as Alternate Reality Games (see Hans Vermy), require new and updated playwriting approaches, open to collective contributions, audience interactions, and the structures or strictures of digital and social media platforms. Indeed, "social media [and the internet] are reshaping both playwriting and the experience of theatrical spectatorship" (Muse 2012, 43). The use of cued questions and script breaks/pauses to allow improvisational moments between performers and the audience is essential for live experiential online plays, adapted or original. I used textual improvisation for *The Etheatre Project* as a method to build the narrative of the pieces: "The improvisational character of the project allowed space for audience interpretation, sharing dialectical thinking and critical participation" (Papagiannouli 2016, 87). Here, performers asked specific questions to the audience to prompt discussion, while blocked cues functioned as transitional moments to link the improvised discussions and inspire audience reflection on the topic.

Postdigital and post-internet theatre practices, such as Tabletop Storytelling (see Mike Sell), also reveal a need for new forms of digital media dramaturgy. A theatre that moves online needs experts in the study of digital/online theatre, who will provide the cast and crew with vital knowledge, research, and interpretation about online audience interaction, different uses of online platforms and digital tools. In 2020, Tasos Angelopoulos, the artistic director of Papalangki theatre (Greece), asked me to help the company move their *Ubu Roi* production online. Following initial rehearsals, we decided to build *UBUmaterial*, a performative archive on Instagram, in order to engage audiences in a virtual modellbook (in Brechtian terms) sharing a series of *material* not just as outputs, but also as evidence of the *architecture* of the work (see Robert Quillen Camp's use of term *material* as *architecture*). Here, performers as "abstracters" (see Sarah Johnson's notion of "abstracters") created and recorded video improvisations, which were then edited, transcribed, and uploaded on Instagram, together with live Instagram events where audience members entered the live streaming and posted messages and emojis via the live-stream's chat-box. *UBUmaterial* engaged followers and participants in an experiential post-dramatic version of *Ubu Roi*, allowing them to enter the live events, interact with Instagram accounts of some of the play's characters and create their own materials:

A POSTDIGITAL RESPONSE • **179**

In UBUmaterial"s deconstructed, digitalworld (really, how happy would Jarry be?), even the very end (?) is still pending to be established as "the end". The performative archive finished with an open invitation to its audiences to send their own videos, photos, thoughts, poems and anything else they can imagine or think that can open a conversation with UBUmaterial. (Angelopoulos et al 2021, 14)

I also worked with Jill Greenhalgh to move her *Daughter's* performance online for the 2021 Online Magdalena Festival. In the case of *Daughter*, the project had already a long and successful running history and "was never conceived for online engagement" (Mastrominico 2021). With respect to the original piece and the personal stories of the performers—*Daughter* follows a refined creative process and intimate presentation structure and style—I started looking for an appropriate platform to re-stage the piece online, as close as possible to the original project. Besides, the eye-contact between the storyteller and the audience member, one of the most essential characteristics of the piece, was already lost as soon as rehearsals moved online—it is impossible to have an eye contact online, instead you can only look at each other's camera boxes. The Ohyay.co platform allowed us to create individual rooms for each performer, each of which would represent a "table," with an image of the storytellers table and two webcam windows, one for the storyteller and one for the listener. Similarly to the live performance, audiences gathered around each "table" (they could only watch what was happening in the room without participating) and witnessed the one-to-one intimate exchange between the storyteller and the listener. When a listener would leave a table, Ohyay.co would randomly bring a new listener from the invisible witnesses inside the room/"table." As a digital media dramaturge, I attended rehearsals to better understand the needs of each piece, and took responsibility of the technical needs of the projects, from finding the right platforms for the performances, to building a virtual room on Ohyay.co and creating an account on Instagram, to "teaching" the performers how to use the platform (in the case of *Daughter*) and creating an Instagram posting strategy for *UBUmaterial*, to supporting the technical needs of the actual live performances.

CONCLUSION

Although online theatre has existed since the 1990s, the history of online theatre "is still recent and directors, performers, and audiences are still finding their paths in this virtual world" (Selim 2020, 7). COVID-19 and social-distancing rules have pushed things forward, making online theatre the new "norm-al." However, it is important to maintain online theatre's experiential, interactive, immersive and live character. This section offers important examples of online experiential theatre (see *Arcana* alternate reality game discussed by Hans Vermy in "Theatrical Immersion within Alternate Reality Games"), immersive performances (see "Mapping Narrative in Pig Iron Theatre Company's Pay Up and Franklin's Secret City" by Robert Quillen Camp) and highlights the role of audience (*partakers)* as co-creators in experiential theatre (see This Is Not A Theatre Company's case study by Erin B. Mee). These examples, along with the rise of online theatre during the COVID-19 pandemic, demonstrate a real need for new and/or updated approaches to theatre and performance training. As Gary Garrison notes in "Reconfiguring Narrative and Experiential Dramaturgy: A Conversation with Professional Educators and Dramaturgs on the Future(s) of Storytelling," "theater training is about 25 years behind the reality of the world that we're living in." "The WildWind Performance Lab: New Play Development through Abstraction" by Sarah Johnson and the use of a creative approach into teaching in "It's Okay to NOT be "Right": Incorporating Creativity Approaches into a Conventional

180 • CHRISTINA PAPAGIANNOULI

Theatre Arts Course" by Rachel E. Bauer offer new training approaches. There is also a need for new playwriting approaches and dramaturgies, translating and adapting plays from stage to cyberstage, and supporting the performers and the crew through an explorative journey of new technologies. The need for new dramaturgies is also reflected in Mike Sell's "The Dramaturgy of Tabletop Roleplaying Games."

Notes

1 I am using the term "online theatre" because it has been used more widely since the Covid-19 pandemic. Other terms that exist to describe this practice include cyberformance, cybertheatre(s), internet theatre, and network performance (see Papagiannouli & Rodríguez 2021, 117; 137–139).
2 I am using the term "Practice Research" in accordance with the Practice Research Advisory Group (PRAG-UK).
3 NTLive is Royal National Theatre's (in London) program of selected performances which are broadcasted live via satellite to cinemas in the UK and internationally.
4 National Theatre at Home is NTLive's initiative to live stream its repertoire on YouTube during the Covid-19 lockdowns in the UK. National Theatre at Home now offers its own streaming service through subscription.
5 Internet Relay Chat (irc) is an open source and free real-time text messaging online system created by Jarkko Oikarinen in 1988.
6 Multi-user Object-Oriented space (MOOS) is a text-messaging online platform released by Stephen White in 1990.
7 The Palace is a 2D avatar-based interactive chat environment created by Jim Bumgardner in 1994.
8 The first online live streaming performance can be traced in 1994, when Nina Sobell and Emily Hartzell launched ArTisTheater, a series of live, weekly, online performances. In ArTisTheatre audiences could see into the artists" studio in real-time through a telerobotic video camera called LabCam, which broadcasted live content on the net. In ArTisTheatre audiences could click on the frame and control the direction of the camera, requesting the next frame in real-time (Hartzell, 1998).

References

Abrahams, Annie, Helen Varly Jamieson, and Suzon Fuks. 2021, January 22. "Before the first [Video]". Vimeo. https://vimeo.com/503467731
Allsopp, Ric and Scott deLahunta. 1999. "On Line," *Performance Research*, 4(2): iii–iv.
Angelopoulos, Tasos, Panayiota Konstantinakou, and Christina Papagiannouli. 2021. "UBUmaterial: Building a Performative Archive on Instagram." *International Journal of Performance Arts and Digital Media*, DOI: 10.1080/14794713.2021.2006486
Crews, Sarah and Christina Papagiannouli. 2019. "InstaStan – FaceBrook – Brecht +: a performer training methodology for the age of the internet." *Theatre, Dance and Performance Training* 10 (2): 187–204, DOI: 10.1080/19443927.2019.1613260
Corcoran, Marelena. 1999. "Life and Death in the Digital World of the Plaintext Players". *Leonardo*, 32 (5): 359–364. doi: 10.1162/002409499553578
Gough, Richard. 2018. "On Reflection." *Performance Research* 23 (4&5): 1–5.
Hartzell, Emily. 1998. "Nina Sobell and Emily Hartzell: Collaborators in Art with Technology." In *Women, Art and Technology* Judy Malloy (Ed.). Leonard: MIT Press
irc Theatre, Live!!! About the Hamnet Players. http://www.hambule.co.uk/hamnet/
Jamieson, Helen Varly. 2012. "Interviewed by Christina Papagiannouli". 3 April. Available at: https://etheatreblog.wordpress.com/helen-varley-jamieson/
Jamieson, Helen Varly. 2008. "Adventures in Cyberformance: Experiments at the Interface of Theatre and The Internet", unpublished Master of Arts (Research) thesis, Australia: Queensland University of Technology, http://creativecatalyst.com/thesis.html; http://eprints.qut.edu.au/28544/1/Helen_Jamieson_Thesis.pdf
Kapsali, Maria. 2020. *Performer Training and Technology: Preparing Our Selves*. Oxon & New York: Routledge.
Kidder, Gayle. 1994. *PCbeth: An IBM clone of Macbeth. irc-play*. Available at: https://www.marmot.org.uk/hamnet/pscript.htm

Mastrominico, Bianca. 2021. *Reflections on Shifting Practice in BODIES:ON:LIVE MAGDALENA:ON:LINE 2021*, https://onlinefestival.themagdalenaproject.org/reflections-on-shifting-practice/

Mitchell, Twyla. 1999. "Terror at the Terminal: How Some Artists View Computers." In Schrum, Stephen Alan. A. (Ed.) *Theatre in Cyberspace: Issues of Teaching, Acting and Directing.* New York: Peter Lang, pp. 9–18.

Muse, John. 2012. "140 Characters in Search of a Theater: Twitter Plays." *Theater*, 42 (2): 43–63. DOI: 10.1215/01610775-1507784

NT [National Theatre] *Immersive Storytelling Studio*, Available at: https://www.nationaltheatre.org.uk/immersive

Papagiannouli, Christina, and Rodríguez, Verónica. 2021. "Online Theatre/Theatre Online: What Can Theatre Learn from the Covid-19 Pandemic?" In Feryal Cubukcu (Ed.) *Toward Digitalism.* Ankara: Nobel Akademik Yayincilik, pp. 113–143.

Papagiannouli, Christina. 2016. *Political Cyberformance: The Etheatre Project.* (Pivot). Palgrave MacMillan. DOI: 10.1057/9781137577047

Papagiannouli, Christina. 2018. "On Line: A Response from a Transmedial, Postdigital and Post-Internet Future." *Performance Research* 23 (4–5): 428–430. DOI: 10.1080/13528165.2018.1506384

Sant, Toni and Kim Flintoff. 2007. "Website Supplementary Article: The Internet as a Dramatic Medium". Interactive and Improvisational Drama: Varieties of Applied Theatre and Performance, July 24. https://www.interactiveimprov.com/onlinedr.html

Selim, Yasser Fouad. 2020. "Cyberformance: Towards a Transnational User-Response Theory", *International Journal of Performance Arts and Digital Media*, DOI: 10.1080/14794713.2020.1722915

Section 3
Performance Technologies and Design Thinking

21
Pedagogies for Design Thinking and Experiential Technologies

Bruce Bergner and Rich Dionne

DESIGN THINKING AND HISTORIES OF AESTHETICS

Every moment is an experience. And life is a composite of innumerable such moments. Each moment has impact, be it cognitive, affective, sensory, or inconspicuous, encoded into our synaptic registries, sometimes triggering action or thought. A moment, an experience, is elemental.

Moments can be made. Preceding the etchings at Altamira, performative storytelling emerged among our ancestors. And since, theatre has shouldered the charge to render moments and animate story. For a duration, beginning ca. 2500 BP, it did so within self-imposed limits, venerating a comfortable partition between performer and spectator. Designers aided by various technological innovations, hewed scenic worlds, bound by the defining perimeters of the boards, to be watched, or at best felt, by a passive audience. Mainstream teachers of design cast curricula after accordant practice, emphasizing exact design, within the margins.

Theatre today, customarily, is breaching its margins. In its experiential forms, it ventures without benefit of its once expected elements, such as linear narratives, conventional performers, and constrained scenography. It stretches into the realms of themed entertainment and immersive installations. It appends interactive museums and commercial pop-ups. Its breadth has become prodigious. There is now a cultural desire for prescribed visceral experience. Experiential Theatre, providing an immediate engagement of host and guest, wrought of intended moments in a constituted environment, is made more in the manner of music and film than architecture. Experience Design (XD)—in service to Experiential Theatre—follows suit, preparing a score or storyboard before plans and elevations. Such new design beckons new training and new understandings of the technologies that allow for deeper forms of experiencing.

New design pedagogies, aiming to divulge methods for devising experience, must regard XD's formulative tendencies. Following theatre's tradition, XD's creative journey usually inaugurates with story. The story may be linear, spatial, or amorphous, and it may arrive fully wrought or may evolve organically within the experience of individual attendees by their very immersion, but remains a primary source, be it prescribed or predicted. The design process, with a quest to convey the story by myriad languages of experience, courses through phases of dramaturgy, including an anthropology of audience, site interpretation, and a tally of accessible idioms, technologies, and materials. For designers of experience,

DOI: 10.4324/9781003188179-25

185

research is a vital skill, as is composition. XD must instill an understanding of the static, dynamic, cohesive, and connective values of fluid, composed experience. The statics of experience involves fashioning moments of distinction and significance—places where one can be, and things one can do—parsed judiciously throughout the environment. The dynamics of experience involve the way of the event, how it moves, its arc, path, and thread. All of this must live in a unified world. That is its cohesion. And all of this must link with the guest attendant, reaching them. That is its human connection. To augment these values, the compositional task might depend on the employment of special tools.

As for technologies, they are the sustenance for design. And XD training can explore how designers approach, encounter, partake, and apply this vital body. First, they learn to identify the wish, what an audience member craves. Their story may call for a moment of high energy and they wish for a way to empower it. Inspired by the wish, their investigation yields a novel technical option, a kind of "magic." It may be a tool, a mechanism, or a trick they discover that generates the energy the moment needs. Technology serves and nourishes the work. From this, they ingest new knowledge to fortify future designs which bolster innovation.

Establishing story, conducting dramaturgy, composing experiential moments, and relishing technology are not solitary exploits. They involve a creative collective. The process is collaborative, and so is the product. This might be lesson one. An experience design progresses through an amalgam of individuals with distinct offerings. The product they bear is co-joined with an audience. Together there is a storytelling that becomes an event. The event might commission a machine to activate its moments, the service of technology. And in the event's environment, a community emerges, a union and a life. This life may contain an impactful experience. And in the end, the experience may present what famed American theatre designer Robert Edmond Jones called our art form's ideal: telling the truth.

THE TWENTIETH CENTURY AND NEW PERSPECTIVES ON AESTHETIC EXPERIENCES

In his prime, Jones became the centerpiece of a young stage designer's inspirational pool. His landmark text, *The Dramatic Imagination: Reflections and Speculations on the Art of the Theatre* (1941), was ubiquitous among training institutions. In it, he laid convincing edification toward what "should" be a novitiate designer's quest. Although some of the references are dated, many of his global philosophies still hold value, even inspiring work in XD. Prior to Jones and his contemporaries, designers were schooled by other classic forms, trade apprenticeships, or their own inventions. Italian Renaissance designers were trained architects, easel painters, and engineers: masters of illusion via mechanical perspective and the marvels of stage mechanics. Later, scenic painting began to flourish, and designers made their way through guilds and the scenic studio system. By the nineteenth century, a few notable figures, such as David Belasco, rebelled against flat, painterly convention and introduced dimensionality to the form. This trend became a guideway for the New Stagecraft. At the turn of the twentieth century, Edward Gordon Craig, Adolphe Appia, and Lee Simonson sowed principles for a new discipline, one that redefined the theatre design aesthetic, escalating the merits of dramatic space, performer, and story, and inspiring Jones' vision, ascent, and legacy. Jones was assisted by Broadway stalwart Jo Mielziner who was later assisted by Ming Cho Lee. Lee donned the mantle of "Dean of American Design" in his long and influential tenure at the Yale School of Drama. At the tails of that lineage emanates a new didactic, teaching XD.

Jones mentored legions of orthodox designers. Through his writings and recorded talks, he forged an ideology of theatre design, rich with visions of the transcendent artist, lush literary references, and a fervent, unique logic. Design teachers, to this day, embrace his scrutiny of the audience psyche, his chase of imaginative powers, his dissection of aesthetic perceptivity, and his charting the imperatives of design. Theatre artists were taught to speak to the collective unconscious of their audiences, to elevate their images and themes toward a resonance with some ancient and universal profundity. Jones conferred these artists with a faculty to metamorphose the actual into the supernormal. They were presumed to change guests' lives by sagaciously formulating dramatic moments that buoyed consciousness into a land of dreams. Jones was aspirational in his service to the audience and taught as such. He revered the imagination, and in the context of drama, viewed it as almost numinous. He expounded: Designers must invoke the imagination as a manner of making. One does not intellectualize design content, one visualizes it. Content springs from something accessed by the designer, deep below the sentient surface. In the greatest instances, the theatre attendee accesses the same. The marriage of imaginations in maker and taker is a unity nearly sacred. And if all goes well, the experience blossoms as poetry, a feature one filters through prisms of perception.

Perception is addressed in both *The Dramatic Imagination* and in the voices of Jones' protégés and peers. In the senses of the viewer, a well-designed stage setting should transitorily impress and then essentially cease to exist, going unnoticed while the action of the text unfolds. This sentiment was echoed by Lee in later years. A theatre production should be perceived as a life in an environment rather than a show on a stage. This notion was frequently parroted by Mielziner. Like Appia before him, Jones saw performance space as a media onto itself, arguing that dimensional placement was an artful and communicative wavelength for perception, and like Czech Scenographer Josef Svoboda after him, maintained that the theatre experience should be felt, not watched. One can trace a scholarly lineage on topics of experiential and experiential design—originating with Appia, channeled through Jones, and inspired by Svoboda—in the works of Arnold Aronson, Jarka Burian, Scott Palmer, and Rachel Hahn.

Inspired by the luminary figures around him, Jones engraved his imperatives, the compulsory actions of design, into the record: A designer must function as a clairvoyant, a seer of souls, a conduit to the cores of text, audience, and performance. They must evoke and not explain. A designer must arrange, placing the walls of the set precisely where the energy of a play, its emotional content, its aura, has its definite physical edges. A designer must be an artist of occasions and orchestrate a dramatic event like a music composer. And a designer, buttressed by the latest technological assets, must enchant the audience attendee, moving them with an impulse toward some higher plane. How synchronously these precepts of yesterday fluoresce upon XD's present (and future) mission. Illuminated by Jones' fluorescence, future teachers of design might engrave their own principles of XD. They might advance design tenets, including the foundational considerations of Story, Language, Form (space), Function (service), Flow (sequence, direction, motion), Detail (especially concerning the experiential proximity of guest to content), and Engagement (points of human connection and how that connection evolves).

PEDAGOGIES FOR DESIGN THINKING AND TECHNOLOGICAL IMPLEMENTATION

In our proposed program for training the design process of experience, a series of studio projects could be cobbled toward emphasizing how one finds a design's inaugural point of story, message, or scenario, the instigation of the creative process. Once such an instigation is fully known and mined via design dramaturgy, the language of experience is indoctrinated. Are a design's colors, textures, haptic elements, and aural or musical natures, the voices that will, like sirens, induce the attendees? How are those voicings orchestrated into a composite, often non-verbal, storytelling? This becomes a type of creating discipline that is teachable. Students could begin studies into the shapes of the event: moments, phases, and pathways that confirm the form of the experience. These can be spatial studies, compositional arrangements, and even musically analogous event plans. And when imagining an event musically, one cannot avoid musing melodically. They might ask: How does the event move? Is it linear, spatial, or liquid? Does it course along a way? Or does it churn with no definitive route? This reckoning with flow is a healthy subject for a day's exercise on a whiteboard. Additionally, they might ask: What do the space and content aim to serve? Each element being considered for an experience design should have a function. This involves a designer's honing. Following that editorial passage, a deliberate attending to detail becomes part of the project's evolution. Find what is appropriate in meaning and what is effective in the context of the attendee's encounter with the detail. And above all else, there should be an uber-arching quest for evidence on how the designed experience reaches its audience's minds, emotions, backgrounds, and spirit. This is a drill in deep reading one's audience.

Such a program might outline the elements of XD and their modes of actuation, such as Experience (the act of conjuring experience from objects, subjects, and thoughts), Design (the act of chasing ideal form, function, and flow), Space (the act of interrogating and apprehending the values of dimension), Time (the act of scoring the event), and Technology (the act of realizing the impactful via devices). Designers should be taught the value of their own creative actions. A design action is fueled by the element of design at its root consideration, a basic component of the end-product that induces a move toward its own attainment. In Experiential Theatre, most practicing designers identify the fundamental components of Experience, Design, Space, Time, and Technological attributes as their root considerations starting out. Like a stage director outlining the motivations of characters in a play, designers might lay out the way they classify these gestational kernels. And this program might promulgate upon the provisions of XD. This may encompass qualities of design, namely: Interaction/Immersion (fostering the visceral, immediate, and tangible), Education/Enrichment (fostering the intellectual and moral), Spectacle/Attraction (fostering wonder, awe, and dreams), and the Emotional/Psychological (fostering the deeper self in generative and receptive ways).

If a standard curriculum were built, its architecture might carry framing rubrics that each advance a distinct priority. At its base may be a Theory Pedagogy, describing the way of the designer, identifying the designer's spirit, their fundamental makeup, accumulations, and world perspective. Such a course could anatomize the tactics of design and research the means of project engagement. And it might stress problem-solving, elucidating a central duty in the honing of XD, one of productive confrontation and irising resolution. A Practice Pedagogy could follow, one that walks through the procedures of XD. It might traverse the collaborative exercise, introducing strategies and examining profiles among living studios. In its discourse, it might trek subjectively from the ideation of the conceptual to the creation of the material. And then it may cross the area of implementation, covering both artistic and commercial systems of realizing designs.

This could be explored via mock/paper process projects, administered by host guides—perhaps from the profession—who can mark the crossroads, landmarks, portages, and scrambles in the journey of making. These would become a set of walking rehearsals for genuine making in the field. And each such guided, risk-free tour might attend to a distinct aspect of creative negotiation and navigation. A kind of map-savvy with regards to efficacy and dexterity of procedural ways is potential survival gear from the ascendant creative.

PEDAGOGIES FOR DESIGN THINKING AND EXPERIENTIAL TECHNOLOGIES • **189**

On a parallel, one might construct a Technology Pedagogy, which will ask questions: how is technology accessed and what are the implications? The rising availability of technology is unprecedented. There are lower equipment costs. Hacker/maker movements have made prototyping easier. The ubiquity of always-connected devices raises and changes expectations. Self-curated entertainment makes passive acceptance of delivered content no longer sufficient for audiences. How do we learn/teach technology? You can't design or create what you don't know is possible. How do we learn what is possible? How do we learn to contextualize what is possible? How does one connect what they can do with what they want to do? And how do we maintain a squared marriage of design and technology? The queries go on. But the answers can be boundless and invaluable. Technology for XD is hard-wired to the webwork of the creative subconscious. Tech and design feed from one another. They trigger each other's circuitry and together fire the primary drive. As discussed earlier, that drive impels a species of "magic." And for a student of XD to become acquainted with that magic's machinery, they will need to earn fluency in both conceptualization and the toolset. This can demand a good degree of inquiry. That inquiry is a set for a future spike in the designer's vocational volley.

And conclusively, there might be a Delivery Pedagogy, one that projects the communication of design. Its curricula might manifest like a portfolio of new standards. As such, it displays the protocols of interfacial communication between designer and client or producer. It posts an assemblage of graphic norms for mood boarding, sketching, storyboarding, scripting, rendering, modeling, and drafting. It archives an album of presentation strategies, how to sell the idea, market/brand, and portray cultural connections. It tells the story of how to tell the story. Of all the parcels in XD, the one most commonly referred to as central to success or failure of projects is this communication package. Getting clarity of vision—on paper (per se)—and establishing the way the vision is prioritized and articulated on spreadsheets, across budgets/calendars, and in construction rolls, is a vital aspect of the functioning field. In our roundtable discussion on experiential design/technology practices, many of the respondents address this exact mantra.

Putting all these proposals into a succinct whole, this becomes but one imagined program. It will take the keen imaginations of future teachers, mentors, and guides (such as those who write here) to prepare those programs which will actually embark in academic studios. But if one summons the same degree of vigor and rigor that possessed Jones, one might set a beacon on which the design world relies and lead us to what he described as "a theatre, a stage, a production, that will be exciting to the point of astonishment" (Jones 1941: 1982, 144).

Simultaneously, as Jones' spread his philosophical vision on conventional design approaches, a related, and very concrete influence—stemming from conventional theatre's architectural trends—became manifest in the educational realm. Schools and departments of theatre became inextricable from their physical plants. The spaces in which one tests and presents academic work became essential. Even an institution's recruitment of desirable prospects included doses of marketing material heralding the facilities these charges might indulge. Many schools' resident makerspaces were modeled after what had become vogue in the profession. State-of-the-art proscenium venues, "Guthrie-esque" thrust stages, polished arena configurations with generous vomitories and adorned lighting grids, and black-box spaces with boundless seating flexibility, sprouted from foundations on campus grounds. Donors were solicited to fund these brick-and-mortar treasures. Dreams were laid as ground was broken. And with such spaces available to house one's craft, ideals of polished, realized productions—often qualitatively competitive with established regional theatres—became an aim, then a goal, then an expectation. From there, a student's polished production portfolio became analogous to the well-made dissertation. A focus was cast on modeling one's educational achievement after the highest regarded professional specimens. And pedagogy often evolved toward teaching a method of craftwork toward a discernable standard, more than fostering a quest for innovation and invention and seeking new definitions of what theatre, design, and technology might mean.

A signature, recent pedagogy of theatre has been built around the realized production. Most academic programs in theatre—and in design and technology—integrate, to some degree, realized production work with classroom content delivery and exercises. The specific ways these productions are integrated may vary from program to program: some programs may have a structured progression of scaffolded experiences (for example, students may be assigned as a painter in the scene shop first, then as a scenic design assistant, and then as a scenic designer). Others may be less structured while still providing opportunities for students to put into practice what they've learned in the classroom. Regardless of the specific pedagogical framework, allowing students to move from theory to practice on realized production work is a staple of theatre education.

This praxis approach to theatre instruction, commencing in the twentieth century, led many institutions to create proscenium performance spaces—some new-built, others renovated and repurposed spaces. These spaces reflected the widely accepted design aesthetic of the time: a fourth-wall and a voyeuristic, representational style, with the audience physically separated from the performance. In the middle to the latter part of the twentieth century, as artists like Artaud, Brook, Brecht, and others began to challenge the validity of representational approaches to theatre and explore more "experimental" ways of presenting theatrical work and relating to an audience, the black box theatre began to become more common. In the 1960s and 1970s, black box theatres began popping up in theatre departments across the country—in some places as the only theatre, and in others as a "second stage" venue for experimental work.

The presence of these spaces—proscenium and black box—both enabled and defined the pedagogy of praxis in theatre education. They permitted students to create theatrical experiences, designing visual and aural worlds for performers to explore and audiences to experience. However, it is impossible to ignore the degree to which they restrict and define both the development of theoretical approaches to space and audience experience as well as the ways of moving theory to praxis in live performance. The proscenium by its nature creates a barrier between audience and performers; the more experimental black box space, while more flexible, often still defines distinct audience and performance spaces. To be sure, other influences inform this, from ticket sales, to space capacity limits, from fire code to ADA accessibility requirements. These theatre spaces represent expensive capital investments, and, as a result, most are still in active use at educational institutions across the country. Many have been updated with new equipment and systems as lighting, sound, video, and scenic automation technologies have evolved in an attempt to "keep up with the times." These venues are typically the primary (or only) spaces for students to apply their learning; as a result, they inevitably define the pedagogy and interaction of theory and praxis. For well or ill, even students learning about experiential theatre may find themselves designing for a proscenium stage during their school years or designing for a black box space that has limits in terms of audience/performer boundaries.

Fortunately, a few select programs—some affiliated with art schools and general design programs instead of theatre departments—have adopted an adventurous spirit regarding experiential, performative space. Space can transcend real estate. It can be virtual. It can be imagined. It can also riff off the gaming design universe. There are several, easily accessible computer programs that allow a participant to create an avatar, walk through an experiential world and encounter a story digitally. These kinds of tools have found their way into commercial design studios where gaming designers are often employed to accentuate the creative collective. Some training programs have reflected the tendency toward melding digital design with the physical mechanics of making live experience, offering curricular electives into animation and gaming arts. Their studios became tooled with copious provisions to dive into the depths of digital design. This adventurous nature nurtures new explorations into actual space as well, with a few training bodies fabricating their own soundstages, or other kinds of palpable proving grounds, to assay the powers of environment. How do area, line, shape, direction, movement, material attributes, imagery, color, light, and texture, stimulate and affect response? How does the surround invest in the story? These proving spaces may never present marketable public events, instead obliging as productive Petri dishes for concocting moments of impression in a laboratory setting.

A palatable experiential theatre event is prepared from an apposite mix of ingredients from a venturesome tester's hearth. The designer is the chef. And any seasoned gastronome will not serve their guests a soup before sampling the nuances between a quarter and half cup of umami miso. Likewise, a designer, especially one of neophyte status, will benefit from the play-safe pantry of an amenable pot to stir their bounty in solace: an open room with tools and toys and no paying guests (although maybe a focus group to partake and appraise the samples). The focus shifts from polishing and finishing to processing and finding.

Regrettably, too many theatre training spaces are indeed patterned after archaic architectural ideals, restraining season planning choices on the kinds of texts produced as much as the way they are designed. And such educational constraints contend with the spirit of Jones, and many of Jones' own peers, other forward-thinking designers, and professors (despite their own proscenium experience). New XD programs might aspire upward and outward. They might chase theories and vocabulary via reconsidered praxes, fertile studio collaboratives and by the inclusive invitation of minds from beyond the shells of the established and understood theatre custom. They may also raise the free and flexible chambers where these studies ensue, pursue, and issue.

SURVEY OF THE SECTION

In the pages that follow, we share the perspectives of practitioners and teachers, who are already exploring both the aspirational possibilities of experiential performance and the development of pedagogies to support those possibilities. These artists—for both doing and teaching are art forms—add their voices to the lineage of Jones detailed here, expanding, and perhaps even existing outside the boundaries of this admittedly White, Western European, male-dominated spatial tradition. The section begins with three essays focused on the blending of theory and practice to set the stage for pedagogical innovation within the realms of design and technology education.

In *Storyliving: A Creative Process*, Justin Stichter provides a new term and a new way of thinking about creating shared narrative spaces: "storyliving." Borrowed from Google Zoo's earlier work in VR design, "storyliving" refers to a design approach that considers not only what we want audiences to experience, but how they experience it—how will they taste it, touch it, smell, and—perhaps most importantly—express what they are experiencing. This invites audiences to become partners in the story creation. Stichter contrasts traditional themed experiences—old favorites at Walt Disney World, for example, like Space Mountain, that audiences passivly receive—with newer, immersive experiences, such as the Wizarding World of Harry Potter, where park attendees wander through recreations of Hogsmeade, are encouraged to dress in costume, invited to "cast spells" with RFID-enabled wands that have effects on the environment, and to interact with other guests who are similarly "living" in the experience. He then takes us through a detailed examination of the use of this storyliving design approach as applied to an immersive experience at

St Louis Aquarium. Leading into questions about the use of immersive technologies, Elizabeth Hunter discusses the impact of virtual, mixed, and augmented realities (collected under the umbrella "XR," or "extended reality") on experiential events in her interview with Joanna Popper, Global Head of Virtual Reality for Location Based Entertainment at HP, Inc., *Theatre Majors and Immersive Technology*. Popper and Hunter talk about the growth of XR to create otherwise impossible experiences for brick-and-mortar commercial spaces and how this has expanded the possibilities for experiential events. They also discuss the importance of creating development teams that include not only coders and technologists, but creative artists and others with humanities-based backgrounds—and how students in those fields might prepare themselves for a potential future working on XR experiences. The XR experiences are further explored both philosophically and in practice in *Interaction and Extended Somatechnics*, by Johannes Birringer. The essay examines the history of interactive or augmented choreographic performance—in which dancers interact with, impact, and often create the environment they are dancing in through the use of wearable sensors. In his work, *kimosphere #4*, he builds on this history to explore both how these wearables not only respond to dancers but also inform their movement, as the limits and functionality of the devices force choreographic choices. Further, he explores how these devices and a combined sculptural and augmented/virtual reality environment invoke "uncommon senses," or those often-subconscious responses to barely noticeable environmental stimuli, by creating environments for those exploring it. This exploration uncovers the potential of deep feeling resonances between experiential performance and the embodied response of the audience.

In a rousing roundtable discussion, Jim Doyle, Adam Bezark, Danny Byerley, Dave Cooperstein, and Drew Campbell talk with Bruce Bergner, Rich Dionne, Sean Bartley, and William Lewis about experiential theatre in general, best practices in the field, and how educators can better prepare students to not only participate in but drive the development of the burgeoning field of experiential design. Through this interview, the reader gains real-world perspectives on the changes necessary to theatrical training for a new set of possibilities. This roundtable is followed by a set of praxis essays that offer practical advice on how to implement the advice offered in the preceding chapters.

Stephen Jones, in his essay, *Unlocking Formal Qualities to Discover the Iconography in Visual Design*, makes a compelling case for changing how we think about visual design of more traditional theatre. His call to action: rather than approach a design primarily from our own response to the narrative being presented, instead we should develop a visual vocabulary based on the iconography that arises out of a potential audience's background, experiences, and attitudes. By centering the design approach on the visual vocabulary of the audience—rather than the designer—we find the potential to create access to more diverse audiences, connecting narratives that might be more traditionally rooted in one community to many others. Samantha Meigs takes us on a journey to the high seas of the seventeenth century as she examines the use of experiential design in the classroom in her essay, *Playing with the Past: Pirates in the College Classroom*. She describes how she uses the framework of "living history" to take undergraduate students from a broad, popular-culture-infused understanding of piracy to a more nuanced understanding of the realities of piracy during the 16th, 17th, and 18th centuries. Her work engages students in creating an immersive environment, recreating the sights and sounds—even the clothes and currency—of the time. Students then live in this environment, role-playing as pirate crews, learning about the world they inhabit; this culminates in a public experiential performance that the students design to teach others about what they've come to know, using the same experiential design principles. Meig's living history pedagogy provides a map not only for how one might incorporate experiential design

PEDAGOGIES FOR DESIGN THINKING AND EXPERIENTIAL TECHNOLOGIES • 193

techniques into a history course but also for how one might teach experiential design—by experience. Liz Fisher, in *Designing an Interactive Production: A Practical Walkthrough*, presents us with a deceptively simple framework for thinking about creating experiential events that take place either in digital/networked environment or with digital/networked platforms. In her essay, she connects some of the ways theatre artists approach understanding and designing for a traditional (in-person, observed rather than interactive) narrative experience to creating digitally augmented experiential events; for those intimidated by the thought of creating the latter, these connections make the process more familiar and approachable. More importantly, she provides ways of thinking about the online/digital tools for creating content—as contrasted to tools for *distributing* content, which she also explores—as well as schema for how to think about incorporating audience participation in a way that is integrated to the narrative. She also introduces the delightful term, "meatspace," to refer to more traditional, real-world environments, for which this author will be forever grateful.

The section is completed with a provocation toward the postdigital. A paradigm shift where digital technologies become ubiquitous, changing our relationship to communication, performance, and design. Hans Vermy and Eric Hoff offer advice on how to take the next step toward new horizons of space, time, audience relationships, and most compellingly a nuanced understanding of responsiveness with digital tech. Their essay offers a both/and approach to the inclusion of technologies as foundational elements for contemporary experiential theatres. Through this approach, a new realm of experience is opened-up for the next generation of educators and designers to boldly lead the field deeper into the twenty-first century.

Observe the fundamental quest of experience in all this work. Experiential Theatres pursue an immediate engagement between story and those once safely passive under other modes of performance. Now, the audience are vested characters. They are world inhabitants, active beings, moving moments along or capturing the moments in space and time, imprinted with some kind of marking by the experience, be it solitary or collective. What is crucial to know is how an experience can be imagined, studied, chiseled, communicated, and then animated intelligently with a deep consideration of the humans who enter it: who they are, from where they come, and where they may go. Equally vital is how an experience can be enriched by technology, effects, moments of wonder and magic, and so on. The prime directive is to build an experience that will leave guests moved or changed. Find a pedagogy or methodology that will foster that quest, at the center. The words below illuminate the academy's task at hand: to devise effective new ways to teach for that cause.

Reference

Jones, Robert Edmond. 1941:1982. *The Dramatic Imagination: Reflections and Speculations on the Art of the Theatre.* New York: Theatre Arts Books.

22
Storyliving: A Creative Process

Justin Stichter

THE CALL TO CREATE

When considering the process of creating it is important to consider the *very beginning*; when the initial process of creation began—before there were created things. It is in this beginning that all creation bursts forth, and it is in this initial spark of creativity that all created things find inspiration and the desire *to make* is founded. We create because we too were created, and this inescapable truth is what drives us to create. We must. We are made to. It is our purpose. And this inevitable need to make manifests itself in a prismatic variety as varied as artists themselves. When we look at the individual's creative process, it is not a discussion of absolutes, but rather a dialogue of trial and error, of preference, and personal expression. The anecdotes to follow are a glimpse into an ongoing exploration of what it means to invite the end user (in this case participatory audience members more commonly referred to as guests) into the ranks of the creators. To engage them in a manner that puts them into the narrative, fostering agency and allowing a story to truly live.

INSPIRATIONAL DRIVERS

As designers, we look for catalysts to guide our decision-making and creative process. These help in answering the barrage of questions associated with the predestined critique of all design, such as:

Why does it look like that?
What's this for?
Who cares?
How is that going to work?

We often find ourselves grasping for reasons to rationalize and validate our creations as a means of explaining them firstly to ourselves and then secondly to others. Some designers might rely solely on the imposed finite variables, and thus the rationale of their decisions can feel formulaic, a sort of $a + b = c$ phenomenon. Other designers will rely solely on their creative intuition, and thus the rationale of their decision can be difficult to articulate, a sort of *happy + square = hippopotamus* phenomenon. What is truly required is a marriage of these two types of rationales …

194

DOI: 10.4324/9781003188179-26

Enter: **STORY**.

Having worked in the attraction industry for almost two decades, the construct of *Story* or *Storytelling* has been ingrained in my daily regimen, and thus every project I work on is driven by story. But stating that one's design process is based on a story is simply not enough. It must be based on a *good* story. A good story is far deeper than a list of what happens first, second, third, etc. It is far wider than a few sentences or a singular image. A good story must include full sensory experiences. It must engage. It must be alive. It must be effectively and affectively experienced. The best stories create lasting memories and inspire the end user but also, and perhaps most importantly, the designer. Good stories are not passive but rather they initiate a response, a call to action.

STORYLIVING

We have determined that regardless of the type of design effort, a good story must be the main catalyst in the creative design process. Story will drive the process and evidence itself in the finished work. That being said, if we allow our story to become too rigid it too can become prescriptive or formulaic, enslaved by the words contained within. For example, if we were to design something based on a specific story, say *The Three Little Pigs,* and through our process of creating we discover that it would in fact be better to have a fourth pig, we would need to allow the story to adjust. Likewise, if we were iterating design options, we would use the story to test the proposition of only two pigs or a ninth or tenth pig. Perhaps those notions are too few or too many respectively. In summary, a story-based creative process is critical and is only successful when the story is itself well crafted, flexible, and clear. We could be so bold to say that as designers we cannot simply rely on storytelling, but rather must invest in *Storyliving*.

Storyliving as a concept has its genesis in the UX (user experience) world and has most commonly been considered by designers delving into VR, AR, and gaming mediums. Google Zoo, Google's internal think-tank, first coined the term while investigating the user experience with VR marketing (Google News Lab 2017). They found that by creating virtual worlds to showcase curated content, potential customers would not only respond to the intended content, but they would begin to craft their own experiences by exploring the virtual world on their own. Their conclusions suggested that marketers (designers) must consider not only the intended content for consumption, but also the methods in which it was delivered, and the space for a user to expand the possibility for engagement. Could the possibility of fully engaging the whole user into an experience help a designer intentionally initiate a deeper emotional response?

Regardless if VR, AR, or gaming (each being a mediated form of experiential theatre) is our medium for a specific design task, the essence of Storyliving can apply directly to the greater design realm. Whether we are painting a landscape, designing a pen, baking a cake, or directing a movie, we as artists can position our designs in a way that the end user can participate in its creation. They can live in the story, and therefore be part of the creative process by becoming creators themselves. To explain this further, we will look at a few constructed examples in the attraction industry and explore the differences between traditional storytelling and Storyliving.

MOVING FROM TELLING TO LIVING

Like most industries, attraction design has continued to evolve over time. From its humble beginnings of individual disconnected experiences (i.e., the traveling county fair) to the current trend of world-building (i.e., The Wizarding World of Harry Potter at Universal

Studios Orlando Resort), much of the attraction industry has transitioned to deliver a more robust guest experience, where guests are placed into an ever-changing narrative and they themselves become active characters, shifting, and influencing the story via participatory interaction. This evolution towards Storyliving has allowed the guest to participate in a self-directed choreography of exploration and discovery. It also allows for a varied level of engagement for guests—meaning guests can now choose their level of engagement in any particular aspect of the overall experience, whereas before, guests had little to no choice beyond the prescribed experience.

Classic Storytelling

When Walt Disney first conceived his Disney Parks, first in Anaheim, California, and then later in Orlando, Florida, he created a plan that included several themed lands. Each land included a variety of individual attractions, shopping, and dining offerings, that were all generally connected by the common theme of the land. For example, Tomorrowland was an area of the park that featured space-themed attractions and futuristic innovations, while Adventureland was a place filled with untamed jungles and wildlife to explore. The individual attractions of each land shared a similar theme and vernacular, but they lacked a deep connection from experience to experience. "Attraction A" and "Attraction B" had no specific relationships, and if a guest should choose to skip any particular attraction in a land, the storytelling wasn't specifically impacted in any meaningful way.

One of the classic attractions located in Tomorrowland is Space Mountain which opened its doors to Disneyland guests in 1975. It is an indoor, all-in-the-dark roller coaster featuring a fast-paced, twisting, and turning exploration of the galaxy. Upon entering the futuristic—now nostalgic—ride building, guests find themselves led through a series of queues as if they were the next generation of space travelers ready for launch. The catacombs of pathways culminate in a multi-leveled mission control spaceport from where small rockets (coaster trains) are propelled into space. The bulk of the ride zips through a planetarium-like cavern with no visual cues to the coaster path. The experience is quite thrilling, and the attraction is beloved by everyone. However, this described level of guest engagement falls into the storytelling category of attraction experience. The guest is not able to influence the experience in the queue or on the roller coaster in any meaningful way. While the ride has undergone several upgrades and enhancements over the years, including audio, lighting, and media effects, the fact remains that guests are not really active participants *in* the story. Additionally, the supporting cast, the adjacent retail, food, etc., aren't directly tied to the space traveling story, thus compartmentalizing the overall Tomorrowland experience.

Contemporary Storyliving

Fast forward to today's modern era theme park, we can find several instances where the notion of themed lands has evolved into fully engaging experiences where guests are active members of the continual narrative by fostering user agency, which empowers the guests by encouraging them to influence the experience. Individual attractions are deeply connected with one another in addition to being individually rich and detailed. They build on each other adding richness to the story. The environments include specifically crafted food and retail experiences, deepening the immersion of the guest. In doing so, the designer has shifted the guests' individual experiences, as well as communal experiences, from being simple tourists of *storytelling* to engaged interactors in *Storyliving*. Themed lands are now immersive worlds where guests take on the agency of their own character in lieu of simply observing the prescribed characters of traditional storytelling.

One of the first and most successful examples of this type of contemporary Storyliving can be seen in *The Wizarding World of Harry Potter* at Universal Studios Resort in Orlando, Florida. Occupying one of the back corners of the Islands of Adventure theme park, *Wizarding World* places the guest directly into the beloved pages of the Harry Potter novels and subsequent movies. Guests meander and explore the cobbled streets of Hogsmeade, roam the cavernous halls of Hogwarts, and most recently speed through the mysterious Forbidden Forest on *Hagrid's Magical Creatures Motorbike Adventure*. The experience is remarkable, and no detail is left undone, and if it were to stop here, it would be undoubtedly memorable, but still categorically based on traditional storytelling.

Where the needle shifts from storytelling to Storyliving is when a design provides a space for environmental guest engagement. By the mere existence of the design, guests cannot help but engage—it becomes intuitive and spontaneous, perhaps pulling at the ancestral desires to create found in all of humanity. *Wizarding World* intentionally provides this real platform, and it gives guests permission to take an active role in crafting of story. When guests activate their individual agency in the experience it comes alive for them. It is no longer simply filled by an audience of tourists, but rather an audience of real-life characters. Through the design process guests are offered different levels of engagement to choose from. They can take on a starring role or become an extra in the immersive background dependent on their level of comfort engaging.

In addition to making a beautiful and detailed environment, the designers of *Wizarding World* removed barriers to intentionally further the sense of immersion by encouraging cosplay, or costumed play. It is common to observe [most] guests donning costumes and props (robes, scarves, and wands—which can be brought from home or preferably purchased at the gift shop). Guests who are wearing their "normal" clothes are seen as Muggles, those who do not possess magical abilities. In this way, everyone is literally a character whether they intend to be or not. No longer are guests living through the eyes of the already known and established characters in the story, but rather *they* are now the lead characters in their own novel built upon the strength of the established story. Furthermore, as guest engagement increases, the richness and depth of the Storyliving increases; my experience is enhanced by your experience and vice versa ultimately creating a combination of personal and shared experiences. The successes of *Wizarding World* have led to many similar developments in the attraction industry. Worlds such as *Pandora: The World of Avatar* at Disney's Animal Kingdom, *Star Wars: Galaxy's Edge* at Disneyland and Disney's Hollywood Studios, and *Diagon Alley* the sequel expansion to the original *Wizarding World* at Universal Studios to name a few. All of these have built upon the notion that Storyliving enhances the guest experience more than traditional storytelling.

Storyliving doesn't just exist in attraction design. *Sleep No More*, a modern take on Shakespeare's *Macbeth*, was written and created by the British theatre company Punchdrunk. Without the use of a traditional stage, the show turns theatre on its head by transforming an abandoned warehouse into a period-specific hotel. For three hours audience members don macabre masks as they anonymously and voyeuristically wander through five floors of the McKittrick Hotel, in a choose-your-own-adventure walk-through experience. With over one hundred "scenes" to explore, the audience opts to follow characters of their choice, or none at all, which means some performances are completely missed. The show is a mixture of pantomime, dance, music, lighting, and void of almost all dialogue. The level of engagement is completely self-directed, allowing for a unique experience at every performance, and depending on the presence of the audience, the actors will modify their performances including interacting with the audience. It is important to understand that the types of examples given could be perceived as only being associated with large budgets, advanced technology, and massive scopes. However, Storyliving is not

198 • JUSTIN STICHTER

directly proportional to the spend. At its core, Storyliving as a product is truly about guest engagement in the story, which can manifest in a multitude of mediums and scales.

STORYLIVING: A CREATIVE PROCESS

Thus far much thought and conversation have been devoted to validating the need for story, specifically Storyliving. We have looked at examples where Storyliving is the product of a creative process, and we have seen how it varies from the more traditional storytelling methodology. We will now turn our attention specifically to the creative process. If Storyliving is the desired outcome for our designs, then perhaps we can use many of the same principles of Storyliving to establish a new type of creative process. What would it be like to allow the process to be engaging and reactive for the designer in the same way that a finished design might be engaging and reactive to a user? The remainder of this essay will use The St. Louis Aquarium at Union Station located in St. Louis, Missouri as a case study, and will show how a Storyliving creative process influenced the final design.

Shark-Train

The St. Louis Area, located in the middle of the United States, has a long history of being an important hub. Dating back to its earliest days in the early 1700s, the region established itself as an important fur trading post nestled near the confluence of the Mississippi and Missouri Rivers. Over the centuries, the city's relationship with the rivers of North America would foster rapid economic growth, and by the mid-1800s St. Louis would become one of the nation's largest riverboat ports. It wasn't until 1867 when the Eads Bridge was constructed over the Mississippi River connecting Illinois to Missouri that train travel boomed in the region. It was at this time when Union Station came on the scene. Designed by architect Theodore Link and opened in 1894, Union Station quickly became one of the busiest train stations in the world. Any freight or passenger destined for the western frontier had to first cross the Mississippi River and therefore came through Union Station, birthing St. Louis' moniker of *The Gateway to the West*. Today the days of romantic train travel are gone, and Union Station no longer serves as a functioning train station. The massive complex has continued to evolve over the decades and its current steward, Lodging Hospitality Management (LHM), has once again transitioned the space into a thriving destination. The Head House, Grand Hall, iconic Clock Tower, and massive Train Shed have blossomed into a boutique Hilton Curio hotel which includes sprawling convention space, as well as an offering for family entertainment including restaurants, shows, and small attractions. But for LHM something was still missing: an aquarium. An aquarium? Prior to the St Louis Aquarium opening its doors, St. Louis was the largest metropolitan area in the United States without an aquarium, and LHM envisioned Union Station as the perfect location to fill this void.

But what does an old train station have to do with fish? Exactly.

As our team began the creative process, we identified project elements that are unavoidable and must be included. Things like existing conditions, budgets, guest capacity, etc. Sometimes these variables that are out of our control can be seen as obstacles, but when we marry them with our innate creativity, they can afford us opportunities. We often approach a design problem by listing challenges, questions, and goals. In "architect-speak" this is often called the program. The program is not the story, but it begins to shape the kind of story we intend to communicate. In the case of the St. Louis Aquarium, our client required that we achieve three specific goals with the project's programming.

First, we were asked to connect the new aquarium to the specific historical significance of our site. Our design was to pay homage to the historical aspects of Union Station, namely train travel and its impact on St. Louis and western expansion; as Union Station flourished, so went St. Louis. Union Station is also a registered national historic landmark, so it was important to highlight the architectural vernacular in our design as well. Second, we were asked to connect the regional significance of our city to the surrounding rivers and watersheds. Leveraging the unique landscape of the St. Louis Area, focusing specifically on its proximity to the Mississippi and Missouri Rivers, became an important differentiator in the selection of species and their associated narratives. No other aquarium could claim to be at the confluence of the two largest rivers in the United States. Third, we were asked to establish connections between the regional freshwater ecology and the world's ocean in order to help educate guests on the importance of conservation and sustainability in their own backyards. We initially joked the solution should be an aquarium on a train that could transport guests from land to river to ocean, hence: Shark-Train. We would come to realize we were not so far off.

The essence of our final narrative was to provide a train ride, reminiscent of the romantic era of train travel once home to Union Station, that would take guests on a fantastical journey to the nearby banks of the Mississippi River. From the Mississippi River, guests would flow through continental waterways until they splashed at the Ocean Shore. They would then descend from the beach to a cavernous Shark Canyon and then drop to the mysterious and dark Deep. Finally, like all good attractions, they would exit through the gift shop (Figure 22.1)! As we have discussed, this kind of Story development is an important backbone to begin fleshing out the design during the creative process. However, it alone is only the beginning of storytelling and has much development required to mature into Storyliving.

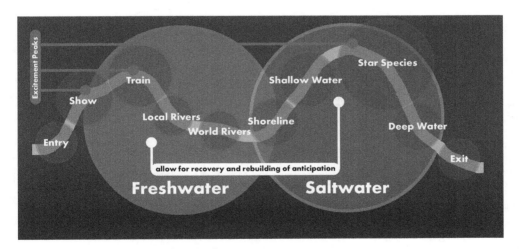

Figure 22.1 Story arc diagram for *Shark Train* concept.

Story Arc diagrams such as this help to establish important moments within the overall narrative. The *River* and *Ocean* bubbles serve as Acts and smaller bubbles serve as Scenes. The size of a bubble suggests importance or relative spatial relationships, as well as the implied level of guest engagement. At this stage, characters, emotions, and settings have not yet been established.

STORYLIVING DEVELOPMENT

The design process is seldom linear beyond having a beginning, middle, and end. There are typically twists and turns, do-overs, and sustained periods of growth and decay. When

200 • JUSTIN STICHTER

considering our development, we were inspired by the notions of Storyliving. We desired to allow the inspirational period of designing to be sustained for as long as possible. We wanted to use Storyliving as the creative process. To truly do this, however, we needed to consider alternatives to the traditional storytelling methods of project development. We had to use traditional tools differently and invent new tools so that as we placed ourselves within the story construct we could manipulate the design in real-time.

Workflow and Tooling

In the attraction industry we typically use one set of tools: sketches, written narrative, flavor boards, etc., to generate the ideas, and a different set of tools: CAD drawings, specifications, cost estimates, etc., for the production of the ideas. Typically, there is a breakpoint where design stops, and production begins, and on large projects, there is typically a division of labor, meaning that a creative team develops, and then a production team produces. In a creative process driven by Storyliving, we try to overlap these traditional divisions of design and production as much as possible, so that design can continue to influence production and conversely production can inform design (Figure 22.2).

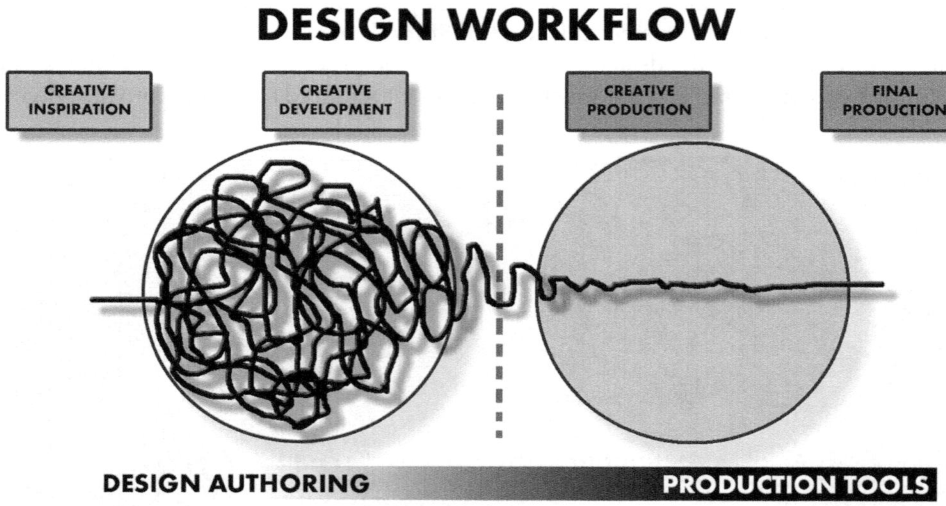

Figure 22.2 Traditional design workflow.

Considering the theoretical aspects of the design workflow are not enough, however. We had to consider the literal processes of how the work was to be completed, especially if we intended to sustain a feedback loop between design and production. We had to develop an interface between traditional creative tools and traditional production tools. Our team was already using specific software that was appropriate for the specific design tasks. Programs like *SketchUp* allow for quickly massing the blocky, low-detailed architectural forms, while *Rhino* and *zBrush* work well for more complex and detailed geometries. *Revit* is the industry standard for production drawings and isn't well suited for iterative design. With all these tools in play, we opted to use 3D Studio Max as a Visualization HUB. The HUB allowed us to filter in the individual components in real-time, combining them into a single robust digital model. Our HUB model was then output using the Unreal Engine to provide the ultimate in visualization. The single greatest benefit to this type of workflow is it allows individuals, regardless if they are design or production minded, to use the tool best suited for their skill set and task (Figure 22.3).

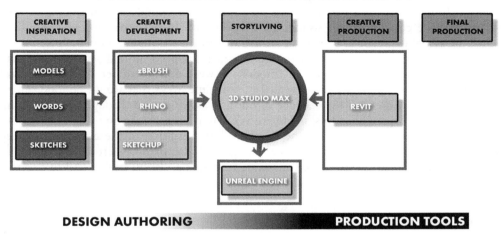

Figure 22.3 Storyliving visualization workflow.

Finding Inspiration

In addition to retooling and workflow development, we turned to nontraditional sources for inspiration. Afterall, our desire was to evoke an emotional response to the design process as a means of immersing ourselves in the story. While developing the initial story structure for the St. Louis Aquarium, I listened to all sorts of things such as recorded train sounds, singing whales, thunderstorms, babbling brooks, dueling banjos, and crashing ocean waves. These sounds were not specifically "composed songs" in the traditional sense of the term, but I found that they echoed memories from my personal life experience and transported me to a different headspace. I was no longer sitting at my drawing board trying to generate ideas, but rather in my imagination I was snorkeling off the coast of La Jolla, California, or splashing in a puddle during a summer rainstorm. With each memory, I was reminded of how it felt, how it smelled, and what the lighting was like. Stories from my own past became alive again and provided a series of moments in which I could build upon, and from those places the sketching and writing began. For me, personal experiences and memories bubble to the surface when triggered by music, for others it might be writing a poem or dancing ballet. As designers we must find these initiators and allow them to spark our creativity. In a way, my real self was giving way to my memory-self, a sort of user agency not unlike the guests roaming through *Wizarding World*.

In addition to being inspired by music, I often use image boards to generate ideas to establish flavor, texture, color, and mood. This technique is common in the design industry and serves as a means of weeding out and refining the creative intent. Some designers will use digital pinup boards like Pinterest, but I prefer having a tangible print to work with. This allows me to quickly group, scramble, and regroup until the right mix is discovered. For the St. Louis Aquarium, we developed a series of flavor boards, each one focusing on individual scenes within each act of the Story. The purpose was to explore guest and animal adjacencies as well as desired layering of view corridors. At this stage, the design is only loosely based on project specifics. Instead, it is more importantly focused on the type of experiences to be established—placing a guest *in* the River surrounding them with fish.

As we continued to develop the digital model of the St. Louis Aquarium, we found that our tooling provided a conduit for adding sophisticated visual components like human and animal artificial intelligence (AI), lighting, and atmospheric effects. Through our software we could visually see how guest AI would stack up in a space, we could dial in the specific lighting levels, and we could see how animal AI would react within their new habitats. But we could also add sound, allowing us to hear how soundscapes would influence the visual experience. Providing AI fish within the 3D digital model allowed us to understand how the physical layout of the design influenced animal behavior. By also placing "sound widgets" in the digital model we were able to direct the attitude and emotion of a space. These widgets revealed in real-time areas that would be loud, quiet, fast, and slow. They dictated the cadence of our gait as we moved through the aquarium, causing us to move quickly or to slow down. We found ourselves composing crickets and frogs in otherwise quiet corners of the River Gallery, resulting in the addition of more speakers and audio channels in the final design. As the pathway crossed beneath an overhead aquarium we pulled in the sounds of a bouncing playful stream. All of this was possible because we allowed our creative process to be dynamic and alive.

Choreography of the Guest Journey

I am not a dancer; however, when considering attraction design, I often consider the guest experience to be a sort of dance as a guest moves through the space. Imagine riding a rollercoaster that after the initial lift hill is a rapid-fire of inversion after inversion. Twisting and turning, the coaster blazes down the tracks until the riders are dizzy and sick. Even for the most aggressive thrill seeker, this experience would be awful. When we design, we must consider pacing. We need to include moments of rest between elements contrasting with moments of excitement. Areas for the eyes and ears and body to seek refuge contrasting with areas of movement. The design becomes an exercise in choreography.

Part of the creative process should include the development of the guest journey. This is a map to help organize the things a guest will do combined with the desired emotional arc a guest will feel. The pace of a guest journey is important to establish to ensure the design is not overly intense or, conversely, overly passive. It also helps to establish spatial relationships. For example, if the guest journey intends for a guest to be pensive and quiet, creating a physical space that will allow for those movements is important to consider. When positioning the guest journey in the context of Storyliving, the design will invite the guest to discover the emotional arc on their own.

Upon arrival at the Aquarium, guests find themselves within the *Grand Lobby* which is reminiscent of the historic *Grand Hall* at Union Station. The space is visually striking being anchored on one end with a giant clock teeming with fish and wrapped by an overhead 8K visual display. The video content and music continually change in a *Fantasia*-like performance that provides for a stunning opening act. By creating a space for guests to be enveloped with music, fish, and media, they are immediately engaged and are encouraged to reconsider what an aquarium experience could be.

Global Rivers is a showcase of habitats from around the world from a fish's perspective. By creating spaces that feel underwater, guests dive below the surface to get nose to gill with a variety of species. They can learn about the differences between North American and South American Catfish and play alongside River Otters. Guests gained a sense of what it's like to live underwater, but they still lacked the ability to converse with the animals and hear directly from them. As a solution to this challenge, we developed *Otter Chatter*, an interactive show where kids could interact with a real-time animated Otter. Through technology, an off-stage actor and digital puppeteer can interact in real-time with guests bringing the animals at the Aquarium a voice. The audience is transformed when they realize that the Otter can "see and hear" them and it isn't a traditional video loop (Figures 22.4 and 22.5).

Figure 22.4 Grand lobby entry exhibitat St. Louis Aquarium. Courtesy PGAV Destinations.

Figure 22.5 *Otter Chatter* interactive exhibit at St. Louis Aquarium. Courtesy PGAV Destinations.

Situated at the bottom of a long ramping pathway that intertwines with 200,000 gallons of oceanic splendor is a curving overhead acrylic vista into *Shark Canyon*. From this vantage point guests are positioned more than 12' below the surface of the water and have deep views into the hypnotic symphony of schooling fish and looming sharks. The space was designed as a culminating "wow!" moment within the guest journey. We intentionally wanted to inspire feelings of awe, wonder, and reverence in an attempt to change the hearts and minds of the guest about their relationship to the ocean—remember St. Louis is far from the ocean shore. To do this we established a particular atmosphere and space that included dimmed lighting, reflective music, and intimacy (Figure 22.6).

Figure 22.6 *Shark Canyon*. A place where guests can take in the symphony of the ocean as thousands of fish school past large acrylic views. Courtesy PGAV Destinations.

REFLECTIONS

As a product, Storyliving engages the end user giving permission to explore and discover within the contextualized narrative, creating agency where the guest loses their real identity and allows them to take on a new one. They become part of the story and in that process, they too become Creators. As a creative process, Storyliving fosters deep creativity within the designer, and it allows for a similar level of agency, by placing them into the design before it is real, fostering exploration and engagement which ultimately affects the design in ways perhaps not imagined. With advancements in technology, the ability for designers to breathe life into their creations will continue to flourish, heightening the realism in which pre-visualization is actualized. The examples and explanation of process discussed are the proverbial tip of the iceberg of what is possible within the Storyliving framework. As designers we will continue to create and our process will justifiably continue to evolve. Just as we are no longer limited to encircling a campfire participating in oral traditions only, we are no longer limited to the traditional methodologies of storytelling. Rather, Storyliving allows us as creators to iterate and react to a living process of design.

Reference

Google News Lab. 2017. "Storyliving: An Ethnographic Study of How Audiences Experience VR and What That Means for Journalists." https://newslab.withgoogle.com/assets/docs/storyliving-a-study-of-vr-in-journalism.pdf

23
Theatre Majors and Immersive Technology: An Interview with HP's Joanna Popper

E.B. Hunter

E.B. HUNTER

We first met when I came to your panel at Augmented World Expo, "Location-Based Entertainment as a Driver for Consumer Adoption of XR". Could you talk about what Location-Based Entertainment, or "LBE" is, and how it differs from other XR experiences a user might have?

> The terminology of immersive technologies is still in flux. In short, virtual reality (VR) headsets attempt a complete visual immersion, while mixed reality (MR) headsets and augmented reality (AR) enabled smartphones insert interactive digital holograms into the analog world. In other words, a user wearing a VR headset could easily trip over a cat in the room, because a VR user can only see the digitally rendered world inside the headset. In contrast, a user wearing an MR headset or using an AR smartphone would see the flesh-and-blood cat (and the rest of the room), but holograms would appear next to the cat. Most relevant to theatre majors is that these tools enable a semi-porous, multi-sensory theatrical design space similar to site-specific theater. MR and AR technologies have become so advanced that some holograms can "sense" the proximity of an analog object, and interact with it. To refer to VR, MR, and AR collectively, people sometimes use "spatial computing" or "XR" (where X stands either for "extended" or "any of the above").

JOANNA POPPER

"Location-based entertainment" is anywhere you go outside your home to be entertained. With the pandemic, we aren't going outside to be entertained now. But generally, it would be a cinema, or a theme park, or a museum, or even a mall with entertainment or "re-tailtainment." In terms of VR, LBE came about because that brick and mortar retail numbers were down. A lot of things had been digitized, thanks to developments like online shopping and Netflix, etc. There was a strong interest from retailers in driving additional foot traffic and new audiences to their venues. Bringing VR into their locations was a way to increase the revenue, from the VR activities as well as food and drink. It's also a way to

206

DOI: 10.4324/9781003188179-27

decrease costs. For example, VR allows a place like Dave and Busters to provide a roller coaster experience to people without the footprint and cost of a roller coaster. And it drives innovation and makes a familiar venue newly exciting to different audiences.

E.B. HUNTER

It has always struck me that live theatre and XR storytelling experiences (LBE or otherwise) have in common that they rely on liveness, the user's sense of being present, and a multisensory, 360° design space.

JOANNA POPPER

Yes, definitely.

E.B. HUNTER

Could you talk a little bit about XR projects you've seen or worked on that are standout examples of these elements?

JOANNA POPPER

A project that HP sponsored, and where I came in as an executive producer, is Kiira Benzing's *Finding Pandora X*, which won the Golden Lion for best VR immersive user experience at the Venice Film Festival last year.

E.B. HUNTER

Oh, wonderful; congratulations.

JOANNA POPPER

Thanks very much. Because of the pandemic, they did the project as live interactive social VR, where all the actors, the audience, and the whole production team were anywhere around the world in their headsets. It's a modern take on Greek mythology.

E.B. HUNTER

Always go back to the Classics. First of all, because there's no copyright.

JOANNA POPPER

[laughs] Yes. That was always important for budgets. The actors were Greek gods, and they interacted with the audience. And the audience had choices: they could go on a journey to help Pandora find the underworld or go somewhere else, and in the end we all came back together. One interesting part was that Broadway actors were involved. Broadway is dark right now because of the pandemic. And VR was a place for them to act, and continue to grow their craft. And this art form is becoming a community—people who have worked on live VR projects like *The Under Presents* and *The Under Presents: Tempest* or with immersive companies like Punchdrunk. And for projects like *Finding Pandora X*, we can send actors the tech and provide some support, and teach them to become technologists as they're learning their lines and rehearsing.

> Released in 2019 for Oculus VR headsets, Tender Claws' *The Under Presents* (Tender Claws) integrated live immersive theatre and multiplayer VR. At any given moment, users might encounter and interact with a live, roving actor, who had logged on from their own space. The live elements of the project ran through September 2020. The standalone non-live elements are still downloadable for Oculus headsets. Since then, the company has released *The Under Presents: Tempest*, an adaptation of William Shakespeare's *The Tempest* that makes use of similar live actor and VR components.
>
> In 2019, *New York Times* theatre critic Ben Brantley pinpointed British theatre company Punchdrunk's signature production, *Sleep No More*—a multi-million-dollar juggernaut of immersive theatre and themed restaurants on West 27th Street in Manhattan—as the catalyst for "[a]round the globe, an ever-multiplying slew of immersive productions" (New York Times). Since the company's launch in 2000, its work has evolved from in-person immersive theatre to projects that "fuse theatre, film, TV, art and gaming into atmospheric experiences that defy categorization, and which leave intriguing spaces for audiences to explore" (Punchdrunk).

E.B. HUNTER

MIT's *Sloan Management Review* recently ran an article titled "Build a Diverse Team to Solve the AI Riddle" (Byrum 2020). It argues that teams solve complex problems more effectively when they take diverse, multidisciplinary approaches. In this case, the author's team hired more English majors to collaborate with the tech folks on an AI tool for the financial sector. If we expand this idea to "arts and humanities" majors, could you talk about how people in XR collaborate across tech and arts/humanities areas of expertise?

JOANNA POPPER

That's what this industry is: technology and content creation go hand in hand. This is a creative medium. So even when you're talking about enterprise, you're still making content that has to engage somebody in learning, even if it's about how to handle an oil and gas rig, for example. It's the blending of different skill sets that drive innovation and engaging storytelling in the industry.

E.B. HUNTER

And you were a humanities major, weren't you?

JOANNA POPPER

Yes, history and international relations and Latin American Studies. I also went to business school. I think the humanities degree teaches you to think—to break down problems. It helped prepare me for a global world, and an environment of working with people who have different backgrounds, different points of view, different ways of thinking, different training.

E.B. HUNTER

Performing arts majors tend to be pretty busy, between classes, rehearsals, too many a cappella groups … add in working, which a vast majority of undergraduates do these days,

THEATRE MAJORS AND IMMERSIVE TECHNOLOGY • **209**

and it's daunting to find time for extra skill-building (CEW Georgetown). How can a performing arts major be strategic with an eye towards the XR industry? What kinds of things should they learn?

JOANNA POPPER

First, if you want to work in this field, it is incredibly important to experience as much of the existing content as possible. That can be harder for people if they don't have a headset when they're in school, but often there are labs and other places on campus that do. Second, it's important to know about game engines and how they work.

E.B. HUNTER

Like an entry level entry-level coding class or two?

JOANNA POPPER

It's not just coding. There's coding, but then there's Unity and Unreal, the two main game engines. It would be a good investment of time to become familiar with those two software environments.

E.B. HUNTER

I'd like to switch gears for our last few minutes. You've done a lot of work on improving gender parity in XR. Could you talk about the XR industry and diversity initiatives?

JOANNA POPPER

The industry is nascent. While immersive technology itself has been around for a long time, it's been mostly in research institutions and the military. We're now at a price point that this technology is becoming accessible to more people. And that means the industry is coming alive at a time in history when there's better recognition of the importance of diversity, inclusivity, and representation. Data point after data point is showing how important it is—both for a company's product and their financial results—to have teams that are inclusive, representative, and diverse.

XR is the future of computing. The previous three generations of computing were built by groups that were not all that inclusive, in terms of demographics. And some of the decisions that were made then have led us to some of the issues that we have today. Hopefully, by bringing diverse voices into the room earlier in the development of XR, we can build a better industry.

It's not perfect. There's still a long way to go. You'll still see companies, sometimes a small startup, without diversity of demographics represented, or only small percentages of people who have historically been underrepresented. But there's a lot of emphasis on making sure that this next wave of computing is the more representative. That way, we can build it to work for all of us, not small subset of us.

E.B. HUNTER

How hard is it for new folks to break into the industry?

JOANNA POPPER

You know, unlike film or other industries where there are people who've been doing it for 30 years, most people haven't been in XR that long. A few people have, like the early

E.B. HUNTER

My last question is about the future of XR. What does it look like? How has the pandemic changed the landscape, and what changes do you think will be permanent?

JOANNA POPPER

We've seen an acceleration of growth during this time period, especially of people wanting headsets for home. For example, I exercise every day in VR now, which I was not doing before, even though I had headsets. The growth of headsets at home is also a result of more gaming at home. And there's strong growth on the enterprise side, because the pandemic has changed how we're able to collaborate at work—we can't look at a design for a new product or be trained like we were before. But companies are learning that VR empowers us to learn, connect, collaborate, and create. And that's driving a lot of the acceleration in this industry.

E.B. HUNTER

Do you think the pandemic will permanently change live storytelling?

JOANNA POPPER

It's like Nonny de la Peña, one of the VR industry's pioneers, says: "If the world is not flat, then why should media be?" When I worked at NBC and I was leading marketing for Telemundo, search engine marketing was new at the time. First, you could only buy words—you know, "click here" or something similar. Then, you could add pictures, and then video. And with each change, the media became more engaging for the audience, and they spent more time interacting with it. They're not selling ads yet in VR—which is a good thing—but as we make media more realistic and interactive, give the user agency and presence—all the things we talked about at the top of this interview—the future of live storytelling is going to be that much more compelling.

E.B. HUNTER

And theatre artists can help shape that future.

JOANNA POPPER

Absolutely.

Joanna Popper

Joanna Popper is a Hollywood and Silicon Valley media executive. She leads HP's initiatives for Go-To-Market and Location Based Entertainment for Virtual Reality. Prior she was EVP of Media & Marketing at Singularity University and VP of Marketing at NBCUniversal. Recently Joanna was executive producer on Double Eye Studios' "Finding Pandora X," winner of Best VR Experience at the Venice Film Festival. Finding Pandora X is a modern-day take on Greek mythology as a live theatre interactive experience in

VRChat. Joanna developed a TV show partnership with NBC and Singularity University for a new TV series on technology and innovation.

Joanna was selected as "50 Women Can Change the World in Media and Entertainment," "Top Women in Media: Game Changers," "Top Women in Media: Industry Leaders," "Digital It List," "101 Women Leading the VR Industry" and is on the Coalition for the Women in XR Fund. She has an MBA from the Wharton School at the University of Pennsylvania and a BA in History/International Studies from Northwestern University. LinkedIn: https://www.linkedin.com/in/joannapopper/

References

Byrum, Joseph. 2020. "Build a Diverse Team to Solve the AI Riddle." *MIT Sloan Management Review*, May 18, 2020. https://sloanreview.mit.edu/article/build-a-diverse-team-to-solvethe-ai-riddle/

CEW Georgetown. ND. "Learning While Earning: The New Normal." Accessed September 5, 2020. https://cew.georgetown.edu/cew-reports/workinglearners/

New York Times. 2019. "33 Ways to Remember the 2010s." *The New York Times*, November 24, 2019, sec. Arts. https://www.nytimes.com/interactive/2019/11/24/arts/2010s-decade-end.html

Punchdrunk. ND. "About | Punchdrunk." https://www.punchdrunk.com/. Accessed January 29, 2021. https://www.punchdrunk.com/about-us/

Tender Claws. ND. "The Under Presents." Accessed January 29, 2021. https://tenderclaws.com/theunderpresents

24
Interaction and Extended Somatechnics

Johannes Birringer

SOMA AND THE EXTENDED CHOREOGRAPHIC

After several years of working with partner art organizations on the five-year European METABODY project, my London-based DAP-Lab ensemble felt that we were reaching a new level of audience and performer experience in the interactive/immersive installations we designed between 2015–19.[1] We had created a series of seven installations that I titled *kimospheres* (kinetic atmospheres), conceived as porous augmented reality environments with unpredictable outcomes. Audience behavior could not really be calculated, we imagined, nor did we intend to design an experiential world based on assumptions about experiences to be had or not. And yet, increasingly over the years of my engagement with new media technologies, the physical and sensorial side of what was becoming a techno-choreographic system design remained always at the forefront of my approach to energizing spaces, affirming bodies within their moving relationships with mediated environments.[2] With system design I mean the computational *dispositif* programmed to enable real-time interactivity in a performance space. For such a techno-choreography to be somatically affective, and emotionally and culturally experienceable, interaction and any coupling between bodies, space, and technical devices need to be probed in all "embodiable" directions (cf. Hansen 2006: 184). This probing of the corporeal (soma) lies at the core of the present essay; the way I use the expression somatechnics is meant to emphasize the deep intertwining of corporeality with technologies and techniques.

Introducing somatic embodiment as a core concern raises an immediate question about the design side of the coupling, implementing technical applications exterior to bodies, with often predominantly visual dissociations of bodies and projected images. We have separated "input" and "output." *Designing experience* had become an eye-catching idea in the early twenty-first century, especially in the design-centered fields (fashion, digital media, mobile media and interaction design, product design, games, etc.), but for theatrical production (stage design) such concern for psychological/perceptual impact or tactile/haptic dimension had been less talked about until *immersion* and an aesthetics of *atmospheres* moved to the fore. Immersive performance became a trend over the past two decades (e.g., Punchdrunk), and so have immersive installations on the impressive scale at which teamLab (*Future World*, now at the ArtScience Museum in Singapore) or Yayoi Kusama (e.g., *Infinity Room*, Museum of Fine Arts Houston, 2016) operate, among others who had been creating overwhelming projections for years, such as Rafael Lozano-Hemmer or Kris Verdonck. And yet,

212

DOI: 10.4324/9781003188179-28

augmented, affective environments have existed since ancient times when sacred dramatic festivals took place in amphitheaters, sanctuaries, temples, and town squares (Javanese *Wayang Kulit* shadow puppet plays were staged in village cemeteries). Immersion is festival, ceremony, ritual. A rock concert can be as cathartic as a Greek tragedy performed in the theatre of Dionysus. Its vibrations are aural but also tactile, fleshy: they can be felt inside bones, organs, skin. Theoretical discourse on *immersive atmospheres* is fairly recent, derived from philosophers such as Gernot Böhme writing on ecological aesthetics, but also from research in cultural geography, legal and spatial studies, as well as architecture (cf. Philippopoulos-Mihalopoulos 2015, McCormack 2013:2018, Durham Peters 2015, Pallasmaa 2014, Zumthor 2006, Thibaud 2011). Böhme (1993) proposed "atmosphere" as a new aesthetic category, suggesting that it can become a concept "if we succeed in accounting for the peculiar intermediary status of atmospheres between subject and object" (114). If we think of atmosphere in regard to the weather, say a rainstorm, or the aura of ancient ruins, this "intermediary status" is not precisely localizable or definable, its qualities remain uncertain and obscure.

In the *first generation* of interactive dance theatre, when "mapping" (gesture to sound, gesture to video, or graphic output) was explored in interface design for performer and reactive environments, an understanding of the system was inspired by the cybernetic vision of feedback control and the modeling of the machine on the human actor. Direct interfaces (flex sensors, micro switches, pressure plates, smart fabric, etc.) required specific techniques which sometimes led choreographers to argue that the dancer acted as a live video editor or musical instrument. But aesthetic and conceptual concerns regarding the emergent techniques eventually led to a search for alternate interfaces. Dance-tech or music-tech collaborations involving direct, gestural trigger interfaces began to decline, even if some practitioners continued to argue that the interface should remain tangible (causal) so that mappings between performative input (gestural) and output (video/sonic) are more easily inferred.

Second-generation interactivity can heighten the experience of human embodiment and sensory affect as the coupling of dancer and augmented environment evolves in noncausal correlation with one another. Ideally, both performer and performance system respond to the other's enaction by undergoing self-permutations on the basis of distinct operational rules which are internal to them. Moving toward indirect interfaces (optical, magnetic, and ultrasonic sensors or machine vision), however, creators of such performance systems often prioritize the development of software techniques over physical techniques. In many performances of this kind one sees mediocre or underdeveloped dancing; in such cases, perfunctory physical techniques are used to patch the interface functionality rather than expanding transformational capabilities of the system or discovering new re-organizations of the body, its expressive metabolism. The situation tends to be worse in interactive installations, inviting an unprepared public to move around and become "co-authors"—having to intuit or learn the system and how it might respond (cf. Birringer 2008, 119ff).

At the same time, a spatial atmosphere is full of potential kinesthetic dimensions: an aura of indeterminate sensorial affect, directionless in every direction, membranic. Atmospheres are spatially "without borders, disseminated and yet without place, that is, not localizable." They are porous, ethereal, ephemeral; carrying "affective powers of feeling, [they are] spatial bearers of moods," of emotions (Böhme 1993, 119). They go under the skin, so to speak. Sound, in particular, is always resonant, spectral, reverberating. Waves haunt the material space, and voices are disembodied and yet physical, just as noise is. But the performer's skin is directly engaged when a sensor is worn on the arm or wrist, when muscular tension elicits signals sent to a computer and the *very nervous system* surrounding the performer, when the actor thus needs to bring heightened attention to feedback loops and palpable excitations in the intermediary states. This notion of palpable atmosphere, originally derived from geography, physics, and chemistry perspectives, is now often brought to bear on architecture/design and microperformativities, to questions of how designed space surrounding cellular bodies affects somatic experience, including imperceptible physiological processes, emotions, and moods in an ecosystem. Speaking of augmented reality in theatre or music performance, some imply that the physically affective is amplified through technical means (sound diffusion, digital projections, lighting, etc). These amplifications are lively, and on various functional (and microscopic) levels they can encompass "mutation processes involving biological, digital, algorithmic and physical parameters," on the vast and often unperceivable spectrum in which *biomediality* is understood today (Hauser 2020, 14).[3]

Thus, in this *third generation* of interactivity an expanded sense of the choreographic is evoked, with alchemical and invisible mutational dimensions, and corporeal and perceptual irruptions. Augmented space enters us, and our receptors receive many (often ambiguous) clues. The space and the objects within it choreograph *us*, so to speak. Thinking of the materials in sculptural spaces, or the emphasis on kinetic plasticity, texture, light, the non-static materiality of scenographic constellations make them prototypes of interactional architectures which alongside augmenting digital technologies become *actionable* in further dimensions (3D, 4D, 5D, etc). This form of engaging the visitors resides on one end of interactive scenography. The other end is the stage where actors engage with interactive instruments or invisible intelligent sensing systems – the "very nervous system" as David Rokeby (2019) called his early sensing environments which would react to the behavior of anyone who entered them.[4] When actors/dancers step into a programmed environment, enacting a "world" for the audience to watch or listen to, they perform a kind of animation, propagation, or continual agitation: they need to engage the nervous system (and its feedback implements) to elicit its responses and play with these according to the dramaturgy that the collaborators have devised.

ACTOR OBJECTS AND ENTANGLEMENTS

In late 2019 I returned to a staged scenography, not involving the audience directly as we had done over the previous years. DAP-Lab's *Mourning for a dead moon* is an interactive work involving several dancers, musicians/sound artists, and designers, further exploring what I call "extended choreographic." The work does not ask our audience to mingle and act inside the theatrical environment. Rather, challenging our own creative team, it places more emphasis on organic/somatic enaction and responsivity to the scenographic architecture and subtextual dramaturgy than on computational interface design and controllers—in fact we had wanted to rehearse new techniques learned from previous experience with the more audience-focused *kimospheres* (one of which is my main case study here). I remember starting to work with concepts of interaction design in dance around 1995, using camera-based interfaces and software (BigEye) long vanished. Since 2004, and after a few years of euphoric telematics—hilariously complicated networked dance with partners in vastly different time zones—the emphasis slowly shifted towards sensors and on-body wearable design (programming with Max/Msp, Isadora, Python, Unity, Unreal, Metashape, Sensestage/MiniBees, etc). DAP-Lab increasingly expanded its ideas on wearables (specially designed sensortized garments/accoutrements) to spatial or architectural materials, working over these years on the *kimospheres* in which visitors became immersants—co-agents of the unstable atmospherics of the "latent commons" (Tsing 2015, 135). There is no objectively and concretely fixed environment; and for each perceptual system there are carriers of significance (*Bedeutungsträger*) specific and consequential for particular organisms in the particular *Umwelt*. The *Umwelt* is not the same as the objective space or environment. *Umwelt* is constituted by those elements or carriers of significance that are vital to the discrete perceiving organism, be that of an animal or insect or jellyfish or human or plant. In an assemblage of perceptual stimuli, this of course also then implies that different perceiving organisms, say in a forest, constitute different forests. The lives of the forests (Figure 24.1).

Figure 24.1 *Kimosphere no. 4*: Dancer Yoko Ishiguro standing still inside one of the 8 ghost speakers; Coral reef on the left; Sound artist Sara S. Belle performs in the background right. The skeleton of the soundsphere is visible in the far back. London 2017 © DAP-Lab.

These lives resonate with the atmospheres of digital installations we designed exploring the notion of an extended choreographic. This extension, and the lives of "being alive" (cf. Ingold 2011), reaches far beyond the theatre. It leaves behind older distinctions between actor, media, embodiment, things, settings, words—touching upon current materialist and ecological concerns with *contaminated entanglements*, as Tsing (2015) considers them—provoking collaboration, gathering, happening, crossing over—something she also calls "interwoven rhythms" (34). In our case of *kimosphere no. 4*, the focus is on lemurs and tamarind trees (on a subtextual level of allusions to migration, for which we used primatologist Alison Jolly's field report on lemurs in Madagascar), on climate change, and concomitant elements of sensory experience (responding to *Umwelt*) through performative constructions of reality as "augmented virtuality."

While the growth of computer-based art and the paradigm of interactivity are accepted phenomena in today's art world and everyday culture, the genre of digital performance is still unconventional. It has also run into limitations that concern both compositional practice (e.g., dramaturgical placement of interfaces for trained performers in a stage work) and the participatory promise of interactive design for audiences (who have not trained with the interfaces or cannot intuitively navigate programmed parameters). In artificial intelligence research, engineers are working hard toward instilling learning capabilities into their creatures: intelligent technical organisms might learn from the behavior of the audience, or the processual systems (artificial life, multiagent populations) develop their dynamic (self)reconfigurations—their emergence. The question of whether

216 • JOHANNES BIRRINGER

participatory design and emergence are actually achievable or desirable in stage-centered performances was addressed by the *Pixelspaces* symposium "Re-Scripting the Stage":

> In performances and installations produced in recent years, more or less successful attempts have been made to put this immanent interactive element in the hands of the audience attending the performance–for example, through the use of various tracking technologies. In addition to the attendant problems associated with people's inability to grasp the connection between cause and effect, the process of enabling audience members themselves to generate sounds or visuals often quickly results in the exhaustion of the performance's aesthetic, emotional or intellectual quality. (2011 ars electronica)

The cause-and-effect connection has always intrigued me, especially after becoming less interested in knowing what "effect" I can cause wearing an accelerometer on my arm, wrist, or leg. Orientation toward affect on one's own proprioception, and the psychological dimension, for example, of wearing encapsulating costumes and accoutrements, are equally fascinating. On a functional level, on-body wearables are somewhat distinctive from other mobile devices or electro-acoustic/digital instruments by enabling hands-free interaction, minimizing the use of a keyboard, strings, or manual input. Devices worn on the body, including headsets allowing voice interaction or head-mounted displays replacing a computer screen, can shift data control of sensor interfaces directly to bodily motion, muscle activity, or breath. "Wireless" interaction with networked, digital environments never really meant "without wires": sensors, electrodes, and data capturing devices have to be applied, stuck, taped to the body in order to produce data transmissions that could affect reactions from the system. In DAP-Lab's forays into wearable design (with Michèle Danjoux's expertise in fashion and electronics), we looked at smart fabrics to explore whether they can replace the wires on the flesh-body, and how they are used in "stand-alone" reactive design or as interfacial, affective design allowing performers to engage with a real-time system. Our performers are actors, so to speak, but they also entangle with objects, they are drawn to them. They do other things than just wear a communication device. The wearable thus acts more as an accoutrement, or indeed becomes a sculptural and definitive style—it plays with "characters" that motivate the performer to move or act in certain ways.

VIRTUAL IMMERSIVE EMBODIMENT

I now turn to such constructions and foraging/tracking constellations in augmented performance. I am particularly interested in asking how performative atmospheres move and affect us, how material/immaterial variations are experienced, and how amplification works as transformational effect through *somatechnics*—through an integration or entanglement of body, wearables, and environment. We can think of performative sensorial habitats as precarious: enactments are perhaps stressful or require caution, kinaesthetic sensitivity. The *things* in the installations have their lives. They could be said to have their various rhythms, and thus contribute to constituting complex relations between rhythm, figures, light, sound, spatial milieus, and elemental infrastructures.

The *extended choreographic* implies not only the sculptural-architectural, but also the unhinging of clear sites of artistic forms. The technically designed space could be an organic one at the same time, "site-specific" in the sense of being else-where, off-site of conventional theatre architectures. It could be contaminated, a kind of artificial plantation. Plantation, forest, rewilding—these are conceptual machines for installation assemblages. They harbor many affective, poetic, and transformative potentials.

Thinking of Oskar Schlemmer's sculpturized figurines or Hélio Oiticica's *Parangolés* as historical precursors to Danjoux's complicated wearables, what are we to make of an encapsulating mask that constrains the wearers or even makes it impossible for them to see what they do?[5] The notion of the costume as mask invites speculation on how a difficult costume (which hides the face and occludes vision) is meant to make the wearer move, prevent them from moving in any conventional way, compelling them to behave in ways they were not aware of previously. Is this similar to the interactive devices we strap on, moving with sensors ("controllers") that send out physiological data—in real-time measured/analyzed by the software—thus constrained/contained within processing parameters? Is the wearable controller a mask or subterfuge inciting me to move in uncertain ways? Am I moving to effect?

When I began to work with Danjoux and noted encumbrances she increasingly built into dancers' garments, the performances we developed with the DAP-Lab gained a dimension that resonated with other "choreographic objects" (Forsythe's term) created by contemporary dance-theatre artists who moved off-site. The things that choreographed me seemed supremely confident and impartial to my exhaustive struggle. They were admirably unsusceptible to my emotional effort. And I did appreciate them, as I could touch them and feel their materiality. This was not my body in code or entangled with coding. Bodies inside affected and opened environmentally to the tentacular: transduced to objectness, gravitational pulls, sweat and quicker breathing, heat and melting down, in the billowing and swinging of the furnishings. The forest of swaying rings prevails.[6]

Danjoux's wearables evoke uncommon senses[7] in wearable space, insofar as the tactility of fabrics and sensortized garment creates hallucinatory sensations, sonic and echoic resonances that become coupled into augmented virtuality design, which is three-dimensional and envelops you. VR worlds are hyper-choreographic objects, exceeding the real, entangling the subject while themselves being meshed and knotted of complex computational physics, graphics vectors, and apparitions. The fact of virtual matter thus also becomes the subject wearing you and making you internally associate various uncouplings and re-accommodations. Garments, however, are sensual and seductive, and velvet, silk, or plastic materials evoke distinct reactions (Figure 24.2).

Figure 24.2 Visitor enacting/embodying what she perceives inside "Lemurs" forest interface with VIVE goggles, conducted by Doros Polydorou, *kimosphere no. 4*. 2017 © DAP-Lab.

218 • JOHANNES BIRRINGER

In *kimosphere no. 4,* a virtual tropical tamarind forest can also play tricks on our minds, becoming an abstraction intensely impacting an unanchored body. I propose to look at different thresholds of perception—here in the context of VR performance installations—which take us across not only various materialities but also diverging modes of physical sensing-thinking. Such sensing strays across registers not necessarily based on visuality alone. It includes subliminal and peripheral sensings, rhythms of sensation, vibrations, proprioceptive and imaginary relations, dreaming, and dancing as a kind of morphing, detailing the imperceptible, surrendering the curves and edges of others and other things. The *un-common senses,* as I recall from a talk by neuroscience philosopher Barry Smith[8], are the ones we are much less conscious or certain about—thermo or mechanoreceptor nerves in fingers, arms, or the spine, giving us tingling sensations; skin and hair sensing temperature and wetness or feeling textures, though not reliably; muscles and ligaments "hearing" how our anatomies, the bones, minerals, and water in bodies, move along and stumble about; how organism and metabolism are comfortable or tensed, affected and afflicted by the environment as well as internal biophysical processes. I evoke these propositions here as I am concerned not merely with technical interface design but with artworks and compositions I consider provocative.

The vitalist impact of *kimosphere no. 4* echoes through my bodily memory, not only of the forests of my childhood but also of an *arborescent movement* class I took years ago, its deep listening focus on skeletal bone nodes in the feet. The be-holding of the faint or barely noticeable is a dynamic I want to emphasize regarding the energetic sides of immersive aesthetics. The sensational, the forces of sensations are the nexus here, the connecting array of trans-sensory fluidity experienced and felt in a saturated environment.[9] Immersive atmospheres are entered into, and they enter into the receptors. They enter through surfaces of skin, through the bones. The underground of atmospheric, ambient interactivity is skin, porous and stretching. Sensori-kinetic control of one's reactions, therefore, would rely on how the organism tunes into an alignment with its habitual sequences or opens out into the errant. Such errancy implies the superposition of disparate rhythms, and it "is a matter of realizing how relations between motor, sensory, neurochemical, and other milieus are given a fragile consistency as rhythmic spacetimes" (McCormack 2013: 82). The refrains of moving or orienting are altered when inside a virtual environment, when one's elemental body or surfaces are affected by shifting from outside to inside a forest generated by VR technologies. The forest is hyperreal. There is no envelope of smell or sound one is familiar with. We are enamored by this without knowing it, wondering how far the unknown body schema can dislocalize sensation, like hallucinogenic experiences described by ethnomycologist R. Gordon Wasson and photographer Allan Richardson for *Life* Magazine ("Seeking the Magic Mushroom"), during their 1957 journey to Mexico and an encounter with the *curandera* Maria Sabina, who gave them mushrooms to eat in the dark, reciting a ritual chant: "I am a mouth looking for you—but you are not paying attention. Come!"[10]

THE MOUTH LOOKING FOR YOU

Immersion takes on a growing significance as a category of attracting forces of affective experience, as the term is now often used not only in theatre and art installations but in conjunction with VR and games, or bioscientific experiments. Immersion is sticky matter. It moves around bodies and their sensory desires. It moves inside bodies. Prostheses create affordances that point to their *Umwelt,* connecting body and world, enabling new qualities of existence, relationships, inhabitations. A wheelchair is a somatechnic wearable.

Immersion requires prosthetic techniques. It can hint at vast imaginary lands. Come here, then, and inhale, kinetic atmospheres say to you. Lift off, dive in, let yourself fall, ascend, fly high, become buoyant, crawl into the tent, get on your knees, roll around, taste the flavor, bounce on the balloon, hang in the rafters, climb the scaffold, balance yourself on the see-saw, touch the screen, tilt your wheelchair, put on the earphone, smell the peat, allow yourself you to be pulled in, follow us.

I propose immersion here as a technique close to performative interactions I have described and return to the *extended choreographic* and kinetic objects. VR designers, such as Jaron Lanier, may dance with their avatars, but their initial questions are very different: they point to *mapping*, i.e., controlling motion in virtual environments, making measurements on the body of someone wearing a capture suit, calculating an aspect of the flex of a wrist to be applied to control a corresponding change in a virtual body. Immersive virtual reality allows persons to inhabit avatar bodies that differ from their own, Lanier (2006) argues. This can produce significant psychological and physiological effects, and Lanier's concept of *homuncular flexibility* proposes that users can learn to control bodies that are different from their own by changing the relationship between tracked and rendered motion. In later research at his Stanford lab, Lanier and his team examined the effects of remapping movements in the real world onto an avatar that moves in novel or unusual ways (Won, Bailenson, Lee, Lanier 2015)—thus shifting the mapping of one's physical anatomy (occurring in the motor cortex) to rather different homuncular "body schemas," avatar creatures that are indeed virtually different. Lanier mentions a lobster with a trio of little midriff arms on each side of its body. What he does not fully explain is how an "alien" body schema can be neurophysiologically and neuroaesthetically incorporated; how it alienates and traumatizes; how it associates injury or delusional states; how it might cause exciting confabulations and morbid distortion to the human perceptual experience.

During the development of *kimosphere no. 4*, and in many of the subsequent international workshops, the virtual differences that interested me were atmospheric, not avataric. Thus I turned to habitats of certain colors, textures (red sand, silver foil, cling film, tree branches, moss), and tropical vegetation (coconut, tropical fruit, palm tree fronds), with dynamic environmental elements that incite immersants to bathe in them, feel the swarm of fluctuations, crawl into them, lie down, dive, surf, and fly across the currents and mutations of such kimospheres: to imagine becoming bird-like or amphibian, participating with flow and uncanny connections emerging from a geomorphological base. The immersant imagines this, rather than delegating agency onto something other or alien. The immersant also feels rawness, affected by physical sensations and tendencies. With tendencies, I mean ambiguous potentials that are plural, virtual, and real, with sensorimotor capacities still quite active. The immersant is not still. The immersant arches backwards, rolls around the floor, stretches out forward, bends down, thus even becomes dizzy, motion-sick, noting imbalances and paradoxes—namely contradictions in the perceptions of their own movements as they are implicated in a VR world (Figure 24.3).

This is the trans-sensory atmosphere I try to conjure up here. When speaking of *augmented reality*, it is implied that what is planted to be physically effective is also extended and *amplified* through technical means (sound diffusion, digital projections, lighting) to be experienced somatically by immersants. An expanded sense of the choreographic as raw, as becoming a multi-perspectival and wearable space, grows out. The material is co-extensive with the immaterial, it stretches.

We are returning to the forest I evoked in the beginning, approaching the ritual force through a growing prehension of these spaces as "latent commons" (Tsing 2015, 255).

Figure 24.3 *Kimosphere no. 6.* Visitor touching branch in virtual forest, inside augmented virtuality space where the sound of the suspended silver foil creates a rustling (of leaves). CNDP Bucharest, 2018 © DAP-Lab.

Amplified and augmented space enters us and our receptors receive many (often ambiguous) clues. But this is not entirely true. One would probably have to carefully describe each stimulus and atmospheric condition to ascertain what is affective, and how, and in what variation, that indeed may exceed any technology of measurement (how do you measure the wind, the cold, and the heat in an environment where fifty or a hundred visitors or more have gathered? How do you measure affect in a stadium during a sports event or a rock concert?). In the workshops and installations I refer to here, the physically affective is composed of various organic and synthetic materials that are embedded in the space. The space is a wider ecology. The materials and aesthetic occurrences are emergent, dynamic, and thus may generate different kinds of attunement. Yet I am still describing it all in terms of affective values (atmospheric qualities) that concern human perceptions, perceptions of a limited number of visitors, say between ten and one hundred. I wish I could go beyond, and atmospheric values indeed point beyond to the elemental, the meteorological, the viral, and bacterial, scaled up and scaled down.

The fullness of the real—the physically affective that is expanded by the virtual and the virtual that is augmented by the real—heats up such densely sensorial atmospheres towards a ritual aura, a ritual sense of performance events that may indeed be "meta"—moving across varying trajectories and speciated desires. There is a ritualistic, elemental quality in such environments, and since we do not know yet what the future will hold, I suggest that the elemental will first of all be an off-site environment—perhaps without any technological interaction whatsoever. A physically affective space, however, will bear traces of the augmented realities we already know because we have experienced them.

Notes

1 The Design and Performance Lab (DAP) was founded in 2004. Filmic excerpts of many of our works are available online. DAP-Lab's website is here: http://people.brunel.ac.uk/dap/. On the website are numerous links to publications, conferences, and exhibitions that featured our innovations in wearable design created by fashion designer and co-director Michèle Danjoux (http://www.danssansjoux.org). For the design philosophy of choreosonic wearables, see Danjoux 2017. The METABODY project is archived here: www.metabody.eu.

2 My reference to techno-choreographic systems goes back to the early 2000s and my work with ADaPT (Association of Dance and Performance Telematics). We first met at Arizona State University's "Intelligent Stage," a laboratory-studio fully equipped with motion capture/sensing systems and programmable computational software interface options for sonic and visual/ graphic as well as networked interactions. See Birringer and Bromberg 2004; Birringer 2001. For a brief video history on telematic performance before the dawn of Zoom, see: https://youtu.be/ 7JAyd8TBMwU.

3 Jens Hauser and Lucie Strecker edited the special issue "On Microperformativity" for *Performance Research* in 2020, probing immersive and emersive microperformativity on many levels (Hans-Jörg Rheinberger speaking of "agency" being "everywhere") of algorithmic art and techno-scientific infrastructures in human and non-human performance.

4 For Rokeby's recent reflections on his early installations and the development of his VNS (Very Nervous System) software, see Rokeby 2019.

5 During the early 1922 Stuttgart performances of the *Triadic Ballet*, Schlemmer was one of the three performers wearing the constrictive costumes himself, discovering that unfortunately he "could not see the scenes in which he performed and hence did not have an overall picture of the performance" (Schlemmer cited in Cramer 2014: 22). He also comments on the differences in techniques, e.g., how trained dancers might wear the elaborate full-body sculptures and oversized masks, compared to non-trained performers. For descriptions of some of the re-strictive garments worn by DAP-Lab dancers, see Danjoux 2014.

6 My reflections refer to Forsythe's *The Fact of Matter*, an installation of suspended gymnastic rings inviting visitors to climb through, at *Move: Choreographing You*, Hayward Gallery, London, 2010–2011.

7 During the run of *kimosphere no. 3*, we invited an audience of blind and vision-impaired persons, who were led through the environment by facilitator Karen Staartjes and our dancers. Or who moved through it quite on their own, following the sensory stimuli and engaging very concretely with all the performers and materials co-present, conversing with our performers, asking questions or giving feedback, touching the costumes, pulling strings, listening to sounds emanating from the atmospherics. They spent nearly two hours with us. It was one of the most rewarding audience interactions I have ever had, as I was invited to listen to our blind visitors' stories: the stories they wrote into the kimosphere.

8 For the radio broadcast on "uncommon senses," listen to philosopher Barry Smith, with sound artist Nick Ryan, "The Uncommon Senses Radio Series," BBC Radio 4, March 2017 (www.bbc. co.uk/programmes/b08km812/episodes/player).

9 In several public engagement lectures/workshops on sensory techniques and somatechnics I addressed this; my thinking about trans-sensory fluidity is partly indebted to collaborations with colleagues in social work, disabilities studies, and the Welfare, Health, and Wellbeing Research Group at Brunel University. I am also inspired by choreographer Fayen d'Evie's ideas about be-holding (2017). For a film version of *kimosphere no. 4*, see: https://www.youtube.com/watch?v= 0aIW6Klfm1g. For a translation of *kimosphere no. 7*, see https://youtu.be/kJfuwG5k048.

10 Quoted from the exhibited book objects and photographs in *Mushrooms: The Art, Design and Future of Fungi*, Somerset House, London, January 31–April 26, 2020

References

Birringer, Johannes. 2017. "Metakimospheres." In *Digital Bodies: Creativity and Technology in the Arts and Humanities*. edited by Susan Broadhurst and Sara Price, 27–48. London: Palgrave Macmillan.

Birringer, Johannes. 2010. "Moveable Worlds/Digital Scenographies." *International Journal of Performance Arts and Digital Media* 6 (1): 89–107.

Birringer, Johannes. 2008. *Performance, Technology and Science*. New York: PAJ Publications.

Birringer, Johannes. 2001. "The Intelligent Stage." *Performance Research* 6 (2): 116–122.

Birringer, Johannes and Ellen Bromberg. 2004. "ADaPT: Telepresent Artistic Collaborations." *Interdisciplinary Humanities* 21 (1): 87–93.

Böhme, Gernot. 2017. *The Aesthetics of Atmospheres: Ambiences, Atmospheres and Sensory Experiences of Space.* Translated by Jean-Paul Thibaud. London: Routledge.

Böhme, Gernot. 1993. "Atmosphere as the Fundamental Concept of a New Aesthetics." *Thesis Eleven*, 36: 113–126.

Cramer, Franz Anton. 2014. "In the Here and Now of Geometry." *Bauhaus: Zeitschrift der Stiftung Bauhaus Dessau* 6: 19–29.

Danjoux, Michèle. 2017. *Design-in-Motion: Choreosonic Wearables in Performance.* PhD Thesis, London College of Fashion, University of the Arts London.

Danjoux, Michèle. 2014. "Choreography and Sounding Wearables." *Scene* 2 (1–2): 197–220.

D'Evie, Fayen. 2017. "Orienting through Blindness: Blundering, Be-Holding, and Wayfinding as Artistic and Curatorial Methods." *Performance Paradigm* 13: 42–72.

Durham Peters, John. 2015. *The Marvelous Clouds. Toward a Philosophy of Elemental Media.* Chicago: University of Chicago Press.

Gaensheimer, Susanne and Mario Kramer, eds. 2016. *William Forsythe: The Fact of Matter.* Bielefeld: Kerber Verlag.

Hansen, Mark B. N. 2006. *Bodies in Code: Interfaces with Digital Media.* London: Routledge.

Hauser, Jens. 2020. "Microperformativity and Biomediality." *Performance Research* 25 (3): 12–24.

Ingold, Tim. 2011. *Being Alive: Essays on Movement, Knowledge and Description.* London: Routledge.

Lanier, Jaron. 2006. *Homuncular Flexibility.* Seattle: Edge Foundation, Inc.

McCormack, Derek P. 2018. *Atmospheric Things: On the Allure of Elemental Envelopment.* Durham: Duke University Press.

McCormack, Derek P. 2013. *Refrains for Moving Bodies: Experience and Experiment in Affective Spaces.* Durham: Duke University Press.

Pallasmaa, Juhani. 2014. "Space, Place and Atmosphere: Peripheral Perception in Existential Experience." In *Architectural Atmospheres: On the Experience and Politics of Architecture*, edited by Christian Borch, 18–41. Basel: Birkhäuser Verlag.

Philippopoulos-Mihalopoulos, Andreas. 2015. *Spatial Justice: Body, Lawscape, Atmosphere.* London: Routledge.

Rokeby, David. 2019. "Perspectives on Algorithmic Performance through the Lens of Interactive Art." *TDR* 63(4): 88–98.

Thibaud, Jean-Paul. 2011. "The Sensory Fabric of Urban Ambiances." *The Senses and Society* 6 (2): 203–215.

Tsing, Lowenhaupt Anna. 2015. *The Mushroom at the End of the World: On the Possibility of Life in Capitalist Ruins.* Princeton: Princeton University Press.

Won, Andrea Stevenson, Jeremy Bailenson, Jimmy Lee, and Jaron Lanier. 2015. "Homuncular Flexibility in Virtual Reality." *Journal of Computer-Mediated Communication* 20 (3): 241–259.

Zumthor, Peter. 2006. *Atmospheres: Architectural Environments – Surrounding Objects.* Basel: Birkhäuser Verlag.

25
A Design Roundtable: The Creative Process of Experience

Bruce Bergner, Rich Dionne, and William W. Lewis

PANEL PARTICIPANTS

Jim Doyle (WET Design)
Adam Bezark (The Bezark Company)
Danny Byerley (Byerley Experience Studio)
Dave Cooperstein (PGAV Destinations)
Drew Campbell (Freelance Creative Producer)

How do you define experiential theatre practices?

Dave Cooperstein

We would define it as an immersive storytelling experience that's created using a fusion of architecture, space, light, sound, media, music, special effects, magic, and people. Because if there aren't people involved, there's not much to experience.

Drew Campbell

I am in the theme park business. We concentrate on fully immersive entertainments, composed of a series of structured experiences arranged in a non-linear landscape. Guests choose the order of the experiences but each one of the individual experiences follows a narrative path. Our goal is immersion in a compelling storyline.

Danny Byerley

It's a nexus discipline. We're pulling from many disciplines. We bring everyone to the table, especially right at the beginning. If you can bring as many stakeholders to the table for the research and get as many different points of view and as much buy-in from every person that may be operating, creating, or paying for this at the very beginning. It creates a roadmap forward. It's like an expanded group project. Everyone's voice really does need to be inserted at the beginning, and then guided forward by the creatives and by the project leaders. We need to identify what we want to make our audience feel. When we build in that layer of what we want guests to feel, not only are we creating experiences, but we're creating transformational experiences. We're tapping into the emotions.

DOI: 10.4324/9781003188179-29

Adam Bezark

The truth? There really isn't a simple, mutually agreed definition of what we do. For that matter, there's not even a simple, mutually agreed *name* for this work. I have to say I've never loved the term "experiential theatre." Isn't all theatre experiential? Isn't *everything* experiential? I kind of prefer "immersive theatre," because that specifically denotes the notion of putting an audience inside a space and events that completely immerse them in story.

But that said, Dave's definition is pretty thorough. We're creating experiences that can only be experienced in a specific location.

And as for "practices," that's challenging to define as well. This is, almost by definition, a prototype business. No two projects are ever the same. We're constantly reinventing the wheel as new ideas and new technologies emerge. It's also an iterative business. It's rarely a single visionary with an idea. It doesn't spring fully formed from the head of Zeus, dictated down from on high. It's almost always generated in a collaborative and iterative process. It's three things: One is that it's iterative. The other is that it's so multidisciplinary. It's a renaissance business where everybody who does this work, does lots of different things throughout their careers. You may get hired to be an architect, but you wind up being a graphic designer, a show designer, a set designer, and an improv theatre person. The third piece of it is that it's a process about puzzle solving, and each puzzle is unique. So it's incredibly challenging to come up with a single description of the practice of creating experiential theatre. The best thing we can do is create a productive, collaborative group mindset that adjusts to each new project.

Jim Doyle

We are given a space to work with, a mall, let's say. The guy building the mall wants something "here." The first question has to be why. Why do you want something here? Rather than have a story and then build the feature around it, you break the experience design down. You have to decide what that experience means. And by means, I mean it's really simple. How are you directly affecting people's senses as they move into this space? Is it warm? Is it cool? Is there a little bit of a breeze?

What do you think is missing from current theatre training? What theories, methodologies, approaches, philosophies, would you recommend that be added to training?

Drew Campbell

There are several themed entertainment programs, each having a different focus, depending on which part of the university it resides in (theater, architecture, computer science, etc.), but I haven't seen any program that teaches what I do: producing. For a program to train a producer, it would have to have an artistic design element, but also train in business, project management, construction, and marketing, as well as broad exposure to technical issues, like lighting, audio, show control, and ride engineering. It would also need to cover issues of copyright and intellectual property.

Danny Byerley

I've identified a lack of communication, public speaking and presentation, development, and design communication. Everyone wants to be able to draw or be a scriptwriter, an architect, or a landscape architect. But how do they bring all those things together and communicate it to the team, client, and guests? How do they present their ideas and thoughts clearly, choosing the right words to express what they're trying to say? If I were to put a focus in any of these programs, it would be on public speaking. If you can communicate, then you're setting yourself up for success. And then you utilize the strengths of the people on the team and all the things they bring to the table.

Dave Cooperstein

What's related to that is a lack of understanding and practice of cross-disciplinary work, of the art, science, and magic of working with people who know things that you know nothing about, and who are better at things than you are. Learn how to communicate with those people, to create and build together, because understanding how to lead teams of people effectively, to bring out the best in all the individual contributors, makes a cohesive whole. A lot of young people miss the opportunity in school to try out new things, new techniques, methods, and skills. They have the freedom and the opportunity to do this while they're still in school. Learn how to take a hobby and monetize it. Or just get so good at it, you come into a new place and teach it to other people because no one else there has tried it. I think you must take advantage of that desire to try new things, while you're in school.

Adam Bezark

The most important thing is still just mastering the basics. Story, staging, performance, stagecraft. Some students try to learn everything; and they wind up mastering nothing. One of the things we try to tell people is: pick one thing that we can hire you for. Be really good at one thing … but be interested in everything. Because once you're in the door, and you're doing well, your interests and your Renaissance nature will draw you into other areas and other opportunities. This is a business that really encourages people to cross disciplines and try new things; but like I said, don't overlook the fundamentals.

Jim Doyle

We not only hire designers. We have a lot of engineers. And one thing we found years ago was that the engineers coming out of school didn't know what the hell a pencil was. How are you going to sit at a conference room table and present anything? Engineering is not described with your hands. Engineering is described with sketches. So, we teach drawing and presentation for engineers. And we teach engineering and architecture for designers. So hopefully, the designer can be in the same room as the engineers and be able to communicate and understand what it is they're doing. And flipside, the engineer needs to be able to sit and throw ideas across the table on the yellow pad. It's really critical.

Adam Bezark

A renowned, retired Imagineer who ran the interactive group at Imagineering for a long time, now teaches a theme design course at USC. They use a workshop approach. They only have a couple of classes. One of them is a practical concept and development semester. You put people in teams, they create concepts, they each work on different pieces, and they present along the way. So, presentation is built into the semester, as part of the project.

Danny Byerley

Communication is how you transform minds and audiences through the message that you're trying to tell. With a class focused on that, you can inspire and get the students to take what they've learned about themselves and communication, and infuse that into the rest of their learnings.

Adam Bezark

In our business. I think you find yourself pitching every day. You have to re-pitch the idea 1000 times to every new person that comes on to the project. You remind people what the project is. So those presentation skills just get used all the time in our world.

Danny Byerley

I've worked a lot with recent technical and production-focused grad school graduates who have the programs, budgets, spreadsheets, and the structure down—but they don't know how to present their ideas to a team. And they don't know how to communicate. So, they've got the skills, but they're not inspiring any passion in the room. And they're not actually communicating beyond the fact that they know how to go X, Y, and Z and fill in the blanks and make the thing happen.

Are there any new trends that you see happening in the industry, whether in technology, theory, practice, story, design, or whatever it is, that made you revisit your own practice and approach to experience experiential theatre?

Drew Campbell

3D Visualization is now central to the design process. We don't do anything without modeling it in 3D anymore. Well before we show the attraction to anyone, we use modeling to kick around ideas and test solutions. We also depend heavily on BIM modeling to avoid cost-spiraling clashes. Projects nowadays must have a dedicated modeling department that receives the work of each vendor and combines it with the General Contractor's model at every step of development.

Adam Bezark

The arrival of BIM as a completely integrated way to design complex projects. Even as a creative director, it impacts what you do. So when we did the pirate ride in Shanghai Disney, the whole ride was built in a BIM model, from the walls to the animatronics. This lets you create an animatic live video fly-through of the entire ride, three years before it opened, where the lighting and animatronics programming were all in there before the installation team ever got on site.

Dave Cooperstein

I would go a little bit further and say that the integration of technology into the design process on a meaningful level, is something that in the last ten years has just become critical. Understanding what the tools can achieve and finding the right people who understand how to take advantage of those tools, leads to incredible results.

On the opposite end of the spectrum, a trend that we've seen recently is the notion of allowing employees to explore their own interests and live their own lives. Make them better designers by the virtue of them just experiencing things, getting out into the world, and finding a work–life balance. Our office created a program where every employee is given a stipend for just about anything, except purchasing hardware. If you want to take a metal smithing class, or if you want to go to Broadway and see six Broadway shows, or travel to South America, these are all things that you can use the money for. It's created a studio of people who are well-rounded human beings, which greatly informs our design process.

Adam Bezark

I'm obsessed with the Pixar book, *Creativity, Inc.; it's* an amazing treatise about exactly what Dave is saying, about how to build a creative community, a creative culture of people who are interesting and interested. The other critical part of the book talks about a culture where every single person from the janitor on up is empowered to speak their mind and give honest feedback on what's going on as opposed to the top-down pyramid-oriented, like traditional director-driven theatre. It's about giving everybody a voice.

Danny Byerley

I build from a cultural perspective of diversity and inclusion in our storytelling. It's something that we should have always been doing as an industry, but have now realized and forced to reckon with it. If we're telling stories about East Asia, and we don't have anyone on the team, or any consultants, or any person from the East Asian region that can help tell that story, then we're telling it through our own lens. How do we make ourselves relevant for the future, to ensure that our guests are all being seen? I mean, look at the Haunted Mansion, for example. I once had a group of African American guests in the stretching room. They looked up at the portraits of white people and I heard them say, "oh, this is a house of white people—a house of white ghosts." None of them are seeing themselves anywhere in this story. And so, when I looked at this, and the new trends in the culture, this is making me think: What are the stories we're telling? Who's telling those stories? How do we bring them into the fold, so that we can propel our stories forward and make sure that we're not having just a traditionally hetero-normative or white-centric storyline? How do we make it more diverse, and reflect the guests that are coming to the parks and expect to see themselves in the stories that we're telling? And if we want to transform lives and give people their own personal hero's journey, that be much more successful if they see themselves mirrored back in the experiences they're having.

Adam Bezark

It's something that we're increasingly conscious of these days. It infuses everything we talk about now. Getting more people into the conversation will change the conversation and improve the product. And part of this effort falls on academia. Bring us those voices! Find us diverse student bodies and bring us more perspectives. I want to go out to high schools, find people before they go to college, saying: "Hey, kids, did you know there's cool things you can do and make in this world that you've never even thought about?" I want to reach people early enough in their lives, so they get sparked up.

What goes into the experience designer's toolkit?

Danny Byerley

It goes to what's your experience, background, and focus. Graphic design was my initial focus and that led me to understand the Adobe Creative Suite. From there, I honed PowerPoint to create layouts that the entire team can utilize, regardless of their technical skill level. So, my toolkit is heavily focused in reference imagery, design, and presentation layout, while being supplemented by writing. It's about how you communicate your design, the project, and the scope. If you're a 3D person, Rhino and SketchUp can become second nature. You can communicate across the table and groom your vision or the vision of the team via a medium. That can even be Excel because we often deal with lists and deliverables. So, what is your background? What are your interests? What have you been playing with and how can you use those tools to express your ideas?

Dave Cooperstein

The best tool is the tool you need to get your job done. Whatever that tool may be—SketchUp, Rhino, Excel, hand drawing, Photoshop, building physical models, whatever—that's the right tool.

Drew Campbell

All themed entertainment people should be comfortable with cloud-based storage and document-creation systems, like DropBox, Google, and Amazon Cloud Services. Very important to understand the capabilities and differences. For design, high proficiency in SketchUp, Photoshop, one of the major modeling programs (Maya, 3D AutoCAD, Houdini, Cinema 4D, etc.), as well as simple video editing, are essential. However, I am still a strong advocate of hand drawing. ALL scenic designers must learn to hand draw. There is a freedom of expression that exists in this medium that is not available on a screen. Plus, this skill is invaluable for a design conference or brainstorming session. But those are the technical tools. I have used three different conceptual toolboxes: a massive library of books, a massive library of images on my computer, and a massive log of attractions (including museums, stadiums, public spaces, aquariums, etc.) that I have visited.

Dave Cooperstein

We also look for people with programming skills, with the ability to author extensions, and plugins and write code. Designers don't always learn those things.

Danny Byerley

We're talking about students that are entering the workforce and want to have a well-rounded toolkit. The work that they're going to be doing for the first ten years of their career is going to be at the very front end of the project. If you're creating a 3D model or a 2D drawing in order to communicate your idea at the blue-sky level, someone else may take it and finish it in a different project phase. What is the program that you're most comfortable with? Lean into that and that hopefully gives you enough background. Then expand from there.

What is the process for accessing the latest information on production technologies?

Danny Byerley

Go to IAAPA and be a continual consumer of our industry. I don't want to mount a Broadway show with someone who has only seen *Phantom* in Vegas and has never seen any other Broadway show. I want people who are consuming experiences, theme parks, and attractions and learning from them when they do. They're turning around when they're on a ride and looking at how the lighting works and where the projectors are, looking at the different show elements and the different disciplines that come together to make these things possible. So, consume them voraciously in the physical space, as well as the myriad of books and tools that are available. There are sources online that can expose people to the multi-disciplinary approach of creating our attractions.

Adam Bezark

And the flip side is you want people who are students of the industry, but not *exclusively* students of the industry. You want people who are out there seeing the world and finding surprising things they can bring back to our world from other industries. Go to museums. Go to art galleries. Just travel the world if you can. Go to electric music festivals. Go where the energy is, and steal that, and bring it back. Don't live in our bubble, which is easy to do.

Tell us about accessing and utilizing technology as a creative in the experience field. How is technology integrated into the creative process? How should young designers learn to chase and apprehend the assets of technology?

Danny Byerley

That goes back to some of our conversations surrounding the Microsoft suite and the Adobe Suite from a visual communication, organizational, and production perspective. How do you want to three-dimensionally communicate your idea? One path is to start in SketchUp. For students to dive into SketchUp as a perspective-building tool and learn how to use it, helps them fundamentally understand three-dimensional space, which can be expanded in other programs. And graphic design plays a role. Many things that we must send out are going to be sent out as a PDF and then submitted to the entire client's team. It should speak for itself and have enough information that it can communicate for itself but isn't overburdened with explanation. It's a balance. Basically, how do you want to communicate your ideas?

Dave Cooperstein

The other key piece of that is giving people the resources and the opportunities to experiment, to try the cutting edge, and to push the boundaries of what's possible, so that they find this new piece of software, they try it out, really pushing the edge of what can be done. It's not always going to work, but occasionally, you're going to hit on something. Continue to draw by hand, continue to do research, finding the right inspiration images, and then learn how to translate your hand drawings and your reference images, and all that research, into amazing 3D. Understanding how all that translates into the 3D environment, or into an experiential model, is key to making technology work for you.

Drew Campbell

Here's the thing: when we did research at Universal Studios Japan about what factor most affected the guest's overall impression of their visit to the park, the answer was … an encounter with a live character. Simply put, nothing replaces the human element. Technology is not always the answer.

Adam Bezark

Of course, it's not the specific app that matters. Technology changes all the time. It'll be obsolete by the time this book goes to print. The common thread in everything we're saying here is that it all boils down to how you use your tools to communicate your ideas. I remember when I first started out, we did our presentations by printing concept art on huge 24×36 inch foam core boards, and we'd lug them through airports and stand them up on easels in our clients' offices. Then along came Keynote, and my life changed forever. Not only could we leave the damn artcase behind, but we could tell our stories better than we ever imagined, with transitions and effects that helped tell our stories. And now, twenty years later, I'm finally starting to look for the next big way to convey ideas that will grab a

230 • BRUCE BERGNER ET AL.

client's attention. But what never changes is the goal: to communicate your ideas in the clearest, most compelling way possible.

What are the good components of a portfolio? What approaches to putting together a portfolio might you recommend or have thoughts about?

Dave Cooperstein

The things that we look for are things that show us how you think as a designer, what's your process, where does the project start for you? How do you take that idea and turn it into something? And what's the result of that thing that you've developed? I would much rather see five pages of a project from beginning to end than five pages of eighteen different projects because I want to know what your process is. And the thing that most students leave out of their portfolio is all the other stuff that they do. What else do you like to do? Do you sculpt? Do you paint? It's not in their portfolio, the hand-sketch of a flowerpot, or drawing anime, or whatever crazy hobby they've picked up over the years. That's the type of thing that people don't put in their portfolios, and they need to. How do you think? Not only do they need to include that, but they also must know how to celebrate it.

Adam Bezark

Show me something surprising. Something personal to you. The thing–that makes you interesting, makes you human. And that shows me, like we said at the beginning, that you're really, really good at one thing, but you're interested in a lot of things. And that makes you someone I want to talk to.

Dave Cooperstein

You should have a different portfolio for every job you're applying for. You're going to sell yourself differently depending on the company—if you're going to an architecture firm, it's going to look different than if you're going to a movie studio to look for a job. You can very easily customize your portfolio because it's all digital anyway.

Danny Byerley

One of the challenges for me, with the promises of academia, is this concept that if you check all the boxes and do everything in the right order, you're good to go. But this industry is an art form. Not just "check the box." How are you expressing yourself in your presentations and in your portfolio to indicate you know this is an art form? And how do you, as an artist, communicate your ideas? What is the thing that radiates joy inside you, that keeps you passionate, and keeps you understanding and driving forward?

In experiential projects, where have projects gone wrong? And why?

Dave Cooperstein

When communication breaks down, the project breaks down. Great communication, both internally and externally, is the single best way for a project to be successful. All the team members work in unison. It lets clients feel engaged with the process. It lets your contractors, subcontractors, and consultants understand what they're supposed to build. It lets investors understand what they're buying. It lets users know what they're in for when they show up. Communication is the single biggest ingredient to success.

Danny Byerley

Ego. Ego has caused a good deal of projects to go wrong and is one of the reasons why there is so much conflict in teams or between vendors. You've got to push that ego aside, immediately resolve that conflict you might have with a team member (or between teams) and move on as adults. And if you can achieve that, you can remove the harboring of resentment that builds up, that starts to infect the team, infects morale, and drains the passion that everyone has. From a process standpoint, remove the ego, right from the beginning.

Dave Cooperstein

Something that we learned in our architectural training, that I think is one big reason projects can break down or suffer, is the understanding of the relationship between scope, schedule, and budget. If you've got a project where the budget is set, and the schedule is set, well, then the scope might have to take a hit. Or if you know you can't change the scope, and you can't change the schedule, you may have to spend a little bit more money. Have that understanding at the beginning of a project. And you must learn how to budget. You must learn how to build a budget, manage a budget, and spend a budget, in the most cost-effective way, to get the most out of that budget.

Drew Campbell

You could run a successful bar in Orlando if all you did was host conversations about why attractions fail. First, there are several definitions of "failure." Sometimes, an attraction never makes it off the page, while other times, it opens to the public and crashes miserably. Sometimes it works fine but doesn't stand the test of time or is ahead of its time. Some thoughts on why shows "fail:"

One: Undercapitalization. Put simply, owners try to get off cheap and don't spend enough money to portray the IP. One example of this is Universal's much-reviled "Universal Wonderland" at Universal Studios Japan. This children's area is quite successful in some people's estimation because it provides an entire day's worth of entertainment to children under six, but it is considered a failure by most creatives because it is very lightly themed and lacks any sense of immersion. The owner simply didn't spend enough to raise the area to the Universal brand standard.

Two: Failure to Meet or Manage Audience Expectation. My favorite example of this is the string of walk-through attractions that Universal built to support whatever tentpole movie opened that year. The attractions began to score poorly because the team had built this wonderful entrance facade that promised a full-blown attraction but only contained a walkthrough with a few effects and some live characters. Guests would wander through the maze, thinking it was a queue line, then emerge at the other end and ask, "Where's the ride? This problem was alleviated over time by clearly presenting the attraction as a walkthrough in signage and maps as well as designing it as a series of increasingly scary encounters. Much attention was paid to the final encounter: an intense scare that would eject the guest back into the park just as they reached the cathartic relief of escaping with their lives.

Three: Technological Failures. Sometimes we try to create a new level of experience, but we never really solve the tech. At Universal Singapore, the team designed a boat ride that included a trip up to the top of a volcano. The boats were deposited at the top of the mountain, where they would slide into a circular flume that took them down, around the mountain and back to the "river" they came from. Unfortunately, the water flow wasn't properly engineered, and the boats would create a wall of water in the flume every time they slid down. Fixing it would have required essentially starting over, which was deemed cost-prohibitive. The ride never scored well and is now scheduled for demolition.

Four: Not Serving the Demographic. It is essential to have a good grasp of who will be coming to see your attraction. Disney's EuroDisney suffered mightily from this error as the designers assumed that the European visitors just wanted a Disneyland like the American version. The best example of this phenomenon was the "Alien Encounter" attraction at the Magic Kingdom. This "theatre in the round" attraction scares the living daylights out of you. The claustrophobia of being tied into the seat, hearing the intense sound effects, feeling the haptics in the chair, and going through the entire experience in pitch black, denying you the visual assurance of the presence of others, making you feel like the beast was stalking you and you alone was ... awesome. But here's the problem: The Magic Kingdom is "The Happiest Place on Earth," designed to be a magical, wonderful, safe place for families with young children. You put a five-year-old in there and you get a screaming meltdown. The point is: know your audience.

Five: Capacity. This may seem like a technical problem that is easily solved, but it has killed more attractions than I can count, so it bears mentioning. In the world of master planning, there is an important relationship between the cost of the attraction and the capacity. This issue makes it difficult to do individualized experiences. Ride vehicles need to be bigger to push capacity up, but larger vehicles mean less movement, less individual experience, and less interactivity. Lots and lots of attractions get through blue sky and into concept before somebody says, "Wait a minute, what kind of capacity are we talking about here?"

Regarding experiential theatre, what is "design thinking?"

Drew Campbell

Lots of ways to answer that one, but in my experience, experiential theatre is:

One: Immersive. We are not trying to show you something. We are trying to take you somewhere. We are trying to separate you from your daily reality.

Two: Visceral. This is a story that you will experience with your entire body and all your senses. In many cases, we are after the Illusion of Danger.

Three: Non-linear. To some extent, the guest will decide on the order of events, including where to focus their attention at any time. Our goal is to make the guest feel like he/she has made a lot of decisions, even if they really haven't (or have been cleverly guided). We want to give them the Illusion of Agency.

Four: Emotional. This is not an intellectual exercise, although your brain is involved. This is an emotional roller coaster.

Five: Story-based. And then this happened, and then this happened, and then this happened, and then oh my God!!!!!!

Adam Bezark

In the broadest sense, I think "design thinking" is really "puzzle solving." It's the ability to take a bunch of things (often provided by the client) that don't make any sense and mix and match until it does ... and to know when you found the right solution. Know how to draw in a lot of ideas, from a lot of people, and edit them down to the solution that works. The most essential part of the design process is figuring out what you're going to make—what's the essence of the story you're going to tell—and figuring out what pieces of the toolkit you're going to use. And to do that you have to have this massive vocabulary of stuff that you can mentally mix together, to create that unique solution that's just right for this project.

Jim Doyle

Welcome to design in the twenty-first century. We don't just work with wood and paint anymore. We have all these amazing things that are out there available to us. And if we don't actively search for new things to put in our filing cabinet, we're going to miss some really important stuff. One of the things we look for is: what do you do besides this? "Well, I'm a musician," but what do you play? "I play cello. And I'm also a ballet dancer," Really? You're hired. That young woman became the head of our design program. And she wasn't hired on the strength of her design. It was on her. It's a hunger and it's the desire to keep looking, because it is getting so big, so fast, that you need to keep your eyes open and see what's available to you. I want somebody that's going to come into my office and say, I just found this cool thing for this thing we're already doing.

Danny Byerley

A format of pedagogy that has infiltrated recent generations has led young designers and recent graduates to believe there is only a single path from A to Z and a specific set of steps. They see that if they didn't do X, Y, and Z, then they won't be able to do what's next and find themselves stuck. But just keep pushing. The pivot is going to eventually happen. One day you're in a meeting or you've met someone at an event and then suddenly you're on a completely different path. You must be open to those paths and to pivoting in a direction that you didn't expect, to fully experience what this industry can offer. Because if you think you have one specific path to go down, you're not going to hit that path, because you're going to say no to things that would have opened opportunities and directions you weren't even aware of.

Adam Bezark

Amen!

26

Playing with the Past: Pirates in the College Classroom

Samantha A. Meigs

INTRODUCTION

In his 2017 *CLADbook* article "Why Immersion Matters," Scott Lukas says "… Immersion is the shared undertaking of story that unfolds over time … immersion is never an easy undertaking, but that is why it is an art" (126). As both a trained early-modern social historian and experience designer (with a background and degree in theatrical design), I am intrigued by the impact of immersion into unfamiliar worlds. When my university instituted a new type of Freshman Seminar class in which faculty were to choose an interesting topic and use it as the focus for a general education class that would address research, writing, and presentation skills, I chose the "Golden Age" of piracy (c. 1550–1750) as an engaging topic that would allow students to explore the contrast between popular culture and historical authenticity. Having now taught the class multiple times, I have realized that the basic structure and premise of the class would work equally well in teaching about other historical time periods and different cultures, while also providing a structure and focus for a variety of design applications. Through prompted immersion techniques, students learn how to research and design authentic environments filled with engaging characters and storylines.

THEORETICAL FRAMEWORK: LIVING HISTORY

The essence of living history is that participants learn about history through a combination of historical and theatrical methods. Good introductions to living history techniques can be found in books by Val Horsler (2003) and David B. Allison (2016). In his chapter "Examining Successful First-Person Interpretation," Allison notes that though different, there are points of interconnection between living history, museum theatre, and experiential theatre. Typically living history is improvisational based on meticulous historical authenticity, museum theatre usually refers to scripted, goal-driven performances, and experiential theatre usually involves some level of immersion and audience agency. All three are based on the idea of fostering audience experience of other "worlds," times or places. In museum settings, experiential elements often include walk-through environments such as buildings and farmlands (sometimes preserved from the past and sometimes created), interaction with animals (researched historical breeds), and almost always, human storytellers dressed in period clothing who take on a first-person identity to speak as though they lived in the created/simulated past. Usually, they are not recreating a

234

DOI: 10.4324/9781003188179-30

specific event, but more often strive to portray accurately how people lived, worked, thought, and experienced life during the period being studied. Living history interpreters are trained through deep knowledge of the historical period gained through research that emphasizes primary sources, and often are involved in experimental archeology research in which they test designs and uses of a wide array of tools and materials from the past.

Conventionally, living history has been used by museums as a way to engage visitors and facilitate conversations between curious visitors and well-informed museum staff. In these settings, the designed/created (or re-created) environments provide the backdrop of immersion, allowing the audience to feel as if they had stepped into another world in which they are a participant. An example of living history as a form of experiential theatre can be seen in the "Weekend on the Farm" program (Conner Prairie, 2004–2007) in which participants were given brief biographies (with pre-experience research suggestions) and spent the weekend interacting with continuously in-character interpreters, helping with the cooking, gardening, cleaning, family recreations, and using the outhouse as needed. The debriefings with the participants were amazing—consistently they remarked on how "real" it felt, and how much they had learned, and many returned for another chance to experience life in 1886. As a pedagogical method, living history is sometimes used in elementary classrooms (most often as a portrayal of some famous person), but little has been studied about how useful these techniques might be with college students.

OVERALL METHODOLOGIES: FIRST-PERSON COMPOSITE CHARACTERS

Based on my own training as a historical interpreter, I chose building a "first-person composite" character as the centerpiece of the class. The freshmen would not only learn about pirates; they would become immersed in a world in which they would experience the life of a pirate. Using Stacy Roth's *Past into Present* (1998), students were given the "Ultimate Character Development List," which includes pages of prompted questions, all in the first-person voice. To construct their character, those questions must be answered through meticulous historical research, not only to find one example of a plausible model but to find similarities across several examples which allow the interpreter to amalgamate the characteristics into a person who could have lived during the time-period. This part of the assignment requires at least a basic knowledge of constructing prosopographies, an analytical method designed to look at characteristics of defined groups of people. For example, a pirate prosopography would yield the information (from trial records, broadsides, demographic records, and other types of primary sources) that the biggest percentage of documented pirates were young men of low economic and social status who lived in port towns and usually lived a life of piracy for less than three years. A student pirate would be "safe" using these norms, but they could also research the exceptions, such as the existence of female pirates or long-term "career pirates." As they are introduced to the historical sources, they begin developing a substantial autobiographical narrative (8–12 pages) in which they describe the character's background, experiences, and thoughts on being a pirate, all substantiated by historical evidence.

PIRATE SPACES: DESIGNING AN ENVIRONMENT

As students are developing their characters, they also begin work on designing and creating the physical world that their characters (and audience) will inhabit. Interpretive spaces typically strive for authenticity insofar as they can be reproduced, but also are designed to provide countless interpretive objects that can help create story, enhance interaction, and help bridge communication between the characters and the audience. For example, we have used reproduction pieces of eight as currency to purchase goods (and which were "stolen") during the event. In creating this holistic environment, students utilize standard theatrical techniques of set, lighting, and costume design, while emphasizing potential multisensory and experiential interactions. Each design element helps form a deeper connection between the student and the world of the past they are studying, and which they will "bring to life." Although the specific layout and design vary from class to class, it has been most effective to create a three-dimensional space that allows us to utilize different kinds of story "zones" such as a tavern, jail, and dock area. Designing the spatial environment (along with the historic clothing they will wear) helps the students identify specific character traits or storylines which they can then bring to life in the final class event. The specific elements of the environment which they choose to include will contribute greatly to the immersiveness of the overall experience.

"PLAYING" WITH KNOWLEDGE

To help encourage student involvement in the project, I organize them into "crews" of four. They select a captain and must choose crewmen for their ship who have a background and skills (drawn from their first-person composite character) that are suitable to that ship's goals. Throughout the semester they are given time in class (with my coaching) to develop a storyline "from the bottom up" for their ship which interconnects and enhances the individual pirate's stories. They name their ship (based on research into the typology of sailing ship names), design a flag, and carefully select the specific type of ship they will need for the waters in which they will be sailing, types of cargo expected, etc. Each captain and/or crew selects one student pirate to serve as the ship's quartermaster to keep track of the personnel and items on board the ship. This list is thoroughly discussed in class with information about what normally was on board a sailing ship and types of commodities associated with different global markets. Students must calculate approximate sizes and weights to show that their ship is capable of carrying the materials selected. There is a great deal of critical thinking that goes into the selection of items and choices that have to be made between necessary tools, stores of food and water, potential plunder, and number of crewmen. It is assumed that there are more sailors than just the four who represent the ship and each ship must furnish lists of the ranks, duties, and skills of at least the most significant members of the crew. During the semester they will be given competitive challenges and scenarios in which they achieve victories or defeats depending on their preparedness and ability to think strategically. If students are not already engaged by the character development and environment design, the addition of the gamified, competitive angle usually produces intense interest and the desire to do more research so they can best prepare for whatever challenges they receive. The pedagogical strengths of incorporating play into learning are well documented for all ages. For a basic analysis of the positive role of play in learning see Stuart Brown's *Play* (2010) and George Kalmpourtzis, *Educational Game Design Fundamentals* (2019).

HANDS-ON SKILLS

Another part of the class focuses on hands-on activities which teach period-specific skills. I vary these each semester depending on the interests of the students, but this part of the curriculum emphasizes the lived experience of daily life and how it would have been different in the seventeenth and eighteenth centuries. Students have consistently shown enthusiasm for period writing (including learning how to cut a quill pen and learning to write in early modern script), fire-starting (with flint and steel or a burning glass), knot-tying, cooking, and period dice and card games. Sometimes the challenges involve the ability to perform some of these activities, so students also end up competing for the highest proficiency levels in these areas. Depending on what they are interested in exploring, each skill can turn into a full-blown performative experience (such as having the class research early modern recipes and ingredients and cook a full meal). Hands-on activities that involve equipment or safety issues that would be too challenging in the classroom are normally done through field trips. These have included taking students to visit a museum in Michigan where participants can help crew a two-masted sailing ship, and meeting with historical reenactors who have taught them how to shoot black-powder weapons.

FOCUSING ON SPECIFIC LEARNING OUTCOMES

Although the first-person composite character and immersive environmental design are always the centerpiece of their semester-long portfolio project, I have experimented with different components, primarily to test specific teaching outcomes, often adjusting the modules to incorporate new strategies into the assignments as needed. For example, though I have always provided a number of pictorial resources (videos and books which illustrate artifacts), I have found that students struggle with the idea that different objects existed in that time period, and what people valued differed according to their needs and background. To try to address this point, last semester I added a requirement that each pirate needed to have a pirate chest in which they would keep their most valuable possessions. The chest and objects had to be three-dimensional and needed to be incorporated into their first-person narrative. The results were amazing. The students built and modified objects, wrote letters with their quill pens, pressed flowers, collected and identified seashells, and connected them with the history and personality of their personae. Several of them commented that selecting special objects helped them understand more about the time-period and helped develop their character. For overall assessment of the semester-long project, I evaluate the final portfolio for excellence in the selection of primary historical documentation, the story arc of the narrative, specific details that help create three-dimensional characters, and students' ability to demonstrate actual proficiencies in pirate skills such as fire-starting or navigation.

PUBLIC PERFORMANCE

The final piece of the "pirate experience" class is to have the learners become teachers through designing and implementing a public event focused on what they have learned during the semester. This event utilizes the design principles of experience design and serves as an excellent illustration of the research-based aspect of the Experience Design field. Since each class designs the event they want to experience, the features vary each semester, but the basic goal is always the same: to teach others what we can learn by studying pirates, and how the popular culture images differ from the actual reality. Using the techniques of theatrical and experience design, students use their characters and designed environment to help their visitors (students and faculty from the campus community) explore the pirate world through multisensory and experiential scenarios and vignettes. In addition to being fun for the students, the event allows me to observe what the students in the class have retained, and what specific things they deem most important to teach others.

PEDAGOGICAL OUTCOMES

This class has shown me how profoundly effective the joining together of history, theatre, and experiential techniques can be in promoting positive student outcomes which are transferable to many fields and majors. There is no question that students learn how to do complex research in this class and gain understanding and empathy for situations and people from the past. Through emphasizing living history techniques students put themselves into novel scenarios in which they also can explore contemporary perceptions and issues. Throughout the class comparisons are made between popular culture and historical reality, so students can learn how to analyze the societal ideas behind the characterizations. They are given the freedom to develop characters that are either similar or markedly different from themselves in terms of gender, race, age, economic status, and so forth. By learning experientially, they vividly understand that life was different in different times and places which helps promote empathy and informed imagination, both skills of use in any discipline.

REFLECTIONS

In her book *Past Into Present: Effective Techniques for First-Person Historical Interpretation* Stacy Roth (1998) observes:

> first-person is more demanding of staff than other types of interpretation and more difficult than third person to present effectively. It requires interpreters to know their historic information, technical processes, and a vast range of peripheral facts. It requires more research, training, and authentic detailing than third-person. It demands proficiency at communication, teaching, and (frequently) theatrical skills. (24)

This is also true when teaching through living history methods. Both the instructor and the students are stretched and challenged by utilizing these techniques. One does not assume knowing everything at the beginning, but rather this style of teaching forces a focus on a type of discovery-based learning in order to explore specific interests or questions that may arise. Students have the freedom to find the things they want to learn about, but at the same time, the class is very carefully orchestrated to keep students moving ahead to the intended outcomes.

To conclude: I offer this essay as a call to action. I believe these techniques could and should be used more extensively in teaching students both specific disciplinary skills as well as an overall understanding of social context and an appreciation for other times and places. The component pieces are easily applied to other classroom settings and pedagogical goals, and my message is immersion works. In the years that I have taught this class, I have found that students respond enthusiastically, often returning the next year to mentor new crews of pirates. They take other experiential classes and become majors in our Experience Design Department, and they retain knowledge and interest in history, design, and research lasting throughout their college careers. In some specific cases, I have seen that this class has been truly transformational with imagination, creativity, and empathy becoming an integral part of students' identity. My faculty colleagues laugh when students greet me with a cheerful "ahoy, Captain!" when they see me on campus, but I am convinced this class is one of the most important pedagogical activities in which I am engaged.

References

Allison, David B. 2016. *Living History: Effective Costumed Interpretation and Enactment in Museums and Historic Sites*. Lanham, MD: Rowman & Littlefield.

Brown, Stuart. 2010. *Play: How it Shapes the Brain, Opens the Imagination, and Invigorates the Soul*. New York: Penguin Group, USA.

Horsler, Val. 2003. *Living the Past*. London: The Orion Publishing Group.

Kalmpourtzis, George. 2019. *Educational Game Design Fundamentals*. New York: Taylor & Francis Group.

Lukas, Scott. 2017. "Why Immersion Matters." *CLADbook*, pp. 1–26.

Roth, Stacy. 1998. *Past Into Present: Effective Techniques for First-Person Historical Interpretation*. Chapel Hill: University of North Carolina Press.

27

Unlocking Formal Qualities to Discover the Iconography in Visual Design

Stephen Jones

INTRODUCTION

The impact of creating a theatrical experience is a celebration of the collaboration between artists and the intended audience. Successful stories that "speak" to those in attendance are ones that allow for creative relevance and challenge opinions based on the visual representations of the source material. This collaboration relies heavily on how the themes buried within the storyline relate. The process of creation begins with unlocking how relevant themes can be highlighted for the contemporary artist and the intended audience. This relevance is imperative because we, as artists, must always remember that our work is created for a wide variety of observers. Their backgrounds and understandings of the story differ from ours due to the diversity of individuals in the audience. We create a container for our story when we consider every object we place in the space, every color we select. Each choice has a different impact based on the person witnessing and experiencing the body of work. We, therefore, have a responsibility to unpack as much of the meaning behind the event or story as possible before we begin to consider how the container for the story will be shaped. These visual road-markers for the setting (including the casting) fall under the iconography of the story.

Traditional analysis of the facts of the story as it relates the visual and designer elements only scratches the surface of how it might be interpreted and received. There needs to be a process of understanding and processing the tropes within individual moments, the motivations behind character choices, and the interiority of a setting in order to create powerful containers that highlight other actions within the story. Why is it important to focus on the container? Consider a fine work of art from the renaissance era. While we celebrate the beauty of the work and marvel at the use of color and composition, the painting takes on a slightly different meaning when placed in a clean-lined modern picture frame from IKEA. In this example, we can compare the different impressions derived when telling a story in a historical theatre ordained with gold leaf versus a modern black box space. The container can stand in as a bridge between the artist and the audience. Even though Aristotle claimed that spectacle was less important than other theatrical elements, I respectfully disagree. This container that houses the story helps audiences to self-identify with and contextualize the themes and style of the story. It also allows the artist to have the freedom to create a container that is fitting for an experiential environment that is specific to the project and story being told. This is opposed to copying a copy of a copy.

FORMAL QUALITIES AND RELEVANCE

By understanding of tropes and motivations within a story, one can begin to identify what we will define as the formal qualities necessary to connect with the audience. While the formal qualities are based in the facts of the story, i.e., Kathleen and Stephen are discussing a serious topic in a coffee shop, these qualities are feelings extrapolated from the intangible artistic motivations gleaned from a careful analysis of the source material. Formal qualities can address how do they drink their coffees. Are they gulping down the drinks, or are they gently sipping? Where are they sitting? Sitting at a tabletop can give the idea of it being a longer conversation while sitting at a bar can give the feeling of being rushed. The designer might ask, "How does the story feel? Dark? Light? Heavy?" While we need to have a grasp of the facts of the story, understanding the formal qualities takes some of the responsibility of connecting with an audience off the shoulders of the text or other source material, and allows visual elements, to carry the load. These visual elements serve to create the bridge that connects the artist, work, and audience through individual experience.

In order to achieve the desired impact, the artist must also have a strong understanding of who the audience is. Generally speaking, what experiences have they encountered that might affect the way they interact with the story? Are they from a background that is completely foreign to the facts and actions of the play? Often when teaching students who have been educated to primarily look at the scenic design to tell a story ... they rarely begin by thinking about who their audience is and how that particular audience creates meaning through visual representation. Young students that are watching *Hedda Gabler* might not find the story, the characters, or the themes as compelling as when Ibsen wrote it. But by identifying the formal qualities within the text we can develop visual elements that make the material more relevant to this audience.

As an example, to help one grasp the ideas of formal qualities, one might set up an exercise where participants are asked to create a relationship with physical space. Ask the participants in the exercise to leave the room with a piece of dialog that involves the need for a character to engage with a chair. Line up three distinctly different types of chairs in an empty room. Ask the participants to return and analyze the chairs with the goal of determining which chair is most appropriate for the moment. In their analysis, ask the participants to verbalize why one chair *feels* better for the moment than another. Is it the color? Yes. The size? Yes. The softness? Yes. The arms or not. Yes. Then ask them to describe the personality of the chair. A fact of the story might be that a chair is needed for a particular environment, however, there is something that goes beyond the need for a chair. What choice could one provide for the audience that heightens the relevance of a moment where a character interacts with this chair? How does it make you feel when you see it? Does it feel correct for the moment? With the chair, how does it feel to the touch? How do your hands and senses respond when you interact with it? When it is sat upon, does it make a noise? Does that noise complement the moment of the scene? The chair has character and *is* a character. The choice of which chair goes beyond serving as a functional object within the composition of the fictional space. By better understanding the character's experience with the chair, the designer creates a stronger experience for the audience witnessing that character's interaction.

Much like choosing the wrong actor when casting a play, the wrong chair can bring the energy of the story to an unintended place. This chair has been selected because of the understanding of the personalities of each character in the story. It has been selected because the designer can speculate on how the audience might respond to it. Perhaps the chair possesses qualities that the audience can associate with comfort or sterility. The choice is in direct relationship to the moment of the story and helps to artistically drive the point of the moment. This understanding of relevance allows for bold and potent artistic choices for the audience to encounter. These choices also allow each mounting of the project to be vastly different.

While a chair is an easy object to consider, let's dig deeper into how understanding these formal qualities can be applied to the story and experience being told. How can we glean ideas about textures, size of space, and how dramatic the transitions between moments can be? We arrive at these ideas from our understanding of the subtext gleaned from our readings and analysis. One element that helps this understanding is the tempo of the text or the moment. Characters speaking in short one-word responses give a different feeling than thoughts that speak more colorfully. This can be a clue that helps us in our understanding of the urgency (or lack of) of a moment. Something else that might help is our interpretation of the texture of the space in the story and how characters might move in the space. Shakespeare's *The Tempest* gives us a good example.

The Tempest

We begin by asking, "How big is the storm in the prologue?" A fact we can derive is that the storm is strong enough to wash the characters to shore. Another relevant question is "How big is their boat?" As we consider the formal qualities of the scene, we can see that there is a quick short dialogue between characters. Orders are being barked, and reference is being made to secure the ship. But how big is the storm, and how do we want our audience to perceive it? Have they ever been at sea? Does it engulf the entirety of the environment that houses the audience? Or is it confined to the fictional space being observed and/or experienced? We can balance the size of the waves with how violent the characters are tossed and more. The subtext of the moment is subjective based on who we are sharing this with, and the freedom we might want to express for the blocking of the scene. While we can base our artistic choices on a balance of dramaturgical research and text analysis to arrive at the artistic inspiration, formal qualities of understanding can help to drive our choices for visual design.

ICONOGRAPHY AND VISUAL DESIGN

For the formal qualities to resonate with the story a designer must also understand the collective social experiences of the intended audience. These hard-to-define impulses that are based in the facts of the story, become a key to discovering how to create such a connection. The relationship between how the story is represented visually and its impact on the audience is often overlooked and/or taken for granted because the iconography is suggested by the playwright. To effectively connect with today's audience, a designer/team must challenge the scripted iconography of a story. Much like the chair, if the audience can not relate to it in some way, the potential of the event can be lost on many.

Within the traditional training of students, the analysis of the text and the reliance on the playwright to dictate the iconography has been the template for design students. Because of this approach to training, most American university productions exhibit playwright-centered iconography versus audience-relevant iconography. The play is cast based on the character descriptions, the setting is suggested through the functional needs of what the characters interact with, and not much is explored regarding theme. Perhaps there is an overarching artistic visual element that might be placed as a backdrop, or the lighting might add a level of drama by pulling our focus to a specific monologue. These factual and functional choices do not fully serve the artistry of the work, nor do they take into context when and where the work is being produced. It certainly is not accounting for who is in the audience.

For example, consider *The Glass Menagerie* by Tennessee Williams. The facts as dictated by the stage directions and playwright's notes strongly suggest that the play is about a Caucasian family located in an economically meager setting. These directions suggest a specific type of iconography that commands a high level of environmental realism mixed with the formal qualities of life in the early 1900s in a tenement apartment. Because there are parameters as laid out by our playwright, there is an inherent repetitive approach to the iconography of how the story unfolds. Tennessee Williams, in creating this piece of theatre does not mention the type of theatre space, nor is there mention of the intended audience. Casting has often excluded people of color and of different sexual orientations. The result can be an emotional and artistic disconnect when telling this story in certain communities. Ironically, the cycle of factual storytelling does not take into consideration how the story might relate to a community that has not experienced similar settings. Because of the playwrights suggested iconography, the story cannot resonate with a diverse array of audiences in the same way. How do we break the cycle and make this story reach a more diverse audience?

We can start by asking what the story is about? Loss, or perhaps regret, the feeling of being trapped? What does it feel like to be living on top of one another? These are not exclusive to Caucasian communities. To break the cycle, we must explore the formal qualities of the human experience. We can look to broader themes and compare them to who we are presenting the story to. In this way we can ask, if the play is about feeling trapped, does the container *have* to be an apartment? If the story is about loss, does the play have to be set in the 1930s? Ultimately, are there opportunities for us to read the subtext of the play to create iconography that is more inclusive? Understanding how the visual design meets the demands of the story being told can allow for a far greater metaphorical arrangement of objects on stage as well as help dictate what type of venue the story should or needs to be told within. Challenging the source material in this way can lead to new ideas about what is truly important in the text or material. From a dramaturgical standpoint, one could even begin to discover that cuts and modifications to the material are needed. In this way, we can squeeze all the relevant messaging needed to make the story potent for the observer.

A celebration of collaboration between the artist and the audience allows the work to sing and resonate for all. We often assume that the visual elements of the play are there to provide functionality. If we are truly creating art that is expressive, we must consider what is challenging the audiences' thoughts. Are our choices creating an environment of imaginative activity or does it allow the audience to become passive as they observe? The collaborative process is not formulaic. It morphs based on conversations, between the artists, and conversations with the audience. Themes and discoveries change as the development process digs deeper and deeper into the formal qualities of the story.

28
Designing an Interactive Production: A Practical Walkthrough

Liz Fisher

FIRST THINGS FIRST

This essay does not pretend to be an authoritative system for the pre-production process of an interactive work of theatre, but rather a supplementary reading raising questions and considerations that practitioners should examine, considerations that focus on concrete digital solutions for engaging audiences. The proposed approach assumes that a production team *wants* to foreground audience participation as an *essential* and *holistic* experience of the dramatic work, where one would consider that the performance would be diminished or impossible without the active role of the audience.

WORKING DEFINITIONS

Before digging into deeper analysis of the production, let's walk through the working definitions that will be used throughout this article.

- *Digital Performance*: one or more of the essential elements of a performance exists within a networked platform.
- *Networked Platform*: any platform that requires the use of the internet.
- *Transmedia Performance*: a performance that transpires across two or more networked platforms.
- *Meatspace*: a cheeky reference to the physical world, embodied interactions (or IRL as it's known on the interwebs), as opposed to ones that take place in a networked platform.

ESSENTIAL FORM AND THEATRICALITY

No matter how your production arrives at its fundamental narrative structure (devised, scripted, or anything in between), an initial feature to consider is the story's essential form. Is it a monologue? Is it epistolary? Is it serialized? Is it predominantly a movement piece? Does it include direct address? With these kinds of questions, you are not identifying a text's locations or evaluating linguistic styles. Rather, you want to discover what is the *core storytelling mechanism*. Identifying this modality can assist in selecting an aligned networked platform. For example, why couldn't an epistolary play be performed over email or a radio play as a podcast?

244

DOI: 10.4324/9781003188179-32

Next, consider any moments of theatricality. While notably difficult to define, for the purposes of this approach, "theatricality" means instances of heightened performance, such as metadrama, intersections with other art forms (dance or music), or key cultural/historical references. While this tends to be a key part of most production teams' pre-production work, these same moments need to be evaluated for interactive and networked possibilities. For example, many traditional ways of embodying a heightened moment on a stage simply don't work as well on the flattened visual field of a video screen. Projections in meatspace can be an excellent way of creating theatricality, but it is less effective when used online. Why the difference? There is no shift in audience experience. In meatspace, the audience's visual understanding shifts from three dimensions to two. It is this shift that creates the audience's experience of the event as "theatrical" because it is an intentional disruption of the storytelling mode and therefore supplies a moment of theatricality that serves the narrative. In the digital world, excluding virtual and augmented realities, projections don't shift our visual frame—projections remain in two dimensions. But what if you sent the audience a text message at that same moment? Now you have introduced a shift in their experience of the play and found a way to heighten that moment. Turning a theatrical moment into a transmedia[1] experience is just one potential way to solve this challenge of presenting theatricality on screens. But some of our meatspace tools can also work in digital spaces. Shifts in sound, especially change between mono and binaural, can bring the same experience of theatricality to digital and meatspace performances.

There is a specific subset of theatrical moments that offer rich opportunity for blending of meatspace and digital elements: "seams of reality." These seams include *memory*, *imagination*, *magic*, and the *supernatural*. We can look to Shakespeare's plays for examples of these seams of reality:

- *Memory* – the story of Claudius' murder of Old Hamlet.
- *Imagination* – illustration of Othello's explicit suspicions of Desdemona's infidelities.
- *Magic* – the masque in *The Tempest*.
- *Supernatural* – Banquo's ghost from *Macbeth*.

Audiences understand these instances as events and characters that exist outside of our natural world and are therefore more likely to accept them when portrayed as alternate frames of reality. When you find examples of these in your production, spend extra time considering how you might bring them to life with the disruption of a separate platform.

ANSWERING QUESTIONS OF TIME AND SPACE

Meatspace theatre is all about focusing time and space for the audience. The same is true for interactive digital performances. When solving for time and space, each production team will have to answer the following questions:

Time
- How does time operate in your performance?

Space
- What is the format of your performance?
- What platform(s) will you utilize during your performance?
- How will you distribute your performance?

When producing theatre in meatspace, creative teams must answer these same questions. But the creation of meatspace theatre requires that the answers to these questions frequently begin with the same answer: a performance venue with areas for actors and audience that are co-inhabited at the same time. With interactive networked performance, you are liberated from this assumption and can make decisions that best fit your production's specific needs.

First, your team must answer the question of **time**. How much of your performance must be synchronous/real-time? How much is asynchronous? Which parts? The performance? The distribution of the performance? Will you blend synchronous and asynchronous elements at any step of the performance? Any combination of live and pre-recorded content is possible when embarking on a digital production.

Next up are questions of **space**: the *format* of the performance will be the first digital spatial element by which other elements are then included or excluded. You can blend formats as needed, thereby creating a transmedia performance. Possible formats include:

- Moving Images/Video.
- Still images.
- SMS/Text Messages.
- Pre-recorded audio.
- Use of pre-existing websites or web applications (Twitter, Minecraft or other MMORPG, Mozilla Hubs, and many others).
- Custom-built website or web application.
- Augmented Reality (AR).
- Virtual Reality (VR).

Each format comes with pros, cons, dependencies, and requirements. Be sure to talk through the implications as a team as you settle on your final form. For example, if you want to do a VR show, then *everyone* has to have a VR headset, including creatives and audience.

After selecting your format, the next major question of space involves determining your *platform*. It is important to separate platforms from the previously mentioned formats since formats have multiple possibilities when it comes to platforms. Video can be created by recording an unedited Skype call or be exported from a video editor, like Adobe Premiere. Skype and Premiere are examples of platforms; the .mov file is the format. By identifying what you need the end-product to be (the format), you can then explore potential platforms that will be best suited to delivering you the required format.

Distribution deals with how your performance is shared with your audience. Sometimes, a platform will also serve as a production's distribution. Zoom fulfilled this need for many theatre companies during the 2020 pandemic, offering both a platform and a distribution model. But production could also blend platforms to achieve different performance goals: streaming a Zoom call over Twitch with OBS (Open Broadcaster Software) and QLab to manage its video and audio inputs. When considering what distribution method your team wants to use, make sure that you are considering the inherent dramaturgy of that distribution. Streaming a performance on YouTube is different from Vimeo and also different from Twitch. Each of these websites has its own identity, core community that they serve, and their own social norms, in addition to any assumptions by the public (and your audience) about the "personality" of these sites. Vimeo is considered the artsy, cinephile video streaming website, whereas YouTube, with a roughly identical feature set, is video streaming for the general public. Think how your production works with (or against) these patterns of behavior. Your choices can have an impact on your audience before they even see your production.

COLLABORATING WITH THE AUDIENCE

The topic of the target audience and how they are desired to interact with the production must also be considered while the team determines format, platform, and distribution. You cannot separate these decisions from the audience's role in an interactive performance. There are three key elements that every production must consider when establishing the audience's role in an interactive performance:

1. Defining and contextualizing the audience's agency.
2. Creating and honoring a contract with the audience.
3. Building into the narrative structure a series of trainable moments that establish the interaction norms.

In order to define the audience's agency in a performance, the creative team must decide the extent to which the audience is a co-creator in this process. Audience co-creation can take many forms, from audience members sitting in the dark and laughing to a complete dissolution between the roles of audience and actor. In this second case, both performer and audience fully inhabit the performance space (be it entirely digital, meatspace, or some combination) and the forward trajectory of the piece is made collaboratively by all parties.

Once the degree of co-creation is established, it is then helpful to contextualize the audience's ability to impact and alter the narrative within the world of the play. How does the audience fit into this world? Sometimes this is called "casting the audience"; giving them a distinct role that fits inside of the narrative structure. While casting your audience can be helpful as you contextualize and support their agency, it should be remembered that audience members cannot be controlled, only invited and encouraged towards specific narrative goals. They remain, finally, agents of chaos. No matter how hard the actors work, the audience will have its own whims and desires that cannot be controlled or expected. The romantic notion of the audience as your scene partner may turn out to be true, but you rely on it at your own peril. Therefore, it falls to the creative team to establish a context wherein the potential for chaos introduced by audience agency is given right-sized narrative guardrails to go in whatever direction it needs, without completely derailing the expected path of the performance.

Once the team has set the norms, context, and boundaries for the interaction, a meaningful "contract" between audience and production is established. And now both sides must honor this agreement. If the production is set up to be a branched narrative that gives the audience the ability to choose their own adventure, then the production should strive to do exactly that. If the production violates that trust by using technology that cannot support the audience's selection or if the team doesn't want to fulfill the audience's decision, then you have broken the trust with the audience and are no longer co-creating interactive theatre. To borrow a term from the tech world, you are selling vaporware.

To help the audience understand the limits of this contract, it can be helpful to build trainable moments into the performance. Training an audience allows artists to build consent with their patrons, wherein the interactions are defined and engagement protocols highlighted. The development of consent and clear boundaries between audience and performer reinforces an ethical and safe environment, ensuring everyone's participation reflects their expectations. This leads to an understandable question of how does one train an audience? Your story and narrative structure will help you answer this question. Is this an original or a canonical production? When working with an established text, you will need to find a moment outside of the published script to train the audience. This could be done through the use of a pre-show or other extra-performative device. One example might be an email with instructions (perhaps a video) that wraps the audience into the world of the play before they enter the theater.

You can have multiple trainable moments, but each moment needs to answer the following questions:

1. What are the boundaries of the audience's involvement around this exact moment of interactivity?
2. When will these moments of interaction happen? (i.e., what is the cue to begin/stop interacting?)
3. How will the audience know if they were successful in their moment of interaction? (i.e., how does the audience know if their actions resulted in an outcome?)

With a new play, it is possible to write the trainable moments into the narrative, such that the characters walk the audience through how they will participate as part of the play itself. For Whirligig's *Deus Ex Machina*, a choose your own adventure play based on *The Oresteia*, audiences were trained on how to text their votes through a pre-show performance that illustrated how a new piece of technology, discovered by the production team, translated prayers into text messages. After the play began, the audiences learned that this same technique would be used for them to vote on the outcomes of the performance, through a modeling process illustrated by one of the central characters in the play, Zeus. A scripted scene allowed the audience to vote on how Zeus should interact with other characters onstage. While this did not impact the overall arc of the narrative, it trained the audience on how and when they would be given control of the story. If you're searching for additional inspiration for other training modalities, look to video games. Every video game trains its audience on how it can be played, which gives us a rich set of examples on which to draw.

GETTING UNSTUCK

As you work through these questions and considerations, you may find yourself stuck on a particular point. In order to get past this block, try describing the ideal audience experience. What is the end-to-end audience journey and experience? How are they physically engaging with the play? What is the emotional journey that you hope they have? Once you've described this perfect encounter, then you can begin to look at the practical considerations needed to achieve it. What equipment would they need? Are there bandwidth requirements? Thinking into questions like this can allow the team's imaginations to run wild, typically moving the team closer to finding a technical solution that fits the narrative needs of the production.

FINAL THOUGHTS

After working through all of these considerations and preparing for that moment when the audience is finally invited into the process, your production now faces the biggest challenge: letting go. This is the easiest one to say and the hardest one to do. You must build the backstage systems by which the entire production company can remain open to whatever the audience asks of them, and then let go. Trust that it will turn out alright in the end. How? It's a mystery, coupled with a whole lot of testing. Inviting sample audiences, even in the earliest phases of the rehearsal process, can help a team acclimate to the unpredictable nature of interactive theatre. This testing, while it can never account for every possible outcome, can build confidence in creative teams, while also learning what needs further development. Embracing audience agency into a performance event requires actors and technicians to be fully in the moment, knowing that it will be different every night, so everyone must cling to the present moment, waiting to see what will happen next. Because no one knows. It is listening and reacting. It is living in the present. It is what is most essential about theatre.

DESIGNING AN INTERACTIVE PRODUCTION PROJECT

Using the above approach, you and your creative teams will develop a concept and produce a short performance for an interactive production based on Euripides' *The Bacchae*.

Concept Statement (25%)

Write a 3–5 pages paper that outlines what your production will be. Be sure to answer the following questions:

- What is the narrative of your production?
- How are you casting the audience?
- How will the audience interact with your narrative?

Production Plan (25%)

This plan includes a variety of written and visual elements that illustrate the plan for implementing the production. It must include

- A written statement that lists the format, platform, and distribution methodology that your production uses
- Storyboards that illustrate the significant action, as experienced from the audience's perspective
  - These storyboards should also identify whether an action is synchronous or asynchronous
- A written outline of the initial trainable moment for your production (if it is not part of your significant action)

Prelim Design Presentation (25%)

Each department must prepare a brief presentation that represents your designs for this production. They must include:

- 5–6 research images that showcase your ideas for the entire production
  - These images should tell the journey through the play, highlighting any key transitions.
- 2–3 research images that showcase your ideas for the significant action

Demo (25%)

Create a demo, or short performance, of the significant actions of your team's production. It should be no longer than ten minutes and include a functionable moment of audience

250 • LIZ FISHER

interaction. The demo must be presented using the distribution methodology that was previously identified.

Note

1 A stricter definition of transmedia would argue that this example should be considered an intermedial example of theatricality. Outside of this essay, you are likely to see people describe transmedia of storytelling that crosses multiple platforms and expands the narrative structure, such as a video game based on the most recent Marvel universe movie that originated from a Marvel comic book.

29

A Postdigital Response: Performance Technologies and Design Thinking

Hans Vermy and Eric Hoff

THE POSTDIGITAL?

What is the postdigital? "Response" is an answer. And we find with experiential theatre design "response" is *thee* answer. More on that later; for now, let's get comfortable. Because this essay is a conversation, some introductions are in order:

Eric Hoff is a writer, director, producer, and dramaturg who focuses on experience design, immersive theatrical events, and themed entertainment. Eric talked with Hans Vermy, an educator, writer, and filmmaker who focuses on histories, theories, and practices of performance, media, and animation. The following is an intertwining.

What does "postdigital" mean? Or, rather, what is the postdigital? Social comfort with digital technology. The postdigital is an innate/native understanding of the digital within an experience.

How does social *comfort* matter to design?

In postdigital art the digital doesn't have to be pointed out, explained, justified, or even shown; it is integrated. It is expected to be one of the layers even if it isn't planned to be. A phone rings and interrupts the show. The digital is active even when no one is looking, tracking us in our pocket for example. Giving us maps as well as making maps of us. Tracking and mapping is just one social convention of space that has evolved. Comfort means we now have many kinds of space to design because there are more kinds of space people are actively social in: cyberspace, virtual space, augmented space, projected space, that space between a user and an interface, in addition to the new *physical* spaces digital design tools help us conceptualize and create. Designers of digital spaces who use digital tools are just now working to deliver experiences to an audience that is comfortable in digitally integrated spaces.

Comfort is not just coziness. It is a physical sense of ease from a prior constraint. Comfort is physical and emotional. Like relaxing in a chair after a long day of working on your feet. Learning to live with the digital *was* a constraint. It hindered us as we learned digital quirks, tendencies, needs (like network access), and social relations/complications (like social media). Now, even the oldest generations have given up a Luddite response to computers as they too navigate the world with digital tools once shooed away as just another interfering gadget.

DOI: 10.4324/9781003188179-33

251

In many of the previous articles (though articulated differently) we sense a striving to convey a new social comfort and connection within digital devices and online experiences; that cyberspace has now become a social space, a type of space we *can* take for granted as being filled with living people *and* bots and apps and embodied responses. This is the postdigital. When we no longer need to attach the words "digital" or "online" or "computer" or "network" or even "embodied" to words or our projects. Digital art *is* Art. Online Zoom-performances *are* Theatre. VR concerts *are* live music performances.

The postdigital is social comfort forged with the digital. We know how it works and what it can do (even if much is yet to come). We no longer need art with computers to explain how the digital is acting, responding, or sensing the audience because we as a society are becoming ever savvier about what the digital can do and what it can grow into.

"Comfort" doesn't just mean comfortable. One can gain some comfort by removing a stone from a shoe, but the rest of the journey will still be rough. Social comfort with the digital brings new conventions and social contracts. The postdigital brings about a re-examination of social contracts. New etiquettes. New forms of consent and conflict arise around anonymity, trolling, doxxing, and globally networked tribalism. We are now in the re-examination of social rules (and how to break them) because we live in and out of cyberspace; and because the in and out of cyberspace is no longer a binary option. Cyberspace has merged with our "analogue" space. What do we make of the hacker? The troll? The viral lie? Ransome-ware extortionists?

The digital arrived and quickly tried to integrate us. Now that we've taken up the digital tools, we find ourselves navigating new social spheres and roles that haven't had much time to pause and consider new social contracts that are needed in new social platforms. Re-examining social contracts lies at the heart of creating exciting experiential design in the postdigital. For many reasons. Mostly because when we ask an audience to participate, we as creators, become responsible for how they will navigate our immersive experience. But in a performance that blends the real and fake, online and off, we as creators must also account for how participants might navigate the borders of our experience and or misinterpret a signal or puzzle and move out of the experience into a real (perhaps dangerous) situation without realizing it. Or a participant may break an explicit rule of the world. Thus, we must be aware of social conventions in the postdigital and how social contracts are necessary to build strong and safe experiences. Listing rules of engagement and etiquette is one way to make such a contract but as creators we have to consider the ever-expanding ways people exist online and on social media.

Thinking about social contracts also includes how we as designers and creators build our teams and communicate. New conventions and contracts need to be drawn up to train postdigital artists and to encourage team structure based on the needs of each new immersive project rather than a formal structure of production. Comfort with the digital means that experiential theatre and responsive art will continue to grow (perhaps exponentially as the digital continues to expand social platforms in addition to generating new tools for creation).

Within all the essays in this section (and thinking about the future of design of experiential theatre) we found a need for more in-depth discussion around:

1. **Device Technologies of the postdigital**
2. **Postdigital Language**
3. **Education in the postdigital**

The following sections explore a braiding of the three: ***Language, Education,*** and ***Device Technology.*** This essay is mostly focused on technology. Education and Language are not exceptions, they are two powerful technologies made by humans. As creators, it is always important to remember that language is one of our most important technologies. And to keep in mind that the digital is also a language, albeit constructed of code (and code put into action). Computer language is focused on code and action, but now more than ever our society *is* a flurry of codes in action. Our creative worlds have expanded so greatly with the digital because it is composed of machine technology (hardware) and social technology (language/code) but also technologies of learning (education and artificial intelligence). Thus, our look at *Performance Technologies and Design Thinking* in the postdigital is a technological braid of *Language, Education*, and *Device Technologies*.

DEVICE TECHNOLOGIES OF THE POSTDIGITAL: INVISIBILITY, COMFORTABILITY, AUGMENTED REALITY, AND VIRTUAL REALITY

We talk in the industry that we want the tech to be invisible. This idea echoes through a lot of technology in performance. For example, the film projector is behind the audience, placing the simple surface of the screen in view and the complex projection machinery out of sight. But in the postdigital it's not that the tech is invisible, it is that it no longer draws so much attention to itself; the technology isn't the subject matter itself. For example, is Instagram a technology or a social platform/place? To many users, it is a place for social communication even though it is also complex digital networked technology. In other words, many technologies of the digital are "invisible" now because we see them as places and platforms for communication as opposed to new social technologies. But the devices themselves that link us to places are too becoming invisible as they proliferate across our bodies and social lives.

Postdigital tech is digital tech that is not in our way; when we don't have to think about technology, just connection and response. In the digital era, looking at a dancer holding a Wii remote was awkward, but in the postdigital, we can take for granted the responsive technology a dancer might use in a performance; we can assume a physically minded dancer would wear a Fitbit. And that the audience has phones to track the dancer's Fitbit. And that the audience might be wearing Fitbits themselves.

New technology in the postdigital appears to be that which layers best with our way(s) of being in the world. The digital integrates best into our lives when it manages to become a helpful layer on top of our real-world experiences. For example, the way the cell phone made internet-accessible maps usable in the moment: layered onto our driving or walking. The digital sutures and merges many kinds of media. Hans has written elsewhere (Vermy 2013) about how the digital embraces composite work in cinematic effects, blending models and miniatures and computer graphics and costume and makeup in order to give us the digital as a suturing layer to many textures of the real. The digital loves layers and it expands best in situations where it is a layer. Thus, we believe technologies that embrace layering onto our real world, technologies that apply the digital as a transparent skin to our embodied experiences are the ones that will continue to grow and create greater opportunities for experiential creations.

Layering brings us to Augmented Reality or AR. Currently, Virtual Reality (VR) is making a hard push to become a technology we are comfortable with. But we believe VR is at a disadvantage over AR. VR blocks out real-world sounds and vision. It's like slipping into a dream world, where we pass the veil entirely. Perhaps because of this passing into a dream quality, the first global in-headset, VR live theatre performance was an adaptation of Shakespeare's *The Tempest*; a play about a social world manipulated by a magician. But AR plays on top of google glasses or on our pads and phones as we navigate the real world, like IKEA Place or Amazon's "See it in your room" AR which allows you to see commodities in your home: just hold up your phone camera to your living room and see if your ottoman choice compliments your old chair. The layers of AR add to our real world. Forcing the media to be responsive to the real world. Whereas VR forces the body and media into a visually-direct responsive relationship. Again, VR places the body and media into a responsive relationship but AR places media in a responsive relationship to our navigating the world. Although it requires much more technological work to become seamless with our experience, AR seems likely to be an integrated part of the postdigital whereas VR seems more likely to remain a technological escape for the few who want to brave the dip into a dream (and the possible motion sickness) of VR.

Being a fully digital dreamscape of immersion, VR has a lot of potential in constructing exciting immersive spaces and performances. VR allows us to test digital models of soon-to-be-built immersive spaces. VR also allows us to test the emotional responses to models. VR will be a place the postdigital experiential artist will continue to create in. But VR will always be a dive into a fully-digital visual and sonic world rather than an experience layered onto our movements. VR never allows us to truly disengage from awareness of technology—we are constantly reminded of the digital when in a VR situation. Is this going to change at some point? Sci-fi films indicate that yes, it's possible, but the tech does not seem to be advancing at a speed that indicates we'll see such developments any time in the next decades.

POSTDIGITAL LANGUAGE FOR EXPERIENTIAL DESIGN: IMMERSIVE, GUEST EXPERIENCE, RESPOND AND RESPONSIVE, AND SOCIAL CONTRACTS

Our social integration of cyberspace as a social place creates a need for a new set of vocabulary: a rejoining of words. As computers evolved from the 1960s into the 2000s, many words and hyphenates were generated to try to understand our shifting world. Computer-generated. Multimedia. Interface. And those three took root. Endless other words failed to and have faded from our lexicon. Academia is still generating new terms around the digital. When working in immersive experience creation the plethora of academic terms should be thrown out for words that breathe with a social over a computer input/output language: such as "experiential" and "responsive" to replace "interactive." We need to coalesce terms for our new social existence by embracing the colloquial and currently professionally developed terms: such as "guest experience" over such philosophically imbued terms like audience trajectories, constellations, or entanglements. "Experience" and "immersive theatre" instead of "multi-media performance." Implicit in this is the need for Theatre and Performance Studies academics to stop seeing themselves as superior to corporate experience designers, Imagineers, and so on. We need to recognize that many things we saw as new with the rise of the digital have now settled into a comfortability with their historical legacies, as Johannes Birringer writes in his essay *Interaction and Extended Somatechnics*, "Immersion is festival, ceremony, ritual." But who are we to say which words should or (and even more ridiculous) shall arise? Our point is that it is happening, and it *should* happen. We as creators should be attentive and choose a language that is people, body, and socially inclined over one that is a legacy of the computational age (when computers were more about numbers than communication).

Rather than thinking about the *trajectories* of our audience or the *constellation* of non-linear spaces for guests to traverse or the immersive point of view we should use a phrase that has long worked well to explain immersive art and spaces: "guest experience." The difference between a guest and an audience member is a social contract; a social convention on how we act in a space: a *guest* can go where they please while following the rules of the house whereas an *audience* is expected to stay relatively in place and watch. A guest is invited whereas an audience is marketed to and enticed. What is proliferating in audience-guest relationships are the social contracts themselves. They are changing and new ones have evolved as new social spaces and practices have taken root in the postdigital. There are different social contracts between creators and consumers of games, plays, theme parks, theatres, etc. What unites experiential creators and gamers, audience members, players, participants, and guests is a call and an answer. The answer is response.

There is something to the word "response." Response from the audience is a major goal that unites art forms. We as designers and creators hope to elicit certain responses. We believe that certain artistic gestures generate certain responses from our audience such as joyous laughter or screams of fear. Responses like empathy, or a change in perspective. Responsive means answering. Immersion is dipping into (A place, an event, an experience, a stream). Respond is an answering to a call made by the (creators of) immersive experience. There is also that element of a pledge, made between audience (I will be there) and creator (I have something for you to respond to).

The root for respond comes from Old French, from *respondre* meaning "to answer." The root is Latin. *Re* is 'again'. *Spondere* is to pledge. Respond thus means to "again pledge." A call is put out. We need not answer. But if we do it is a pledge, a promise to be a part of the call and response experience. The *re* part of the word, to again answer, means already in a way that a response isn't a one-time thing. It is an engagement with a whole performance of call and response.

Respond also removes a kind of optic-centric language that plagues performance: *show*, to sit and *watch*, and the word "theatre" itself is promoted to have come from the Greek for "seeing place" instead of the more logical translation "place to behold." An audience is never only its eyes; it responds to sounds and architectural space and textures on the seat fabric (or lack of) in addition to what is seen.

Each experiential project is an experiment on responsiveness (with guardrails on some responses). As creators of experiences, we have to ask how truly free or real is the response from the audience? Some art is more immersive than responsive. Or, rather, experiential art takes on various levels of responsiveness. When we build immersive art, we are also renegotiating *responsiveness* with each new piece. How do we want the audience to respond? How do we want them to move through these non-linear spaces? Or reply to a fictional character's Insta account?

The postdigital magnifies response as an important concept because the postdigital has expanded the number of responsive channels in society. As creators of experiences in the postdigital it is important to think beyond designing for a single response from guests. Instead, we must respond to the fact that the digital responds to us and then we in kind respond to it. We are working with tools that can respond back to us and that create a kind of feedback loop. We see responsive feedback loops in performance all the time. For example, when a comedic actor has a good night and the audience is responding uproariously, the actor feeds off that responsive energy from the audience and answers with perhaps a bit more daring in a joke's timing or flare in a gesture. But in the postdigital era we not only work with responsive computer programs, but we are creating for an audience that is itself now consistently linked to their own responsive, networked phones. In other words, we are designing for the responses not just between the people on stage and in the house, but for a much bigger combination between the people onstage, the digital devices onstage, the audience, and the audience's digital devices. The feedback loop between four (and more) responsive possibilities is vastly more complex and offers more creative possibilities than the response pattern between performer and audience. For example, the digital systems on stage that control projections and sound could be responding to tracking data from the audience, the dancer, *and* the audience's phone history. Or just the performer and the audience's phone data. In Birringer's essay we read how DAP-Lab's work evolved from wearable sensors on dancers to applying the techniques from wearables onto spaces, allowing the audience to become participants in the responsive creations. There are exponentially more combinations possible of response between social systems because we have expanded the social to include the digital.

Kinetic technology is an obvious way to talk about looping response in a postdigital world. But it is not just digital devices that highlight *response* and its feedback loops. Response is central to creating experiential performance. Response is the guest experience to story and story-driven design. In Justin Stitchter's essay, *Storyliving: A Creative Process,* we learn about the St. Louis Aquarium relying upon a narrative journey ushering guests from the railroads of St. Louis to the Mississippi and the ocean depths beyond. The guest response is to what they see along the way. Fish. And since fish are living creatures they will generate an infinite number of human responses to their grooming, hiding, feeding, mating, and sleeping. The story of the journey for the guest of the St. Louis Aquarium aims to bring them closer to the creatures that will evoke varied responses, where humans respond to the fish and the fish respond back, both by noticing humans and by being themselves.

Experiential postdigital performances have a very different relationship to time because the postdigital does as well. Some online shows can go on for a long time and when and where the audience will enter or when depends maybe on when they normally check their social media accounts. These shows respond to the responses from the audience and as creators of experiential art we also need to be more responsive to how the audience is helping build the narrative world with their responses. We must ask, how do we allow real-time interactive moments in these highly mediatized spaces? Then, how do we as creators respond to that media world?

This is very different from Theatre with a script—set in stone, that can be licensed but must get permission to change one word—but with immersion we engage with real-time responsiveness. The experience is responsive in a way that is immediate and live. A director, a puzzle maker, an actor, cannot simply stand back and let the script roll when there is a responsive component. During the run of an immersive project, we must be flexible and present as a creative team.

When we allow for audience response to impact our shaping of the world an interesting thing is being yielded. *Yield* in the context of creation might mean allowing audience/guests ahead of us in the narrative. Creators of projects that allow the audience to contribute to the narrative have to build in a response, where creators yield the story to the unpredictable nature of participants. To work in experiential art you have to respond to the realities of the world along with those responding to the art. Experiential theatre absorbs all things (even its audience); how will you respond to the real-world needs of your project?

And "response," with all the etymological baggage of a pledge, highlights *social contracts*; yet again. Pledge means a promise, but in law language a pledge is a thing that is given as security for the fulfillment of a contract. Instead of talking about an experiential or immersive audience vs theatre audience or participant vs audience vs gamer, there is a need in the postdigital to recognize that all experiential theatrical audience relations are *social contracts* and *social conventions* that need attending to. In this way we can always come up with new experiences because we can imagine new conventions and contracts that allow guests to navigate safely and with purpose.

Designers are as much a part of this as those on the narrative and performance side of production. For example, with an immersive space, a designer has to account for where people go but also how they may act in that space. A set decorator has to consider that audiences might open drawers, and read from books on shelves. A lighting designer must consider social contracts as well. Can the audience turn a lamp off and on? The audience will do what they can if the rules indicate they're allowed to play. What do light and dark do to affect story/immersion and what happens if they use their bright phone screens and camera flash? Will it aid or detract from the experience? In one immersive production Eric directed, someone called a phone number inside a prop book that was on the ground. The guest assumed that number would lead to a clue or some kind of furthering of the story; in reality, the phone number was just there, and the book had been purchased at a thrift store (Anderson and Cassidy). Actors need to be fully wrangled within the world. Otherwise, an actor might improvise a line that feels "out of world" for an audience member. Or an actor might make improvised jokes that seem to be making fun of the immersive experience itself. All improvisation should aim to have fun within the world of the play while not making fun *of* the play.

EDUCATION IN THE POSTDIGITAL: SOCIAL CONVENTIONS, CREATIVE ROLES, ACADEMIC DEPARTMENTS, AND CREATIVE PITCHES

To create postdigital experiential work and to design it well we need to think through social conventions and contracts that will surround and protect the guest experience. It is important to start with social contracts because audience rules and etiquette and behavior are often where we draw lines between performance art forms. "The audience strolls through a non-linear themed space" instead of "staying in one place watching a stage" is the difference between a theme park and theatre for the guest; and we design for the guest.

Performance asks us to constantly re-examine social contracts in environments that are akin to but not too far removed from the reality in our everyday lives. That includes a renegotiation of the social contracts with how we interact socially online and offline and onstage and off and in-game and out-of-game. A simple example of this is that at the start of shows we tell people to silence their phones. That is a (very simple) new social convention and contract developed as cell phones became prevalent.

Social contract is inextricably linked to guest experience. We may not notice all the contracts because they have been inherited (via generations, our upbringing, childhood conventions, childhood lessons), like when to applaud (when the actors bow), when to stand up (when the house lights come on), etc. These traditional audience contracts are different from those that govern a guest experience, like Star Wars Galaxy's Edge at Disney theme parks, where the audience is encouraged to play a part, ask questions "in-world," etc. In creating the award-winning Alternate Reality Game *Arcana*, Eric and the team set up rules on the game's Instagram page that laid out what times characters would be available to chat, when the game play was active (only during certain hours of the day) etc. Laying out these rules and having them be present and repeated is an important way to think about contracts between guests and the experience.

Contract is also about the conflict of social settings and coming to contractual terms with them. For example, as creators we need to think about how we inform guests about how they are allowed to participate. Like whether they're allowed to speak or not. Eric recently saw a show where one actor told the audience, "Ask many questions." But the next actor said, "Only speak when spoken to." This is an example of a very diluted social contract being made between performer and guest. Contracts need to be clearly drawn up and presented.

Drama itself, a favorite story form of theatre, plays out conflicts of social contracts in social settings. For an early example, King Oedipus breaks the social contract/taboo of incest and ignorantly reigns in the social setting of the royal court. Social contracts elicit drama because not everyone agrees with the reasoning behind the rules. This is the drama response *between* guests in an experience. In *Playing with the Past: Pirates in the College Classroom,* Samantha Meigs explores how changing social conventions around teaching history creates an immersive experience to help students be a part of history rather than read it. Immersive experiences are an exploration and re-examination of social contracts.

Another social contract and convention that needs to be reassessed is the structure of education in the fields that all coalesce around postdigital experiential art (theatre, visual studio art, architecture, digital media, film, etc., etc.). Education needs to look to other team structures apart from media and repertory theatre production. Teams need to be assembled with more layers in the organizational forms and shared directorial importance, such as puzzle makers being equal with directors and writers and producers. Academically we need stronger ways of helping students prepare for these structures and design fields and the demands to have better communication.

We, Eric and Hans, both work in many fields but think of the theatre as a kind of intellectual home base. A theatre degree may be a way to open more doors to opportunity but not if the connections made lead only back to a narrow form of performance presentation and traditional design methodologies. Rather than thinking beyond the theatre department, we who toil in the theatrical need to embrace that Theatre is the performance art that absorbs the world and shows it back. Theatre is bigger and more diverse in form than many departments and professional programs will allow or encourage thus shutting off avenues of opportunity for young theatre makers to also be experience makers at theme parks and virtual reality production houses. In other words, theatre departments are good at training students to be smiling performers at theme parks, but not good at turning students into experience creators.

The structure and course work of the B.A. in theatre needs to radically change for the postdigital world. Set designers for film and television often come from architecture and theatre. Perhaps a Theatre Department is where students should also be learning immersive architecture in conjunction with their introductory scenic design work. Perhaps we need to build (many) more experiential art creation departments. But having immersive art education somewhere is better than nowhere. As long as departments are flexible and embrace the merging of media that has come with the postdigital, there is a way forward.

Exposure to more. Students need exposure to more experiential pieces, yes, but way more importantly students need access to the creation of experiential art. Students need to experience the roles themselves which so often remain hidden in corporate team models. Let's recall that experiential theatre is not new, and it can be found in more places than we often remember. Immersive experiences date back to ritual call and response dance, promenades, passion plays, and other on-site or site-specific theatrical experiences/festivals/balls/rituals.

A major roadblock to creating experiential theatre is that every project is unique, resisting formulaic constructions. And it is hard to explain and communicate a complex responsive experience. The very existence of exponential layers in the postdigital means that a lot must be explained to pitch an immersive theatre experience. Film, television, and theatre all have models whereby ideas move from writers to production. With agents, executives, developers, and producers in the mix. But experiential performance can start with code or a projection animation or a concept for mass group tracking. We rarely need to start with a script. What we really start with is a pitch. Students need to work on the communication of their ideas. Good creators are always working to better explain ideas, simplify, and excite their prospective audience with a taste for the experience to be made. Designers need to practice their communicative approaches more than most because the visual is difficult to translate into language. So practice. In front of people. Practice with your team and without. Practice making that pitch more exciting, clear, quick, and engaging. Can you describe the excitement and power and experience of your idea in one sentence? You can. So work on it. And always be ready to share it.

Welcome to experiential creation within the postdigital.

References

Anderson, Eva and Michael Cassady. 2017. *AMOS: A Play with Music*. Monk Space. November 2017.

Vermy, Hans. 2013. "Diectic Feet: Performance as the Index of Animation." *Mimesis Journal. Scritture Della Performance* 2 (2): 57–77.

30

An Afterword: Experience and Theatre Education

William W. Lewis and Sean Bartley

As we noted in our introduction, experiential theatre is *not* a new phenomenon. Theatre artists and those from connected disciplines and traditions have integrated experiential, embodied, and site-based techniques since before theatre as a term emerged in Ancient Greece. Instead, we see today a resurgent movement of community-based, socially-engaged, and experientially-framed modes of performance that exist both inside and outside conventional notions of theatrical form. A formal rethinking and reshaping of the limits and tenets of our discipline, perhaps akin to the artistic revolutions of the 1960s and 1970s, seems firmly underway, begun in earnest before the COVID-19 pandemic, and is newly understood as an economic and artistic imperative today. These developments are fueled, not threatened, by the new modes of digital interaction arriving regularly, which offer us a chance to more affordably, equitably, inclusively, and openly return to some of the roots of our craft. We have offered a taxonomy for these varying new forms, explored from many different angles by our contributors: Immersion, Participation, Game Play, and Role Play. The pressing question now: what to *do* with all of these new ideas, techniques, and practical elements?

EVOLVING VIEWPOINTS

In this collection, we have outlined a series of possibilities for change. We have argued for structural shifts to the university programs we call home, shared techniques, exercises, and lesson ideas for specific courses within those programs, and detailed the evolving skill sets our students will need to thrive outside the academy. Now, we must consider the changes we need to make as faculty members in our own research, teaching, and scholarship to facilitate these shifts. This book serves as a starting point rather than a comprehensive manual, a way of pushing our thinking towards experiential performance in more aspects of what we do. First, we need to attend more immersive, experiential, and digital works on our own time to ensure we stay conversant on these rapidly changing forms. For educators in locations with less professional performance groups, this requires devoting time and resources to accessing digital performances in live-streaming or archival formats as well as planning travel opportunities to engage with new performance modes. We also must continually reengage with contemporary performance theory and pass those new theoretical voices on to our students (alongside Aristotle, Lope de Vega, and Artaud). Next, we need to begin teaching these works in the classroom—and not just in courses on devising

260

DOI: 10.4324/9781003188179-34

or "experimental" theatre making. Play analysis and dramatic literature syllabi must evolve as the work evolves. As we will discuss below, they must also engage with and learn from other academic fields and disciplines. Finally, we need to reconsider the basic structural underpinning of our programs that divides coursework from a mainstage season of performances. How might our seasons program new experiential forms alongside Shakespeare, Churchill, Chekhov, Nottage, Ibsen, and Morrisseau? How might we make experiential processes visible to our audiences (and, hence, stress their urgency to our students)? How might experiential coursework *become* the mainstage season itself?

Many of the exercises and activities outlined in this collection make for excellent class projects. In many programs and departments, we tend to think of the mainstage season as our public-facing, culminating effort and practice classes as laboratories to develop skills and techniques rather than to generate final performance material. But what if our mainstage seasons shed light on the processes *behind* new and canonical theatrical works? What if a course like Samantha Meigs' "Pirates: Truth and Legend" concluded with students designing an experiential, immersive pirate voyage for members of the campus community? What if Mike Sell's experiments teaching TTRPG dramaturgy to students produced a massive, department-supported role-playing game that took place not on a tabletop, but across a football stadium or campus quad? What if our mainstage seasons included not just new plays and revivals, but original *experiences* born in the classroom?

PRIMED FOR EXPERIENTIAL PRACTICES AND PRODUCTS

While the term experiential theatres may seem novel to some, these forms of performance and production creation are actually closer to the expectations of college-aged students. As shown by many of our contributors, experiential theatre practices are already engrained in these students' ways of understanding and navigating their daily lives. They thrive on anything that gets them involved and active in the stories they encounter. The concept of immersing themselves in an experiential format is ubiquitous across their various social domains, whether it be a technological interaction with their gaming, audio, and entertainment devices, the feeling offered by the surround sound format of the cineplex, the embedded learning experience of a study abroad trip, the active engagement asked for in their daily purchases, or simply the marketing jargon inviting them to do more than passively consume. They are actively bombarded by the term immersion and this expectation of non-stop personalized exchange carries over to their expectations for all of their media, theatre included. Their social media tools ask them to actively participate in a variety of ways. They post, repost, comment, edit, challenge, and create using these tools on a near-constant basis. Just look at the wild success of the *Ratatouille* Tik Tok experiment that emerged during the early days of the pandemic. Like other fan-generated content found in Reddit forums, the various memes floating around the internet, or even digital gaming products like Minecraft and Fortnite, they seem to be most engaged when they can participate with one another in a variety of creative ways. They also engage with gamification constantly whether they are aware of it or not. From the constant awards given from their health tracking devices to the points given through their various rewards-based purchase programs, they seek validation and achievements for their every activity. In each of these instances we see that these students seek to be engaged in new and exciting ways. The Experience Economy has been discussed in various places throughout the volume, but what we haven't touched on is that each of these modes of interactivity harness the power of the Attention Economy. Experiential theatres are uniquely suited to both of these economies because they engage with the audience and hold their attention through the various modes of experiential exchange.

If you are reading this book, you are most likely already placed in an advantageous position to have a ready and willing audience clamoring for deeper and more meaningful moments of engagement. All one needs to do is reconfigure their perceptions of what theatre is and can be for these students. After all, they are the audiences and makers of the future. While it is too early to fully track the impact of COVID on theatre attendance, preliminary numbers are concerning. The Broadway League statistics as of mid-December 2021 show that even with shortened production weeks (avg 6.76 vs 8 shows per week) and twenty-six versus the usual forty productions running, attendance is hovering at around eighty-one percent capacity for Fall 2021 (Broadwayworld.com). Broadway's normal audience composition is sixty-five percent tourists (as of 2019) so that could account for some of the drop with COVID restrictions still in place in New York City[1]. Even with the tourists accounted for, the average annual salary of these Broadway attendees is $261,000 per year (Broadway League). For touring shows, the average salary of the audience is $100,000 (Broadway League). These numbers are nowhere near the median salary for everyday Americans, showing there is a baked-in accessibility issue with the commercial theatre we hold up as the standard to follow. Rethinking what we value broadly and adapting to social currents might help us foster new audiences who can engage in the exciting ways each of our contributors has discussed. Our current ways of making theatre and training students for expanding models can change to invite a broader range of audiences because of the wider horizons of experience we can give them.

Speaking to colleagues in a wide range of academic departments, we've heard that production attendance in fall 2021 for shows with either live or mixed live/streaming productions has been around fifty percent or lower than pre-pandemic numbers. In spring 2022, when restrictions began to lift and masks removed, those numbers seemed to be improving but there was still a drop in the previous numbers. The pandemic has possibly hastened the trends away from "conventional" formats of theatrical storytelling, specifically for younger audiences. For theatre educators and the departments they work for this means diversifying both forms and content while marketing to the audiences we have on our campuses. This means programming work that speaks to students' expectations, motivations, and understandings of the world around them. Instead of programming seasons modeled after the expectations of donors and educators who have largely experienced theatre in a pre-21st century model, it is time to program for today's younger generation, especially if one of our educational mandates is to help build audiences of the future. With experiential theatres this might mean taking the work to the audience versus asking the audience to come to the work. Moving beyond the conventional model of proscenium-bound theatrical events, it is time to develop engaging theatrical experiences away from the safe confines of the theatre building. It is time to create work for our students where they are (physically and metaphorically) and even, in the best of cases, with their creative input beyond the audience interaction model. This is the beauty of experiential theatres: they are collaborative and inviting in multitudes of ways.

EXPANDING THE FRAME/INVITING NEW COLLABORATIONS

In order to enact the change we wish to see in our system of training, we also need to rethink the pedestal on which we place the limited theatrical forms that regional, commercial, and institutional theatres have reinforced as "conventional". Usually lifelong theatre artists, we understandably tend as university educators to privilege the canons of work that delimited the commercial and institutional theatre culture we grew up and practiced in. We need to embrace a larger frame of performance that deemphasizes the arbitrary divide between theatre and other cultural products. This is essential to train our students for survival in a postdigital, multimodal reality. But just as importantly, these new forms and cultural products are already proving to be more responsive than institutional theatre structures to the concerns of students and artists today: concerns over degree applicability in a new, post-COVID economy and arts landscape and concerns over diversity, equity, and inclusion in both the academy and the professional theatre.

In our introductory essay, we stated that there are multiple currents potentially moving against our students as they graduate and move beyond their formative training in theatre. COVID has exacerbated these issues but has also brought about a sizeable moment of reflection and reflexivity about our processes and practices. In the professional sphere these moments of reflection have largely been activated around issues of well-being and equitable labor practices that coincide with long-ignored issues of safety and consent in rehearsals, casting, and production. The movement toward shorter work weeks and more humane use of time is becoming stronger day by day. Within academia many have also been actively engaging with efforts to diversify our student populations and our workforce through initiatives that largely have dealt with issues of content. While we argue these actions are necessary, much more needs to be done to also address structural issues in our pedagogies, production processes, and products created. One of the core arguments our contributors have presented is for how experiential theatre processes emphasize issues of audience and artist agency, interdisciplinarity and diverse community building, holistic and structural thinking, and ethical perspectives on the work we make. This is why we argue that expanding form in the way experiential theatres requires opens us up to better addressing the issues we face. The basis of the practices and pedagogies we are promoting is to better understand the human condition by looking at the central experiences of our audience members. Instead of simply focusing on telling stories, we engage in the process of crafting deeply felt and personal experiences. Doing this ethically means fully investigating each other as individuals, communities, and social fabrics.

This newfound openness towards new experiential forms and cultural products invites us to reconsider how our programs interact with the universities around them. Along with our outdated notions of what is (and what is not) theatre, we often rely on an overly simplistic notion of interdisciplinarity. This often means performing plays about particular topics of interest to other departments (*Copenhagen* for Physicist colleagues or *1776* with American Historians, for example) and inviting them to watch and comment on the work. We offer two additional proposals. First, we need to view cross-disciplinary collaboration less in terms of exporting our craft to others, but more in terms of bringing those others into our devising and rehearsal processes to help shape and author both the content *and the form* of our experiential works. Finally, we must move from a self-serving notion of interdisciplinarity toward a more even-handed feedback loop of *transdisciplinarity*. Rather than simply considering how we can learn from colleagues outside our theatre programs, how can we use our new systems of experiential performance to move, inform, and shape *their* disciplines, too? Through performance, can we learn to collaborate in a cyclical and experiential way, creating a feedback loop with our colleagues and their own disciplinary concerns?

A CHALLENGE

To close our collection, we invite our readers to turn again to the experiential capabilities of our students. The suggestions made by the contributors in this volume, some as small as in-class exercises and others as large as season and curriculum shifts, will not be easy to implement overnight. Theatre educators feel exhausted and anxious following the COVID-19 pandemic and the seismic shifts taking place in both the academy and institutional theatres today.

But while we have invited professors to broaden their own exposure to contemporary performance modes and theories, the task now is *not* to start from scratch or to command an all-encompassing knowledge of new experiential work. Rather, our job is to give our students an entry point into these emerging modes of performance making, to leverage what they know and understand, and follow along with what they create. Because they have grown up in a postdigital paradigm, they often intrinsically understand these works in a way that we might not. Rather than comprehensively defining and explaining these modes for the students (as we might do with a theatre history topic, for example), we need to start jogging in the relay race and then hand the baton off to them. This is not just effective pedagogy, but a model for collaboration in praxis.

Note

1 The Broadway League suspended full accounting of attendance numbers and gross receipts for much of Broadway's seasons for 2020–2021 and 2021–2022. In the third week of March 2022, they began posting numbers again which showed a minor increase in overall attendance but still with far fewer total shows being produced than pre-pandemic. Per the reporting from Broadway world in mid-August 2022 overall attendence for the 2022 season was less than 83% capacity compared to the approximately 90% capacity for 2018 and 2019 the last full seasons prior to the pandemic.

References

Broadwayworld.com. 2021. "Broadway Grosses for Week Ending December 12, 2021." *Broadwayworld.com.* https://www.broadwayworld.com/article/Broadway-Grosses-for-Week-Ending-December-12-2021-20211214

Broadway League. 2019. "Demographics of the Broadway Audience: 2018–2019 Season." *Broadwayleague.com.* https://www.broadwayleague.com/research/research-reports/

Broadway League. 2018. "The Audience for Touring Broadway: 2017–2018 Season." *Broadwayleague.com.* https://www.broadwayleague.com/research/research-reports/

Appendix 1
Glossary of Experiential Terms

AFFECT/AFFECTIVE

Pertaining to the sensory response of the body. A feeling generated inside the body through moments of interactivity.

AFFORDANCE

A tool implemented within an interactive structure to assist audience members.

AGENCY

The ability to do something. The sense of freedom, free-will, and/or purpose an audience member feels. Agency may be related to narrative formation, movement/action, and/or affective response.

ALTERNATE REALITY GAME (ARG)

Interactive game and/or performance that blends real-world events/locations with fictional narrative elements. ARGs often blend digital and non-digital storytelling and interactivity.

ATTENTION ECONOMY

Model of economic exchange where a consumer "pays" for a service or good using their attention or engagement. Social media sites use attention economy models by offering "free" information in exchange for the user's time, focus, and data.

AUDIENCE-CENTERED

Model of spectatorship where an individual audience member is the central focal point of interaction within a performance or game.

265

AUGMENTED REALITY GAME

Relative of alternated reality game that utilizes a technological device to create a separate layer of reality. AR games and apps superimpose graphic content over a live visual feed, usually from a phone or tablet. Games such as *Pokemon Go* and *Ingress* utilize AR technology in conjunction with GPS technology to create digital visual layers over real-world locations.

BOUNDARIES

The furthest point of engagement within a system of interaction. Also, the point of no-return for safe interaction within consent-based systems.

CONTRACT

The often unspoken set of rules an interactive audience member agrees to with the maker or distributor of a performance. See boundaries.

DISTRIBUTION

The formal mechanism for sharing a performance with an audience member when using digital platforms. Also, a method for delivering the transitive properties of agency between a performance/performer and audience member.

EMBODIED

Pertaining to the activation of the human body. To bring into and live within the human body. Often used in opposition to traditional, sedentary, and proscenium-bound theatrical forms.

ENCOUNTER

The moment of interaction between an audience member and an object, person, or environment.

ENGAGE/ENGAGEMENT

The actionable moment where agency is activated. Requires a measurable amount of commitment on behalf of the audience member.

ENVIRONMENT/ENVIRONMENTAL

The envelope in which an audience member interacts. An environment can be designed, imagined, or realized and may or may not be based in spatial reality.

ESCAPE ROOM

A form of interactive/immersive game where audience members are tasked with solving puzzles and games in a set amount of time in order to open a locked room in which they are trapped.

EXPERIENTIAL

A framework that encompasses multiple forms of audience interactivity. Experiential aspects of an encounter are often measured by agency, affect, and engagement. See immersion, participation, and play.

EXPERIENCE DESIGN (XD)

A design framework where teams develop strategies for delivering the best possible user interaction. Experience design is most often attributed to software development but has quickly spread across media and product spaces.

EXPERIENCE ECONOMY

A marketing and economic system where elements of exchange are based on delivering an experience versus simply a service or commodity. The consumer places value based on the quality of the experience. Coined by B. Joseph Pine II and James H. Gilmore in *The Experience Economy*.

EXTENDED REALITY (XR)

A format of interaction that relies on the blending of in-person realities with digital realities. An enveloping term for the multiple forms of digital augmentation such as VR, AR, and MR.

FACILITATOR

A member of an interactive event that serves to guide the action between the audience and either performers or other audience members.

FEEDBACK

The direct response from input stimuli. Feedback is what drives engagement and is the basis of liveness.

FIRST-PERSON

The focal and embodied perspective of one who is interacting within an interactive event.

FLOW

A deep sense of mental and embodied immersion one feels when they are fully engrossed and engaged within an event.

FRAMEWORK

The overarching configuration used to design, conceptualize, or structure an event. Also, a specific viewpoint one might utilize during the process of ideation and creation.

GAMES

A specific form of play that utilizes structures, rules, objectives, and rewards.

GAMIFICATION

The social process where everyday interactions implement a system of objectives and rewards to increase engagement. Gamification is often invisible: for example, gaining badges for completing exercise tasks in a health app. One does not have to actively know they are playing the game to engage with the process of gamification.

GEOTAGGING

The process of adding digital identification data to real-world locations. Geotagging operates as the hidden backbone of GPS-based systems of interaction in many ARGs and social media interactions.

GEOCACHING

Utilizing geotagging as a mode of game play by hiding clues or objects in everyday physical locations and tagging their location for others to find. Often associated with scavenger hunts.

GUEST

The terminology used for audience members who interact with themed entertainment attractions. The term is used as a way of emphasizing the fact that they have been invited into the experience.

IMMERSIVE/IMMERSION

A mode of experiential exchange where the audience member is enveloped within a physical, digital, or mental environment. The level of immersion relies on how deeply the affective and psychic feedback are received.

INSTALLATION

An event-based physical construction that allows a performance piece to either be displayed or experienced. In experiential terms an installation is something an audience member has the opportunity to either physically interact with or move in and through. Installations can be temporary or permanent constructions.

INTERACTIVE

An encounter where the agency of the audience member influences levels of feedback and response.

INTERFACE

The boundary at which point information is exchanged. In software and user experience design it is often the element that allows interaction between user and product. For example, the user interface of a smartphone is the screen.

INVITE/INVITATION

The act of bringing an audience member into the realm of experience. The invite sets up the rules and contracts of exchange within an encounter.

ITERATIVE

The developmental process or repetition brought about through conceptualization, actualization, testing, and review. Games and interaction design require an iterative process in order to fine-tune both the interface and the modes of experiencing.

LARP

Live Action Role-Play. A performative mode of embodying a fictional character in order to live the reality of that character within a specific narrative frame. Larp uses real-world places and layers on fictional strata to allow experiential exchange.

LOCATIVE MEDIA

Technologies that utilize geotagging and GPS to establish location-specific modes of communication.

LUDIC

Referring to any form of interactivity that utilizes play and playfulness.

LUDOLOGY

The study of play structures bound by rules and how these rules impact the way one interacts within a system.

MAGIC CIRCLE

A term established by Johan Huizinga in his book *Homo Ludens* that refers to the space where the rules of everyday life are suspended and replaced by the rules of a game system. Within the Magic Circle, a new reality exists for those to experience.

MEATSPACE

A playful use of language to refer to the world of organic life as opposed to digital life.

MECHANICS (AS "IN-GAME")

The formal rules that structure the interactive qualities of game play. Game mechanics establish the systems of input and feedback for users and players.

MEDIATIZATION

A meta-process where multiple forms of media influence other systems of everyday life. Mediatization is often analyzed in conjunction with politics, entertainment, culture, and business. Mediatization is not a stable process and relies on interplay between media and the multiple systems it acts upon.

MIXED REALITY

An interactive framework in which physical and digital worlds blend.

NARRATOLOGY

The study of the ways narrative structures impact perception.

NORDIC LARP

A specific formal system of LARPing that was established and continues to develop in the countries of Northern Europe. Nordic larp often emphasizes collaborative creativity and a deep sense of immersion in more "serious" fictional environments.

OPEN-WORLD GAME

A game structure where the boundaries seem almost limitless and game play is based on exploration versus objective completion.

ORCHESTRATOR

A member of an experiential event who serves as both member of the fictional world and guide through that world. Orchestrators are put in place to keep interaction flowing within the boundaries established with the rules given.

PAIDIC

A form of play that does not rely on rules or objectives. Play for the sake of creative freedom instead of play for the purpose of goal attainment. See Open-World Game.

PARTICIPATORY/PARTICIPATION

A form of experiential exchange where the audience member is presented with agency to engage with choice-making opportunities. The choices made may or may not directly impact the narrative, world, or event, but deepen the sense of investment within an experience.

PERFORMANCE CONVENTIONS

Cultural and social systems of expectations for how one receives and responds with a mode of performance.

PLATFORM

A digital space on which an experience might occur.

PLAY

An activity that occurs with the intention of creating meaningful fun and/or joy.

POSTDIGITAL

Referring to a moment where digital interactions become completely commonplace to the point of impossibility for separating the digital from the analog.

PRESENCE

Being in the moment or present to the act of interactivity. The more present one is, the more open they are to the affective resonance of an experiential encounter.

RESPONSE

The direct relationship between an action and its counteraction. See Feedback.

ROLE PLAY

A form of experiential exchange where the audience member takes on the persona of one other than themselves. Role-play operates as a form of co-authorship within the experience and is often combined with other forms of interactivity.

ROLE-PLAYING GAME (RPG)

A game where the basis of play is predicated on a player faithfully performing through the characteristics and traits of a fictional persona.

SANDBOX

The foundational playspace of creative and agential control within a game. The sandbox is the space in which a player is given freedom to impact how they play and with what elements they will play.

SENSORY

Relating to systems of input and their elements of response. Embodied senses are engaged within immersive experiences while digital senses are utilized to drive feedback and action for technological implementation.

SITE-SPECIFIC (SITE-BASED, SITE RESPONSIVE)

Designed for and/or bound to a specific, real-world physical location. In these sited works, geography, topography, and history combine to frame and organize the performance or events.

SPACE/SPATIAL

Referring to the environment in which an experience may occur. Space does not have to be physical and is highly malleable.

STORYWORLD

The fictional space driven by a narrative framework.

SYSTEM

A set of interlinking and interworking elements put into relationship with each other. Systems are designed with specific purposes based on the framework utilized. Examples: computer system, game system, ecosystem.

TABLE-TOP ROLE-PLAYING GAME (TTRPG)

A genre of role-playing game where game content is primarily communicated through speech. A Game Master typically designs and explains the scenario while other players assume characters and improvise words and actions.

THEMED ENTERTAINMENT DESIGN

A field in which designers create experiential spaces for audience members and customers. These spaces might include theme parks, zoos and aquariums, restaurants and retail outlets, or museums, and might utilize VR and AR techniques alongside a physical playspace.

THROUGHPUT

The volume of a product, service, or experience that can be delivered in a given span of time. In experiential performance, this might refer to the number or audience members who can experience a performance each hour.

TRAJECTORY

The structural sequencing of an audience journey through an experiential encounter. Trajectories are defined as canonical or participant. The canonical trajectory is the ideal pathway as defined by the maker. The participant trajectory is the pathway taken based on audience member choice and agency. Ideal journeys allow for individualization by the audience members and orchestration to keep them on the canonical pathway.

USER

Terminology used to discuss an individual who interacts with a product, specifically a digital product. Synonymous with audience member, guest, immersant, participant, and player within experiential theatre productions.

VIRTUAL REALITY

An experience, usually crafted through digital technologies, that encompasses the viewer in a visual and/or multisensory world. Virtual Reality might adhere closely to the rules of everyday life or depart starkly from them. Often achieved through headsets that block out other visual stimuli or with sophisticated systems of linked projectors that superimpose the VR over a physical space.

WEARABLE

Referring to digital sensors that are embedded within clothing items and worn on the body in order to receive input often based on location or movement.

Appendix 2
Companies, Organizations, and Ensembles

THE BEZARK COMPANY

https://bezark.com

BLAST THEORY

http://blasttheory.co.uk
Operation Black Antler, Karen, A Machine to See With

BYERLEY EXPERIENCE STUDIO

https://byerleyxps.com/philosophy

CANDLE HOUSE COLLECTIVE

https://candlehousecollective.com
Ghost Light, The Lucky Ones, Black Box

CONEY

https://coneyhq.org
Adventure 1, Remote, Telephone

DESIGN AND PERFORMANCE LAB

http://people.brunel.ac.uk/dap
METABODY, Mourning for a dead moon, kimosphere no. 4

FABULA(B) THEATRE + NEW MEDIA LAB

https://fabulabsite.wordpress.com

COMPANIES, ORGANIZATIONS, AND ENSEMBLES • 275

HOBO THEATRE

http://www.hobotheatre.co.uk
Washing Machine, People Vs Democracy, Things Might Have to Get Worse Before They Get Better

INTRAMERSIVE MEDIA

https://www.intramersive.com
Balls, Hawthorne Moon, Blackthorne Winter

MEOW WOLF

https://meowwolf.com
Glitteropolis, The Moon is to Live On, Habitats

NEW PARADISE LABORATORIES

http://newparadiselaboratories.org
Freedom Club, Prom, Batch: An American Bachelor/Ette Party Spectacle

NOCTURNAL FANDANGO

https://www.nocturnalfandango.org
Iterations, Therapy & Dreams, Retreat

OPTIKA MODERNA

https://www.optikamoderna.com
Walking La Llorona, Las Quinceañeras, Portaleza

PGAV DESTINATIONS

https://pgavdestinations.com

PIG IRON THEATRE COMPANY

https://www.pigiron.org
Zero Cost House, Pay Up!, Hell Meets Henry Halfway

POWERPLAY INTERACTIVE DEVELOPMENT

https://www.unh.edu/powerplay

PUNCHDRUNK

https://www.punchdrunk.com
Sleep No More, The Drowned Man, The Masque of Red Death

SHUNT

https://www.shunt.co.uk
Money, Tropicana, Dance Bear Dance

THE SPEAKEASY SOCIETY

https://www.speakeasysociety.com
The Kansas Collection, Ebenezer: An Immersive Christmas Carol, Under the Big Top

SPELLBOUND THEATRE

https://www.spellboundtheatre.com
The World Inside Me, Wink, Grow!

SWIM PONY

https://swimpony.org
Welcome to Campus, SURVIVE!, The End

TENDER CLAWS

https://tenderclaws.com
Pry, Virtual Virtual Reality, Tempest

THINKWELL GROUP

https://thinkwellgroup.com

THIRD RAIL PROJECTS

https://thirdrailprojects.com
Then She Fell, Roadside Attraction, The Grand Paradise

THIS IS NOT A THEATRE COMPANY

https://www.thisisnotatheatrecompany.com
Ferry Play, Café Play, Versailles 2015

VERTICAL CITY PERFORMANCE

https://verticalcityperformance.com
All Good Things, Youtopia, The Rouge Show

WET DESIGN

https://wetdesign.com

COMPANIES, ORGANIZATIONS, AND ENSEMBLES • 277

WILDWIND PERFORMANCE LAB

https://www.depts.ttu.edu/theatre-dance/programs/signature-experiences/wildwind-performance/index.php

ZU-UK

https://zu-uk.com
Hotel Medea, Binaural Dinner Date, Viva the Live!

Index

Note: Page numbers in *italics* type refer to figures.

abstraction 160–165
actors, training 53–62, 80–85
Adams, Matt 64, 70–73, 105
aesthetics: histories of 185–186; new perspectives on 186–187
affect/affective 106, 110, 147–149, 195, 212–220, 265
affordance 30, 76, 100–103, 106–107, 127, 218, 265
agency: actor/audience symmetry 53–62; audience 30–31, 39, 75, 94, 105, 109–110, 125, 135–136, 194, 196–197, 234, 247, 249; co-creation 47–51, 142, 205; definition of 265; facilitating agency 76–79; narrative agency 74–76
alternate reality games (ARGs) 32, 171–174, 178, 257, 265
Appia, Adolphe 186–187
Arcana 172–173
attention economy 265
audience: background and composition 240–243, 261–262; collaborating with 240, 247–248; experience 2–8, 29–32, 39–44, 55–59, 64–66, 72–73, 74–75, 100–103, 105–108, 123–125, 127–128, 146, 151–153, 158, 171–174, 185–186, 190, 197, 207, 214, 234–236, 244–245, 254–257; online 176–179; rehearsing as audience 61–62
augmented reality (AR) 99, 118, 206, 212, 214, 219, 246, 253; definition of 266

Barton, Bruce 64–65, 69, 71, 73
Bay-Cheng, Sarah 106, 110, 119
Beast, The 171
Blast Theory 12, 16, 105, 108, 274
Bly, Mark 29, 151–152, 154–157, 159
Boal, Augusto 80, 91
boundaries 59–61, 67–68, 75–76, 88, 92, 107, 135, 137, 166, 173, 190–191, 229, 247–248; definition of 266

brainstorming 100–101, 118, 161, 166–170, 228
Byerley, Danny 223–231, 233

Caillos, Roger 10, 31, 36
Call of Cthulhu 130, 133, 137
Campbell, Drew 223–224, 226, 228–229, 231–232
Carlson, Marvin 4–5
Causey, Matthew 13
Chemers, Michael 131, 138
collaboration 17–18, 25–30, 28–29, 107–108, 137; developing methods for 64–73, 98–71, 116–118, 166–167, 169–170; and knowledge 46–48; comfort 251–252
Complicite 28
Coney 10, 64, 71, 274
contract: audience 69, 92, 247; definition of 266; social 252, 254–258
Cooperstein, Dave 223, 225–226, 228–231
COVID-19 1, 11–12, 16, 117, 125, 130, 145, 171, 175, 177–178, 260, 262–263
Craig, Edward Gordon 186
Cramer, Florian 12–13
creative learning 47–49, 92
creative process of experience 223–233
creative thinking 166–170

Davis, Khalia 64–66, 69–70, 72
Debord, Guy 9
de Certeau, Michel 122–123
De La Guarda 12
design thinking 185–193; histories of aesthetics 185–186; new perspectives on aesthetics 186–187; pedagogies and technological implementation 187–191

278

INDEX • **279**

devising 26–31, 56, 67–69, 72, 76, 78, 80, 98, 103, 107, 117, 120–121, 131–132, 154, 164, 171, 185, 244, 260, 263

Disney 2, 20, 196–197, 226, 232, 257

distribution 132, 246–247; definition of 266

Doyle, Jim 223–225, 233

dramaturgy: dramaturgical grounding 56–58; of guest experience 173–175, 254–258; table-top role-playing games (TTRPGs) 130–139; training 116–119

Dungeons & Dragons 130

Dwyer, Carly 151, 153, 156–158

Elevator Repair Service 28

embodied/embodiment 2, 14–16, 19, 21, 35, 42–44, 91, 106, 141, 147–148, 244, 253, 253; definition of 266

encounter 2, 6–8, 14–15, 20–21, 56, 62, 74, 86–87, 229, 231–232, 266

engaged/engagement 2–8, 15, 36, 41–41, 55, 65, 73, 91, 93, 96, 107, 110–111, 127, 142, 172, 187, 195–199, 214, 244, 261–262; agency of engagement 74–75, 77; definition of 266

environment/environmental 4, 107, 109, 185–187, 192, 213–218, 235–236, 240–243; definition of 266

escape room 101; definition of 266

experience/experiential: definition of 267; dramaturgies 175–180; experience design (XD) 185–189, 267; experience economy 267; experiential theatres 1–18, 7; theatre

education 260–264; trajectories 98–103

extended reality (XR) 192, 206–211, 267

facilitate 31, 40, 50, 55–56, 68, 71, 74–79, 91, 106, 107, 235

facilitator 47, 50, 94; definition of 267

feedback 44, 267

first person 267; first-person composite characters 235; Fischer-Lichte, Erika 44

flow 267

Forced Entertainment 12, 28

Forum Theatre 80

framework 268

Frantic Assembly 28

Fuchs, Elinor 111

game(s) 10, 46, 77–78, 94–96, 125–127, 171–172, 257; definition of 268

game engine 209

game mechanics and design 35–44, 60, 68, 93–94, 125

game play/gameplay 6, 29–32, 36, 93–94, 99–100, 260–261

gamification 10–12, 66, 236, 261; definition of 267

Garrison, Gary 151–159

Gilmore, James 14–15, 110–111

Google Zoo 195

guest 55, 58, 143, 194–205, 225, 227, 231, 232; definition of 268

Hamnet Players 175–176

Hansen, Pil 64–67, 71

Harlem Unbound 137–138

Hotel Medea 92–93

hot seat 81–83

Huizinga, Johan 10, 31, 36, 92, 269

immersion 6, 7, 42–44, 43, 55–56, 66, 109, 151–152, 171–174, 216–219, 251–259; definition of 268

installation 268

interaction/interactive 2–16, 30–32, 35–48, 42–44, 55–56, 60–62, 66, 78, 80–85, 101–103, 105–112, 131–132, 147–149, 202–203, 212–215, 244–250; definition of 268; technologies and media 8–13, 176–177, 206–210, 216–217, 246

interdisciplinarity 16–18, 28–29, 117, 263

interface 8; definition of 269

invite/invitation 58–59; definition of 269

iterative 30; definition of 269

Jenkins, Henry 11, 111

Just, Julianne 64, 66–67, 72–73

kimospheres 214–215, 215, 217, 218, 220

Kolb, David 18, 98

Lanier, Jaron 9, 219

larp (live action role-play) 32, 39, 46–47, 49–50; definition of 269

Lavender, Andy 6, 15

Lean UX 30–31

living history 234–235

Living Theatre 9

locative media 10; definition of 269

lore 56–57

ludic/ludology 269

Machon, Josephine 6, 15–16, 42, 56, 61, 106, 111

Magic Circle 39; definition of 269

maker culture 9

Manovich, Lev 109

mapping 101–103, 120–129

McGonigal, Jane 10, 31–32, 36, 55, 171–172

meatspace 193, 244–247; definition of 269

mechanics, dynamics, and aesthetics (MDA) 36–37

mediatization 270

Meow Wolf 275

mixed reality (MR) 105, 206, 224, 270

Morrison, Elise 106

Murray, Janet 39, 110

narratology 270

No Proscenium 171

Nordic larp 46–52; definition of 270

280 • INDEX

Oddey, Alison 29
offerings 58–59
open-world game 270
orchestrator 270

Pace, Chelsea 53
paidic 270
Parker-Starbuck, Jennifer 107
participatory/participation/participant 2–4, 6–7, 9, 14–16, 36, 42, 55–58, 62, 64–73, 74–79, 91–96, 99, 105–111, 141, 147, 171–174, 176–178, 260–261; definition of 270
Pig Iron Theatre Company 116, 118, 120–128, 275
Pine, Joseph II 14–15, 110–111
platform 177–179; definition of 271
play 6, 10, 29–30, 94–95, 234–238, 257–258; player 31–32, 36–44, 53–62, 93–96, 125–127, 130–137, 172–174; playtesting 74–77; definition of 271
Pokémon Go 10
postdigital 12–14, 105–111, 175–180, 251–259; definition of 271
PowerPlay Interactive Development 80–81, 275
presence 106–107; definition of 271
prosumer 111
Punchdrunk 12, 74, 197, 275

Rancière, Jacques 47, 142
rasa 140–150
relational 47, 49–50, 92
response 36, 41–42, 59–62, 76, 82, 94, 149, 255–257; definition of 271
ritual 46, 49–51, 65, 92, 109, 124, 175, 213, 218–220, 254, 258
role-play/roleplay 6, *7*, 42–44, 46–49, 80, 91–96, 99, 130–133, 260; definition of 271
role-playing game (RPG) 130–139, 271
Rosa-Shapiro, Marisol 64–65, 68–69, 73
Rovegno, Mia 64–65, 67, 72
Royal Shakespeare Company (RSC) 177–178

sandbox 271
scaffolding 40, 47, 190

self-care cues 59–60, *61*
sensory 140–150; definition of 271
site-specific (site-based, site responsive) 10; definition of 272
Sleep No More 151, 197
space/spatial 65–71, 186–193, 251–259; definition of 272
Stevens, Tassos 29, 64–65, 68, 71
sting/reward system 61–62
storyliving 196–204
storytelling 151–159, 196
storyworld 272
Suits, Bernard 36
Svoboda, Josef 9, 187
Swim Pony 35–44, 276
system 31, 70–71, 93, 96; definition of 272

table-top role-playing games (TTRPGs): definition of 272; dramaturgy of 130–139
themed entertainment design 196; definition of 272
Third Rail 12, 276
throughput 66, 98; definition of 272
trailheads 59
training actors 53–62, 80–85; exercises 81–84
trajectory 6, 100–103, 107, 149, 247, 254; definition of 272

user 8–10, 26, 29–31, 42, 71, 107, 193–195, 201, 206–207, 251; definition of 273
user experience (UX) 8, 26, 29–32, 107, 195

virtual reality (VR) 9–10, 273
visual design 240–243
Vygotsky, Lev 47–49

Warren, Jason 151–155, 158–159
Weinbloom, Jenny 64, 66, 68, 70, 73
White, Gareth 16, 58, 141

XD (experience design) 185–189, 267
XR (extended reality) 192, 206–211, 267

ZU-UK 91–96, 107–108, 277